D0772399

Praise for *Really Good Schools*

"Ten years after his pioneering book *The Beautiful Tree*, James Tooley has taken his argument about the transformative power of low-cost private education to a new and revelatory level in *Really Good Schools*. The deeply researched first part of this volume makes the compelling argument that decentralized, self-organized teaching and learning offer the best hope for children in the poorest parts of the world, from Kenya to Ghana, from Liberia to Nigeria, from Gujarat to Gansu. But Tooley wants us to understand that we in the developed world—with our sclerotic systems of public education, our over-priced private schools for the wealthy, and our insufficient schemes for reform—also have much to learn from the spontaneous order of the countless slum schools he has visited. This is a bold and inspiring manifesto for a global revolution in education."

> —**Niall C. Ferguson,** Milbank Family Senior Fellow, Hoover Institution, Stanford University

"In the fascinating and provocative book, *Really Good Schools*, James Tooley applies his immense learning about low-cost, entirely-private schools around the world to develop a daring and truly thought-provoking proposal along those lines for the United States. En route, he engages in lively virtual arguments with both Charles Murray and Milton Friedman! Check it out."

> —**Chester E. Finn Jr.,** Distinguished Senior Fellow and President Emeritus, Thomas B. Fordham Institute; Senior Fellow, Hoover Institution; former U.S. Assistant Secretary of Education

"Based on James Tooley's extensive knowledge of educational systems in developing countries from around the world, his pathbreaking and superbly written book *Really Good Schools* provides the essential understanding of how low-cost, private schools extend access to high quality education for the poor. Reading this book will allow educators and parents, academics and students, school reformers, policymakers, and the general public at last to have the proven and authoritative know-how to allow children to transition from failing government school systems in the U.S., U.K., and elsewhere, into inexpensive, first-rate schools. This makes *Really Good Schools* utterly essential reading!"

> —**Sir Anthony F. Seldon,** former Vice Chancellor, Buckingham University; Co-Founder and First Director, Institute for Contemporary British History; President, International Positive Education Network

"Based on remarkable and fascinating, personal, worldwide experience and meticulous research—both conveyed with engrossing detail—James Tooley's book *Really Good Schools* reveals the surprising successes of low-cost private schools pioneered by conscientious entrepreneurs (including himself) in the slums of developing countries where resources are frequently scarce, and danger often lurks. Careful to acknowledge and respond to critics, Tooley makes the case for the comparative advantage of low-cost private schools that merits respect and serious attention. *Really Good Schools* has relevance to both those interested in international development as well as to readers in advanced nations that are experiencing educational ferment given the social and economic problems of contemporary times, including the threat to educational attainment posed by the coronavirus pandemic."

—**Donald A. Downs,** Alexander Meiklejohn Emeritus Professor of Political Science, Law and Journalism, the Glenn B. and Cleone Orr Hawkins Emeritus Professor of Political Science, and Co-Founder of the Center for the Study of Liberal Democracy at the University of Wisconsin, Madison

"Here in *Really Good Schools* is perhaps the most beautiful and neglected story in the world. Unremarked and unreported, low-cost private schools have sprung up to serve some of the poorest places on Earth. For 20 years, Professor Tooley has been seeking to bring this heartening development to wider notice. He has travelled the shantytowns of Africa and India. He has found ultra-cheap independent schools even in China. Again, and again, he has heard how slum-dwellers make sacrifices to avoid the listless and perfunctory education offered in government schools. Here, in his most complete analysis of the phenomenon, he examines why it continues to expand, despite the disdain of Western aid agencies and the outright hostility of local authorities. And he ponders how some of the principles of self-organized learning might be imported into the United States and other wealthy nations. I guarantee that, after reading *Really Good Schools*, you will feel more cheerful."

—**Daniel J. Hannan,** former Member, European Parliament; bestselling author and columnist, *Sunday Telegraph* and *Washington Examiner*

"James Tooley, rightly celebrated for his discovery and promotion of private schools serving the poor in Africa, India, and China, now in *Really Good Schools* argues that the logic of his findings could transform education in America and Britain. Tooley would abolish government's role, even in the form of support for vouchers and charter schools, allowing a 'spontaneous order' of education to emerge through the decisions of entrepreneurs and parents. A stimulating reading for a time when, as he points out, COVID-19 has brought much of formal schooling to a standstill and invites its reinvention."

—**Charles L. Glenn,** Professor Emeritus, Educational Leadership and Policy Studies, Boston University

"In *Really Good Schools*, James Tooley presents a compelling argument for education in contradistinction to schooling, a difference seemingly lost in the bureaucracies of public education. He identifies the possibilities and promise of private education as a ground-up, spontaneously ordered enterprise that can serve even the lowest income individuals more effectively than can the Administrative State."

> —**John W. Sommer**, Knight Distinguished Professor Emeritus, University of North Carolina at Charlotte; former Dean, School of Social Science, University of Texas at Dallas

"In *Really Good Schools*, James Tooley takes us on an adventure across some of the most difficult parts of sub-Saharan Africa and South Asia, revealing the extraordinary revolution of low-cost private schools taking place. But he also takes us on a journey back to the West, to Britain and America, to show the relevance of his findings for education there too. *Really Good Schools* is a manifesto for educational freedom—the emancipation of education, as he calls it—and how we can move towards it."

> —**Sir Robert G. W. Balchin** (Lord Lingfield), Chairman, Commission on Special Needs in Education; former Pro-Chancellor, Brunel University; Founder Chairman, League of Mercy; Chairman, Centre for Education Management; former Director-General, St. John Ambulance; author, *Choosing a State School: How to Find the Best Education for Your Child*

"James Tooley is an invaluable authority on private schooling. In *Really Good Schools*, his advice on the provision of accessible, affordable school choice options has never been more timely or necessary."

> —**Frederick M. Hess**, Resident Scholar and Director of Education Policy Studies, American Enterprise Institute

"I strongly support the idea of expanding the affordable independent sector: variety in education is the spice of life especially in this drearily conformist age. So, more ammunition from James Tooley and from his book *Really Good Schools*."

> —**Lord Robert J. A. Skidelsky**, Emeritus Professor of Political Economy; University of Warwick

"The author of *The Beautiful Tree* has done it again. His truly unique and exceptional book *Really Good Schools* is another must-read about how some of the most disadvantaged people on earth are taking matters into their own hands to provide great, low-cost educations for their children. But, Tooley goes much further in *Really Good Schools* and provides a new clarion call for those who believe in the power of education to empower individuals to live their best lives—a call for education-choice supporters to recognize and embrace the notion of 'self-organized learning environments' in order to reclaim the education of youth from those who prize uniformity and government control over schooling."

> —**Benjamin Scafidi**, Professor of Economics and Director, Education Economics Center, Kennesaw State University

"Dr. James Tooley has uniquely challenged all of us with his revelations on low-cost private schools. *Really Good Schools* is a trailblazer for a grassroots transformation of education and illuminates the rewards that follow a system that is left in the hands of those closest to children. Tooley takes us with him in his journey, exploring the privatizing of education across the world, and through his clever insights, leads us into a new world that will change the course of education for generations to come."

> —**Jeanne R. Allen,** Founder and Chief Executive Officer, Center for Education Reform

"Well-read, well-travelled, and thoughtful, James Tooley has created compelling starting points for a lot of critical conversations. Tooley imagines that his, 'task is simply to write it all up, in the hope of inspiring and motivating others to get involved.' In *Really Good Schools*, he has written it all up, and it is inspiring, but he is far too modest. He has discovered and directly demonstrated that freedom and entrepreneurship can produce excellent, low-cost schools that very few others thought possible, even when they have already existed, against long odds, right under their noses."

> —**John D. Merrifield,** Professor of Economics Emeritus, University of Texas at San Antonio

"In the well-trodden field of education studies, it is rare enough for a researcher to supplement the public's understanding of a well-known issue. But in an earlier book, James Tooley revealed a massive, striking, largely unknown phenomenon: the existence of ultra-low cost, high-quality private schools in developing countries. Now in *Really Good Schools*, Tooley expands his descriptive and empirical research to other developing and war-torn countries, while offering a thoroughgoing reflection on the significance of this still under-studied reality. Interesting enough on its own terms, Tooley's book has acquired an unexpected aspect in the wake of COVID-19—might we see the rise of such schools within developed countries like the United States? Tooley argues, persuasively, that it's possible. For it to happen, would-be entrepreneurs, policymakers, and parents would be well-advised to learn the lessons that Tooley teaches."

> —**Max C. Eden,** Senior Fellow, Manhattan Institute

"In *Really Good Schools*, Tooley reminds us through vivid examples from across the globe that we don't have to turn to government for education; that even in the poorest and most remote areas, it is private schools, not public schools, serving the needs of families. And when so many continue to insist that 'accountability' comes from government oversight, Tooley shows yet again how market-based education creates the ultimate form of accountability by making schools responsive to the needs of parents. His book on the promise of low-cost private education comes at a pivotal moment: the COVID-19 pandemic has shuttered public schools and led many families to turn to private options. At a time when the pandemic has given us the opportunity to rethink the structure of education, *Really Good Schools* provides a must-read guide."

> —**Lindsey Burke**, Director, Center for Education Policy, Institute for Family, Community and Opportunity, Heritage Foundation

"*Really Good Schools* picks up on James Tooley's previous revelations about the wondrous and (at the time) unknown existence of low-cost private schools and sketches a future built on them. This underlying structure of a radically different education system breaks out of Mumbai and heads for America. It not only builds a case for a new future but artfully dissects the arguments of those still holding hope for making today's schools better. Warning: this is not a book to be skimmed but one to be intellectually grappled with."

> —**Eric A. Hanushek**, Paul and Jean Hanna Senior Fellow, Hoover Institution

"*Really Good Schools* provides an interesting review of educational entrepreneurship around the world."

> —**Kent Grusendorf**, Senior Fellow and Director, Center for Education Freedom, Texas Public Policy Foundation; former Member, Texas House of Representatives and Texas Board of Education; former Chairman, Texas House Public Education Committee

"James Tooley's work documents the ubiquity of low-cost private schools in the poorest countries and poorest villages of the world. It is hard to read this book and do nothing. *Really Good Schools* illustrates both the deep-seeded desire for education that exists among humans regardless of income and the many efforts by private individuals to help the poor who otherwise would not be educated."

> —**Eugenia F. Toma**, Wendell H. Ford Professor of Public Policy and University Research Professor, Martin School of Public Policy & Administration, University of Kentucky

"There is no one who matches James Tooley when it comes to giving a global perspective on the widespread availability of well-performing and low-cost private schools serving children from Africa to India. Importantly, his research gives him the unique ability to analyze why similar low-cost private education is not plentiful in the U.S. and to challenge American education reformers to rethink some of their basic assumptions. Tooley does not merely challenge, however, as he also gives hope for U.S. parents by laying out a business model for low-cost private schools in America. *Really Good Schools* is a must read for all those interested in expanding and improving the education options for children."

> —**Lance T. Izumi**, former President, Board of Governors, California Community Colleges

"In the midst of a pandemic, many parents in developed countries have become keenly aware of the inability of government-operated schools to educate their children. In response, these parents are struggling to form affordable and effective micro-schools. The wonderfully readable book by James Tooley, *Really Good Schools*, has arrived at exactly the right time to offer models and lessons from how parents in developing countries have managed to succeed in educating their own children without state assistance."

> —**Jay P. Greene,** Distinguished Professor and Chair of the Department of Education Reform, University of Arkansas

"*Really Good Schools* is a valuable follow up to James Tooley's remarkable 2009 book, *A Beautiful Tree*, which showed us that in some of the world's poorest slums, with dreadful public schools, a large share of students were enrolled in small private schools started by local entrepreneurs. In this innovative book, Dr. Tooley updates the reader with more case studies and research on this bottom-up educational phenomenon and suggests potential lessons for the U.S. *Really Good Schools* makes an important contribution to policy discussions regarding school choice and education reform."

> —**Michael J. Podgursky,** Chancellor's Professor of Economics, University of Missouri-Columbia

"James Tooley has done it again. With *Really Good Schools: Global Lessons for High-Caliber, Low-Cost Education*, he has produced another excellent volume on how the power of markets and choice can help drive high-quality school options for poor families. The global revolution of low-cost private education that he profiles shows us how school-reform entrepreneurs across the world are achieving genuine equity. *Really Good Schools* is a must read for citizens, school leaders, and policymakers alike who want to embrace a larger vision of how to make equality of educational opportunity real for the kids who need it most."

> —**Jamie Gass,** Director, Center for School Reform, Pioneer Institute

REALLY GOOD SCHOOLS

Also by the Author

The Beautiful Tree
  *A Personal Journey into How the World's Poorest People Are
  Educating Themselves*

Imprisoned in India
  Corruption and Extortion in the World's Largest Democracy

E. G. West
  *Economic Liberalism and the Role of Government in
  Education*

From Village School to Global Brand
  Changing the World through Education

Reclaiming Education

Education without the State

Government Failure
  E. G. West on Education

The Global Education Industry
  Lessons from Private Education in Developing Countries

Disestablishing the School
  *Debunking Justifications for State Intervention in
  Education*

What America Can Learn from School Choice in Other Countries
  Edited by James Salisbury and James N. Tooley

INDEPENDENT
I N S T I T U T E

INDEPENDENT INSTITUTE is a non-profit, non-partisan, public-policy research and educational organization that shapes ideas into profound and lasting impact. The mission of Independent is to boldly advance peaceful, prosperous, and free societies grounded in a commitment to human worth and dignity. Applying independent thinking to issues that matter, we create transformational ideas for today's most pressing social and economic challenges. The results of this work are published as books, our quarterly journal, *The Independent Review*, and other publications and form the basis for numerous conference and media programs. By connecting these ideas with organizations and networks, we seek to inspire action that can unleash an era of unparalleled human flourishing at home and around the globe.

100 Swan Way, Oakland, California 94621-1428, U.S.A.
Telephone: 510-632-1366 • Facsimile: 510-568-6040 • Email: info@independent.org • www.independent.org

JAMES TOOLEY

REALLY GOOD SCHOOLS

Global Lessons for High-Caliber, Low-Cost Education

INDEPENDENT
I N S T I T U T E

OAKLAND, CALIFORNIA

Independent Institute
100 Swan Way, Oakland, CA 94621–1428
Telephone: 510–632–1366
Fax: 510–568–6040
Email: info@independent.org
Website: www.independent.org

Cover Design: Denise Tsui
Cover Image: John P Kelly / Getty Images

Library of Congress Cataloging-in-Publication Data

Names: Tooley, James, author.
Title: Really good schools : global lessons for high-caliber, low-cost education / James Nicholas Tooley.
Description: Oakland, California : Independent Institute, [2021] | Includes bibliographical references and index.
Identifiers: LCCN 2020054354 (print) | LCCN 2020054355 (ebook) | ISBN 9781598133387 (cloth) | ISBN 9781598133394 (trade paperback) | ISBN 9781598133400 (ebook) | ISBN 9781598133400 (mobi) | ISBN 9781598133400 (pdf)
Subjects: LCSH: Private schools--Developing countries--Cross-cultural studies. | Alternative education--Developing countries--Cross-cultural studies. | School improvement programs--Developing countries--Cross-cultural studies.
Classification: LCC LC57.5 .T66 2021 (print) | LCC LC57.5 (ebook) | DDC 371.02--dc23
LC record available at https://lccn.loc.gov/2020054354
LC ebook record available at https://lccn.loc.gov/2020054355

Contents

Acknowledgments

MANY PEOPLE HAVE helped and motivated me to write this book. I've been inspired by thousands of educational entrepreneurs across the world. I can only name a few—Ken Donkoh, Orji Emmanuel, Bawo Sabo Elieu Ayeseminikan, Umedsinh Sodha, Ekta Sodha, Yajuvendra Jadeja, Massimo Mazzone, George Mikwa, Mohammed Anwar, Charles S.W. Smith and Chris Gray. At the E.G. West Centre, Newcastle University, I would like to thank Barrie Craven, Pauline Dixon, Gopalkrishnan Iyer, Steve Humble, Sugata Mitra, David Longfield and James Stanfield in particular, for their insights and friendship. At the University of Buckingham, I wish to thank Matthias Klaes, Len Shackleton, Martin Ricketts, Andreea Dogar and Alex Hammond.

At the Independent Institute, thanks to David J. Theroux, for commissioning this book; the two editors, Roy M. Carlisle and Stephen Thompson, for their encouragement and kindness; Christopher B. Briggs and George L. Tibbitts for their attention to detail; Anne Healy, Allison Britton, and Elizabeth Kuepper for their copyediting and proofing prowess; and Denise Tsui, Ayelet Arbel, and Mike Mott, for their design expertise.

List of Figures and Tables

List of Figures

List of Tables

Introduction

"A general State education is a mere contrivance for moulding people to be exactly like one another ... ; in proportion as it is efficient and successful, it establishes a despotism over the mind, leading by a natural tendency to one over the body."
—John Stuart Mill, *On Liberty*

"We are going to emancipate ourselves from mental slavery because ... none but ourselves can free the mind."
—Marcus Garvey, October 1937, in a speech that inspired Bob Marley's "Redemption Song"

MALALA YOUSAFZAI, THE youngest person ever to win the Nobel Peace Prize, is a brave and resolute young woman. She has become a twenty-first-century icon of global education,[1] instantly recognizable in her pink hijab with yellow embroidery and for her serious dark eyes.

She had started campaigning in the picturesque Swat Valley, Pakistan, her home region, about the virtues of girls' schooling and became known to the Taliban, the murderous regime from neighboring Afghanistan, which also thrives along the Pakistan-Afghanistan border. One morning, as she was on her way to school, Taliban thugs against women's education tried to murder her. Miraculously, she survived and is now a forthright young activist, completing her degree at Oxford University.

But there is something strange about the way her story is told. Something crucial to her experience is always omitted when her life and mission are described by international agencies and the media. Education International, the global federation of teachers' unions, is typical. Malala is campaigning, they say, so that all can benefit from "equitable public education."² The BBC summary of her talk to the United Nations on her sixteenth birthday highlighted only "her campaign to ensure free compulsory education for every child"³—"free" and "compulsory" being the buzzwords for "public" or "government" education for all. Meanwhile, Gordon Brown, erstwhile British prime minister, now UN special envoy for global education, used the same event to "renew the call for all governments to guarantee equitable quality education for all."

But it wasn't to government that Malala and her family turned to enable her to get an education. In fact, everything in her life story—related beautifully in her autobiography, coauthored with journalist Christina Lamb— points to something importantly different.

In her life story, she's not standing up for the right to public education. In fact, she's scathing about public education: it means high teacher absenteeism and teachers abusing children. Public-school teachers, reluctantly posted to remote schools, "make a deal with their colleagues so that only one of them has to go to work each day." On their unwilling days in school, "all they do is keep the children quiet with a long stick, as they cannot imagine education will be any use to them."⁴ She's surely not fighting for the right of children to an education like *that*.

But if not public education, what is she standing for? In fact, Malala's life story shows her standing up for the right to *private* education, and for the kind of private education that has been my passion for the past two decades: *low-cost* private education.

The school she attended, on her way to which she was famously shot by the Taliban, was in fact a *low-cost private school* set up by her father. This reality gets totally obscured in media reports: not untypically, Education International describes her father as a "headmaster." *Time* magazine describes him as a "school administrator." Headmaster, school administrator? No. Not at all. Her father was in fact an educational entrepreneur.

In 1994, he started a private school in Mingora, a city in the Swat Valley, seeing few other private schools there and recognizing that there was market demand for English-medium schools,⁵ because the area was "a tourist destination."⁶ He and his friend invested their entire savings of PKR 60,000 (about US $1,754 at contemporary exchange rates). It was a struggle, but they eventually succeeded. When Malala was born (July 12, 1997), the school fees were PKR 100 (US $2.47) per month. That's a low-cost private school, accessible to poor families. (In chapter 1, see section, "Toward a Definition of Low-Cost Private Schools.") Her father joined the Swat Association of Private Schools and quickly became vice president.

Government officials tried to make him pay bribes to get his school registered—the going rate was about PKR 13,000, or around one-quarter of what he had been able to invest to get his school off the ground. He encouraged other school owners to fight this corruption: "Running a school is not a crime," he told them. "You are not running brothels; you are educating children!"[7] Pretty soon he was president of the organization; under his leadership, it expanded to four hundred schools.

This is all remarkable and surely part of Malala's story. Shouldn't it at least be mentioned, if not celebrated? Against the odds, her father, with four hundred other educational entrepreneurs, has created *private* schools for the poor in a remote region of the world, because even poor parents don't want to accept the mediocrity and abuse of public schools. But it's all studiously ignored by the international agencies and media, and most definitely by the international federation of teachers' unions, Education International, which continues to use Malala's story to push the case for public schools. This is precisely the opposite of what her life story shows—that she and her family are interested in private education. Why?

Perhaps readers might think it's because what happened to Malala is exceptional, relevant only to that most remote, Taliban-infested part of Pakistan where girls aren't allowed education. If readers think that, then they are mistaken. What is happening in Malala's native Swat Valley is happening everywhere across the "developing world."[8] Malala's story points to a global movement, in which Malala's father is a far from unusual player. Low-cost private education, private education for poor and low-income families, is in fact ubiquitous.

I first discovered for myself the extraordinary revolution of low-cost private schooling in 2000. I was in Hyderabad, in south-central India, doing consulting work on elite private schools and colleges for the International Finance Corporation, the private finance arm of the World Bank. As an outcome of my doctoral work at University College London's Institute of

Education, I'd become an expert on private education. But this meant there was a severe disconnect in my life. Everyone knows that private education is for the well-to-do, for the elites. For various reasons, I felt that my life should be about serving the poor and disadvantaged. And yet I was stuck with being an expert on something that clearly didn't fit with what I wanted my life to be about.

But my life was about to change. On a fateful day, Indian Republic Day, January 26, 2000, I read in my *Rough Guide to India* that the slums of the Old City were behind the Charminar, the Arc de Triomphe of South India. I took an autorickshaw (what motorized rickshaws are called in India) down to these slums, curious to see what I could find—indeed, excited by a hunch from my research about what I might find. Down one alley, I found a small school in a residential building. It wasn't a public school. It was a low-cost private school, charging in those days about US $1 per month. Then I found another, and another, and soon I was connected to the president of a federation of five hundred of these low-cost schools, serving poor and low-income communities across Hyderabad. I spent as much time as I could in these schools after finishing my meetings in the elite colleges that had brought me to Hyderabad. I watched lesson after lesson, where energetic young teachers taught, some in an extremely impressive way.

I remember going back to my hotel room, in an upmarket area of the city, and thinking that the different parts of my life could fit together after all. I was an expert in private education, and I had discovered that private education seemed as much about the poor and disadvantaged as about anyone. My life suddenly felt complete. It was a wonderful feeling that has stuck with me for the past twenty years.

But I also had many questions about this low-cost private education. What proportion of children did these schools serve? There seemed so many of them. Perhaps I was not gauging this properly by traveling around town only with federation members. I needed to find out for myself and do some robust research.

How good were these schools? The buildings didn't look great, but certainly the teachers seemed eager and confident, and children busied themselves in their books and on their chalkboards. Were children doing well in these schools? As well as those in government schools? More research was urgently needed.

But there was one question that I immediately could ask the parents—mostly Muslim mothers of children in the schools in the Islamic quarter of the Old City that I was visiting. Why were they sending their children to private schools, which cost money, when they were poor, and the government schools were free and provided free food at lunchtime, free books, and sometimes free uniforms? One mother answered, "In the government schools, our children are abandoned." Others concurred with this sentiment. I had to see for myself.

So, my hosts arranged for the district education officer (DEO) to accompany me to a nearby government school. The visit will stay in my mind forever. It was in an impressive building, more spacious and airier than the private schools. We went upstairs. In the first classroom we visited, 130 children were seated on the floor among the swarming mosquitos, doing nothing. They sat there, all bright-eyed and bushy-tailed, excited by having a visitor, eager to hear what he had to say, eager to learn. But only two teachers were present at the school. And with remarkable and admirable candor, the DEO explained that only two teachers were present every day. The same thing was happening in urban India that Malala had observed in rural Pakistan, where teachers came in only occasionally, following an informal schedule that allowed them not to be there most of the time.

It broke my heart the first time I saw it. "Abandoned," the Muslim mother had told me. The word rang true.

But it wasn't just because the government schools were bad, and the children within them were abandoned. During my first visit to the Hyderabad slums, I realized there was something else going on. One day, while I was sitting in the office of one school owner, taking in as much as I could about this strange new phenomenon of low-cost private education, a mother dressed in a hijab came to visit. She owed money for several months. There I was, a well-meaning foreigner with a wad of rupees in my pocket. I did what I guess many would have done: I pulled out the number of rupees she owed and handed it over to her.

Her response was emphatic. She held up—not out—her hand and spoke to the proprietor in Urdu. He translated her response: "I don't want your charity. I can stand on my own two feet, thank you very much." This struck me deeply. What was it about her desire for independence? The proprietor explained it a bit more: "Independence, self-help, for sure. But she wants the school to be accountable to *her*, not to you. By paying her own fees, in small amounts each month to cover her arrears, she knows that she keeps me on my toes. Don't ruin it by stepping in between us."

I went back to the World Bank in Delhi, and then to the International Finance Corporation in Washington, DC, fired up by all I had seen. Did colleagues know that there were an amazing number of low-cost private schools in poor parts of India? The response? "Calm down, Tooley, calm down. You've seen a small number of businessmen ripping off the poor.[9] And in any case, it's only happening in Hyderabad, nowhere else." Ripping off the poor? I'd seen the proprietors running sports competitions and science fairs on their weekends—was that the sign of someone abusing the poor? And was it true that I had just happened to uncover something that only occurred in the places I'd visited? Was this just a chance discovery or something that, in any case, was relatively minor?

I had to know. Fortunately, I received a grant from the John Templeton Foundation to see if the same phenomenon was occurring elsewhere and to answer these two questions: What proportion of children is served? And how good are the private schools? Two more questions also seemed important: What is the business model for these schools? Can it be replicated and improved? I'll be addressing these questions further throughout the book. Suffice it to say now that in poor urban areas, it is common to find 70 percent or more of children in low-cost private schools, while in rural areas there is a substantial minority in private education. Children in low-cost private schools outperform those in government schools, after controlling for all relevant background variables. And the schools do it for a fraction of the per-pupil cost.

It is an incredible success story, and I've been championing it ever since.

For the research, I always went to places on my own first, to check that the phenomenon of low-cost private schools existed there and to satisfy myself that the places were safe for researchers to visit. Then, often with Pauline Dixon (who started as my doctoral student, then research associate, and ended up as a professor in her own right), I created a team in each place and managed them in the conduct of the research.

I went to places like Kibera, one of the largest slums in East Africa, in Nairobi, Kenya. The old Uganda Railway line runs through it; the railway was built by the British to link the port of Mombasa with Nairobi and then Kisumu, on Lake Victoria, where steamboats could connect you with the old capital of Uganda, Entebbe. Before I started my research, if one had noticed any children at the edge of the slum, you'd assume that they were either in public school or out of school. But I went with these children into the slum and found that they were very frequently in low-cost private schools. We found more than one hundred low-cost private schools in the slum of Kibera alone.

And I went to places like the fishing village of Bortianor, in the district of Ga, outside of Accra, Ghana, where there were seven low-cost private schools. Later, in one of them, I helped make a film that followed one of the students, Victoria, through her daily routine.[10] We went out on her father's fishing boat at 3 a.m., riding the surf in the bay out to the Atlantic. The family lived close to the public school, and Joshua, the father, told us in detail of how he or his wife, who worked all day smoking the fish that they would sell, saw how late in the day the public-school teachers arrived, how little teaching they did, and how early they left. Mostly the children played outside.

Joshua told me how, as soon as he could afford to, he sent his daughter to the private school. "The reason the private school is better than the public," he said, "is because there is a private owner. If the teacher doesn't teach as required, he will be fired and replaced." He understood precisely the dynamics of the situation. In a parallel way, he knew that if a fisherman didn't turn up to the fishing boat before it left in the morning, he'd be fired unless he had a very good excuse. He could see the same accountability operating in the private schools.

Low-cost private schools even existed in rural China. I was asked to speak at a major conference in Beijing, and I told the large audience about what we'd found in India and sub-Saharan Africa. At the end of the session, I asked, "Could the same thing be happening here in China?" A rather embarrassed silence followed. Had I not seen how wealthy China was now, what with Beijing's multiple circular ring roads and countless plush high-rise office and apartment buildings? Of course, it was a silly question to have asked. I felt ready to concede that there wouldn't be low-cost private schools in a country growing as wealthy as China.

In the break time after my talk, an Englishman came up to me. He was from the Department for International Development (DFID), the British government aid agency. He told me that they were working in the poorest part of China, in the northwest, the Gansu province. They were working in the poorest villages. There were no private schools there, I could take it from him. Perhaps I had found low-cost private schools in India or Africa. But in China, there were none. Here private schools were only for the elite.

This was like a red rag to the bull in me; the same had happened wherever I sought to find out about low-cost private schools. I would arrive in a country and meet with academics or even sympathetic think-tank leaders from whom I was seeking help with the research. They would tell me: I'm sorry to say this, but whatever you've found in other countries, in *our* country, private schools are for the upper classes, not for the poor. I would hear the same story repeated time and time again by government officials or those working for aid agencies. But in every single one of the countries in which I had worked, I would go into the slums and poor areas, and within a few minutes I would find a low-cost private school, then another, then another, and realize that this phenomenon seemed to be well-nigh universal, wherever there were poor people—well-nigh universal, but also well-nigh universally ignored.

So, when the Englishman from DFID told me that there were no low-cost private schools in rural China, couldn't this just be the same as I'd been told so many times, in so many different places? I had to go back to England the next day, but I vowed to return and find out. And as luck would have it, a few days later a young Chinese man came to see me in my office in Newcastle. His name was Liu Qiang, and he's a professor now at Beijing Normal University. Then, he was a young man who wanted to sign up to do a doctorate with me. "Where are you from?" I asked. "China," he said. "I know you're from China," I said, "but where in particular?" "Gansu province," he said. "Are there low-cost private schools there?" I asked. "Of course," he said. "Do you mind if we put off registering for your PhD for a couple of months and go there together?" I asked. "Of course," he agreed.

So it was that a week later we flew into Lanzhou, the capital of Gansu. We drove out into the valleys of the most beautiful highlands, getting up early to go to markets and talk to women and men, asking whether there were low-cost private schools in the remote villages they had come in from. We found a few leads, drove out into the highlands, then abandoned our car and hired one of those three-wheeled vehicles that carry goods and passengers into the remotest mountains. We traveled along mountain routes in late September, seeing peasants harvesting—as they had harvested for hundreds if not thousands of years, gathered in a family circle, cutting with scythes. We went through a narrow gorge. There we found our first low-cost private school in the Gansu mountains: Ming Xin, People's Hearts private school, where the husband-and-wife team greeted us warmly, and the husband gathered his school choir to sing to us. "No more turn your cold eyes away from these innocent children," they sang.

Over the next few days, we visited five similar low-cost private schools in these spectacular highlands. The head of international relations in the government office in Lanzhou was nonplussed that I'd been out looking in the mountains myself but was eventually convinced that it was a legitimate research interest. And so, we got a large research team organized and out into the mountains, and the team found 586 low-cost private schools. DFID had been right, but only to a point. They were working in what they considered to be the remotest, poorest villages of Gansu, the poorest province in China. In those villages, it was true, there were no private schools. But if you pushed farther, traveled for a day beyond those villages, then there were even poorer communities, beyond the reach of the state. And there we found the low-cost private schools.

I went to places like Makoko, Nigeria, the shantytown built on stilts in the dark waters of Lagos Lagoon. Makoko has probably played one of the greatest individual roles in highlighting globally the significant role played by low-cost private schools.

Many foreign visitors arriving at Murtala Muhammed (Lagos) International Airport make their way to Victoria Island, the upmarket part of the city. As you travel there over Third Mainland Bridge, you can look down and see Makoko, with its thin veneer of smoke emanating from the open cooking fires, and you'll see its fishermen out in the lagoon. When I first traveled across that bridge, I pointed down to Makoko and said to my host, "That's where I want to go to find low-cost private schools." "Too dangerous" was the response.

So, the next day I went without him. The taxi I took stopped on the edge of the slum, also implying that it was too dangerous to go on inside. Instead, I went by canoe, found some children, and asked where they went to school. Little eight-year-old Sandra said, "KPS." "What does that mean?" "Kennedy," she said, or at least that's what I heard. "Kennedy what?" I asked. "Kennedy Private School," she answered, and then she took me to see it. It was not, in fact, named after the American president but instead was *Ken-ade* Private Secondary School, on the edge of the waters. It turned out to be one of thirty-two private schools that my researchers found in that slum alone.

Makoko and Ken-ade Private School (and its amiable, committed proprietor, Bawo Sabo Elieu Ayeseminikan, whom everyone calls "BSE") have featured large in what happened next in global public awareness of low-cost private schools: In 2010, after thirteen years in opposition, the British electorate returned the Conservative Party to power, in coalition with the Liberal Democrats. Prior to the election, I'd been talking to the opposition shadow secretary of state for international development, the Right Honourable Andrew Mitchell, about the virtues of low-cost private schools, and he'd become convinced that they had an important role to play in reaching "education for all." When my book *The Beautiful Tree* was published in 2009, he had circulated it to his entire team, making sure that they understood the importance of this phenomenon. Later, when the Conservative Party was in power, their "Green Paper on International Development" expressly referred to low-cost private education, and future prime minister David Cameron mentioned its importance at a press conference launching the paper.

I was in Ghana, doing teacher training in low-cost private schools, when the 2010 election result came in. Andrew Mitchell's political assistant phoned me. He said, "You know that Andrew is convinced. Now you have to convince the officials in the Department for International Development." So, when I returned to England, I went to visit Mark Lowcock (now Sir Mark), then head of policy, soon to become the department's permanent secretary, the most senior civil service position. He appeared skeptical that such schools could exist in any numbers or be of the quality that I was reporting. I was used to this. Ever since I first started talking about low-cost private schools, senior academics as well as government and aid officials have been dismissive.

But then an opportunity arose for Lowcock to go and see for himself, accompanying Mitchell, who was now secretary of state, on a visit to Lagos. From Ken-ade Private School's computer, Lowcock wrote me an email: "In twenty-seven years of working in development, I have had few surprises. This is one of them. I am impressed by both the quantity of private schools I have seen, as well as their quality." From that moment on, he became an ally in this work. A few months later, he invited me to the Department for International Development's education retreat in southwest Scotland, where he told the gathered education advisers from all over the world that they must always report back to him on the number of low-cost private schools in their communities. He said to me afterward, "Why have they never told me about these schools? They're serving a majority of the urban kids, and significant minorities of rural ones. Why didn't they think I'd be interested?"

The next year, David Cameron, the prime minister, was also in Lagos as part of his tour of Africa. His political adviser, Steve Hilton (now a commentator on Fox News Channel), wrote about the trip in his book *More Human*: "When we were accompanying the prime minister on a 2011 visit to Africa, Rohan [Silva] and I asked to see one of James Tooley's schools in one of the worst slums in Lagos." While it's flattering to be mentioned in this way, the larger point is that there are literally hundreds of thousands of these schools that have nothing whatsoever to do with me or any foreigner at all. They've been built and set up by local entrepreneurs.

Hilton continues:

Whereas the UK-government-backed school, run by the state and financed via the Department for International Development (DFID), was a disaster, the Tooley-backed for-profit school was a sensation: eager children in pristine uniforms learning literacy, maths, science— with the help of a solar-powered computer. This is in the middle of a slum. Literally. To get there, Rohan and I had to pick our way through stinking, festering garbage, open sewers, ramshackle structures that could and would be washed away by the next rains. To arrive at that school, peep over the makeshift wall, and see rows and rows of eager pupils happily studying in the midst of utter chaos and squalor was completely astonishing, incomparably inspiring.[11]

It is most definitely all those things and more. It's the inspiration I still get each time I visit such a poor area. As a result of my team's research in Lagos State, and the film that we made in Makoko in 2005 for *Newsnight*, the BBC's flagship news program, DFID decided to conduct a thorough census of all the private schools in Lagos—in part, I guess, to verify that the data I was giving them were correct. They invited the young researcher Dr. Joanna Härmä to lead this census, and I made sure that the Association for Formidable Educational Development (AFED), the huge and vibrant private school association of which I'm a patron, fully cooperated. The census found 12,098 private schools, serving 1,408,420 children. This census, the first full census of low-cost private schools that had been conducted in any major city, led to other projects by the Department for International Development, including DEEPEN—Developing Effective Private Education in Nigeria—to help foster the environment for low-cost private schools in Lagos State and elsewhere. Härmä, too, has contributed enormously to the research effort on low-cost private schools in Lagos and in other states and countries.

So, by degree, in large part because of my teams' research work, people became aware of the role played by these low-cost private schools. Critics of this work have been many, and you'll be hearing from some of them in this book. But one criticism did challenge me. Some critics charged that when I said, "Private schools are good for the poor," I had only looked at Ghana, Kenya, Nigeria, India, and China. Those countries are hardly the world's most difficult places. For the *real poor*, the most disadvantaged children, how can you say that private schools are good for them?

I have taken this challenge seriously. The world's most difficult places are not hard to find: they are in war-torn, conflict-affected states, especially in sub-Saharan Africa. So, again with funding from the John Templeton Foundation, I created research teams in Sierra Leone, Liberia, and South Sudan, looking to see what we could find. Would the extraordinary phenomenon we'd found in the rest of the world also be present in these settings, the world's most difficult places? I'll take up this story in the next chapter, but it's not too great a spoiler to say that yes, they were there too, in extraordinarily large numbers, doing pretty much the same as they were doing in the other countries I'd visited already.

So, there is truly a global revolution, a grassroots social entrepreneurship revolution—what I call "education, by the people, for the people," in my own version of the Gettysburg Address. What's happening in developing countries is radical.

Three Parts

This book has three parts. Part 1, "A Global Revolution," looks at the current state of the debate on low-cost private education. Here I have a dilemma. I've been working in this area for nearly twenty years now; it is my life's work. I've already written a book (*The Beautiful Tree*) on the subject, published a decade ago. One aim of part 1 of this book is to update the reader on some of the important debates and examples that have emerged since that book. However, in the space available, it would be impossible for me to bring out *all* the examples and challenge *all* the arguments that have emerged since then. In any case, some readers may not be familiar with low-cost private schools, so they would need a more introductory approach, while some challenges to the arguments would require going back to earlier cases already made.

So, part 1 of this book aims to give a *flavor* of some of the important debates that are live in this area now. As I shall outline at the beginning of the next chapter, there seem to be seven themes or dimensions that commentators consider the most important to address, gleaned from sources evaluating developmental impact. These dimensions are *scalability* (or *ubiquity*) and *affordability* (chapter 1), *quality* and *value for money* (chapter 2), *equity* and *choice* (chapter 3), and *sustainability* (chapter 4).

It's my contention that if you are satisfied that low-cost private schooling compares favorably with the public alternative along these seven dimensions, then you will be convinced that low-cost private schooling has an important role to play in development. In each of these chapters, I give an example or description to illustrate the dimension, and then I explore some of the evidence to support the theme. Readers seeking a watertight case defending the role of low-cost private schools, however, may need to go back to some other referenced articles, reports, and monographs. Nevertheless, I am hopeful that part 1 of this book gives a clear enough picture of the direction of travel of the evidence and arguments to satisfy many readers.

All of this is a defense of low-cost private education against critics who feel that governments, not the private sector, should be doing education. But there are also independent arguments against letting governments have control over education, particularly in conflict-affected or war-torn states, such as Sierra Leone, South Sudan, and Liberia. The arguments may even be applicable more widely, to countries such as Nigeria and India, and perhaps even to the United States and the UK. Part 1 concludes with chapter 5, which examines these arguments, drawing the themes together with a look at implications of the Universal Declaration of Human Rights. Part 1, then, is an update to *The Beautiful Tree*, a survey of the current landscape of the extraordinary phenomenon of low-cost private education.

But this book also aims to move the discussion forward in other respects. The existence of this alternative private education sphere in developing countries raises fundamental questions about the role of government in education in general, as applicable to the West as to developing countries. This is linked to the growing interest in "self-organized learning environments." My friend and colleague Sugata Mitra, PhD, has been at the forefront of this movement—he won the first US $1 million TED Prize and is an internationally acclaimed educator, hugely in demand for his folksy, charming, and inspiring talks. Sugata and his team coined the phrase "self-organized learning environments," or SOLEs, when we were working together in Hyderabad, India, to set up the first of these learning laboratories in low-cost private schools there. "Self-organized" means that there is no central control that has led to the order that emerges. When people think of "self-organized learning environments," they may tend to think of Mitra's work, of how children can learn by themselves, without the aid of a teacher. It's all remarkably interesting, deserving of the attention it is getting.

But there's another usage of the term *self-organized learning environments* that is equally, if not more, exciting: a way of designating the emergence of the schools I've been describing already. The extraordinary rise of low-cost private schools is itself a dramatic manifestation of self-organization. There is no central control that has led to their emergence. They are organized completely outside of any external state authority. Individual entrepreneurs set them up, using their own template, to satisfy the community, which organizes itself to learn, without any input from government or international agencies.

I have come to think it's useful to explore the rise of low-cost private education under the terminology of self-organized learning for two reasons. First, it's a popular term at present and, seen in a positive light, a virtue-signaling term. More seriously, once one starts to look at the rise of low-cost private education in this light, it brings to the surface important ways in which these schools' self-organization is impeded. For there is one crucially important aspect whereby self-organization is not typically permitted: in what I call the "framework of education," the curriculum and assessment systems, the system of compulsory schooling, and the organization of schooling, all imposed by governments and monitored by governments and international agencies.

As I research schools in different countries, work with large federations that contain so many schools, manage some schools myself, and keep up to date with the academic literature, I worry about the curriculum and assessment systems that get imposed on children in these schools, a framework typically imposed by governments. It has many side effects that seem to be negative. Some of these may appear trivial, yet they are all crucially important:

- I worry why school often seems so boring, particularly to older children.
- I wonder why school can be so demotivating for children, or, to turn it around, why we as educators don't exert ourselves more to motivate students.
- The way we measure educational outcomes seems so primitive—why wait until children have finished high school to decide how well they've done?
- Why do we treat children as if they are age-batches in some factory rather than individuals with their own learning pace?
- Why do the widely accepted international measures of education focus not on outcomes related to the goals of education but instead on tests of what is taught in schools?
- And I worry that schooling as we see it leads to what the educational sociologist Ronald Dore called in 1976 the "diploma disease." Rampant "credentialism" or "qualification inflation" leads to an arms race of stu-

dents piling up certificates whose sole purpose is to provide a signal to employers; the certificates don't appear to add much in the way of valuable skills or knowledge and thus waste everybody's time and resources.

These are not new questions, but in the developing world no one much seems to be worrying about them, at least not in public. It's almost as if those in developing countries should be grateful for all the "education" that gets handed out to them—as if it would be churlish of them to question its worth. Part 2 of the book, "Reclaiming the Framework of Education," is devoted to exploring and proposing answers to some of these questions:

- How far can self-organized learning go?
- Can it encompass even the framework of education?
- Could freedom to challenge the existing framework of education lead to increasing the motivation of children?
- Could educational freedom crack the diploma disease?

The discussion brings in new perspectives on these questions, which are also of relevance to education in the West.

Let's be clear: part 1 of the book is based on evidence, while part 2 is somewhat speculative. Pointing to problems that arise from the framework of education being under state control, it suggests what could happen if education were fully self-organized, a fully spontaneous order. I'm not necessarily trying in part 2 to convince anyone; instead, I want to illustrate alternative ways forward.

In part 3, "Off to America," I'm assuming that readers will by then be convinced of the virtues of the spontaneous order in education and open to exploring its applicability to America (and by extension to the United Kingdom, Australia, New Zealand, Europe, and so on). However, a few words of caution: When American reformers sympathetic to the private sector speak about education reform, typically they talk about top-down initiatives, like giving parents vouchers to use at any school of their choice, public or private. Or they promote charter schools, which are funded and regulated by the state but otherwise have independent management. This is far from what we see in developing countries, where individual entrepreneurs run their own schools, providing high-quality and low-cost education completely independent of the state. But could there be mileage in exploring why there is this difference and whether the solution found in developing countries—burgeoning low-cost private schools—could be relevant to America (and Britain, and others) too?

Perhaps I wouldn't be asking this question if American education reformers were successful in bringing about vouchers or charter schools. But in my view, they are losing an uphill struggle. Less than half of 1 percent of children in America are in voucher programs, and I can't see it ever realistically exceeding 2 percent. I'm all for seeing a glass half-full rather than half-empty, but this glass appears to be very nearly empty.

Perhaps there are currently no low-cost private schools in America because public education is nowhere near as bad as that found in, say, Nigeria or India. There won't be the same incentive for parents and their children to seek out independent alternatives. This is not to say that dissatisfaction, even extreme dissatisfaction, is absent. However, it won't ever be as widespread as that found in developing countries.

But recall that this was not the only reason why parents I first spoke to —in the slums of Hyderabad, India—desired to send their children to low-cost private schools. There was also the issue of accountability and control. In a way, this inverts the whole question of why there are private schools: Why would you *not* want control over your children's education? And if you do, then why would you acquiesce in public education?

In the past, when giving talks about my work, I've often been asked whether I think there would be any interest in low-cost private schools in America or in England, depending on where I'm giving the talk. My stock response has been that public schools in America (or England) do not suffer from the parlous conditions of government schools in sub-Saharan Africa or South Asia, so perhaps that's why low-cost private schools haven't emerged, and why they won't.

But then, a couple of years ago, I did some research in the less wealthy neighborhoods of Newcastle upon Tyne, in North East England, interviewing opportunistically selected parents on street corners, in marketplaces, and the like. Newcastle includes some of the most deprived neighborhoods in England. In part this is because it used to be a significant industrial city, important for shipbuilding and coal mining in the nineteenth and early twentieth centuries, that declined as these industries declined. It is now finding its feet again as a "postindustrial" city, with new industries in software and finance emerging.

My sample was not random; nevertheless, it showed some interesting results. Around one-fifth of participants thought they could afford a school costing around £50 per week. The survey seemed to suggest that there could be demand for private education if fees were low enough. I got together with two other educators in North East England and created a business plan for a chain of low-cost private schools. The idea quickly captured the interest of those in the British media—the BBC, the *Daily Telegraph*, the *Times*, the *Sunday Express*, the *Sun*, and the *Daily Mail* all ran stories on it, and several television production companies asked to do documentaries on the first year of the school chain. And, most important, more than 150 parents expressed an interest in the school, even before we got government permission to open. Perhaps we'd hit on a market niche that was capturing the imagination, one that nobody else had thought of before. I'll have more to say about this later, when we examine what was happening in education before the state got involved, which has remarkable parallels to what we see in developing countries today.

Let's be clear about what we mean by *education*. I've used the word loosely so far, in the way that it is typically used in public discussions. That is, it's been referring to the institutions in which it commonly takes place, so *education* has been used as a synonym for *schooling* or *schools*. This is a widely accepted usage, and we'll carry on with this kind of usage throughout part 1, where we focus mainly on schools—low-cost private schools—and mainly, too, on what is typically described as K–12 education—that is, schooling from kindergarten through twelfth grade.[13]

I was originally a philosopher of education, and the tradition in that field is to be careful about the use of the word. Because if we use *education* to mean schooling, we may preempt the answers to some important questions concerning how and where young people should become educated and the role of government therein. For instance, the nineteenth-century member of Parliament and pamphleteer William Cobbett begins his *Advice to Young Men* with "What need had we of *schools*? What need of *teachers*? What need of scolding or force, to induce children to read and write and love books?"[14] Cobbett was dismissive of early government intervention in what he derisively dubbed "Heddekashun," or mandatory education in schools; he saw that genuine education readily took place outside of institutions called *schools*. Some economists later agreed. For example, Milton Friedman wrote in his influential essay "The Role of Government in Education" that it is important to distinguish *schooling* from *education*: "The proper subject of concern is education. The activities of government are mostly limited to schooling."[15]

Why do we need to make this distinction? There are two major ways in which education can be understood: (1) the preparation of children and young people for adult life, including for the world of work (the economy), the family (social), and society (political), in all aspects of knowledge, skills, disposition, character, and values, or (2) the initiation of children and young people into the "best that has been thought and said in the world"—that is, initiation into knowledge and culture that is "good for the soul."[16]

It doesn't take much reflection to realize that many of these—knowledge, skills, disposition, and values—can be, and often are, inculcated outside of formal schooling: in the family, in religious communities, through play, through participation in political processes, and, of course, in the world of work itself. Similarly, initiation into the best that has been thought and said in the world can also readily take place outside of any formal schooling— even before the internet, there were libraries, reading rooms, concert halls, and radio and television broadcasts, all of which are vehicles for this kind of initiation, whether one is learning as an autodidact or within sympathetic groups. The internet has transformed the potential here so that the world of learning about high culture (as well as much else, of course) is literally at the fingertips of much of the world's population.

The concern of this book, which will come to the fore in parts 2 and 3, is with education broadly understood; it remains an open question whether or not its components can best be introduced through schooling or through other mechanisms.

This book was completed before governments across the world put countries into "lockdown," reacting to the global coronavirus pandemic. To keep up to date with this crisis, I've inserted a few paragraphs at various points into the text to raise some potential implications.

In large part, I find it very hard to predict what the impact of this crisis will be on education, and on anything else. It really is "too early to say," as Chinese premier Zhou Enlai said of the impact of the French Revolution.

A lot depends on whether the rapid lifting of lockdown restrictions that are taking place as I write now (July 2020) will continue, or whether further lockdowns will be imposed later this year. If the former, then the impact of the crisis on education may be minimal, and we may return very quickly back to normal—not a "new" normal, as some are putting it, but just normal. If further lockdowns occur, then clearly there will be a much bigger impact on how we view education.

One impact has been immediately apparent. Across the developing countries that I discuss in the first part of the book, governments acted swiftly to close all schools, including low-cost private schools, and as I write they still have not been allowed to reopen. These governments meanwhile offered no safety-nets to mitigate their actions. This has caused great hardship to so many school operators; many will go out of business as a result. This is a terrible outcome. However, if schools can reopen soon, then they may be able to bounce back, as long as country economies have not been sent into freefall.

Concerning the impact on "developed" countries (those in the West), there has been a mix of experience. Governments closed all public schools, and for many children this has meant a long, extended time of educational inactivity, which is likely to have been harmful to most. For some parents, however, government closure of public schools may have led to a bit of a renaissance in their educational thinking—and this may be the only silver lining to the crisis. Some parents have seen the indifference of public schools to their children—and their teachers' lack of engagement with them online—and been led to think differently about how education can be delivered, and how their children's learning can be transformed. Other parents have experienced homeschooling for the first time and been led to question why governments have a near-monopoly on schooling. Even if these parents don't wish to continue homeschooling much into the future, they're very likely to be more open to the arguments of this book for engaging with educational alternatives.

With that in mind, let's return to our text: Where did this idea of low-cost private schools come from? In the next chapter, we'll journey to Liberia, to give a flavor of what is happening across the developing world, with implications for the future of education in the rest of the world. That will come after we've outlined the seven important themes or dimensions that will frame the discussion in part 1.

PART ONE

A Global Revolution

THIS BOOK IS about the global revolution of low-cost private education. Part 1 catalogs our current state of knowledge of this phenomenon. I started writing about it back in 2000.[1] One influential development expert, Kevin Watkins, recently director of UNESCO's *Education for All Global Monitoring Report* and now CEO of Save the Children UK, wrote in 2004, "Professor Tooley and his like-minded colleagues are ploughing a lonely furrow. Nobody, it seems, is listening to them. Long may it stay that way."[2]

Sixteen years later, the furrow is much less lonely. Hundreds of researchers, activists, philanthropists, investors, and new entrepreneurs are active in this field. Many of the researchers and activists are deeply antagonistic, however. The furrow may be less lonely, but it is sharply polarized.[3]

Why the controversy? Painfully, to many in the development industry (academics, officials in aid agencies, and teachers' unions), the very existence of low-cost private education shows that the people themselves are not embracing the education solution they are supposed to accept. They are not embracing the accepted wisdom that came about with the Universal Declaration of Human Rights in 1948, that free and compulsory public education is the only way forward. It's hard when the people themselves reject seventy years of development consensus.

I

Ubiquity and Affordability

PEOPLE TEND TO take one of three positions concerning the relevance of low-cost private schools to development. First, some argue that low-cost private schools are irrelevant to the promotion of education for all, which should be done through universal, free public education.[1] Second, low-cost private schools can be tolerated for now, given the parlous state of public education, but only until we get public education back on track.[2] Finally, my own view is that parental preference for low-cost private schools, coupled with the parlous state of public education, should make us think differently about the roles of public and private education for development. Indeed, private education alone seems to be able to offer a route to providing educational opportunities for all.

What might be beneficial to know in order to adjudicate between these three positions? Using criteria that I've gleaned from sources evaluating developmental impact,[3] I suggest that there are *seven* particularly important issues that would apply in general to any development-proposed solution—in this case, low-cost private schools:

1. *Scalability/ubiquity*: Is the solution (i.e., low-cost private schools) found across many different types of low-income communities? Does it serve the poor and hardest to reach, in the most difficult countries? Does it exist at scale, or have the potential to scale, in these communities?

2. *Affordability*: Is the solution affordable to low-income communities? Is its cost competitive with existing alternatives, including that offered by government?

3. *Quality*: Is the solution better than other alternatives, including anything offered by government? Is it amenable to being further improved?

4. *Value for money*: Is the solution financially sustainable? Is it more cost-effective than any alternatives, including government alternatives?

5. *Equity*: Does the solution help narrow gender gaps and gaps between ethnic, religious, caste, and other minority groups? Is it better in this respect than existing alternatives, including government alternatives?

6. *Choice*: Is the solution an option desired by the poor themselves?

7. *Sustainability*: Is the solution sustainable—that is, able to continue over time without ongoing external support?

Let's look at scalability/ubiquity first. Synonyms for *ubiquitous* include *universal, pervasive, global*, and *abundant*. I don't think it's at all contentious now to point out that low-cost private education satisfies this epithet splendidly. In *The Beautiful Tree*, I presented research from five countries: Ghana, Nigeria, Kenya, India, and China, with smaller forays into Zimbabwe. Personally, I've now seen the phenomenon of low-cost private schools in twenty-two countries on four continents. The British government aid agency, the Department for International Development (DFID), recently commissioned a "rigorous literature review," supposedly a comprehensive survey of evidence about low-cost private schools in a total of eleven countries: India, Pakistan, Bangladesh, Nepal, Nigeria, Kenya, Tanzania, Ghana, South Africa, Malawi, and Jamaica—and these were just DFID countries of interest. Other studies show low-cost private schools in the Philippines and Indonesia as well as in Latin American countries, including Peru, Brazil, Honduras, and Guatemala. In other words, we can easily talk about this phenomenon as ubiquitous in the sense of global. It truly is a global phenomenon.

Moreover, we can also show that, within countries researched, the phenomenon is abundant; serving, more importantly, an abundant number of children. In sub-Saharan Africa, the most detailed research has been done in Nigeria. Lagos State is the most studied: extrapolating from a recent census, it is estimated that enrollment in private schools in Lagos State alone is now 2.78 million, of which around 2.12 million are likely to be in low-cost private schools. There are likely to be 14,000 low-cost private schools in that one state of Nigeria alone. And the proportion of children served by the private sector is high—around 70 percent of preschool and primary-school children are in private schools.[4] These figures seem typical of major urban areas across West and East Africa. Recent research reports from Nairobi (Kenya), Kampala (Uganda), and Accra (Ghana) support this.[5] The highest percentage is from Kampala, where 84 percent of primary-school children in deprived areas are in private education.

India is the most studied country in Asia. Extrapolating from recent research, we can make some estimates of the numbers of children in low-cost private schools there. In India, there are around 300 million school-age children. Assuming a 69 percent rural, 31 percent urban split (in line with the split across India), there would be 93 million urban and 207 million rural children. In rural areas, 30 percent of children, according to the comprehensive *Annual Status of Education Report (ASER)*, are in private schools, the vast majority of which are low cost. That is, around 60 million children in rural India are in low-cost private schools.

In urban India, it is estimated that around 70 percent of children are in unaided private schools (ignoring government-aided private schools, which would increase the number further, but which are often counted as government schools). This gives a figure of 65 million children in private schools in urban India. It has been suggested by one study that 49 percent of these could be low cost,[6] so that would give a figure of around 32 million children in urban India in low-cost private schools.

Hence in India, I estimate that the total number of children in low-cost private schools is around 92 million. Supposing the average size of a school is 200 students, this gives an estimate of around 450,000 low-cost private schools in India alone.

Indeed, it is well recognized in India that the growth of private schooling is leading to an emptying of public schools. In the year 2015–16, 5,044 government schools were *empty*; yes, you read that correctly—more than 5,000 schools had no pupils at all. But this didn't stop them from employing 6,961 teachers. A total of 12,196 schools had five pupils or fewer (employing 19,419 teachers), 31,963 had ten students or fewer (employing 26,186), and altogether there were 1,047,895 public schools in India with fifty students or fewer.[7]

And let's be clear, this is not because of any drop in India's child population; it has been growing during the period that the emptying of public schools has been taking place. No, the emptying of government schools "is largely the result of an exodus of students from government schools and migration towards private schools."[8]

These estimates are based on research. Anecdotally, one gets the impression that other countries across South Asia and sub-Saharan Africa are similar. Extrapolating from a few studies, I've estimated that there could be about 74 million children in sub-Saharan Africa in low-cost private schools. Indeed, the figures from India and sub-Saharan Africa suggest a common figure of around 75–80 million children in low-cost private schools per billion of population.

One important corollary of all this is that any figure for out-of-school children given globally must be taken with caution, because many of the children are in low-cost private schools that are unregistered and therefore off the official radar. So, it is likely that the global figure for out-of-school children is much lower than suggested, because many of the children will be in unregistered low-cost private schools.

There is no doubt that low-cost private schools are a ubiquitous phenomenon across developing countries. Because of this fact alone, low-cost private schools possess scalability.

One of my questions for ubiquity pushes the concept to its limits: Does it serve the poor and hardest to reach, in the most difficult countries? This is where some might balk. Indeed, a criticism of my earlier work for *The Beautiful Tree* was that I'd said that private schools are "good for the poor," but are they really reaching the most difficult places? Only if they did so would they really satisfy my claims.

With research teams in these countries, I directed a study in Liberia and Sierra Leone, countries recently torn by civil war, as well as South Sudan, still in the throes of bloody conflict. What is happening in those countries is extraordinary. It has huge implications for the way we see the role of government in education in the developing world and beyond.

In the world of international development and education, Liberia has recently featured prominently because the government has contracted out management of some public schools to the private sector, funded by international charities. The project, Partnership Schools for Liberia (PSL), has been covered in, among other publications, the *Financial Times* and the *Economist*.[9] Because the American chain of schools Bridge International Academies—funded by, among others, the Bill and Melinda Gates Foundation and the Chan Zuckerberg Initiative—is involved, this has aroused the ire of international teachers' unions and nongovernmental organizations (NGOs).[10]

This focus is a shame. Something else is happening in Liberia—and other war-affected countries—that in my view is far more noteworthy, as I found out when I first visited Liberia back in 2012. It has nothing to do with any outsider agencies, charities, or for-profit companies. Instead, it has to do with individual educational entrepreneurs, battling the odds to create something of immense value.

Emancipation in Liberia

When one thinks of Liberia, *emancipation* is an obvious word that springs to mind. Liberia—literally, the "land of the free"—was the place where emancipated slaves from America went or were sent. But the history of Liberia is a terrible example of how one person's freedom can become another person's oppression. Public education was an important vehicle of that oppression.

In 1816, white Americans formed the Society for the Colonization of Free People of Color of America, commonly known as the American Colonization Society (ACS), to address the issue of what should be done about the increasing numbers of free black Americans. Their idea, inspired by what they had seen the British create in Sierra Leone, was to resettle the people in a new state in West Africa. But where could the new state be established? In 1818, ACS representatives first went to the British colony of Freetown, in what is now Sierra Leone, but they were not welcomed there, so they moved along the coast looking for a suitable site, one where local African leaders might sell them land; none agreed. In 1821, with the aid of the US Navy, they went again. Still, African leaders refused to sell them land. This time the navy captain "persuaded"—presumably with the threat of violence—the local leader, King Peter, to sell them land, and a thirty-six-mile-long peninsula, Cape Mesurado, was acquired by the society. The local African tribes were antagonistic from the beginning, attacking the (black) colonialists for taking their land. The colonialists suffered, too, from diseases and the climate.

By 1835, six more of these embryonic colonies had been established, including one by the US government itself. Meanwhile, Cape Mesurado had been extended, as the indigenous Africans had feared, sometimes through purchase of land, sometimes by brute force. These colonies agreed to create the Commonwealth of Liberia in 1838, with the capital of Monrovia—named after James Monroe, who had been the American president when the first colonies were established. More colonies joined in 1842 as the size of the state increased. After the abolition of the Atlantic slave trade, slaves freed by the US Navy were brought to Liberia (just as slaves freed by the British Navy were set ashore in Sierra Leone), whether or not that was the area in Africa from which they had originated. (There seems to have been at best ignorance, at worst a despicable laziness here—anywhere in Africa appeared to be suitable as home for someone black, never mind the thousands of different languages, tribes, and ethnic groups that there were in Africa.)

Up until 1841, the colony had been governed by the white members of the ACS. In that year, the first black governor, J. J. Roberts (the international airport and Robertsport are named after him) was appointed. He was what was by then called an "Americo-Liberian"—someone of African American descent, usually a freed slave. Many of these were of mixed race, with some European ancestry.

In 1847, the Americo-Liberians proclaimed independence, and the Commonwealth became the Republic of Liberia. Its constitution was modeled on the US Constitution, with one key difference—only people with black African ancestry were permitted to obtain citizenship and to own land. This aspect of the 1847 Constitution is still in force today.

So, this brief historical survey immediately gives the lie to the common misconception, which often finds its way into trivia questions,[11] that Liberia was one of only two countries in Africa (the other being Ethiopia) that were not colonized. Liberia, it is true, was not colonized by the European powers in their carve-up of the continent, the "Scramble for Africa," from the late nineteenth century. But that was because it had already been colonized by Americans of African descent some sixty years before.

Soon, the Americo-Liberians started to behave like colonists of any race. They began to take their own slaves from among what was called the African Liberian population, the indigenous people of the land. Although the Americo-Liberians were of African descent themselves, they had lived, sometimes for generations, in America and saw themselves as a cut above the African Liberian population. And so, although they made up and still make up only around 5 percent of the population, they dominated all aspects of society and created political, economic, and social institutions that promoted their own interests over those of the African Liberians.

A coup in 1980 brought to power the first African Liberian, Samuel Kanyon Doe. Many hoped this would transform the opportunities available to the indigenous people of Liberia. It was not to be; the coup simply transferred power and privilege from one ethnic group to another. Civil war was the result—from 1987 to 1996, and 1997 to 2003. I'll have more to say later about the way public education was implicated in these civil wars.

I first arrived in Monrovia early on a Sunday in late January 2012. Roberts International Airport, previously a US Air Force base, is some eighty kilometers outside of the city. It's connected by a straight and relatively flat paved road, so it's only just over an hour's drive away.

When I was planning my trip to Liberia, I'd written to someone at the Tony Blair Faith Foundation, who replied that unfortunately it was not a good time to be coming to the country, because "all the people you will want to see will be busy with the presidential inauguration." The assumption is that any Westerner visiting such a place is most interested in meeting with senior government officials. Actually, the people I wanted to see did turn out to be busy, but they were busy running schools, not busy with official ceremonies.

I had chosen a budget hotel not too far from what I'd heard was one of the largest slums in Monrovia—West Point. Wanting to head out straightaway, but not sure I could trust the hotel security, I put my wallet, bursting with US dollars—there were no ATMs that I would be able to use, so I had to bring enough cash for the whole visit—and camera into my leather bag and set off into the streets.

Crossing the wide, American-style boulevard outside the hotel, I eventually found a taxi. There were no individual-occupancy taxis on the road this Sunday afternoon, but there were plenty of multioccupancy vehicles. The driver said that for one US dollar, he could take me to the end of his route, the closest he would get to West Point, and drop me there. His—and everyone else's—accent was extraordinarily difficult for me to understand at first. It was like a very Deep South drawl. The syllables seemed to slur together so much that, at first, it was hard to find any words in among them. Over time, it got easier.

When we ended up in the center of the city, I was the only passenger left. "Do you know where West Point is?" the driver asked. I didn't, of course. He said he could take me there for an additional five US dollars. I then asked if he could guide me around and then take me back to my hotel, for US $5 an hour. He agreed.

Edward, for that was his name, clearly enjoyed showing me around as we proceeded toward West Point. He pointed out buildings and landmarks, including the UNESCO building, with its high walls mounted with razor wire. "They like keeping their distance," he mused. I told him the purpose of my visit, that I was there to find low-cost private schools in the slums and poor areas of Monrovia. He said, "They don't exist. Only high-cost private schools exist in Monrovia."

Was I perturbed by that? I'd been hearing that for years now. I'd heard it in India, Kenya, Ghana, Nigeria, Zimbabwe, South Africa, and China. Always people with power and influence told me, "In our country, private schools are for the rich. There are no private schools for the poor." But always, there were private schools for the poor. I published these accounts of being told they didn't exist and then finding they did once you looked for them in my book *The Beautiful Tree*. Now, of course, in countries I described in that book, no one can deny their existence anymore. But it's sometimes a source of wry amusement to me that people in positions of power and influence now tell me that this phenomenon exists in _____—and they list the countries in which I've done research—but not anywhere else. So, Liberia? No, the schools didn't exist there. People didn't seem to get that it was only after my teams' research that we knew the schools existed at all. So, wasn't it possible that if someone did research elsewhere, they would also find the schools there? I'd gone to Liberia after hearing the development experts tell me I wouldn't find anything of interest. Now with Edward telling me the same, this was slightly more concerning, as taxi drivers usually know better than government and nongovernmental organization (NGO) officials about the local environs.

Anyway, I told him to continue to West Point. Searching for something mythical is what I've been doing for years now. (It's why my friend, the late Andrew Coulson, once described me as "the Indiana Jones of Education Policy.") One day I may meet my government nemesis. But I had a good feeling about Monrovia.

We arrived at the entrance to the slum of West Point and started driving down its narrow paved road. It was pretty much like many slums I'd been to in sub-Saharan Africa: the same crowded streets, with market stalls—run by plump women selling ripe tomatoes, onions, and yams—encroaching onto the road and young men pushing wheelbarrows tottering under heavy loads or running with empty barrows to pick up new goods. There was the same crowded, shared housing, made from poles and wood, mud and tin roofs; the same flimsy wooden and tin structures for shared bathrooms, either perched above the black waters on which this part of West Point had been built, or on small plots of land, with open drains. And there were open drains down every alley, carrying raw sewage as far as it could go until it seeped into the ground or spilled over.

There was the same contrast between the filthy surroundings and the striking cleanliness of the people: women were doing the washing and hanging clothes to dry in the back alleys, and the clothes that people wore typically looked sparklingly clean. Somewhere in every alley, there seemed to be small naked children washing, covering themselves from top to toe in soap, under supervision from an older sibling or young mother.

Another thing strikes you as you go into slums like West Point. There was that best-selling book first published in the early 1960s, *The Wretched of the Earth*, by Frantz Fanon, that influenced me greatly in the early 1980s as a young man, when first I thought of going to work in Africa. From a title like that, you expect to find the *people* wretched—miserable, unhappy, grief-stricken, sorrowful, despairing, cheerless, woebegone. Certainly, the conditions in which people live in the slums appear wretched—harsh, hard, stark, and difficult. But the people strike you as altogether different: women and girls sit contentedly outside their houses braiding each other's hair and gossiping; children gaily play in the dirt; men sit, also gossiping but about soccer and politics. If you just saw the people without seeing their surroundings, the tin shacks and filthy latrines and dirt tracks, you wouldn't think they were poor at all. Certainly, there's no poverty of spirit in these slums. But would there be in West Point the spirit of educational entrepreneurship that I'd found in other countries? That was what I needed to find out.

So many people were in the streets that Edward had to navigate his way slowly. Eventually, I asked him to stop the car; we got out and asked a man seated at the entrance to a tin shack about private schools. He directed us to a woman in the shack next door, who knew of one such private school nearby. She was about to go that way in any case, she told us, so after getting her things ready, she guided us down tiny, narrow alleys, where women and girls braided hair, boys bathed, and men sat and chatted.

It was very hot and humid. Edward offered to carry my bag for me; he indicated that a white man carrying such a bag might attract attention, so it would be better if he carried it. I hadn't thought about that until he mentioned it, but I did have quite a bit of cash, plus my camera and smartphone, all in a rather nice leather bag. I supposed it could attract the wrong sort of attention. He seemed a decent man, so why not?

I handed it over to him. And, of course, nothing happened. He was trustworthy, and it seemed an insult to think that he could have been otherwise. For the rest of my time in Monrovia walking around the slums, he offered to carry my bag and I let him. But it was not because I was worried about anyone else. As for all the other people I've met in the slums—in West Point and elsewhere—I've never had anything to fear. It's only remarkable how peaceful and friendly everyone is, and there is no threatening behavior. In fact, it's always just the opposite: people going out of their way to assist me.

The next day, I came back to the slum of West Point with an Americo-Liberian lady from an NGO who had kindly agreed to show me around. I told her excitedly about what I had already found and said that we should go back there in order to continue these explorations. She had been very reluctant to drive her rather plush 4x4 SUV there but eventually agreed. As we arrived on the crowded main street going into the slum, she said, "These are bad people." I asked her why she should say that. "They will steal from you," she replied. "You must watch your bag. They're very bad." We halted where I had asked

Edward to stop the day before, and she rolled down her window and called a man over. When he didn't immediately respond, she crossly ordered him to "come over here" as if she were talking to a servant. She refused to leave her vehicle to see what I'd already found in the slum, so the visit to West Point was not particularly successful, and we continued our drive somewhere else. We spoke to just one school owner—because his school was by the roadside—and she immediately asked him, "What tribe are you?"

But back to Edward and the kind lady showing us around: we came into a large open area, a sandy, mostly flat playing field stretching down to the sea, crowded with children and older boys playing soccer. Just on the edge, the woman pointed out where her daughter was going to school. I smiled and got out my notebook. It was a low-cost private school in a ramshackle tin building supported by rough wooden poles: Kru Beach Elementary and Junior School, West Point, my first low-cost private school in Monrovia.[12]

Someone went to get the proprietor, Mrs. Munroe. She unlocked the main entrance to the school and sat me down on a wooden chair inside in her office, in the darkness under the tin roof. The kind lady came to join us. Mrs. Munroe had two hundred students in "grade school," she told me, using the American expression that I was not used to encountering in Africa (more often I'd heard such schools called "primary schools," the British term). Her school charged student fees of just over US $4 per month, made up of various daily and semester fees. The school opened in 2000, and she owned the small plot of land. She had eleven teachers, three administrators, and two cooks. The head teacher, the highest paid, received LRD 3,500 (around US $50) per month; the lowest-paid teacher received LRD 750 (around US $11) per month.

I started with a standard, introductory question: Why do children come here, when the government schools are free, whereas here they have to pay? She shrugged. "Sometimes the government school is full," she said noncommittally. The woman who had brought us there was more forthright. I wrote her exact words in my notebook as she slowly spoke: "Teachers in public school don't pay full-time attention with the children." And so, I found my first low-cost private school in the slums of Monrovia.

Although finding low-cost schools is what I've been doing for years in many different countries, it's still a moment of some elation for me when I find a low-cost private school where people have said I won't find any. Finding a low-cost private school run by a proprietor in the slums of a war-affected country in Africa was especially awe-inspiring for me.

Although it was not the greatest idea to look for schools on a Sunday, I felt inspired to continue my quest. Edward was agreeable, so we returned to his taxi and painstakingly navigated our way through the crowds of people down to the end of the main street to a spot where a huddle of latrines reached by wooden planks stood over the dark waters of the lagoon. By the roadside was Kingdom Life Academy (motto: Excellent Knowledge). The school was a simple building made of used zinc sheets held together by wooden poles, with a substantial concrete foundation and tin roof.

The proprietor's wife was sitting outside, and she called her husband, Charles S. W. Smith. Charles had gone to Nigeria as a refugee during the war and went to school and university there. To support himself, he had taught in a low-cost private school, which may have influenced his desire to start a school of his own. The previous year, his first year of opening, he had seventy-five students, from preschool to grade 5. This year he hoped to go up to one hundred students. He charged around US $25 per semester (US $50 per year or US $5 per month).

I asked him my usual question about private versus government schools. "Government school is free," he agreed, "but they pay little attention. They don't give students the time, they write the paragraph and then the teachers sit, they are only there for thirty minutes." He continued, "It's about atmosphere. That's why the parents prefer the private schools. Here teachers take up time with the kids; they care and love the kids."

Moreover, he said, "government schools have one hundred to a class, and they are not really free." He then told me something that I hadn't heard before: "Because the teachers don't get paid, they create 'pamphlets' made up from photocopied notes from the textbooks and some problems solved. They then sell these to the students, who *have* to buy them if they want any teaching."

He told me that many of the parents were not working and that "many of the children come to school hungry; teaching children who are hungry is difficult." Those parents who were working did jobs like pushing wheelbarrows, shoe shining, selling fruit and vegetables in the market, and "picking rags to sell."

Initially, Mr. Smith had rented a temporary building near the old Methodist church, but because of church politics he had to move on. He was renting his current little plot, on a thirteen-year lease, for LRD 9,000 per year (around US$150). He said he would like to buy the land, which was 1.5 lots, but it would cost US$2,000, "because it's in the center of the city." In slums, property prices still relate to how close you are to amenities. (I realized later that this was some of the most expensive land around, since I'd heard of lots going for as little as US$200.) A lot, he told me, is the size of where you can put "a big house and a yard." The total cost for his building was US$1,500. "My dream," he said, "is to purchase the land and build a storey building"—*storey building* being the term used throughout West Africa for a multifloor building. "How much would that cost?" I asked. It would be around US$11,000 for a three-story building, which could house at least three hundred students.

Although it was getting very hot, and the taxi had no air-conditioning, I wanted to get a sense of whether there were schools in other slums, so Edward agreed to drive me to New Kru Town, a slum area nearby. As usual, I took potluck about where we should go. Edward stopped to turn down a narrow alley, just wide enough for the car, and called across to a tall, elegantly dressed man who was making his way in front of us. "I beg you," Edward called, "to help us find private schools." The tall man replied, "I am a principal of one." He got in the car and showed us around New Kru Town, for he knew many other schools here too.

So, game on. There clearly was a burgeoning market of low-cost private schools in poor parts of Monrovia; over the course of the next week, I visited around thirty low-cost private schools in different slums and low-income areas as well as out in some rural villages. I traveled around with Edward, who became my driver and guide for the next several days. He heard me ask the same questions over and over, so eventually he started helping me, taking over by asking my questions in the interview, especially if he saw that I was getting overwhelmed by the terrible heat and humidity.

Ubiquity

I conducted research in Liberia because I was curious to see whether the ubiquity of low-cost private schools found in other countries across Africa and

Asia would also apply there—in one of the most extreme environments, in the slums of a war-torn country. So, I researched seven of the major slums of Monrovia with a local partner, Abraham Karnley, a personable independent consultant who taught part-time at the Wesleyan Bible College of Liberia, and David Longfield, a researcher from Newcastle University. We researched West Point and New Kru Town, the two slums I had visited on my first day, together with the largest of the slums, Doe Community, and others with use-fully descriptive names: you can probably guess why the slum Chicken Soup Factory is so called. But you'd be wrong if you guessed about Red Light—it's named after the functioning traffic light on the main road nearby.

Our detailed research revealed an extraordinary picture of thriving low-cost private schools. In the seven slums of Monrovia surveyed, the researchers located 430 schools serving more than 100,000 pupils, in preschool, elementary, and junior high school levels. There were only two government schools in these slums, serving just over 1,000 pupils.

Experts I'd spoken to before my trip to Liberia had said that I might find a small number of church or NGO schools, but nothing more. In fact, a majority of schools were run by men and women entrepreneur proprietors, like Charles S. W. Smith and Mrs. Munroe, who had set up small businesses in order to cater to the demand for quality education. A majority of students, 61 percent, were in schools run by these private proprietors, while schools run by small independent churches (which show similarities with the private proprietor schools) provided places for 23 percent of all pupils. Private proprietor schools were certainly the most significant provider of education in the slums. It was interesting that this type of school, providing the majority of school enrollments, appeared to be simply ignored as a possibility by the development experts I spoke to before my visit.

The proprietor schools we classified as "for-profit" schools—but that's not to say that they make large, or even any, surpluses. It just indicates where control lies: if any surpluses are made, these are available to the person who owns the school to use as he or she wants. This often includes reinvesting in the school but could also include personal use. Typically, for-profit schools do not have any outside source of funding other than student fees.

Other private management types (NGO, community, church, and mosque) we classified as nonprofit. Under nonprofit management, any surpluses made are only available to be used by the nonprofit organization, not by any individuals. Nonprofit management can also solicit grant funding from outside bodies, which they can do to supplement income from student fees.

It was clear that there were many low-cost private schools in the slums. But the school survey didn't provide me with one figure I needed: the proportion of children from these slums attending private schools and the proportion attending public schools. Our survey wasn't able to tell us about this because some of the children may have traveled outside of the slums to public schools (or, of course, private schools) elsewhere.

Therefore, we conducted a study of nearly 2,000 households (with more than 4,000 children ages 3 to 14) in Doe Community. The results were startling: fully 71 percent of the children (ages 5 to 14 years old) in the community were attending private schools, while only 8 percent were in government schools and 21 percent were out of school—that is, only about one in ten school-going children was attending a government school.

The overwhelming majority of children in the slums of Monrovia were in private schools. The figures were like those found in other countries, including in Lagos State, Nigeria, possibly the most studied private education market in the developing world.

These findings from Liberia are like those found in two other war-torn countries researched, Sierra Leone and South Sudan. In both of those countries, we found substantial numbers of low-cost private schools and a large proportion of for-profit schools as part of that contribution.[13]

Another factor in low-cost private schools was revealed when we mapped the locations of the private and government schools, as we did for our study of Juba, the capital of South Sudan, and its environs. It showed that low-cost private schools—and in particular, for-profit schools—reach areas that other school management types do not reach. They not only serve the most difficult countries on the planet but also serve the most difficult places within those countries.

This was suggested in our first couple of days of work in South Sudan. When I first traveled to Juba with my colleague David Longfield, we began our search for diverse types of schools almost immediately after we landed, in the brutal heat of the afternoon. Starting near the center of the city, not far from Bulluk, the area that hosts many of the city's government schools,

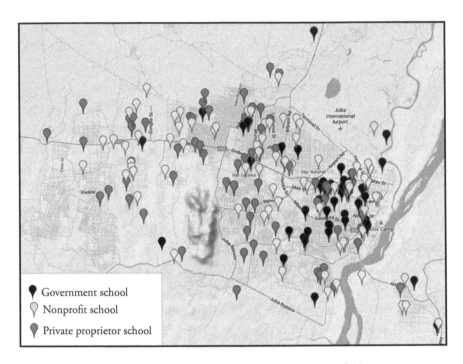

Source: Locations provided by author with colleague, David Longfield, using
Google Maps.

Figure 1.1. Schools Mapped in Juba and Environs, South Sudan

we went talking to people on the streets and in the marketplaces and were
told that there were only government and church schools to be found. Other
experts that we consulted before we went to South Sudan had (as per usual)
said the same thing. Indeed, that's all we found for the first couple of days.
We increased the area of search, slowly moving farther away from the center
of the city—and here we found what we were looking for, what we had hoped
might be there. In the more remote areas of Gudele and Munuki, the poorest areas bordering the city, where many refugees from the war had settled
in mud and brick buildings with tin roofs that glinted in the bright sun, we
found our low-cost private schools.

We were able to precisely record the location of each school researched
using GPS technology (see Figure 1.1). The White Nile is seen on the east
of the city of Juba. There is a heavy concentration of the black markers for

government schools in Juba (city) payam (district), while as you move farther away from the city center to the more remote payams of Gudele and Northern Bari, private proprietor and nonprofit schools predominate. In other words, for-profit private schools are certainly serving children in the more out-of-the-way or remote places than are government schools, reaching the parts that other school types do not reach. Government and the established NGOs are settled in the comfortable parts of the city. It's the low-cost private schools that reach out to the most difficult-to-reach children.

Low-cost private schools are most definitely ubiquitous and scalable. They serve a substantial majority of children in urban areas and a significant minority in rural areas. This is even true in some of the most difficult places on earth—war-torn countries in sub-Saharan Africa. So, the first of the seven dimensions is satisfied.

Affordability

What about the second dimension, affordability, by which we mean affordability for the poor?[14] At first glance, this seems to be a no-brainer. The low-cost private schools we've been discussing are found in poor slums and villages within poor countries, so clearly, they *must be* affordable to the poor; otherwise, no one in those communities would be able to use them! However, it turns out that affordability is one of the major contested areas in the current debate about low-cost private schools. How can that be?

It may be useful to see what DFID's "rigorous literature review" on low-cost private schools has to say about this issue. Concerning affordability, the report concludes, "The evidence on whether the poor are able to pay private school fees is ambiguous. Most is neutral, some is negative but *there is no positive evidence.*"[15]

One of the sources of evidence is from rural Uttar Pradesh, India, which shows that "an average-size family in the poorest quintile" needs to spend around 30 percent of the average household income to send one child to a low-cost private school.[16] Similarly, the report points to evidence from rural Ghana that shows that enrolling "just one child" in a low-cost private school "by a household in the poorest quintile would require about a third (29.8 percent) of its income."

If poor parents do indeed have to spend around 30 percent of their household income to educate one child in a low-cost private school, then such schools would certainly appear to be unaffordable. But, of course, that can't be the end of the discussion. The *very same* literature shows that significant minorities of the poorest *are* using low-cost private schools. The same research from Uttar Pradesh shows "10 percent of children from the poorest quintile" using the private schools—and this is the poorest quintile of the population from very poor villages, so they are the poorest of the poor.[17] Similarly, the research from Ghana also found parents from the lowest-income quintile sending their children to low-cost private schools.

It's odd that the development experts themselves don't see the strange logic here: low-cost private schools are unaffordable to the poorest; meanwhile, significant minorities of the poorest are using them.

The confusion is unnecessary. The researchers focus on answering the question "Can the poorest families afford the *average* fees and other costs incurred by those who send their children to private schools?" The answer to that question is sometimes no—the poorest families sometimes cannot afford these average amounts. But this does *not* mean to say that there are not private schools that are financially accessible to them.

There are three important factors to consider here. First, low-cost private schools show wide variation in fees between schools, even those serving similar areas. The study from the villages of Uttar Pradesh, India, for instance, showed the average (mean) school fee to be INR 39 per month, but the fees ranged from INR 27 to INR 60.[18] The fees at the lowest-cost school were *less than half* those at the most expensive and were roughly two-thirds of the fees charged at the average school. Similarly, a study from urban Nairobi, Kenya, showed an average annual fee of KES 2,861. But the fees ranged from KES 615 to KES 6,150. The fees at the lowest-cost school were *one-tenth* of those at the most expensive one and about *one-fifth* of the average fee.[19]

This large range of fees suggests that using averages is not likely to help us understand the affordability of private schools. Poorer families will be able to look for a school that is affordable to them, which may have fees that are only a fraction of the average school fee.

Second, the advertised fees charged by schools—and reported by researchers—are not necessarily the fees that the poor pay. In many schools, there are

Table 1.1. Annual per-Student Expenditure on Fees and Other Costs:
Public, Private (Average), and Private (for Poorest). Numbers
in INR (Indian Rupees)

Items of expenditure	School type		
	Public	Private (average)	Private (for poorest)
School fees, including exam and other	37	309	143
Books, stationery, and uniforms	258	437	258
Private coaching	16	61	0
Transportation	4	52	0
Board and lodging	6	22	0
Total	321	881	401
Ratio: Private/Public		2.7	1.2

Source: Adapted from Tilak (2002), 38.

concessions for families, so you can, for instance, "buy two, get one free"—if you enroll two children, your third can come for no fee.[20] Or parents can often negotiate a lower amount, depending on how much they can afford.[21] In other words, the headline fees that researchers report are probably higher than fees paid by many parents. Overall, the *average* fees reported for low-cost private schools are going to be considerably more than the fees that the poorest are required to pay.

Third, researchers looking at affordability obviously must consider the "other costs" of schooling, such as uniform, stationery, books, food, extra tuition, and transportation. Again, researchers tend to report the average amounts. But poor families are likely to have some control over these costs and, where necessary, pay well below the average amounts recorded by the researchers.

We can illustrate how these three factors appear to have led development experts astray by looking at one of the seminal pieces of research, from India, which purportedly showed how unaffordable private schools were for the poor compared with public schools.[22] Table 1.1 shows the averages found for public and private consumption (columns A and B), and also what our discussion here suggests might be more likely figures for private schools for the poorest families (column C).

The conclusion drawn by the researcher is clear: the cost to a family of sending a child to private school is 2.7 times higher than the cost of sending a child to public school. Private education, therefore, is likely to be unaffordable to poor families.

However, we can see how each of the three factors listed above will radically affect the affordability of private education vis-à-vis its public counterpart. Let's consider a poor family wanting to move their children from public school into private school. These figures are put in column C.

First, there is likely to be a wide variation in fees charged by private schools. Perhaps (as in the example above), there could be schools that charge roughly two-thirds of the average school fee. This would mean the poorest families could likely find schools that charged around INR 214. Second, even this fee is likely to be reduced for poor families, based on their ability to pay. Perhaps they will get three children in the school for the price of two, reducing the fee down to as little as INR 143 per child. Or families might be able to negotiate a reduction in fees paid, whatever their family size.

Third, looking at the other costs of schooling, we can see how poor families are likely to be spending *much* less than the reported average costs. Poor families are unlikely to need to spend anything on extra tuition ("private coaching"), as they are choosing private schools because they feel teaching is better. Let's omit this expenditure completely.

Similarly, regarding transportation—the finding that the families using private schools spent thirteen times more, on average, on transport than those using public schools is irrelevant to a poor family wishing to choose a private school. It's a feature of low-cost private schools that they are ubiquitous, so they are likely to be found in areas where the poor live, allowing children to walk to school. We can omit transportation costs entirely, irrespective of what an average family was found to be spending.

Similarly, we would not expect poor families to spend anything on board and lodging (though some parents with children in private school clearly do), as again the family could choose a local school close to home (or even have the child board inexpensively with relatives). Even in terms of the category "books, stationery, and uniforms," the poor may be able to source cheaper alternatives or take advantage of the flexibility offered by private schools on purchasing items such as uniforms when they can afford them rather than as a condition of entry into the school, as is often the case in the public schools. But in the absence of figures to this effect, let's leave this cost as it is for now.

These considerations suggest a more realistic view of how a poor family could afford private school (Table 1.1, column C). With these assumptions, the total cost of sending a child to private school could be as little as 1.2 times the average cost of sending a child to government school. Or to put it the other way around, the average cost of sending a child to government school might be 80 percent of the cost of sending a child to private school. Private schooling is much more affordable to the poor than some academic researchers lead us to believe.

We can say more about the affordability of private schools by creating a scientific definition of what we mean by "low cost," and then looking at some of the real data we found in our studies in war-torn countries in Africa to illustrate the use of this definition.

Toward a Definition of Low-Cost Private Schools

The traditional approach in the literature starts with average school fees and checks affordability against average household income. In contrast to this, our proposed model starts with household consumption or expenditure information to explore what fees would be affordable to families with these expenditures. We can thus define low-cost private schools according to internationally accepted poverty definitions. Our method has five steps:

1. *Poverty line.* Start with a poverty line—e.g., the internationally accepted US$1.25 or US$2 poverty lines.[23]

2. *Convert to local currency and bring up to date.* The US$1.25 and US$2 poverty lines need to be converted to the local currency and brought up to date, using the country's Consumer Price Index.

3. *Consider a typical family.* Calculate the total annual expenditures of typical families on these poverty lines. This will be for the average-size family using national or regional data or the specific household size data from local studies.

4. *Find the "maximum amount" for total school fees.* Specify the maximum percentage of annual expenditures that a family can afford to spend on

their children's education. We've used 10 percent below,[24] but this percentage can be adjusted higher or lower as more is known about what families on the extremes can afford.

5. *Calculate the maximum annual total school fees.* Divide the "maximum amount" by the number of school-age children in the family. This gives the maximum annual per-child school fees affordable to families on the poverty line.[25]

We've done these calculations for a variety of countries and settings. For Monrovia, the capital of Liberia, for instance, we worked out that a family on the US$1.25 poverty line could afford to spend up to LRD 5,300 (US$73) per annum on each child and keep within the 10 percent spending limit for private education. Schools of this price range we dubbed "lowest cost." Families on the US$2 poverty line could afford to spend up to LRD 8,530 per annum on each child, again keeping within the 10 percent spending limit. Schools with these fees we called "low cost." Finally, "medium-cost" schools were those charging up to LRD 17,060 per annum, and "high-cost" schools were greater than LRD 17,060.

What we found in the slums of Monrovia is perhaps unsurprising, given that they are poor neighborhoods in a poor country: the vast majority (78 percent) of proprietor-owned (for-profit) private schools were lowest cost, and a further 16 percent were low cost. The proprietor schools are like the private independent church schools (76 percent lowest cost) but different from the established church schools, where a slight majority (52 percent) were lowest cost. The small number of public and NGO schools were all lowest cost.

The important fact is that a large majority of schools that we found in the slums of Monrovia are affordable to families living on the poverty line, spending not more than 10 percent of their total income on private education for all their children. The studies in Sierra Leone and South Sudan showed a similar picture.

Something else, which relates to the earlier discussion on relative affordability of private and public schools, is important to note. A common reaction from critics of low-cost private schools is to question how we can say that they are desirable for poor families when public education is free. But public education is not free. This is easily seen by looking at the relative costs of sending

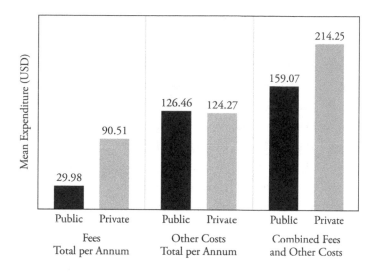

Source: Data collected by author, household survey, Doe Community, Monrovia, Liberia.

Figure 1.2. Comparison of Costs of Sending a Child to a Public and Private School, Monrovia, Liberia

a child to a public school compared with private, using data gained from our household surveys (see Figure 1.2).

Average fees and levies (such as building, development, and examination levies) at the public schools came to US$29.98 per annum, a third of the US$90.51 average fees at private schools. Private schools are much more expensive. However, we need to include all the additional costs of schooling in these calculations. Sending a child to any school—public or private—incurs costs such as those for shoes, uniforms, books, transportation, lunch, and so on. In our household survey, these extra costs were close to the same in both types of schools. In public schools, they were US$126.46 per child per annum, compared with US$124.27 in private schools.

So, to compare affordability of public and private schools for poor families, we need to add together these two amounts. Overall, the cost of sending a child to a public school came to US$159.07 per annum, not too far short of the US$214.25 of sending to private. That is, the average cost to a parent of sending a child to a private school is 1.3 times the average cost of sending to a public school. Or to put it the other way around, sending a child to public school costs 74 percent of the amount to send a child to private school. These figures roughly coincide with those given in the example earlier. They clearly show that the common assumption about the unaffordability of sending a child to a private school is unwarranted—it's not much more than sending a child to a public school.

The research findings indicate something quite extraordinary to celebrate concerning what is going on in the slums and poor areas of Liberia, and of Sierra Leone and South Sudan too. A majority of poor parents are sending their children to low-cost private schools. And these schools are affordable to them; indeed, they are not much less affordable than sending a child to public school.

The low-cost private schools, in other words, are *ubiquitous*, are already taken to scale, and are *affordable*. These findings apply not just in the war-torn countries examined, but also across the developing world. It truly is a global revolution.

2

Quality and Value for Money

IN A FISHING village on the Gulf of Kutch, in rural Gujarat, India, we were talking to parents about the condition of education in the local public (government) school in the village. One father said that his son was in Class 5 (fifth grade) and had only learned how to write the number *1*; that was it. A woman gathering her four children around her told us about the school day. The teachers arrived from the city at about 9:30 a.m., the children having been in school for an hour, and immediately sent the children home for breakfast. The children returned at 10:30 a.m., and there was an hour or so of assembly, prayer, and chores. The teachers maybe then did something for half an hour in the classroom or maybe not; in any case, they were gone by noon. The children learned nothing, she said.

One father, a fisherman, had become so annoyed with this constant neglect of his child that he went to the school to complain. The teachers, seeing this fisherman in their school—*How dare he*, they must have been thinking, *doesn't he know his place in society? This dirty, illiterate fisherman, when we are government-trained and accredited teachers!*—called the police and had him arrested. His extended family had to scrape together the money for his bail and payment of court fees and incidentals.

Meanwhile, the school continued as before. He wouldn't go to complain anymore; he knew his place.

Their stories inspired me to help set up a low-cost private school in their village, and many of the children now attend. They certainly seem happier in this school. Like parents I encountered in Liberia, Sierra Leone, and South Sudan, and in India, Nigeria, Kenya, Ghana, and China before that, such parents are not satisfied with the quality of education in public schools. That's an important reason why they choose private schools.

How Good Are Low-Cost Private Schools?

But are they right? It hinges on how good private schools really are—whether they're academically better than public schools. This is a major source of contentious debate about low-cost private education.

Many critics are adamant. Writing in the *Times of India*, for instance, one social commentator noted, "That private schools improve learning outcomes is a myth." Parental choice of private schools, he said, "ironically, has little to do with outcomes." Instead, he maintained, parents are hoodwinked into thinking private schools are better, liking children in smart uniforms, or thinking (wrongly) that a private education will give them a better chance in life.[1]

Whether it's because of school fashion or misguided aspirations, parents are fooled. It's a line of criticism that persists. Poor parents are considered "ignoramuses," I reported one senior government official saying in *The Beautiful Tree*.

So the question of how good low-cost private schools are must be resolved.

We could jump straight to looking at research on the relative performance of public and private in key academic subjects. But if you talk to poor parents—any parents, really—what they are looking for in a private school is not that simple. Some parents I've talked to spoke about the atmosphere in the classroom—that teachers showed love and care toward their children; they didn't say it was only, or even most importantly, because their children scored better in standardized tests. Some parents talked about the hidden curriculum—how the lessons their children learn from public schools are wholly negative. The children learn by example that you don't have to work hard to achieve in life; all you've got to do is find a government job and you can do what you like.

Harvard professor Lant Pritchett has written engagingly about why "education ain't schooling"—that is, education is much more than those academic subjects that can be easily measured. He distinguishes between two major parts of what we consider to be education: the skills/factual knowledge component (foreign languages, algebra, music, test preparation) and the beliefs/

attitudes/disposition component (love, loyalty, faith, duty, honor, patriotism)—what others have called "character."² The point is that education is not just about how well you do in mathematics and English tests, it's also about your character; and while the first may be easy to measure, the second certainly is not.

Forget these highfalutin ideas and concepts; parents might prefer a private school simply because it is closer to their home, so their young child doesn't have to travel a long distance with all the danger that entails—particularly for girls, perhaps. Parents could prefer private schools for purely pragmatic reasons like this.

All this could sound like excuses. Yet when we turn to look at relative performance in subjects like mathematics and English, we are looking at only a small part of what is important in education. There are other key features of education that are highly valued by parents, not necessarily captured in these data.

So, what does the research show?

Research on the relative merits of public and private schooling (including low cost) has, it turns out, been almost overwhelmingly *in favor of* private education. There is no need to make any excuses! After conducting a "rigorous literature review" commissioned by the Department for International Development, the team members, while not particularly fans of low-cost private education, nevertheless were satisfied by the evidence on achievement.³ They wrote, "Pupils attending private school tend to achieve better learning outcomes than pupils in state [i.e., public] schools."⁴ They pointed to studies from South Asia and sub-Saharan Africa that show these results—children in low-cost private schools outperform those in government schools—after doing the proper statistical controls.

This finding is tempered by the caveat that there aren't many good studies available—indeed, they point to only three of high quality. But they were only looking at studies from the past five years, so they missed many of the pioneering studies. But this aside, what, in general, constitutes a good study?

Ideally, good studies that seek to compare achievement in public and private schools should select children at random, but they usually select *schools* at random, and children within these, so there is a cluster effect that can distort the results. Then the studies test children using standardized tests in key subjects, usually including mathematics and English (or another key language). Typically, children from the private schools will do much better at these tests than those in the public schools, but it is arguable how much of this is to do with the school and how much with children's family backgrounds. It is argued that the slightly better-off poor families send their children to private schools and that these families have more advantages at home, such as parents who give children time to do homework, a quieter space in which to work, and so on. Hence, good studies must administer questionnaires to the children and their families so that these family background variables can be statistically controlled for. By gaining these extra data, you can create predictions of how well an average child would do in a private or a public school.

This method goes some way to helping solve the problem. However, it's harder to get a grip on the key difference, that some families have chosen to send their children to private schools, while others have not. In that very act of choice, there could be some other factor, some missing variable—"selection bias" in statistical parlance—that we don't know about but that could be the reason why children are doing better. So, testing children over a time period rather than just on one occasion (conducting a longitudinal rather than a cross-sectional study) can chart change over time, which can more clearly show the value added by the school itself rather than by simply the family.

In any case, for defenders of private education, there appear to be reasons to be cheerful. Even if there were no definitive evidence in this regard, the "good enough" studies show that private schools are better than government schools, and so parental choices, at least with regard to academic achievement (ignoring the myriad other reasons why parents might prefer private over public schools noted above), seem to be sensible ones. Parental choices appear vindicated—parents are not being hoodwinked by unscrupulous providers or falling prey to the latest fashions or vain aspirations.

At least that's what I thought—until a friendly critic (they are not all friendly) sent me a link to some research that had just been published on the internet. This was, he said, a nail in the coffin of my work. The article by two young Indian academics, Karthik Muralidharan and Venkatesh Sundararaman, was later published in the most prestigious of economics journals, the *Quarterly Journal of Economics*. The article begins in the same vein as the

Department of International Development review (in fact, it's even more scathing): "There is very little rigorous empirical evidence on the relative effectiveness of private and public schools in low-income countries. Non-experimental studies have used several approaches to address identification challenges and have typically found that private school students have higher test scores, but they have not been able to rule out the concern that these estimates are confounded by selection and omitted variables."[5]

In the authors' view, the published research on public-private differences had been unable to control for the problem of selection bias mentioned above—until theirs, that is. Their work, featuring a randomized controlled trial (RCT) with a "unique two-stage randomization" process, was held up as the "gold standard" by which other research in this area of public-private differences would be judged.[6]

Their evidence was not encouraging for those in favor of low-cost private schools.

Their research concerned a "school choice" experiment in Andhra Pradesh, India.[7] Their findings showed that poor children offered vouchers to attend private schools do *not* academically outperform those not offered vouchers, who remain in the public schools—statistically there is the same level of academic achievement in public and private.

My friendly critic wrote telling me that this gold standard research didn't show what I had been saying, so shouldn't I retract and apologize? Never mind that this was about a voucher experiment and that giving parents vouchers to use at private school could produce quite different effects from when parents choose to pay for private schools themselves. Never mind that parents might choose private schools for other reasons to do with character and convenience. All that was beside the point. This research suggested that academic performance in public and private was the same.

This was disheartening.

I'd devoted two decades of my life to low-cost private schools. I'd spent so much time in poor areas and visited so many public schools where teachers didn't turn up, or if they did, they didn't teach; I'd talked to so many poor parents who said they had chosen private schools because those schools were better; and I'd visited so many private schools and seen teachers at least present and teaching, even if sometimes their standards were not high. I'd been telling anyone who would listen about all I had found. Now "gold standard" research was showing that these parents were wrong, at least about academic standards. I'd been the one championing these parental choices for years. I began to understand how those on the opposite side of the debate might have felt as I had publicized my own and others' research over the decades. They had devoted their lives to promoting public education in developing countries, devoted their energies to ensuring that international aid supported the state endeavors. They had been champions of the state and all it can do. I could see how bad it must have felt to be told that public schools are not up to the mark, that they're eclipsed by private education. It would have hurt; I could see that now. Anyway, now the boot was on the other foot. It was time for me to hurt.

The research findings from the "gold standard" work began to be widely reported in popular media as heralding a conclusion to the debate about the relative merits of private and public schooling. In an Indian weekly newspaper, it was asserted, "The empirical evidence is increasingly pointing towards private schools not being able to add value as compared to government schools."[8] The *Times of India* opined, "The findings of the Andhra Pradesh School Choice research aren't encouraging for voucher systems supporters. Private school kids performed better than government school ones in only the first year; in subsequent years, government ones performed just as well. ... The findings dispel a popular myth that private schools lead to better learning."[9]

There was some comfort. Although there was no reported difference between public and low-cost private school *achievement*, private schools were on average doing the same for less than one-third of the cost. So, although not more effective, private education certainly offered better value for money.

This alone was enough for some supporters of school choice, who used it to rally to private schools' defense; writing in response to the *Times of India* article, one of the foremost defenders of vouchers and a good friend, Dr. Parth Shah, commented, "If I were to write the title for the *Times of India* story, it would be: At three times the cost, government schools are no better than private schools. The *Times of India* headline is: Private schools are not adding value. You be the judge!"[10]

The research was certainly thorough. It examined the impact of the Andhra Pradesh School Choice Project, which conducted a voucher experiment in five districts of rural Andhra Pradesh, in south-central India. Half of the 180 villages were randomly assigned to be "voucher villages," and the remaining villages continued as before. Within these voucher villages, children in the public schools were randomly selected to be voucher recipients. Baseline tests in Telugu (the regional language of Andhra Pradesh) and mathematics were given to experimental and control groups. Tests in Telugu, mathematics, and English were conducted at the end of two and four years, while tests in science and social studies and Hindi were given after four years. Overall, nearly a quarter of government-school children in the voucher villages were reassigned to private schools.

Interestingly, the baseline tests themselves (conducted when students were at the end of preschool or at the end of elementary grade 1) showed a large and statistically significant difference in favor of private schools, after controlling for family background variables.[11]

However, no such improvement was found for children given vouchers to use at private schools ("lottery winners") compared with those who were not: "After two and four years of the program, we find no difference between test scores of lottery winners and losers on Telugu (native language), math, English, and science/social studies." For the researchers, this suggested that the huge "differences in test scores across public and private schools" found in the baseline assessment had to do with things other than what private schools bring, or even to do with family background.[12]

Private schools were more cost-effective: "The mean cost per student in the private schools ... was less than a third of the cost in public schools."[13] Because they were able to more efficiently allocate teaching time across different subjects, private schools also taught Hindi, whereas public schools did not. This is, of course, the *national* language in India, so it is a huge advantage that private schools give to their children over what the public schools achieve. In summary: "Private schools in this setting deliver slightly better test score gains than their public counterparts (better on Hindi and same in other subjects), and do so at a substantially lower cost per student."[14]

To me, this was too-faint praise; it seemed pretty damning to my championing of low-cost private schools.

Or was it?

A couple of years earlier, I'd been working to help create a chain of low-cost private schools in the Old City of Hyderabad. Hyderabad was then the capital of Andhra Pradesh, India, the state where the voucher study was conducted. We had wanted to see how well the schools were doing compared with other low-cost private schools as well as the local public schools. (All of us working in chains of schools want to know how well we are doing compared with the competition. There's little point in doing our work if we are not doing better than public schools, so we always want to keep an eye on comparisons.)

The policy organization that I'd commissioned was run by Naveen Mandava, someone whom I feel proud to have initiated into the world of education policy, having known him since he was a bright young man of nineteen. (He's now a highly successful educational entrepreneur—featured in a Harvard Business School case study, no less!) Moreover, he had been a field researcher on the Andhra Pradesh voucher study, so he was an obvious person to conduct tests in our schools to see if they were up to standard.

His organization did the study and presented the results. I'm never content with receiving results in a slick PowerPoint presentation; I always want to check behind the scenes to see what has been done. So, I sat in his office, going through a random selection of test papers and questionnaires. It dawned on me that something was rather odd. For mathematics, the test papers for the public schools were in Telugu, the regional language, while those for the private schools were in English. Different test papers had been used in the comparison. That couldn't be right, surely? The same test had to be used for public and private schools; otherwise, the results would be suspect. I asked him for an explanation. He confirmed that that was what his team had done.

Now reading the gold standard research in the prestigious *Quarterly Journal of Economics*, I remembered what he had told me then—he confirmed that this was what his team had done because this was the method they had used in the Andhra Pradesh School Choice Project!

I wrote to one of the authors of the paper, Karthik Muralidharan, and asked if this was true. He confirmed that it was: the language used in the mathematics (and other nonlanguage) tests "tended to follow the medium [of instruction] of the school, with English-medium private school students taking the test in English and Telugu-medium students taking the test in Telugu (the split was roughly 50 percent each)."[15]

Indeed, it was roughly 50-50: of the private schools, 50.4 percent were English medium.[16] So different tests had been used for mathematics and science/social science. For the public schools and half of the private schools, the tests had been in Telugu. For the other half of the private schools, the tests were in English.

Why is this so important—and so damning to the research findings?

The aim of creating a randomized controlled trial (RCT) is to ensure, as far as is humanly possible, that participants in the two groups—the "treatment" and "control" groups—are treated in exactly the same way, apart from the intervention you're trying to measure (in this case, school vouchers). This supposedly gold standard research had violated this fundamental principle. It had treated the two groups differently, by using two different tests for mathematics, science, and social science: one in English, the other in Telugu.

Even if it wasn't obvious in what ways this difference could lead to bias for one or other groups of participants, it still called the results into question because this was not the way RCTs should be done. Everything apart from what you are investigating must be the same. However, in the case of this study, it is very easy to see how the different tests could cause very serious bias: If it was a comparison between performance in public and private schools in well-heeled urban communities, it may be thought that it was less of a problem—the children in English-medium schools were being taught in English, so why shouldn't they be given tests in English? However, in poorer rural (or urban slum) areas of India, the "English medium" appellation carried by low-cost private schools is typically more of an aspiration, at least in the lower grades, than a reality. As a professor who had been actively involved with the project put it, "The medium of instruction is as claimed by the school authorities. In the rural setting, while these schools could have more transactions in English, *they are some distance from being truly English medium.*"[17]

I agree. I've written elsewhere how it is an "oft-repeated criticism" of low-cost private schools that they are "English medium in name only." The low-cost English-medium schools in fact typically operate as hybrid schools—teaching only in the mother tongue in the lower grades, sometimes using English textbooks translated by teachers into the mother tongue as they go along, with the aspiration of bringing everyone up to speed in English by the higher grades.[18]

Hence, even in a simple comparison between public and private schools in rural areas, it would be unfair to give tests with instructions in English to children in private schools (supposedly English medium but, in fact, teaching in Telugu in the lower grades), as this would penalize them against those being given tests with Telugu instructions. In this particular voucher experiment, the situation appears worse, because it turns out that those who had been accepted for private school were the lowest-achieving children.[19] So the voucher children switching from Telugu-medium public to English-medium private schools had the worst grasp of language and mathematics. Trying to figure out mathematics questions in English may have presented huge difficulties for them.

Let's be more concrete: I can illustrate the kind of difficulty that would be faced by these poor voucher students doing tests after being moved to English-language schools by translating some questions for the reader. Here are three of the questions from the mathematics test translated from English into Telugu. (I'm assuming that not many readers understand Telugu; if they do, they'll need to translate into a language they don't understand.) Readers will probably have little difficulty with questions like this one:

కింది దిపరిష కరించండి

5.57 + 3 = _____

Although the instruction is in Telugu, it is in effect repeated in the mathematical language too, so as long as we know how to add together two numbers (while taking into account place value), we can get this one correct, irrespective of the language of the test (the Telugu instruction is "Solve the following").

But this next question is entirely different:

ఏ అంకెల సంఖ్య 2345 లోపంద నో థసంలోఉందో?

Without knowing Telugu, it is impossible to answer, however good we are at mathematics. (The question is "In the number 2345, which digit is in the hundreds place?") Similarly, we will not be able to solve this question unless we are fluent in Telugu:

వర్తశాలె ఒక హన్ సిల్ విలువ రూ కనుగలు కోరుకుంటున్ నరు. 4. ఎన్ ని 50 పర్తైసల నణాలు ఆమహన్ సిల్ కనుగలు అవసరం ఉంటుందీ?

(Vaishali wants to buy a pencil worth 4 rupees. How many 50 paisa coins will she require to buy the pencil?)

The point is that the difficulties we have with these last two questions illustrate precisely the nature of the problem faced by voucher children moved to an English-medium private school. However good they are at mathematics, they will not get these answers correct, except, of course, through lucky guesses.

So how could the testing have been made fair? It might be assumed that testing the children in English-medium private schools in Telugu could also have been unfair, especially in the later years of the experiment, as by then voucher children's English may have improved because of their greater exposure to the language. However, it must not be assumed that the language children will learn in English lessons is the same language they will need in mathematics, or that there is an equal degree of English-language immersion in language and nonlanguage subjects, especially in the grades tested. It is plausible, for example, that mathematics teachers were less fluent in English than the language-subject teachers, and so they placed a greater emphasis on teaching in Telugu than language teachers.

The only fair way of assessing the students in different language-medium schools would be to follow one of the two methods that researchers working in India have devised to solve this problem.[20] First, you can ensure that mathematics (and other nonlanguage subject) tests are word-free—for example, arithmetic operations only and/or wordless cognitive puzzles. Or, you can ensure that the instructions given in mathematics (and other nonlanguage subjects) tests are in both languages *on the same paper*, to ensure that students can choose which language to use for instructions on how to address each individual question.

Even in the second case, problems of translation will occur—it's hard for researchers (even those familiar with both languages) to be sure that word questions in mathematics have been identically translated. And even minor changes in the wording of mathematics questions can drastically alter student success rates.[21] For this reason, the first solution may be preferable, even though it does limit the type of mathematical questions that can be asked.

But neither of these solutions was used in the gold standard research. They used different tests altogether. So, we simply do not know what the impact of having used these different tests would be on student performance. That is, the summary findings of the Andhra Pradesh study are not valid. The findings that have been heralded as the end of private schools are nothing of the sort.

We can rephrase the summary findings of the Andhra Pradesh School Choice Project as follows, given that the results are for both English- and Telugu-medium private schools combined, compared with Telugu-medium-only public schools:

- In Telugu, the regional language, there is *no significant difference* between achievement of those in public schools and those receiving vouchers to attend private schools. However, private schools spend significantly less time on Telugu, so they are *much more efficient* than public schools.

- In mathematics, science, and social science, we *do not know* what advantage or otherwise the private or public schools have. As children took different tests, *there is no basis for comparison.*

- In Hindi, the national language, children with vouchers in private schools *perform better* than those in public schools.

For English, the situation is also complicated because of a further problem: the English tests "were carefully designed to assess the common curriculum in government and private schools so as to ensure that there was genuine comparability."[22] But English is taught from first grade in private schools, but only from third grade in public schools. Now, if the tests measured what the private-school children had covered, then they would be unfair to the public-school children. If they measured what public schools had covered, then they would be too easy for the private-school children, leading to a "ceiling effect" on what the private-school children were able to demonstrate.

It turns out that there was likely to have been such a ceiling effect. The researchers, aware of the low level of achievement of all students, designed the tests to include items from the tested grade and several lower grades too.[23]

This means that the English results were likely to underestimate the true private-school effect.

It is obviously disappointing that we can't say anything more about mathematics (or science and social studies) achievement. What we can say is that the summary findings concerning the voucher project are incorrect.

However, as roughly half of the students in private schools (those in Telugu-medium private schools) *did* take the same mathematics and science/social studies tests as those in public schools, can't we look at the results for these children to get a fairer comparison between public and private? For in the Telugu-medium private schools and public schools, it would be fair to compare the children's performance.

Helpfully, the researchers did explicitly compare these groups.[24] What they found is powerful: "The estimated impact of attending a Telugu-medium private school is positive for every subject."[25] The results are as follows:

- In Year 2, estimated score differences between private and public schools are positive in favor of those having vouchers for all subjects apart from Telugu.

- By Year 4, estimated score differences are positive for every subject. The impact when subjects are combined is large and positive, and statistically significant. Importantly, this is not simply the effect of Hindi distorting the results: Combining mathematics and science and social science also gives a large, positive, and significant difference.[26]

So, this is clear: once the unfairness of giving different tests to children in different management types has been overcome, children given vouchers for private schools outperformed those in public schools in *all* subjects (Telugu, mathematics, English, science/social studies, and Hindi). The combined result shows a large, statistically significant difference in favor of private schools. This is a hugely positive finding for the voucher debate. Children in private schools significantly outperformed those in public schools, for a fraction of the cost.

So, the results didn't "put the nail in the coffin" of private schools after all. The fact that I chanced across the reason why the study's summary findings were not valid was neither here nor there.

Angus Deaton, Nobel laureate in economics, says that too often researchers unquestionably accept the results of RCTs, being curiously in awe of them.[27] Perhaps this is what happened to the reviewers for the *Quarterly Journal of Economics*. They were so enamored with the research design that they forgot to ask rather basic questions about the research implementation, including whether the same tests were used for all children.

I've looked at this study in detail because it has been held up as *the* piece of research that shows there are no significant differences between achievement in public and private schools. Going into detail here is also to show why we must always look carefully at any study, and not just trust the summary findings. The consensus (including from the Department for International Development's "rigorous literature review") is that other studies from Africa and South Asia have produced the result that private education is better. So, all existing studies point in the same direction; even this study from Andhra Pradesh that appeared to show something different shows the same. Of course, newer studies will come up, and their results will need careful checking. But the "direction of travel" of existing studies seems to be clear.

Poor parents are not making rash decisions based on irrelevant factors. They may consider the relative merits of private and public schools from all sides, considering far more than academic achievement in two or three subjects. But whatever else they consider, they are correct in their assumption that low-cost private schools are better academically than public schools.

Value for Money

Research shows that low-cost private schools achieve higher academic quality than public schools. It's not that they have "better" children or "better" parents; private schools really do add value. Some critics say that this can only be the case because private schools are better resourced than public ones—that's the only way they could possibly be better. Everyone knows that public schools in developing countries are poorly resourced; therefore, children in them don't do well.

This certainly wasn't true in the Andhra Pradesh study reported above. The private schools achieved higher standards at only a third of the cost of the public schools. It turns out that other studies show the exact same thing.

One of the earliest and most notable was from Pakistan, the Learning and Educational Achievement in Punjab Schools (LEAPS) (for international audiences, it is normally referred to as the Learning and Educational Achievement in *Pakistan* Schools). This project tested 12,000 children in public and private primary schools in 112 villages in Punjab, Pakistan.

First, the research shows that private schools are ubiquitous and growing, just as we've reported in different countries around the world. In rural areas, "the one-school village" has been replaced by villages offering a "selection among public and private schools." A typical village had about eight schools, of which three were private.[28]

Lest readers think that this is down to an expansion of madrassas, schools that teach a dogmatic adherence to the Quran, the authors note that such "religious schools are rarely used," serving only 1 to 3 percent of rural children. This number has not increased over the years. Instead, the growth in private education in Pakistan is in secular schools, typically, as we saw in Liberia, "self-owned, for-profit private schools."[29] Such schools have dramatically increased in numbers, just as we saw in Liberia (and, of course, Pakistan is also a conflict-affected, fragile state). In the six years of the study, the number of (registered) private schools in the state grew nearly 50 percent (from 32,000 to 47,000). One-third of all schoolchildren in the rural villages were enrolled in private schools, while nearly 20 percent of the poorest third of families sent their children to private schools.

Second, the research showed that children in the private schools performed significantly better than those in the public schools, even when they came from the same rural village: children in the private schools were between 1½ and 2½ years ahead of their public-school counterparts. Importantly, the "public-private learning gap is much larger than that across children from different socioeconomic backgrounds," where parental literacy and wealth are included in these background indicators: "The gap between public and private schools in English is 12 times that between rich and poor children. The gap between public and private schools in Mathematics is 8 times that between children with literate and illiterate fathers. The gap between public and private schools in Urdu is 18 times the gap between children with literate and illiterate mothers."[30]

Third, just as in the Andhra Pradesh study, the private schools do more for less—they are a much better value for the money: "Educating a child in a public school costs twice as much as in a private school."[31] Annual fees in private schools on average (median) were PKR 1,012, or around US$15 at the time. This was less than half the PKR 2,039 reported as the median amount spent in the public schools—that is, at the point of delivery, excluding government administration costs, and, indeed, excluding rent of buildings or the opportunity cost of capital of the buildings, all covered by private school fees.[32]

Finally, the researchers worked out the "value for money" of the private schools, combining these costs with the test scores in English, Urdu, and mathematics: for all three subjects they found that "for every Rs. 1 that a private school spends on an extra percent correct on a test, the public system spends Rs. 3."[33] The private schools were thus three times better value for money than the public schools—as it happens, the same result found in the Andhra Pradesh study.

The LEAPS study also explored parental satisfaction, something I shall address in the next chapter. Parents were much more satisfied with the private schools than the public schools: they were "26 percentage points *less* likely to rate a government school as 'good' or 'excellent' compared to their private counterparts." The conclusion is clear: from this study in Pakistan, similar to studies in India, "whether we look at test scores, costs, or parental satisfaction, private schools look a whole lot better."[34]

Inspired by the method of the LEAPS study, we used a similar method to explore value for money of public and private education in Sierra Leone.[35] We worked this out for grade 4 children in English and mathematics, using the costs of teacher salaries rather than total schooling costs (but teacher salaries are likely to make up the vast majority of these costs). Of course, public schools have additional resources available, such as those devoted to the government ministry of education. If these were added in, the case for private schools would be even more pronounced.

The results, for English reading, comparing public schools with lowest-cost and low-cost private schools, are shown in Table 2.1. (Recall from the previous chapter, the definition of "lowest cost" was a private school affordable to families on the US$1.25 poverty line, if they were to spend no more than 10 percent of their income on school fees for all their children. Similarly,

Table 2.1. Value for Money, Public and Private Schools, Western
Area, Sierra Leone

Column		(A)	(B)	(C)	(D)		(E)		(F)	
		Mean monthly teacher's salary (USD)	Mean class size	Salary per pupil (USD)	Percentage score		Cost per reading percent (USD)		Value for money	
					Boys	Girls	Boys	Girls	Boys	Girls
Public		103.05	47.4	2.2	16	11	0.14	0.20	1.0	1.0
Private— Lowest Cost	For-profit	50.50	23.7	2.1	24	22	0.09	0.10	1.6	2.1
	Nonprofit	43.70	25.2	1.7	26	21	0.07	0.08	2.1	2.5
Private— Low Cost	For profit	59.06	19.8	3.0	30	30	0.10	0.10	1.4	2.0
	Nonprofit	44.96	16.0	2.8	31	29	0.09	0.10	1.6	2.1

Source: Data collected by author, school survey, Sierra Leone.

"low-cost" private schools were those affordable in the same way to families
on the US$2 poverty line.)

We calculated value for money using the following six steps:

First (column A), we worked out the average monthly salary of teachers
in these different school types—our researchers had asked the teachers for
their gross salaries. Public-school teachers were the most highly paid—with
an average monthly salary of US$103.05, more than double the salary in
the lowest-cost private schools (US$50.50 in the for-profit and US$43.70 in
the nonprofit). Indeed, the only teachers paid as much as the public-school
teachers were those we found in the for-profit, high-cost private schools (not
shown in the table). It may also be worth noting that at each level, teachers in
for-profit schools are paid higher than those in nonprofit. Critics may have
expected the opposite, given their penchant for accusing for-profit schools of
acting always to maximize their profits and thereby screwing down tightly
on teacher salaries. This was not found to be true at all.

Second (column B), we calculated the average class size—our researchers
physically counted all children in the class in grade 4 on their visits. Average class size in public schools was typically around twice that in the private
schools (for example, 47.4 in government, compared with 23.7 in the lowest-

cost for-profit schools). The fact that private schools have much smaller classes penalizes them in the value for money calculations.

Third (column C), we calculated the average teacher's salary per pupil. Both salaries and class sizes were about twice as large in public as in private, so this meant per-pupil salaries evened out somewhat. In the public schools, the average per-pupil salary was US$2.20, compared with US$1.80 and US$2.10 in the private lowest-cost (for-profit and nonprofit, respectively).

Fourth (column D), we worked out the predicted scores based on our data. Our researchers had tested 3,000 pupils from public and private schools in reading, mathematics, and spelling and had collected background data on students and their families from questionnaires. The data had been analyzed, using statistical methods ("multilevel modeling") designed to take away any advantage that private schools might have through family socioeconomic background and cluster effects of schools. For English (reading) in a government school, an average boy would achieve 15.5 percent, while a girl would achieve 10.8 percent. In a low-cost private school, the boy's result would nearly double, while the girl's result would nearly triple, to 30.2 percent in for-profit or 29.0 percent in nonprofit. Even in the lowest-cost private schools, achievement is also significantly higher than in public schools.

The fifth step (column E) was to calculate the cost of a percentage point in reading (and mathematics and spelling), by dividing the per-pupil salary by the cost per reading percentage point. This showed that boys in public schools had a cost of 14 cents per percentage point, compared with 9 or 7 cents per percentage point in the lowest-cost private (for-profit and nonprofit, respectively).

Finally, we set the cost in the public schools as our baseline so that we could see how competitive the private schools were against these. Column F shows the results. In all cases, the private schools offered better value for money, in the range of 1.4 to 2.5 times better. Lowest-cost, for-profit private schools are 2.1 times more cost-effective for girls and 1.6 times more cost-effective for boys. Nonprofit schools are 2.5 times more cost-effective for girls and 2.1 times for boys.

Just as in the studies from India and Pakistan, our own study from Sierra Leone (with comparable results from Liberia and South Sudan) showed that not only are private schools more effective academically than public schools, but also they are more cost-effective, offering better value for money.

What's Not to Like?

In chapter 1, I gave examples to illustrate the ubiquity of low-cost private schools across developing countries, highlighting first the situation in Liberia but also pointing to the extent of private schools elsewhere. Because they are ubiquitous, this means that low-cost private schools have already solved the issue that perplexes development experts: scalability—they have already shown how it is possible to achieve great scale. And they've achieved great scale without any outside assistance from governments or international agencies.

I have also shown how low-cost private schools are affordable to families on the poverty line and that the cost of sending a child to a low-cost private school may not be much higher than sending the child to a public school, once the extra costs of schooling are taken into account.

With ubiquity and affordability covered, this chapter then looked at two of the other important dimensions, quality and value for money. It's clear that the research to date, including work held up as "gold standard" research using methods such as randomized controlled trials, reveals that children in low-cost private schools outperform those in public schools. Of course, it's hard to do really good research in this area—there is the great likelihood of missing variables or not correcting properly for selectivity bias and cluster effects. There are also unforeseen dangers lurking—such as which language to use for your nonlanguage tests—that can surprise and undermine even the most seasoned researchers, publishing in the most prestigious journals. Finally, we must never forget that achievement in key subjects is not the only thing that parents look for when they choose private schools: things like values, disposition, and character formation could be as important to parents, and even practical concerns like proximity to the school and safety for their girls loom large when they choose a school.

Nevertheless, a clear picture does seem to be emerging—of children in private schools doing better academically than children in government schools. It's not just because the children in the private schools come from slightly better-off families that they do better—there appears to be something genuine in the effectiveness of private schools. Nor is it because private schools are better resourced. In fact, the opposite is true. The private schools perform better for a fraction of the cost of public schools. Overall, study after study shows that they are much better value for money than public schools.

A picture is also emerging of some of the major virtues of low-cost private schools. They are serving huge numbers of children, they are affordable, they are of higher quality, and are better value for money.

But are they equitable—that is, are they fair to disadvantaged groups? In the next chapter, we'll focus on what is often considered to be the most important issue of fairness: fairness to girls. The evidence on this front turns out to be pretty clear, whatever the protestations of some development experts.

3

Equity and Choice

BALUCHISTAN IS THE state of Pakistan that borders southern Afghanistan and eastern Iran. On April 25, 2014, terrorists from an organization calling itself Al-Furqan, an offshoot of the Taliban, the group that had tried to murder Malala Yousafzai, began a vendetta against low-cost, English-medium private schools in Baluchistan.

The first school they attacked, in broad daylight, was Oasis School in Panjgur, a district on the Iranian border. Major Hussain Ali, the school's owner, was driving children in the school bus when he was dragged out and beaten up. The thugs then set fire to the bus.

The major had been warned. Al-Furqan had been distributing pamphlets for a few days to all private schools in Panjgur. The pamphlets, in Urdu, told all private-school managers to immediately cease educating girls. Covering all bases, Al-Furqan also told van, taxi, and auto-rickshaw drivers to immediately stop transporting girls to school. But Ali, like most other private-school owners, ignored these threats. To him, educating all children, girls as well as boys, was what he did and what he would carry on doing; he would not be thwarted in his mission by threats from pesky terrorists.

In Panjgur, as across much of South Asia, low-cost private schools are burgeoning. As one journalist reported, "Most parents in the region prefer their children, particularly girls, to receive uninterrupted education."¹ But in the government schools, education is far from being uninterrupted. Just as Malala showed that was true of the Swat Valley, here it is also reported that public-school teachers are generally absent. Parents know this and are abandoning public schools en masse, so "government-run schools in the region have all but gone extinct."[2] Conversely, private schools are thriving. They first appeared in Panjgur in 2000, it is reported, and by 2014 they had grown to 22 schools with more than 16,000 students enrolled and 500 teachers employed.

Let's be clear: the terrorists know that in this conflict-torn place on Pakistan's troubled borders, parents are turning to private schools for the education of their girls. The terrorists want to stop girls' education and know that targeting private schools is an effective way to do that.[3]

In the terrorists' pamphlets, they declare that girls' education is "*haram.*" *Haram* is the Arabic term for "forbidden." This word might be familiar to readers: we've all heard of Boko Haram in Nigeria. That's the terrorist organization whose most famous obscenity was the kidnapping of more than 200 girls from a public high school in Chibok, in Borno, a state in northeast Nigeria. Reportedly there was another "mass kidnapping" a few months after the Chibok abductions, in the town of Damasak.[4] Here it was a private school that was targeted. Again, it was the fact that girls were being educated that was a major source of the terrorists' hostility.

"Boko Haram" wasn't the founder's first choice of name—he originally called his terrorist organization Jama'atu Ahlis-Sunna Lidda'Awati Wal-Jihad ("People Committed to the Prophet's Teachings for Propagation and Jihad"). It was locals who came up with the catchier title "Boko Haram," which in Hausa, the language of the Muslims in northern Nigeria, literally means "Books (Boko) are forbidden (Haram)." This short phrase conveys the enemy that the founder of Boko Haram, Mohammed Yusuf, was fighting against: "Western education," the means by which we access books, should be forbidden. Anything that is in contradiction to what is written in the Quran and Sunnah is *haram.* As Boko Haram believes the Earth to be flat and doesn't accept that rainfall is caused by anything other than the will of Allah, "geography teachers are ranked alongside Nigerian security chiefs and senior politicians as prime candidates for assassination."[5]

On a journey to northern Nigeria in 2013, I first heard the expression "Western education" used to describe the kind of schooling we take for granted. For all its faults—and we'll certainly be discussing some of these in part 2—you start to think something must be valuable once you realize that terrorists are out to murder those involved with it.

I visited only Sokoto and Zamfara, two states that are much safer than others where Boko Haram is most active. True, shortly before my visit, two foreign hostages, the British Chris McManus and Italian Franco Lamolinara, had been killed in Sokoto during an attempt to rescue them, but they had been kidnapped in the neighboring Kebbi state, not Sokoto itself.

Sokoto has a wonderfully tiny airport—with one flight a day on Arik Air from Abuja, the capital of Nigeria. A tent serves as the VIP lounge; otherwise, the airport is entirely open-air. Security is lax, although bottles of water are confiscated: apparently one could have taken bombs or guns onto the flight, but not your rehydration therapy.

With my guide, Abubakar Ladan, a delightful gentleman in his late fifties, resplendent in flowing robes and *zanna* (the northern Nigerian traditional cap), I went into impoverished areas of the city of Sokoto. These neighborhoods, like so many others in West Africa, had very rough dirt roads, crisscrossed by sluggish flows of sewage trying to carve its own course, as there were no drains or even open sewers. Houses were mainly simple block structures with tin roofs, with families living all in one room. Cooking was all done outside; latrines in haphazardly created wooden shacks were shared by several such houses.

I'd been in touch with Abubakar before my visit, and he'd produced a list of nearly two hundred low-cost private schools. As we traveled around for him to show me these, we found more; indeed, there were low-cost private schools in abundance.

This was odd. I had been told by officials in the Department for International Development in Lagos and Abuja that there was only a tiny number of low-cost private schools in the north, making up only 3 percent of total enrollment. Although I was unable to conduct a detailed survey, certainly in the poor areas of the city, they seemed very much like the poor areas of any city in West Africa that I'd already visited.

On the signboards for these schools in Sokoto, I first saw that explicit description: "Western education" written after the name of the school, the very thing forbidden by Boko Haram. Some of the schools also offered "Islamiyah education"—Quranic religious schooling—in the afternoons or evenings; occasionally, a school offered either option throughout the day. When I asked people—parents, teachers, and school proprietors—what "Western education" meant to them, they said it was about the freedom to educate children to be what they wanted to be—doctors, engineers, teachers, whatever. It was also education that would give you the freedom to travel overseas, to expand your horizons. A few used the synonym "missionary education," linking it with that Western tradition.

Gilbert Ekpo was the proprietor of Wisdom Academy, in the neighborhood called Fakomidi. His school adjoined the Eid praying ground. He looked apprehensive as we arrived. "Are you from the Ministry of Education?" he nervously asked. He was from Kebbi State, and it turned out that my guide had also lived there for a while, in a neighboring village, so there was much hand shaking and warm shared laughter as they discovered they were "brothers" in this way. Thus, at his ease, he told us about his school, which he had opened in 1998; it had around five hundred students, from preschool to ninth grade. His fees ranged from NGN 2,800 (US$7) to NGN 5,000 (US$12.50) per term. All his parents were farmers or small-scale market traders, he told us.

Nearly all his children—99 percent, he said—were Muslims. Ekpo was a Christian himself, he told us, but of course he recognized that he couldn't have any Christian teaching in the school. Why had he set up the school? There were three reasons, he told me. "First, I had a calling to train the children. Second, I feel that education should not be only left to the government. Third, also I need to have some kobo [coins of the Nigerian currency] in my pocket."

There had been an arson incident at the school—a politically related incident, in which part of his school and many other buildings had been set on fire. This was in April, during the election. "We did not pay baksheesh," he laughed. Presumably, the politician's thugs required some reward, and as he wouldn't pay this, his school was set on fire. "Thank God my neighbors rescued the school," he said. "They made me know that what I was doing was needed here."

But there was something else going on in these Nigerian schools, which was again odd, given what the international community continually tells us about northern Nigeria. This brings us back to our observation about terrorists targeting private schools because they educate girls.

The accepted wisdom about northern Nigeria says that there is a large problem with girls' education. One fact sheet says that "only 4 percent of girls complete secondary education in northern Nigeria"; its map suggests that Sokoto is one of the worst states, with 87 percent of girls not in secondary school.[6] UNICEF (United Nations International Children's Emergency Fund) reports from 2015 showed that around 60 percent of the out-of-school children in Nigeria are girls; it is currently running a project, with the British Department for International Development, in the badly affected "five Northern States of Bauchi, Katsina, Niger, Sokoto, and Zamfara."[7] It is reported that Sokoto has the highest number of out-of-school children in Nigeria, the majority of whom are girls.[8]

But, curiously, in my visits to the low-cost private schools in Sokoto, all schools I visited had more girls than boys, at all levels of schooling. I was told this by the proprietors, and at first I didn't believe it, so I went counting. In the first school where I counted, there were thirteen boys and nineteen girls in first grade (primary 1), five boys and fourteen girls in sixth grade (primary 6), and then in the first grade of junior high school, there were four boys and twelve girls. I asked the older class why this was the case. "Girls are more brilliant," said one girl, who stood up respectfully to respond to my question. The boys looked bemused but did not challenge her. The headmistress shrugged, "I can't say why it is; I only know that *is* the way it is." I told her about the reputation of northern Nigeria, that we heard that the Hausas didn't like sending their girls to school. She said, "All I know is that here in my school, I have more Hausa girls than boys."

And it was even true as I moved out of the city, to the village of Sifawa in Bodinga Local Government Area (LGA). In the low-cost private school I visited, girls were 60 percent of enrollment, and the percentage was just as high in secondary as primary school. "The nature of the school is conducive to girls," the young headmaster told me. In addition, "married women" had their own section, with around 150 girls in junior high school and senior high school. At first, I assumed this meant older married women going back to school, but it turned out that these were young women who had married around age fourteen and wanted to carry on with their schooling.

When I arrived, the boys were on cadet drill in the compound. The girls were in the classrooms along the compound's edge. Ostensibly studying, most were looking out onto the compound, engrossed in the disciplined marching and neat uniforms on display.

It occurred to me that one reason why official girls' enrollment is so low in northern Nigeria could be that parents are sending their girls to private rather than public schools. Because many such schools are unregistered and so do not appear in official data, these girls are invisible to the authorities. Rather than being out of school, as the development experts believe, girls are actually being privileged with a private-school education. This intriguing possibility will have to await further research, but it certainly was suggested by my initial visits.

Perhaps it should be no surprise. It is, after all, a basic plank of what Boko Haram is out to condemn. "Western education" is forbidden for everyone, boys and girls alike, men as well as women, because what it teaches supposedly runs contrary to the Quran. But Mohammed Yusuf, the creator of Boko Haram, was very clear: Nigerian education is especially *haram* because it educates girls.

In two strife-torn settings, northwest Pakistan and northern Nigeria, terrorists target low-cost private schools *because they educate girls*—even though the development experts say that low-cost private schools are not doing this. What does the evidence show? How do we explain the disconnect?

Why the Disconnect?

Critics of low-cost private schools seem to present them as if they are bastions of male privilege. Here's one, Prachi Srivastava, associate professor at the University of Ottawa: "Given the full costs of low-fee private schools, most disadvantaged households have to make difficult decisions about whom to send. This choice most often favors boys and aggravates gender inequities."[9]

She was summarizing the Department for International Development (DFID) "rigorous literature review" on low-cost private education in the British newspaper the *Guardian*. It does seem to be an accurate reflection of what the DFID report conveys. But is it really what the literature behind it says?

Here we encounter a deep difficulty. Most academic researchers are unsympathetic to low-cost private schools. Occasionally, you will find someone who seems supportive, but only to the extent that private schools are a short-term expedient until public schools improve. And—it's hard to put this delicately—some academic researchers appear to look at the evidence through lenses colored by their prejudices. Nowhere is this clearer than in the DFID report.

Let me give four examples of what they considered to be evidence *against* private schools to highlight their general approach.

First, the DFID report pointed to a study from rural Tanzania that gave "further evidence ... of inequality of access for girls to private schools."[10] This study compared twenty public and six private secondary (high) schools. In the conclusion, the author of the Tanzania study did indeed observe that "our secondary school enrollment figures *for mixed gender schools* suggest that girls still do not have equal access to boys when it comes to school attendance."[11] This is the comment that was decisively picked up by the DFID team to show that private schools are unfair to girls. However, they completely misread the study. That is not what it says at all.

The italicized phrase is important. If you study the research carefully, as the DFID team clearly did not, you'll find that for the *public* secondary schools, which are *all* mixed gender, there *are* more boys than girls (4,369 boys and 3,482 girls, so 44 percent girls). However, *this is not true in the private schools*. There are two *private* mixed-gender schools, and even in these there are more girls than boys (284 girls and 254 boys). But there are also three private single-sex girls' schools and one private single-sex boys' school. In these private schools, there are 1,100 girls and 150 boys. In total in the private schools, there are 1,384 girls and 404 boys—that is, the private-school population is 77 percent girls. So, whereas the *public* schools cater to more boys than girls, the *private* schools are more favorable to girls than boys.

Adding up the totals in public and private gives 50.5 percent girls (4,773 boys, 4,866 girls). In other words, private schools are much more favorable to girls than public schools, leading to rough equality of girls and boys overall.

Curiously, the DFID report goes on to use this article to flesh out reasons for gender unfairness *in private schools*: The Tanzanian study, they write, "explains gender disparity through household-level and socio-cultural factors, including ... a tendency to invest more in the education of sons, inadequate access to latrines and water at schools (which may prohibit girls' attendance during menstruation), and concerns about the safety of the environment for girls, who were often perceived by parents to be particularly vulnerable to sexual assault."[12] Unnecessary reflection, it might be thought, on gender inequality in private schools when the research finds the opposite.

This kind of misreading and misunderstanding categorizes the DFID report's approach to gender equality. They review twelve relevant studies altogether (one of which is the Tanzanian study, held up as negative evidence against private schools) and conclude, "Most of the evidence reviewed indicates that girls are less likely to access private schools than boys."[13] The evidence from rural Tanzania is clearly *positive*, not negative, evidence. It is hard to think that anything but the prejudice of the DFID researchers against private education made them so blatantly misread the evidence.

A second study, giving evidence from five Indian states, was reported by the DFID report as being "neutral" with respect to gender parity. In fact, it is clearly *positive*, as any thorough reading of the research will quickly convey: it reports that "a significantly larger proportion of boys (60% as opposed to 40% of girls) are ever-enrolled in our sample while a larger proportion of ever-enrolled girls (19.6% as opposed to 15.6% of boys) go to private schools. If however we consider the proportion of total boys and girls going to private schools, *the proportion is very similar* (around 11% for both boys and girls)."[14] That is, more boys are enrolled overall in school, but private schools are more favorable to girls. Considering this differential enrollment, in the end there *is* equal enrollment of boys and girls in private schools. This is quite remarkable given that the evidence was collected some twenty years earlier, from rural communities across India, when it should have been anticipated that more conservative social norms prevailed. Today, as conservative social norms have progressively become more relaxed across India, one would expect an even more favorable outcome for private schools.

A third study from Pakistan was held up by the DFID report as being "negative" evidence against gender equity. The study finds that "conditional on enrollment, girls are not any less likely than boys to be enrolled in private schools. Indeed, except in the 20–24 years age group, girls are significantly more likely to be enrolled in fee-charging private schools as compared with boys ... in terms of girls' enrollment, private schools in Pakistan cater as much for girls as for boys."[15]

How can anyone read this as negative evidence for the impact of private schools on gender? Again, the reviewers must have been reading through glasses colored by their prejudices.

Fourth, another study from India, again reported as negative evidence, also appears to have confused the DFID report authors. The paper provides evidence that the greater the number of private schools, the better the impact on closing gender differentials: "Higher private school share is associated with significantly higher literacy for all age groups while it is associated with significantly lower gender gap in literacy ... among 10–14-year-old children."[16]

This is a fair summary of the DFID report's approach to the negative (and neutral) evidence. Often, they appear to be misreading what is there to judge against private education. The team, however, did find two pieces of positive evidence for gender equity in private schools. One was from Pakistan, which reported that "in settlements without private schools, females are 16 percentage points less likely to be enrolled compared to boys. When there are private schools in the settlement, the enrollment by all children increases, but female enrollment increases more so that the overall gender gap decreases to about 8 percentage points."[17] That is, in places with private schools, the gender gap in enrollment is halved, showing how private schools improve the situation for girls.

Curiously, while the DFID report set out to comprehensively survey *all* the literature from the previous five years, they omitted several sources that were entirely positive about gender parity in low-cost private schools. For instance, while Joanna Härmä's work in India (which draws negative conclusions about private schools) is very well represented (with three articles cited as major sources of evidence, all using the same data set), her magisterial large-scale studies from Lagos, Nigeria, are not included.[18] What do these omitted studies show? Her 2013 summary of her large-scale survey summarizes the position neatly: "Slightly more girls than boys are enrolled in private schools ... indicating that families *do not select school types according to their child's gender.*"[19]

This is true for primary, middle, and high school equivalents. No fuss, a straightforward finding: private schools are fair to girls, a study completely ignored by the DFID-commissioned report.

My own recent studies from Nigeria, Liberia, Sierra Leone, and South Sudan all support the same claim of gender parity in private schools. In Western Area, Sierra Leone, for instance, 52 percent of children in schools are girls. Girls make up a majority of pupils in all three categories of schools—government, nonprofit private, and for-profit private—and at each level of primary school.

In the slums of Monrovia, Liberia, likewise, there are more girls than boys in school overall, with enrollment being, again, 52 percent girls. Moreover, private proprietor (for-profit) schools have either more girls or equal numbers of girls and boys, at preschool, elementary, and junior high school. In our household survey, we found no significant differences between boys and girls in those out of school, in government school, or in private school.

There's no other way to view it: private schools are favorable to girls—they promote gender equity. In many countries, like Nigeria, Sierra Leone, Liberia, and parts of India, there is gender parity between girls and boys, or more girls than boys, in low-cost private schools. In other places, such as rural Pakistan, where there are entrenched cultural objections to girls' education, private schools act to improve the position of girls.

The terrorist groups Al-Furqan in Pakistan and Boko Haram in Nigeria know what they are doing. They are clearly more aware of what is happening on the ground than those academics appointed by international agencies to research them. Disrupting low-cost private schools because girls' education is *haram* is perfectly intelligible given the evidence that private schools are, indeed, fair to girls.

We've looked at gender equity as being perhaps the most important aspect of equity or social justice that critics of low-cost private schools are concerned about. Although there is not space here to apply the same detail to discussion of other disadvantaged groups, the same finding is true for them too. Regarding equity for other disadvantaged groups, after reviewing the evidence, we've been able to conclude, "Research evidence shows that low-cost private schools geographically reach the poor. There is no suggestion of a geographical limit beyond which they have not or cannot pass. Low-cost private schools also appear better to narrow achievement gaps for disadvantaged groups than do government schools ... [and] private schools are improving education for girls in developing countries."[20]

A Real Choice

The evidence for low-cost private schools is growing increasingly robust. But another criticism needs to be addressed: that parents are choosing low-cost private schools not because they want them, but because they are forced into making that choice. Their choice is so heavily constrained that it can't be described as free choice. The evidence on this is weak.

Several studies have been undertaken that ask parents a simple question like "What is your preferred type of school?"[21] From one study in rural Uttar Pradesh, India, the answers showed a *"near universal preference for private schools."* Indeed, "94.4 percent of sample parents answered, 'private school.'"[22] Similar results have been found from many other studies around the world.[23]

The researcher who conducted the Uttar Pradesh study gives graphic descriptions to show readers why parents prefer private to public. She writes, "The government schools had virtually no teaching activity." In the public schools, "there was an air of chaos and neglect, as the teachers simply read the newspaper or chatted with friends, while the children came and went, played and fought in front of them." Most disturbingly, parents reported "teachers encouraging children to fight each other, or one child to corporally punish another child."[24]

I read such descriptions of child abuse and neglect and cannot stop feeling anger well up inside me. This was all in complete contrast to what was going on in the low-cost private schools. In these schools, "there was always an air of seriousness and discipline, with children sitting in orderly rows ... working diligently on their own in their copybooks and then bringing these to the teacher to be checked." In general, there was "an overall discipline enforced" in the private schools that was completely absent in the public: "It was this and the fact that children learn basic material that parents seized on in their comparisons of the school types."[25]

The researcher is clear about why this contrast is there—it has to do with competition and accountability: at the low-cost private schools, the head teachers and proprietors see "the need to keep standards relatively high in order that parents will see some benefit in paying fees." This is what leads to "greater teaching activity" in the private schools: "these standards are maintained through the promise of instant dismissal of teachers if standards drop. This was clear from all respondents in the study."[26]

By contrast, there is no accountability in public provision, just as Malala observed was true of schools in rural Pakistan. Even though public-school teachers "are extremely well-paid," they are "permanent government employees with no accountability for the work they (fail) to do." The researcher's own observations and discussions with parents showed clearly that "these teachers have no motivation to teach well even small numbers of children." The teachers didn't keep regular hours: "The most profound problem is teacher inactivity at government schools during official class time."[27] It is, of course, no wonder, given these contrasting pictures, that parental preferences are as they are.

Can we say, however, that these reflect parents' *true* preferences? The researcher who reported the above, Joanna Härmä, wants to qualify this unequivocal finding. She can't deny that she found this "near universal preference" for low-cost private over public schools. But it is only there because of "current conditions in the government sector"[28]—that is, it is not a *real choice*.

What does she, and others like her, mean by this? She conducted some small-scale focus group discussions among parents in her study and reported that "the *universal desire of parents* interviewed was for government schools to improve, *as expressed by one mother.* … 'They should just improve the quality of the [public] schools. We don't have the capacity to send our children to the private school, so this is our only option. The quality of the education should be like the private school.'"[29]

OK, so these are one mother's comments. This mother mentions public schools as parents' "only option" if they're too poor. In passing, one can note that this should be a comment crying out, in a focus group context, for explorations of other possible options, such as targeted vouchers, to let the poorest attend private schools. In any case, what parents really want, Härmä says, is "a well-functioning, well-staffed government school, inspected regularly and sincerely to ensure accountability."[30] But what is the status of that suggestion?

Suppose we were to ask shoppers using a branded grocery store if they would prefer to shop there or in an identical store, with identical standards, but one run by the government, where everything was given away for free? We might well get quite a few takers for this second option. But what implications could we possibly draw from that? Getting a well-run government store with standards as high as the branded supermarket's while giving products away is not going to be possible within the foreseeable future, and it is unlikely ever to be possible, not even in theory, let alone practice. It would probably be far better not to ask this sort of impossible question.

It is similarly the case with parents in the poor villages of Uttar Pradesh, India. High-functioning government schools are not likely to be available to them soon, and perhaps they never will be. So, it's best to focus on parents' actual choices *now* rather than ask them for their opinions about what might be better in some abstract sense.

Considering this argument, I was reminded of the work of the Bengali Nobel laureate, philosopher, and economist Amartya Sen. He made what seems to be a parallel argument in his magnum opus, *The Idea of Justice*. His work is a critique of social philosophy, such as that espoused by John Rawls, that "concentrates its attention on what it identifies as perfect justice, rather than on relative comparisons of justice and injustice."[31] He believes that the subject of justice should not be about "trying to achieve … some perfectly just society or social arrangements" but instead should be about "preventing severe injustice." He gives the example of the abolition of slavery, which "did not require the search for a consensus on what a perfectly just society would look like." Instead, it required a "diagnosis of the intolerable injustice" of slavery and then the taking of appropriate action.[32]

To further illustrate this point, Sen gives the example of someone wanting to make a choice between two paintings, one by Dalí and the other by Picasso. Someone else chimes in that the best painting in the world is the *Mona Lisa*. Sen says, "It is not at all necessary to talk about what may be the greatest or the most perfect picture in the world, [in order] to choose between the two alternatives we are facing." It is irrelevant to know that the *Mona Lisa* is the best painting in the world "when the choice is actually between a Dalí and a Picasso."[33]

Likewise, we can make a parallel move in our discussion of choice with regard to public and private schools. Researchers ask parents whether they would prefer existing low-cost private schools or an ideal model of egalitarian, high-quality, free public schools. This choice is currently unavailable. It may always be unavailable. It's much more helpful, implies Sen, to focus on the actual choice facing parents now. That choice is between existing low-cost private schools and public schools—the public schools, that is, where teachers don't regularly turn up and whose incidences of child abuse the researcher so clearly catalogs. When making *that* choice, that real choice today, parents' preferences are clear and unequivocal.

In several research studies, I've examined how parents make choices in more detail. It turns out that they are generally well informed. They balance many different dimensions to move toward a decision about their choice of public or private—further evidence, I believe, against the notion that we should dismiss their choices as being forced, not genuine.

The household survey we conducted in the slums of Monrovia, the capital of Liberia, for instance, interviewed more than two thousand heads of households. Overall, 82 percent of the families indicated that they preferred private schools over government schools, with just 13 percent preferring the government schools.

In the household survey, the interviewee was given a list of fifteen issues and asked whether each applied to "public schools only," "private schools only," "both public and private schools," or "neither public nor private schools" (there was also a "don't know" option). For a majority of the issues, all respondents, whether using public or private schools, referred more favorably to private schools. For example, both categories of parents more often indicated that "a safe place for girls," "near to my home," "class size good," "discipline good," "responsive to my complaints," and "children are well looked after" applied to private schools only. Conversely, both categories of parents indicated more often that "overcrowded" and "teachers go on strike" applied to public schools only.

Overall, the perceptions in the community were much more positive about private than public schools. More than twice as many regarded the teaching as good, the discipline as good, and the schools as safe for girls, referring to private schools, than said the same was true of public schools. More than three times as many believed that the children were well looked after in private schools and that these were near their home. Less than a quarter regarded the private schools as overcrowded or believed that the teachers went on strike, compared with those who said the same of the government schools.

A household survey I directed in Lagos State, Nigeria, asked a similar set of questions.[34] This was a representative survey of 1,005 households with 2,290 children. Families were predominantly using private schools for their children: 69.8 percent of children were in private schools, compared with 26.4 percent in public. Elementary school was predominantly in the private sector, with 72.8 percent of primary children in private school. Preschool was essentially private—91.0 percent of preschool children were in private school.

The major source of information to inform school choice was school visits—used by 75.5 percent of families—followed by talking to the families' network of friends, neighbors, and relatives (53.9 percent), and observing children from the school (35.5 percent of families).

The three main reasons given by parents who chose low-cost private schools were proximity to home (61.7 percent), better-quality teachers (46.1 percent), and better-quality school (45.1 percent). Asked to choose one reason only that guided school choice, better-quality teachers came in at the top (chosen by 22.8 percent of respondents), followed by better-quality school (19.5 percent), good discipline (13.4 percent), and proximity to home (12.3 percent).

Some parents had moved their children from one school to another; a substantial majority had moved their children from one private school to another (79.9 percent of 380 movers). This makes it clear that some parents discriminate between different private schools in terms of both cost and quality. Moves from private to public were mostly (75 percent) because the parents could no longer afford private school, while moves in the opposite direction were largely because of dissatisfaction with the child's academic performance (71 percent).

We asked parents which school type was better, public or private? Families overwhelmingly believed that private was better than public. They believed that private schools were open the hours they required, were responsive to their complaints, and were near their homes. Affordability was the only issue where public schools rated higher. For all quality issues, such as school facilities, class size, discipline, and teacher quality, families in each of the wealth categories favored private over public schools.

In other words, household surveys seem to suggest that parents are making informed choices about whether to send their children to private schools, and that one of the key factors here is the perceived quality of education.

For what it's worth, the DFID "rigorous literature review" seems to be largely in agreement here. Their summary finding about choice is that a "majority of studies ... indicate that perceived quality of education is a priority for users when choosing between schools, and that private schools are often perceived to be of higher quality than government ones."[35] Moreover, they find positive support for the statement that "users make informed choices about the quality of education" where "informed choice implies users have adequate information on the performance of schools to be able to judge them."[36]

Interestingly, the report did *not* count it as evidence of informed parental choice when parents said that they chose private schools because of "English-language instruction," "a short journey to school," or "small class sizes, scholarships, free meals, and friendly teachers."[37] It's hard to see why these are not legitimate reasons for school choice. It seems the researchers were only ready to accept choices as legitimate when parents focused on academic exam results. Pointing to a study from Punjab, Pakistan, they noted that "when parents were informed that their school performed worse than expected according to exam results, they did not respond by enrolling their child elsewhere—i.e., pursue the exit strategy."[38] This seems to imply that academic exam results should be the only reason on which choice of school is based. But there could be a myriad of other reasons, including those listed above, that made parents still prefer this school even though the exam results were not as good as they had expected.

Demand for private education is driven by the choices of the poor. This is the key: parents are not compelled to use private schools; they are doing so out of choice, sometimes because of positive advantages (like better results, English language, more attentive and friendly teachers, accountability, and so on) and sometimes because of negative concerns (dire standards in government schools or government schools too far away). Indeed, it's taken for granted in much of the research literature, but it's worth stating explicitly: private schools are massively preferred by the poor.

There's still one final dimension to look at: The Holy Grail of sustainability, and the role of the educational entrepreneurs who ensure this sustainability. These are the subjects of the next chapter.

4

Sustainability and the Rise of Educational Entrepreneurs

WHEN I MET with the managers of the very first low-cost private schools I found in Hyderabad, India, I initially assumed that the schools must be run by charitable organizations. They were in low-income areas, serving poor children, so it was hard to imagine that they could be anything else. But when I went to the fifth, and the sixth ... and the fiftieth and the sixtieth, I began to realize that this phenomenon was clearly not predominantly a charitable one, but one sustained by business. I began to ask questions of the proprietors of these schools about their financial model and realized that, by and large, the low-cost private schools were profitable, making a small surplus that supported the entrepreneurs and their families and allowed for some reinvestment in their schools.[1]

This itself was a remarkable finding, for if a vast majority of the low-cost private schools I was investigating were profitable small businesses, then they neatly solved the problem of sustainability that concerns those involved with development. Sustainability is an issue because, normally, projects to improve the living conditions of the poor in developing countries require funding, usually involving external partners such as aid agencies and donors. What happens when that money runs out? Great projects become defunct projects. Aid agencies and donors go to great lengths to ensure that project proposals show ways of continuing after the funding runs out—that is, that they are sustainable. It's extremely hard to demonstrate this and much harder to accomplish.

But not for low-cost private schools. The ecosystem of low-cost private schools funds itself internally. The small profits generated inspire educational entrepreneurs to enter the system and build schools. These are funded largely by school fees, which are set low enough to be affordable to most parents in the community. Parents like what they are offered, they pay fees to the schools, and so the entrepreneurs are satisfied and continue within the system, while others are also attracted. The system is fully sustainable, because it is fully self-funding and contains all the incentives within itself required for it to continue.

The Holy Grail of development is clearly satisfied.

The Spirit of Educational Enterprise

What is it like being one of these educational entrepreneurs? When I meet with these proprietors of low-cost private schools, I feel I am experiencing something remarkable about the tenacity and endurance of the human spirit. The contrast with what we find now in education in America or Britain is strong. In the countries I've been working in, it's a huge leap of faith to think of opening a private school—and then an even bigger leap to think of opening one for poorer communities. Nevertheless, hundreds of thousands of entrepreneurs are doing it every day.

I reflect on the extraordinary spirit of the educational entrepreneurs I've met. It's not easy being an entrepreneur and setting up a school in these kinds of places—I have tried it myself and know a lot about the trials one goes through. I've been behind small chains of schools in India (Hyderabad and Gujarat), China (Beijing), Uganda (Kampala), Honduras (Tegucigalpa), Nigeria (Lagos State), and Ghana (Central Region), and I know how difficult it is to get it all going.

For those entrepreneurs opening schools in some of the world's poorest and most difficult areas, the process they go through is quite remarkable. First, you must have an idea, the concept of what you want to do. You want to build a school, but what kind of school? What features will make your school different and attractive to parents in your chosen community? Is it the school ethos? Is it the curriculum or teaching methods? Or perhaps use of technology? Or your reputation in the community, which will make parents know you are a safe pair of hands? You must decide this, and then decide on the location. You must select an area that appears to have enough children for your school, and where there aren't too many other low-cost private schools as competitors, unless you feel confident about what you are offering. So you have to research the community—it's likely to be near where you live, so this may not be too difficult—to see how many children are out of school and visit or at least observe the other private schools to get a sense of how much they are thriving. You must sense whether parents would be interested in what you are offering.

Next, you must find a site. Often this will mean getting a piece of land (the alternative is to find an existing building to convert to a school, or indeed find a defunct school to reopen). There are probably not too many pieces of land available, so you won't be overwhelmed by choices. But you have to be reasonably sure that it's within walking distance of your clients and that there are no major obstacles—like a main road or canal or river (which may flood in the rainy seasons)—that will stop children from getting to your school. You'll need to save up to buy this land or save up for a couple of years' annual rent (the way rentals often get charged in poorer countries). Your spouse may not be sympathetic to money being saved in this way, so you'll have to convince him or her that your school is going to be a success, that it's all going to be worthwhile.

Then you must negotiate an excellent rate for the land. Importantly, you have to check that no one else has a claim on it, as multiple sales of the same piece of land are not unusual in poor communities with dubious land titles. This is much more difficult than it appears; even government records are often out of date. One method used, I was told when we first started Omega Schools in Ghana (a chain of schools I cofounded that grew to forty schools and twenty thousand students in only four years), is to tip a small pile of sand on the land you want to buy. If there are other putative owners, their contacts in the neighborhood, after seeing the heaped sand, will soon inform them that someone appears to be transgressing on their property. You'll soon hear of other claimants on the land.

So, you find your land, negotiate the price, and then build your school. Land in many of the poor coastal areas I've worked in is prone to flooding, so you may have to fill it with sand and stones and rocks to prevent this. You buy whatever building materials you can afford, such as poles and zinc sheets and tin roofing, using all your savings and probably borrowing money to do what is required. So, you'll need to get a good deal on your loans. Money will always be a source of worry and moneylenders a source of distress.

You'll need to hire people to help you build, negotiating on price and making sure that they don't steal the materials you've collected, and that they're not skimping on building standards so that the school becomes a future trap for your children.

Then you need to furnish it, with chalkboards, and desks and chairs, and teacher chairs and tables, and something for the head teacher too and the office. All the time you must keep negotiating on price because you can't afford much. Then you have to buy the textbooks and stocks of exercise books and chalk or marker pens, cuddly toys and manipulatives for the younger children. Computers, too, if you can afford them. And you have to transport all this stuff over to your new school site, and somehow keep everything safe and secure, so you hire someone to sleep there overnight, to avoid it all being stolen and you being taken back to square one.

Then you've got to find teachers. You let it be known that you need teachers, probably by word of mouth rather than formal advertisements, and get your first applicants. You interview them and perhaps arrange a mock lesson with kids from the community to see how they are with children. You'll need to work out how much you can afford to pay them and negotiate with them over price too. And then you hope that, as opening day dawns, the teachers won't be lured by a competitor offering slightly better conditions of service. And you must find someone you can really trust to help with the accounts. Perhaps you, or your spouse, do this yourself at first, as this is such a fraught area, but eventually you'll need someone with greater financial expertise than you—someone you can trust.

An entrepreneurial idea is like a child: it has a life and needs of its own. One day you're likely to find that your idea needs another thousand dollars that you hadn't accounted for—perhaps for a marketing idea or a building improvement. So, what do you do? You can't just let your idea die; you must feed it, give it the nourishment it needs, so you must find the money.

Perhaps you borrow money from people that your spouse doesn't know about—and if your spouse does find out, she or he may even leave you. You've spent so much time on your entrepreneurial idea, lavished so much time and attention on it, and then out of nowhere you realize that it needs something extra. You find that extra thing; you may have to borrow to get it—you can't just abandon it. You believe in your idea; you know you can do it.

Then one night in the small hours of the morning, you stop believing in it. Perhaps you start to get doubts about whether you can really get children to your school. As an entrepreneur, you must have nerves of steel.

Sometimes, of course, businesses fail. Entrepreneurs know this. It's much easier to get a job, have an employer, and do what he or she wants you to do rather than be on your own, having to do only what you know needs to be done, what you intuit needs to be done, what you guess needs to be done—and when. If your business fails, you can only blame yourself, not an employer. If you fail, you lose everything. In schooling, everything can be beautifully organized—excellent teachers, wonderful building, everything right—but if it's in the wrong location, it will fail. And conversely, you can have done lots of homework on the location, get it exactly right, but if only one of the other ingredients is not right, you'll fail too. Business is cruel; being an entrepreneur is hard. Even people with nerves of steel can fail.

Then you have to satisfy the government officials that what you're doing meets all the regulations; probably these guys will demand some "unofficial payments," or bribes in money or in kind, and you'll have to negotiate your way through these tricky waters. You've got to get all the appropriate syllabi and make sure that what you offer satisfies these government regulations. It'll take a lot of time and perseverance as you make many trips to government offices to get all this done; you'll get used to being in these unwelcoming places.

And finally, you've got to find children. You have to set your fees to what you think parents can afford and are willing to pay to you. You'll have thought through possible payment options: you know that parents will find it hard to pay term or semester fees in advance, so you might consider monthly, weekly, or even daily fees. You'll prepare some marketing materials—posters, flyers, banners, whatever you can afford—although much of your marketing is likely to be by word of mouth. Perhaps you hire someone to distribute your flyers, but most important, you go into the community to talk to parents about why they should send their children to your school.

And then you see what happens as opening day arrives.

The entrepreneurial spirit is an extraordinary one: there must be underneath it all a confidence that what you are doing is worthwhile, that you will be able to get parents to buy into what you are doing. It's all a substantial risk with an uncertain end, and such risk-taking by those who have little money to start with means putting everything in their lives at risk for uncertain returns. I admire the entrepreneurs constantly.

How many sleepless nights must these entrepreneurs have gone through as they saw their building rise; as they encountered recalcitrant officials always on the lookout for a bribe; as nature came and hurt them, with unexpectedly heavy rains or strong winds collapsing their roof or felling their wooden poles? And as opening day draws near, entrepreneurs know that they may not be able to recoup the funds they have risked. Will they get any children at all? Do they wake up in a cold sweat when they realize this? How will they explain that to their spouse, who has backed the plan only reluctantly?

Then when opening day does arrive—and the uniforms are ready, and the desks have been delivered on time, and there are water and chalk and chalkboards, and exercise books are all in place—then, even if only five or ten children appear, your heart can soar, at least for a moment, as you thank God for giving you the chance to prove yourself. Because now you have a school to run, and the really challenging work begins.

I admire the spirit of these educational entrepreneurs. And I feel discomfort when I read the opinions of so many in power and influence, like my academic colleagues, experts in international agencies, officials in international teachers' unions, and unsympathetic journalists, who disregard all that the entrepreneurs have accomplished. They dismiss them as businesspeople setting out to hoodwink or exploit the poor. I would like to see some of these experts try to open a school under these circumstances. It's not something you can take on lightly. It's certainly not something where you know you will instantly succeed, as these critics imply, as if there is no risk. In any case, the rewards at best are only ever going to be small. It would be extremely difficult to rip off the poor even if you wanted to.

Why do these entrepreneurs go through all of this and take these risks for an uncertain reward? The basic motivations are clear. They want to provide a service to a needy community. Yes, and they want to make money, to earn a living. There might be the desire to amass riches in whichever version of the afterlife the entrepreneur believes in. But through it all, their business and educational needs coincide neatly.

When I meet the parents, I marvel at their spirit too. Just as with the entrepreneurs, they show something about the human spirit of tenacity and endurance. It's a spirit of hope too. Parents love their children; they know they must provide the best for them; they know they have to feed and clothe them and provide a roof over their heads. And as basic as these needs are, they know they must school their children too, a basic need felt by all poor parents. Wanting to educate their children—to prepare them for adult life—seems as natural a desire as wanting to feed, clothe, and shelter them.

So, you're a parent. Where can you send your child to be educated? You know there is a government school on the edge of the slum where you live. For younger children especially, you're nervous about sending a child too far. You've heard about child abduction; you know that some evil things can happen to children who travel on their own for even a mile or two. And you know there's traffic on the main road, so your child can easily get hurt that way too. In any case, you hear stories about the government schools—how teachers don't turn up, and if they do, they don't care for the children; you hear how they abuse children, how they get them doing their own chores and neglect their learning. You hear how your child could very easily get lost in a huge class.

You don't have much money, but you must satisfy your child's basic needs, and one of these basic needs is education. There are private schools nearby, and parents you know are positive about them, perhaps even your own family members. So, you decide to send your child to a private school, knowing that it will mean at least the chance of something better. You must scrimp and save, of course. Sometimes you will have to beg the proprietor to let your child come to school even though you haven't yet paid. But you have a spirit of hope and optimism because you trust the entrepreneur to help your child in the way that you are certain the distant government officials will not.

When I talk to parents, I admire their pragmatism and their hope for the future. And again, I feel anger at those academics, development experts, and union officials who decry what these parents do. Some are explicit: parents shouldn't be allowed to send their children to private schools, because it undermines public provision and further exacerbates inequality. I'd like those experts to come to these slums, look a mother in the eye, and tell her that she cannot do the best she can for her child—and see how that academic responds to her anger. The child has only one opportunity in life for education. She is going to grasp it with both hands. How can anyone want to stop her? I always feel blessed to be meeting them, entrepreneurs and parents alike, as I visit low-cost private schools in the poorest parts of the world.

From Lonely Furrow to a Movement

Over a decade ago, in 2006, the International Finance Corporation (IFC) and the *Financial Times* launched their "Private Sector Development" essay competition. There were more than five hundred submissions from seventy countries. I submitted an essay titled "Educating Amaretch: Private Schools for the Poor and the New Frontier for Investors,"[2] which outlined my research findings on low-cost private schools and pointed to several innovative ways that investors and entrepreneurs could get involved in this education revolution sweeping the developing world. One of the key innovations I proposed was to create chains of low-cost private schools.

In my essay, I quoted the late C. K. Prahalad, who, in *The Fortune at the Bottom of the Pyramid*, challenged the "dominant assumption" that the poor are not bothered about brand names: "On the contrary," he wrote, "the poor are very brand-conscious."[3] So in low-cost private education, branded chains of low-cost private schools could emerge to satisfy parental demand: "Buying into trusted brands would be one way of overcoming the information problem," I noted; that is, poor parents could judge if one private school in their community was better than another. I continued, "Already, small embryonic brands are emerging in the educational markets explored, as educational entrepreneurs expand their own, or take over other, schools, because they are providing what more parents want. Some proprietors have four or five such schools now, and are eager to extend further."[4] I had in mind a couple of such small chains of schools I'd seen in India and West Africa.

I pointed to various ways in which investors and entrepreneurs could get involved. These included creating loan funds for low-cost private schools to help them expand from a small number of schools to a greater number, creating specialized education investment funds aimed at chains of schools emerging in the low-cost market, and funding joint ventures between local entrepreneurs and outsiders.

One of the really important areas that these new chains of low-cost schools would have to engage in, I noted, was research and development—R&D— into the best ways of delivering high-quality but low-cost education models to the poor: "Such R&D would explore the technology, curriculum, pedagogy, and teacher training requirements for the successful *educational* model, and the quality control, financial and regulatory requirements for the brand-name chain. The setting up of a chain of 'budget' private schools, serving poor communities, would seem an extraordinarily exciting and innovative project for investors to engage in."[5]

I pointed to how the chain of schools would benefit parents—solving the information problem for them—and children, too, would rather be in one of these chain schools, as they would "prefer to be in a brand-name school, benefiting from the improved curriculum, pedagogy, technology, and teacher training in their school. They would be part of a much larger organisation, and benefit from the networks and opportunities this creates. And as the brand name became well-known, future employers and further education institutions will trust where children have been educated, giving the pupils an edge for the future."[6]

The brand-name chains of schools would have an impact on existing low-cost school providers, of course, but this would only lead to benefits for all children, as quality improved through competition and replication:

In the short term, [existing schools] could suffer, perhaps even go out of business—but only as a result of parents shifting their children to the school where they perceive educational quality to be higher. But in the dynamic market of education, two things are likely to happen: first, individual educational entrepreneurs will seek to improve what they offer, in order to retain children or win back those who have left. Second, most fundamentally, if the financial and educational viability of an educational brand name is demonstrated, others will soon enter the market, setting up competing brand names that offer quality education at a low cost.[7]

I concluded with Prahalad's observations about an innovative and large-scale health care project, the Aravind Eye Care System, that provides cataract surgery for large numbers of the poor. The founder, he said, was "inspired by the hamburger chain, McDonald's, where a consistent quality of hamburgers and French Fries worldwide results from a deeply understood and standardised chemical process."[8] "There is," I said, "every reason to think that a similarly 'deeply understood and standardised' learning process could become part of an equally as successful model of private school provision, serving huge numbers of the poor."[9]

A pleasing surprise, the essay won the Gold Prize. It was this prize, I believe, that began to draw the international community's attention to the reality of the low-cost private-school sector and its potential. After the prize (and an article I wrote in the *Financial Times* summarizing the ideas[10]), I had a couple of key visitors to Newcastle in late 2006.

One was a secretive billionaire investor. He told me he would come and meet me in Newcastle, at the airport, and I worried about how I could meet someone so important in the rather down-at-the-heels coffee shop there. "Don't worry," he assured me, "we'll meet on my plane." And so, our first meeting was on his personal Boeing 737. His visit led me to take two years of unpaid leave from the university to live in Hyderabad, India, to assist in setting up chains of low-cost private schools, there and elsewhere.

In Hyderabad, it was a heady time, as potential investors and entrepreneurs came to visit to learn about the model. One of the visitors was Bob Pattillo, an American investor, who came with Steve Hardgrave. Bob established another of the ideas that I'd mooted in my prize-winning essay, a loan company explicitly for low-cost private schools. They learned from the model I'd created with the Educare Trust with funding from Theodore Agnew—now Lord Agnew, parliamentary undersecretary of state for education in the British House of Lords. They translated it from the small scale we'd created to the extremely impressive large scale of the Indian School Finance Company, which now serves 100,000 schools. Steve later left to create his own version, Varthana, based in Bangalore.

Some people had noticed the ideas on low-cost private schools even before that prize-winning essay. Notably, Chris Crane, then president and CEO of Opportunity International, had invited me to their annual conference in Manly, Australia, in February 2006. He then decided to steer Opportunity International to set up loans for low-cost private-school proprietors, and when things weren't moving as fast as he wanted, he left to set up his own organization, Edify, giving loans only to low-cost private schools.

Others inspired by the work included Irene Pritzker, who set up a loan and development program called Rising Schools in Ghana. A brilliant young entrepreneur, Ken Donkoh, came to visit me in Hyderabad; eventually we went on to create Omega Schools together in Ghana. Many others involved in the sector now, like Paul Skidmore (who created Rising Academies in Sierra Leone) and Stacey Brewer (SPARK Schools, South Africa), also got in touch to discuss how to create their own chains of low-cost private schools.

Sir Michael Barber, who had been Prime Minister Tony Blair's right-hand man, once pointed me to Arlo Guthrie's classic anti–Vietnam War protest song of the 1960s, "Alice's Restaurant." In the beginning, the song says, if there's just one person who says something (in the song's case, "you can get anything you want, at Alice's restaurant"), then people might think that person is just a little odd. If two people say it, they're still just odd. If three people say it, then people might start to think there's some organization involved. But if fifty people say it, then "it's a movement." Sir Michael said that was what it had been like with low-cost private schools.

One other important visitor to Newcastle in late 2006 after my essay won the prize was Jay Kimmelman, a serial entrepreneur who had just returned from China with his wife, Shannon May, who had been doing fieldwork for her PhD there. He was looking for an education project after a previous life in Silicon Valley. He had read my essay and was captivated by the idea of a chain of low-cost private schools. I showed him my data, and I focused him in on Kenya as being a great place for a new chain to start. Everything seemed right there—a huge existing market of low-cost private schools, showing how parents were totally open to this; a government sympathetic to low-cost private schools (I had visited several times with the ministers of education and they had been positive about my research findings); and a congenial climate and beautiful environment to boot. We exchanged emails and continued our discussions in person, and he was soon set up in Nairobi, Kenya, with his wife, and the two (along with one other) founded the education company that was to be renamed Bridge International Academies, now the largest and best-known school chain in the world.

From opening its first school in a Nairobi slum in January 2009, with infrastructure similar to that of existing low-cost private schools in the slums, it grew to four hundred low-cost private schools in Kenya; expanded into neighboring Uganda, where it now has around one hundred schools; opened in Lagos State, Nigeria, where it now has forty schools; and is working in Liberia and India too, using a public-private partnership model. It has a truly impressive standardized model of curriculum and assessment, where scripted lesson plans are relayed to all teachers on their tablets; teaching is done in a slick, standardized manner; and frequent assessments are analyzed in its head office to monitor progress throughout the world. Because it is so successful, Bridge has attracted a great deal of flak, especially from the global federation of teachers' unions, Education International, and fellow travelers. There have been court cases in Kenya and Uganda, the outcomes of which are still ongoing, based on the schools' not meeting all the required regulatory standards.

But the simple fact remains, parents flock to Bridge schools because the education is better in them. They know that government schools don't meet the required regulatory standards either, and they are not convinced that regulations concerning inputs only—things like the size of playgrounds and classrooms, and teacher pay and certification—are necessarily the key to a great education. It's true that, in general, low-cost private schools do not pay their teachers as well, nor are they as highly certified. This is also the case with Bridge. We saw earlier, however, that this doesn't mean the teachers in the low-cost private schools are any worse than those in the government schools—on the contrary, they bring out much better results than those in public schools. My guess is that the same will be true of Bridge too.

Could it be argued that chains of schools like Bridge could become too powerful and take on the bureaucratic and hierarchical characteristics of a public-school system? Of course there's a danger. But it's much less of a danger if there is competition. If other companies come into the same markets as Bridge and respond more closely to parental concerns than Bridge does, then they will prosper at the expense of Bridge—and, of course, this is likely to make Bridge sharpen up its performance to win back parents. Even small-scale entrepreneurs can compete with Bridge; the barriers to entry of school businesses are not high. Small-scale entrepreneurs have a massive advantage over companies like Bridge, in that each individual entrepreneur has genuine skin in the game, and much more to lose, than the school managers appointed by Bridge.

Bridge is so well known that I could make a prediction that, one day, low-cost private schools *in general* (that is, not just the company's schools) could become known as "bridge" schools, just as we do the "hoovering" in England even if we're not using a Hoover-branded vacuum cleaner, or we Xerox something, even though we may be using another brand-name photocopier.

On one level, it would be a shame if this happened, although hardly anything to worry about. I just hope the following doesn't get lost: Bridge and the other operators that have come from outside to set up chains of low-cost private schools didn't create the model. They didn't create the idea; they were all only "jumping into the saddle of a horse that was already galloping," in E. G. West's memorable phrase.[11] West was referring to the way the state got involved in education in nineteenth-century England and Wales, but it's an equally good way of describing the ways that educational entrepreneurs from outside have created chains of schools in Africa and Asia today.

The educational entrepreneurs from outside were able to see what some of the hundreds of thousands of existing educational entrepreneurs were already doing. The outsiders came in and asked the existing entrepreneurs for details of their income and expenditure and learned the model from them. They asked how the existing entrepreneurs dealt with the regulatory regime—both how it was officially on paper and how it worked on the ground, de facto—and so were able to plan how they, too, would deal with the regulators. They used the parents in existing schools as sounding boards to explore what kind of schooling experience was desirable and what was missing from current providers. They looked at the existing buildings and planned their own based on what they had seen.

Sometimes this all gets lost: I've been to conferences and read some of the literature, and it's as if low-cost private schools were an outside invention, brought to Africa and South Asia by American or British entrepreneurs. It's important to stress that low-cost private education is an industry indigenous to Africa, to Asia, to Latin America. The outsiders have merely jumped on the bandwagon, moving the model forward for sure, but not creating it. They are greatly to be admired, of course, and nothing I've written here is meant to undermine that. But let's give credit also to the giants whose shoulders the outside entrepreneurs are standing on.

My own attempts at chains of low-cost private schools have been rather lower key. It seems I'm good at inspiring others to get going, but my own attempts have been less successful. I'm an accidental businessman, an inadvertent entrepreneur. I had been writing about the business of education and the creation of chains of schools, and was sucked into doing it, in part, to prove the model. Of course, I learned so much by being involved in this way—being an operator makes me realize just how difficult it all is, how many mistakes one can make in business. One learns from these mistakes, although they don't necessarily prepare you for the new mistakes you will make next.

Seven Lessons of Educational Entrepreneurship

These seven lessons are not necessarily in any order, and I'm not saying that there are no other critical issues to explore. Nevertheless, they are important lessons that are worth stressing and are sometimes ignored.

1. Why create chains of low-cost private schools?

First, why is it considered worthwhile to create *chains* of low-cost private schools rather than just stand-alone schools? One set of reasons has already been considered earlier in this chapter—the importance of brand names in overcoming the information problem for parents. Parents are faced with a genuine information problem: how can they judge if one school is better than another? A brand name will help parents make judgments in an informed way. As the brand becomes well known, employers and further-education institutions will trust where children have been educated, giving the pupils an edge for the future.

A second set of reasons concerns teacher issues. In ordinary low-cost private schools, teacher retention is a problem. School proprietors may be reluctant to engage in teacher training, whereby experienced, trained teachers may leave for more lucrative employment. Within a brand-name chain of schools, loyalty to the brand, together with the possibility of new career paths through the chain (for example, as teacher, mentor, trainer, or quality inspector) can encourage teacher retention and hence make extensive teacher training more viable.

Third, there can be investment in quality improvements and innovation. Parents, students, and entrepreneurs alike, as well as critics of low-cost private schools, all agree that quality improvements are desired in the schools in terms of teacher and management training, curriculum, technology, and administration. However, an individual mom-and-pop school usually finds it hard to fund curriculum improvements, teacher training, or better ways of doing learning, because their school surplus is far too small. If we bring enough schools together in a chain, then their combined surplus can be enough to support something positive in this direction.

A note of caution here: our R&D overheads should not be so massive that they require too many schools and students to support them. They must be fit for purpose, as lean as possible, so that break-even and profitability can be achieved more easily.

Bringing schools together also can create economies of scale. If you have two hundred children, no supplier is going to be that interested in selling you uniforms, or books, or desks and chairs, or computers at a special discounted rate. If you have twenty thousand, or two hundred thousand, then it's a whole different ball game. You're likely to be able to negotiate with suppliers for very competitive prices.

A lot of people get excited about chains of schools because they see that technology is playing a large role—made possible in part because of the economies of scale that a chain can bring. Chains like Bridge and Omega relay their lesson plans to teachers via a tablet or smartphone, and school managers use tablets to relay all data regarding the school back to the head office. Other chains use technology in a blended-learning model, where children sometimes learn using adaptive software on a laptop or tablet and other times learn in a traditional classroom setting. So, this could also be an advantage that a chain can bring: being able to afford the research and development to create these kinds of innovations, and then being able to bring economies of scale to bear on the purchase of technology.

There is still virtue, however, in creating stand-alone schools, not just chains. Stand-alone schools have the unalloyed advantage that it is the entrepreneur him- or herself who is on the line if the school doesn't succeed. In a chain of schools, the person fronting the school is likely to be an employed manager with incentive, for sure, to keep standards high, but this is surely never as strong as the incentives of the entrepreneur. Indeed, recent research from Lagos State, Nigeria, compared the Bridge International chain of schools with existing low-cost private schools and public schools. It found both types of private schools always doing better than public schools. No surprises there. It also found that Bridge schools did better than existing private schools in literacy *but not in mathematics,* where both types of private schools came out equally as well.[12] So it seems as though the existing low-cost private schools have many virtues that must not be overlooked.

2. Always remember, it may seem low cost to you, but to parents it's a luxury

Low-cost private schooling may seem "low cost" to us, but to a poor parent it must seem an insult—"It may be low cost to you, sir, but it isn't low cost to me." To a poor parent, in fact, so-called low-cost private schools should typically be thought of as a luxury item.

And as with a luxury item, the mantra of any low-cost private-school business must be this: great customer service. Every parent who comes to visit must be made to feel important, must be made to feel that his or her concerns matter to us. And every staff member in the school—the school managers, the teachers, the janitors, the kitchen staff—all must make sure that children and parents alike know that they are valued, that having them come to our schools really matters to us.

It really does matter. In the low-cost private-school world, margins are very tight; if we lose even a small number of customers, our business is threatened.

3. Getting the most out of teachers

One of the key features of the low-cost private-school model is low-paid teachers. It's an often-leveled criticism against low-cost private schools, that they employ low-paid teachers and so must be low quality. There's no way of escaping the first part of that criticism: there is inevitably a correlation between teacher pay and student fees. If you want low fees—which, of course, we do if we're interested in the low-cost model—then you must hire low-paid teachers.

However, the second part of the criticism, that the low-paid teachers are therefore of low quality, is not valid. First, all the existing research, as we've noted already, shows how these low-paid teachers in low-cost private schools deliver better academic results than the highly paid teachers in public schools, even after controlling for the background of the students' families. So, the good news is that we can start from a higher base than the government alternative.

The fact that low-cost schools hire low-paid teachers means that teachers are going to be less qualified or less experienced (or both) than higher-paid teachers. Neither of these may be the disadvantage that critics proclaim. It may be that those who are more experienced, who have been in the education system longer, develop bad habits, making them less effective in the classroom than teachers who are new and unqualified; more experienced teachers may be increasingly bored with teaching or may have acquired bad habits from being in a low-performing government system.

Nevertheless, it's clear that if we're running a low-cost chain, we'll want our teachers to be performing at as high a level as possible, so our low-paid teachers may need additional support.

What do we do? First, we need to examine what skills and knowledge highly qualified or experienced teachers have that less qualified/experienced teachers are less likely to have. One is the ability to do good lesson planning—writing lesson plans and following them. A second is the ability to create good questions for classwork and homework. A third is creating good assessments, both formative and summative. Fourth, there is likely to be better subject knowledge. Finally, more experienced teachers may have the ability to use a range of teaching and learning techniques, such as group work for peer learning.

It turns out that there's a simple way of addressing each of these skills or kinds of knowledge that may be lacking in the lower-paid teachers: creating scripted lesson plans. Scripted lesson plans can address *all* of those issues. These lesson plans can be created by a team of expert educators at a head office or contracted to teams outside: Bridge International Academies has a team based in Massachusetts; Rising Academies used contractors from the

UK; Omega Schools has a small team based in Ghana. The lesson plans then provide the basis for all assessments, also created at the head office, and teacher training, planned and delivered by the head office.

Scripted lesson plans are where, for each class in every subject and at every grade, the lesson is broken down into the steps the teacher needs to take. They specify what the teacher says and does, and what the students are supposed to say and do at the time. Someone who follows the lesson plan conscientiously can deliver a lesson at a much higher standard than without using a lesson plan. Using scripted lesson plans is widely recognized as a very effective delivery method of instruction in numerous academic studies.[13]

There are four major practical reasons for following the scripted lesson plan approach. First, by providing detailed lesson plans, and the formative assessments associated with them, teachers can function at levels far higher than would be the case without these supporting materials. This means functioning higher in terms of both *subject content knowledge* and *pedagogical learning techniques*. This is because the lesson plans incorporate material that helps teachers revise their subject knowledge and never leaves them open to getting incorrect answers to questions. Lesson plans can guide the teacher in terms of preferred pedagogical approaches. So, a lesson plan might recommend teaching to the whole class, then getting children into groups or pairs for peer learning. Whatever the desired pedagogy, lesson plans can embody this.

Second, a low-cost-education chain requires standardization across all schools within the chain in order to ensure consistency of provision. The lesson plans and associated student exercises, homework, and assessments can provide this consistency. Moreover, a chain of low-cost schools requires data on student attainment (summative assessments), to be used for monitoring performance at student, class, school, and school-cluster levels. These data would be valid only if all students at any level were following the same curriculum; standardized lesson plans ensure this.

Third, the scripted lesson plan approach avoids the need for teachers to create new lesson plans each year. The scripted lesson plans themselves embody and incorporate learning philosophy, so this *will be* followed by teachers who are using the materials and are trained in their use. Within the plans, formative assessments given during each unit of learning are used to provide differentiated learning for slower and faster learners, enabling all children to master essential knowledge and skills before moving on to the next unit.

Teacher training and mentoring is not in a vacuum—it is focused precisely on the prepared lesson plans and formative assessments, which ensures focus and clarity for all training, and ensures that lessons learned in teacher training are carried across to the classroom. I've seen much wonderful teacher training that was wasted because the teachers who were trained had no incentives to incorporate all the things they had learned in teacher training into their normal classrooms. This is not the case if teacher training is based on lesson plans that are available for teachers to use in the class after the training is finished.

Finally, lesson plans can also be a critical component of building the brand. Children, teachers, parents, and regulators see the consistent use of identical materials across all schools in the chain and recognize this as part of the brand image.

Some object to scripted lesson plans, saying that they undermine the teacher's professionalism. This is the vociferous criticism from the teachers' unions and Education International.[14] But do they really? For a start, no one, not even the most ardent defenders of scripted lesson plans, would forbid teachers from adding something of their own—their own flair, if you like—to what they were following if they were so inclined. What they're not permitted to do is *subtract from* what is in the lesson plans, because they are the essentials that need to be covered.

When people talk about undermining teachers' professionalism, I think of another profession—that of the actor. Actors, particularly those performing in Hollywood or Bollywood, are among the most highly paid and highly respected professionals the world over. The Academy Awards, the BAFTAs, and so on all show the esteem in which actors are held. If they're on the stage, in London's West End or on Broadway, then even if they're not so highly paid, their esteem is if anything even greater, for they are seen to embody a purity of their art that may be lost on the big screen. Now—let's spell it out—when they speak, they are not speaking words they have written. Occasionally the director may allow some ad-libbing, but typically the actor, in rehearsal, is reading from a script that someone else, the playwright or screenwriter, has written. When it comes to performance, the actor has deliberately and painfully learned by heart that script that someone else has written.

Now no one says that because actors don't write their own scripts, or even plan their own actions, that they are undermined. The profession is still held in relatively high esteem.

The same can be true of a teacher.

Mentioning actors, of course, makes it clear that scripted lesson plans cannot be valuable if the teacher arrives to teach a lesson without having studied the lesson plan previously. This would be rather like expecting actors to arrive at a theater with a script that they are encountering for the first time, and then make a decent attempt at delivering their part—a recurring nightmare for me and perhaps others too.

A final point about lesson plans. Isn't it nonsensical that in most schools, great teachers prepare lesson plans, perhaps modifying them a little year after year, but then nothing ever happens to these lesson plans apart from their use in that teacher's class? These lesson plans are rarely passed on to other teachers. They are created by an expert, and each new teacher who joins has to reinvent the wheel, year after tiring year.

When I first started teaching three decades ago in Zimbabwe, the mathematics teacher whom I was replacing had the insight to hand over her lesson plans to me. I felt guilty. It seemed like cheating somehow to use her work for my own purposes. It was soon made clear to me by the school authorities that it was most unprofessional to use those lesson plans, that I had to make my own. And so, I took part in the weekly ritual of having to submit my lesson plans to the head teacher, who diligently and carefully went over my and every other teacher's lesson plans. Such a waste of time, such a reinventing of the wheel, year after year. Chains of schools (it doesn't require chains of schools at all, of course, to do this) can cut through this and create lesson plans centrally, and these can be used more than once, by all the teachers across the chain, for many years running, with updates each year.

4. Embrace the sachet economy

The term *sachet economy* is used to describe goods that are marketed to poorer families, where instead of buying, say, a normal-size bottle of shampoo or cooking oil or jar of coffee, the family buys a small portion—a "sachet"—of each of these items. They can't afford the bottle or jar, but they can afford the small portion. We tried a parallel approach in Omega Schools in Ghana, and it seemed to be popular with parents.

This aspect is clearly not de rigueur for those who are running chains of low-cost private schools, because most are not attempting it. However, in the case of Omega Schools, some schools in the neighborhoods have adopted this innovation in order to better compete with us, so it seems that once it is an option in the market, its desirability becomes apparent.

The idea came out of our knowledge of the local communities we wanted to serve. My business partner, Ken Donkoh, was living in these communities, while his sister had run a small low-cost private school. Two things were clear from this local knowledge and research.

First, typically the cash flow of the poor is daily. If you're poor, you don't get a paycheck every month or even every week. You're likely to be a laborer who is paid each day, or you may sell tomatoes and spinach in your market stall to bring in money daily.

Second, we'd often encounter poor parents who said that they couldn't afford to send their children to private school. When probed, what it appeared they meant was that they couldn't afford to *save up* for the school fees, which in Africa are typically levied at term intervals (three times a year) or in semesters (twice a year). In part this was because if you're poor, you always have additional calls on your money—for example, someone gets ill, or there's a funeral to pay for—so it's always difficult to save money. But in any case, parents told us that even if you *could* save for these school fees, then you'd only get hit with other costs, such as for a uniform, books, PTA, and exam fees. These sometimes hidden, always-extra costs meant that private schooling was perceived as unaffordable.

So we hit on the idea of an *all-inclusive daily fee* to cover these eventualities—what we called "pay as you learn," or PAYL.[15] It was *daily* because the cash flow of the poor is daily, and *all-inclusive* so that there would be no hidden or extra costs. What you paid per day would be all that you would be expected to pay, ever. In other words, we amortized the cost of a school uniform, a schoolbag, books, and so on over the whole year and divided the payment by the number of days. We also threw a nutritious lunch, deworming, and medical insurance into the package.

It's important to note that the daily fee is not compulsory in Omega Schools—parents are given the option to pay weekly, monthly, or by term as well. But 80 percent of our parents choose daily, which suggests that it is positively received as a benefit.

When we started the first Omega school, all of this, plus tuition and a tiny margin, came to GHS 200 per year (in those days roughly the equivalent of US$200). As there were 215 school days per year, dividing one by the other gave a daily fee of GHS 1 (US$1) per day, plus fifteen free school days—we gave parents "Get into School Free" cards to use on days when there was no cash in the household, which they could use whenever they wanted to.

The GHS 1 per day fee was considered very low cost by parents. In many government and private schools, there was a "feeding fee" for lunch, and this was often GHS 1 per day, or only slightly less. For our GHS 1 per day, the student got lunch, but also everything else. Children in the neighborhood soon realized that we were the cheapest school around and, in the ways of children, started to taunt our students. Walking past our gates on their way home (our school hours were longer than those of other schools), they shouted, "Omega 1 cedi, I'll give you 50 pesewas." In other words, I'll give you half a cedi—implying that although we were dirt-cheap, we weren't even worth one cedi. Our students didn't seem to mind.

Moreover, once we'd worked out this model, we realized that our all-inclusive fees were not actually much more expensive than the costs of sending a child to a public school. We spoke to mothers in a fishing village where we wanted to open a school. They told us that they couldn't afford to pay for private school. Their children were in the public school. We asked, how much do you pay for a uniform? GHS 40 for the year. How much for books? GHS 15. How much for notebooks? GHS 5. How much for a feeding fee? GHS 0.50 per day—that is, around GHS 100 per year. Even with these figures alone (and there are many other costs in public schools), the cost of sending a child to public school would be at least GHS 160 per year, compared with our fees of GHS 200 per year, the equivalent of US$150 at the time. In other words, we were only marginally more expensive than the supposedly free government school. The cost of sending a child to a public school was at least 80 percent of the cost of sending a child to our private school.

There are two possible approaches to the daily-fee model. The first is that it is strictly "pay as you learn" (PAYL); you pay for school if you attend that day, and you don't if you do not. The second is an installment payment plan—that is, we still tell parents, "You are paying GHS 200 for the whole year, but we allow you to pay for this in daily installments. This means that if your child is absent on one day, then you still owe the fee."

We've been back and forth on this—I prefer the PAYL model, thinking that this is the fairer, market-driven approach. But it does have one serious drawback, inability to pay, which eventually made me think that the alternative approach may be preferable.

What happens when parents can't afford the school fee? Many private businesses serving poor areas are likely to offer a degree of credit. If I'm a regular customer at a particular stall that sells bread, then on days when I'm particularly hard up, I'm likely to be able to take a loaf of bread with me, on the guarantee that I'll pay for two loaves tomorrow, or next week, or whenever. Such is also the case with low-cost private schools in general. They'll usually allow a child entrance even though fees haven't been paid in full, on the agreement that eventually all the fees will be paid. At some point or other, of course, the child will not be able to come to school anymore if fees are not paid. Different schools have their own ways of working that out.

It's hard and it breaks my heart if this ever happens, which is one reason I'm a reluctant businessman and need someone harder than me to eventually turn a child away. A not-very-satisfactory reply to critics here is that the child can now go to the public school, which, in any case, the critics are saying is the desirable place to be—so it's not that we are denying them a place in school altogether. A much better response is to say that this is the reason we've created a hardship fund for children whose families fall on particularly hard times. And that's why we had the fifteen free days initially, to be able to smooth over periods when things weren't going so well financially for families.

The sachet economy for education may be growing, and not just among the poor. In response to COVID-19, mandated school closures have been ubiquitous across the globe and parents have had to adjust accordingly. Filling this void, enterprising educators have begun making curricula and materials they developed available to parents, educating their children at home during the COVID-19 school closures for low to no cost. This version of the sachet economy holds tremendous promise for the development of education markets to meet demand from parents to purchase alternative curricula, in whole or in part, for their children. And, as an emerging market, it is not regulated by government, nor is it dominated by large textbooks companies. Families suffering from the economic impact of COVID-19 are in special need of a low-cost alternative for education that the sachet economy offers.

5. Differentiated learning

In any lesson in any classroom—it's true of low-cost private schools as well as most high-end private schools and government schools—you'll find that children fall, roughly, into three groups. There will be those children who quickly understand what the teacher is talking about; indeed, they may know as much about the topic as the teacher does. Second, there are those in the middle, who get to understand adequately the topic by the end of the lesson. Finally, there are those who will not understand the topic by the end of the lesson or even in any catch-up sessions.

This is an acute problem in many subjects, but especially in mathematics, the most hierarchical of subjects. Here educational progress is hampered by the way children progress as a class, coinciding with the performance of the average child. Those who have not mastered the topic get completely left behind: for instance, without mastering addition with two addends, you will not understand addition with three addends, and so on. And those who have mastered the topic quickly can get very bored and disaffected.

In a chain of schools, where we have resources (including time), we should focus on ways of dealing with this problem. I've seen a couple of interesting possibilities. One of these involved using adaptive-learning technology. I was watching a fourth-grade class learn a topic in fractions. One of the girls, Jennifer, had no clue as to how to proceed. The teacher tried to help for a bit, but she had to give up, because she couldn't get Jennifer to progress. She left her on her own and focused on other members of the class. Under normal circumstances, it is likely that Jennifer would forever be lost to mathematics. However, this school had an innovative program where children used an adaptive-learning program on tablets or laptops. The software found that Jennifer couldn't answer any of the questions at her grade level. As a result, it then guided her to questions that looked at her understanding of the prerequisites for the topic she was working on. She couldn't tackle these questions either, so the software then guided her to even more basic topics—at second-grade level. These, Jennifer could answer. Thus, with her confidence built up, and required building blocks in the topic established, she was able to move on to harder and more complex topics. After only a ninety-minute period—only a ninety-minute period!—she was able to come back to the fourth-grade fraction work that had left her completely lost.

The school was participating in a trial of this software. At the end of the trial, we asked the children whether they enjoyed the work and why. Jennifer was one of those eager to say she had enjoyed it. "Because I love fractions," she said. But that had not been her attitude when she couldn't do anything in the mathematics class. The software had really changed everything for her. Perhaps she had missed a week or two when the topic had been covered two years before. In schools, we normally let children like her go—we let them fall behind and be those who can't do mathematics. In chains of schools, we have no excuse to let this happen.

Another approach to tackle this same problem uses peer learning. Here, children were put in groups of about four or five, with one of the children in each group selected as someone who was able to grasp the subject very quickly. The teacher would go through the subject and then the peer leaders would help the other children with their difficulties.

6. For-profit and nonprofit motives

There are two concerns here. First, should your chain of schools be on the for-profit or nonprofit model? There are some famous nonprofit chains of schools—a huge chain run by BRAC (Bangladesh Rural Advancement Committee) in Bangladesh, for instance, and PEAS (Promoting Equality in African Schools) in Uganda. Both charge fees to students, which are expected to cover most, or all, of the operational costs of the schools, but then philanthropic funding comes in to pay for the buildings and head office costs.

Interestingly, BRAC is changing its model and wants to move toward a much more thoroughgoing cost-recovery model, where surpluses are reinvested. The reason is that Bangladesh is transitioning from an extremely poor country into a middle-income country. And this means that BRAC's current biggest donors, the British and Australian aid agencies, will not be able to provide donations in the future, as this is not allowed to middle-income countries. (The British aid agency Department for International Development recently stopped its aid to India for this reason.) Hence, BRAC knows that it cannot rely on donations, so it is moving toward a different model.

This illustrates the general reasoning behind companies such as Rising Academies, Omega, and Bridge, which are for-profit companies: while there may be some people who might be willing to give money away to a good cause, there are more people who would be willing to give money to a good cause *with the prospect of getting it back*, with interest, or a dividend on their investment. There are many potential investors out there now who are willing to look at a "double bottom line," and so they will not be after a high financial return, if you can match whatever financial return there is with the satisfaction of seeing a larger number of less-fortunate children gaining a quality education.

Then there's the self-interest of the entrepreneur. I remember being disappointed listening to a panel of young education entrepreneurs at a conference. Each of their businesses was for profit, and so they were each asked, "Why?" They came out with often long-winded answers that the best way to serve the poor was through raising investment, and only for-profits could bring this, and so on. Not one, regrettably, came out with the simple answer that they would like to make some money. There's nothing wrong with the desire to make money. It will never be the only motivation for someone working in this area—it simply is too difficult to work in these environments, the risks so great, and the rewards so distant. But we're only human. If people are motivated by the eventual financial reward that could come, somewhere down the road, from making money creating a successful chain of low-cost private schools, there's nothing wrong with that.

The for-profit business model must be sustainable. It's no good building a model that depends upon philanthropic donations to provide the computer lab, say, because what happens when those donations stop, or what happens if you can provide computer labs for only half of your schools? This isn't any good; you want consistency across your brand. However, there may be a very strong place for philanthropy, the second area where the nonprofit/for-profit discussion comes in. For instance, philanthropy can be used to provide targeted scholarships for the poorest students. This will always be desirable to do, if the moral-hazard problem can be overcome—that is, parents who pay for their children's education even though they themselves are poor may resent other children coming into the school for no fee. In Omega Schools, we ran a parallel scholarship fund, for two types of families: First, some parents suffer severe hardship, such as the loss of a job or of a partner, which means the child who was in an Omega school can no longer attend. The Hardship Fund helps such families with a medium- or long-term scholarship so that their children can continue to attend the school they have chosen. Second, the poorest of the poor in communities served by Omega are unable to attend because they cannot afford the daily fee. These children may be attending government schools, where education is likely to be unsatisfactory, or they may be out of school altogether. The Hardship Fund can provide places for these children. Importantly, as the daily-fee model covers food, books, uniform, and so on, a full scholarship provides all that is required for a child to attend school.

7. Buy and build, or just build?

Omega Schools expanded by building new schools in selected locations. The same is true of Bridge International Academies. However, it is clear in many of the locations and countries in which chains of low-cost private schools are being set up that there are many existing schools in these countries. Indeed, often wherever one seeks to set up a new school, one will find existing low-cost private schools nearby. So, the question arises: Why build new schools, instead of buying or leasing existing schools? Some education companies are finding that this alternative route has much to commend it, including two that I've helped set up, Cadmus Education in Gujarat, India, and Dream Africa in Uganda and Nigeria.

It wasn't necessarily something that the school owners had thought of doing before we approached them. But there were good reasons why school owners could be willing to sell or lease their school business.

Sometimes the schools are very successful, but the owners still feel like parting with them: perhaps the school had been set up by a husband-and-wife team, but one has died, and the other doesn't feel like continuing. Sometimes the school had been set up with the idea that the founder's children would take over in due course, but the children are settled in America or England, and the founder must accept that someone else should take over.

Alternatively, sometimes the schools are not successful. Because there are so many low-cost private schools now, sometimes a group of businesspeople get together and decide to build another school, thinking that they can make some money relatively easily that way. However, sometimes it turns out that it's more difficult than they thought. The school doesn't have the enrollment it needs to be sustainable. Such groups may be willing to sell a school.

Of course, not just any school whose owners are willing to sell is the right one to buy—the potential buyer needs strict criteria to isolate those schools that are suitable: Is it in a decent-size catchment area of low-income communities? Does the school have some impediments to enrollment, such as a busy road that needs to be crossed by students? Does the school have a clear land title, without family or other disputes? Is the land threatened by developments such as slum clearance or road upgrades? Is the school registered with the appropriate authorities? And so on.

Once suitable schools have been located that satisfy these and other criteria, negotiations can then be undertaken over purchase price. You must be careful to think of "the school" as the business: you probably want to purchase the business, but this may involve leasing the buildings and land rather than purchasing them. Too often people think that running a school business requires the school building to be owned, but there's a good case to be made for not tying up capital in that way and leasing the buildings instead.

The Spirit of Enterprise in Education

The spirit of enterprise in education is alive and well. Educational entrepreneurs across the developing world have created stand-alone schools, serving low-income neighborhoods, to the extent that in urban areas, these schools serve most children—70 percent or more—while in rural areas they're a substantial minority—perhaps 30 percent. Without any assistance from outside, these entrepreneurs have created schools that outperform those provided by the state even though public schools have considerable additional resources, including from international agencies. Now other entrepreneurs, inspired by what they've seen already achieved, are creating chains of schools that build on the success of the stand-alone schools and bring in large investments, partly to be used for further improving and refining the low-cost private school model. Some of the lessons I've learned in helping build chains of these schools have been enumerated to show some of the considerations when working in this sector.

The argument in favor of low-cost private schools is beginning to take shape. They are ubiquitous, reaching even the most difficult countries and the most difficult places within them. They have already achieved considerable scale, so the development aim of scalability is being met. They are affordable to families on the poverty line—indeed, there's not much difference in cost for families between sending a child to a low-cost private school versus a government school. They are of higher quality than public schools in terms of academic achievement, and they are much better value for money. They are fair to girls and other disadvantaged groups. Parents hugely prefer private schools and can make informed choices about them. And the system of low-cost private schools is sustainable; it doesn't require funding from outside to be at scale.

But these are not the sum of private education's benefits. Progressively removing education from the state brings further advantages. We consider this by first returning to problems of government involvement in education in war-torn states; then we argue for its applicability in countries that are not war-torn, through consideration of the writing of the Universal Declaration of Human Rights.

5

Education and Domination

LOW COST PRIVATE SCHOOLS offer a route to providing educational opportunities for all. A spontaneously arising education system that is ubiquitous, sustainable, and scalable, of higher quality than the alternatives, the preferred choice of parents, fair to girls, and affordable to the poor, cannot be dismissed.

But are there stand-alone reasons why we should prefer educational freedom as a permanent option for parents and children? The reasons go to the heart of why wresting education away from the state is important. They also begin to set out why this must include getting hold of the *framework* of education too—the curriculum, assessment, structure, and organization of schooling.

Endorsing the move toward educational freedom—that is, to *increase* the involvement of the free enterprise education sector—is also endorsing a *reduction* of government involvement in education. Reducing the involvement of government in education can (1) reduce the size of government overall and hence the potential for corruption; and (2) reduce the potential for governments to use education as a means of domination, coercion, oppression, and patronage.

Reduction in Corruption

Corruption is a hugely significant problem in most developing countries, including those we've been looking at throughout these chapters. In the latest Corruption Perception Index, South Sudan is ranked 179th out of 180 countries, ahead of only Somalia. Nigeria is ranked 148th—that is, in the bottom quintile of most-corrupt countries. Kenya is 143, Sierra Leone 130, Liberia 122, and Pakistan 117, all within the bottom two quintiles of the most-corrupt countries. Only Ghana and India (jointly ranked 81) make it, only just, into the top half of all countries.[1] That means they are still very corrupt. In each of these countries, education makes up a significant part of the budget.

Putting these two facts together—level of corruption and amount of budget earmarked for education—it could be argued that the more education can be removed from governmental budgets, the less potential there will be for corruption, at a multitude of levels. For instance, the officials who sell government teaching posts for bribes;[2] head teachers who create "ghost" teachers to get more money from the government payroll, or who inflate the number of students on the roll to increase government subsidies[3]—each of these problems could be reduced, or even eliminated altogether, the more we move away from government funding.

Of course, private organizations could also be corrupt, but the discipline of the market is much better at keeping them in check than any potential accountability that's in the public sector. For example, it is common for public-school teachers in developing countries *not* to instruct their students during the week, but to demand money from them to attend after-school or weekend sessions, where teaching does take place. The same thing could happen in a private school. If it did happen there, however, it would likely be discovered by the proprietor, who would probably dismiss the teacher and end the practice. But even if the practice didn't end, parents would have the choice of moving their child from the private school to a different school. In the public-school example, teachers are highly unlikely to be reprimanded for this practice, and in a situation of government monopoly, parents can't move their children elsewhere.

Reduction in Oppression

Reducing government involvement in education can also help reduce the potential for governments to use education as a means of domination. On one level, this is straightforward: a better-educated populace could be one bulwark against governments oppressing their people. Evidence shows that the private sector is better able than governments to deliver superior educational standards. So, the more we move education outside of government, the more likely we are to bring up better-educated young people, who are more likely to be able to stand up against government oppression.

There is also a more complex set of reasons. These reasons are clearly relevant to war-torn countries, but they could also be applicable to countries where there may be the risk of governments using education for their own coercive ends, such as Nigeria or India. These reasons can be applicable to anywhere in the world.

Let's go back to schools in Liberia slums. A typical view held by many in development is that the major reason why people use low-cost private education there is because of the parlous state of public education. Certainly, the public schools in Liberia are not good, and this could be a valid reason why parents are choosing to go private. Many development experts hold that if we can improve public schools, then the demand for low-cost private schools will diminish and eventually disappear. But there is another possibility: that parents want control over their children's education, and this, too, is an important reason for choosing private education.

"Parents wanting control" can be rephrased as "parents *not* wanting government to be in control." Part of the reason for that may be because parents know that governments are always tempted to, and do, use education as a tool of oppression. The history of Liberia—in common with the history of the other war-torn countries we looked at, but also in common with other countries across the developing world—shows how government has been using education precisely to dominate citizens.

In Liberia, what is particularly poignant is that it was the freed American slaves who became the colonial oppressors (the Americo-Liberians) against the indigenous peoples (the African Liberians). Those in power restricted educational opportunities to keep the indigenous Africans in check.

Indigenous African Liberians were not given the franchise until 1963. Crucially, education was used as a key tool of oppression. In 1848, Americo-Liberians passed a law that prohibited the education of the African Liberians, the indigenous people. Most formal education was concentrated in Monrovia and the few other cities where most of the Americo-Liberians lived. Formal schooling was particularly geared to educating the Americo-Liberian society, with only "bush" schools serving the indigenous population. These indigenous schools ("Poro" for boys and "Sande" for girls) played an important role in providing basic education and training, including discipline and the communication of indigenous culture. But they were not able to bridge the educational gap between the indigenous people and the urban settlers.

When the civil wars came, from 1989 to 1997, and 1999 to 2003, one of the key grievances leading up to them expressed by the people was the education, or sometimes the lack of it, provided by government. The Truth and Reconciliation Commission, set up to explore the issues leading up to the civil wars, indicated that key causes of the conflict were found in the "entrenched political and social system founded on privilege, patronage, politicization of the military, and endemic corruption *which created limited access to education* and justice, economic, and social opportunities and amenities."[4] Ordinary Liberians "spoke of the connections they saw between education and conflict, as well as of the importance of education for their children, for the nation, and for the sake of peace."[5] One interviewee commented on the divisions and patronage in education and society:

> The indigenous people were deprived of high-level positions. In the entire history of Liberia to 1980, only one indigenous person was a minister of foreign affairs. None minister of internal affairs, none speaker of the house, and none head of the senate. So all these factors [contributed to the war]. Before the fighting, the education standard was very low. The University of Liberia never had graduate studies. Because the descendants of the elite went to America. They were only here for high school. They went abroad on government scholarships. So the system reproduced itself.[6]

Liberia's educational history is strikingly similar in this regard to that in Sierra Leone and South Sudan. Each seems to demonstrate how, in education, the "revolutions and radical movements" came in to replace "one tyranny with another."[7] The colonialists used education to control the population, but as soon as the new governments came in at independence, they used education as a form of social control too.

Over the years, governments have been using education to stifle freedom and opportunity for ordinary people. Governments have been abusing education, and this has been one of the causes of conflict. Development experts are clear about this. The UNESCO Global Monitoring Report for 2011, *The Hidden Crisis: Armed Conflict and Education*, expresses it like this:

> Education is ... often an underlying element in the political dynamic pushing countries towards violence. Intra-state armed conflict is often associated with grievances and perceived injustices linked to identity, faith, ethnicity, and region. Education can make a difference in all these areas, tipping the balance in favour of peace—or conflict.[8]

There are three areas in which "education can make societies more prone to armed conflict." First, there is the problem of governments providing "too little education."[9] That is, "when large numbers of young people are denied access to decent quality basic education, the resulting poverty, unemployment, and sense of hopelessness can act as forceful recruiting agents for armed militia."[10] Second, there is the problem of governments creating "unequal access to education": "If education policy is seen by disadvantaged groups as a source of diminished life chances for their children, it is likely to generate a deep sense of injustice that can call into question the legitimacy of the state itself."[11]

Third, there is the problem of governments promoting "the wrong type of education." That is, governments can actively use "school systems to reinforce prejudice and intolerance": "In several armed conflicts, education has been actively used to reinforce political domination, the subordination of marginalized groups, and ethnic segregation. The use of education systems to foster hatred and bigotry has contributed to the underlying causes of violence in conflicts from Rwanda to Sri Lanka. And in many countries, schools have become a flashpoint in wider conflicts over cultural identity."[12]

Government education can lead to textbooks "explicitly or implicitly" disparaging certain social or tribal groups, reinforcing "social divisions."[13] For instance, the Sudanese government in 1983 "revived the Arabized-Islamised education system for all schools in Sudan," which Southern Sudanese reported as "a deliberate act of aggression towards their culture, values and languages." One-third of all Sudanese were not Muslim.[14] Southern Sudanese educators were particularly troubled by the fact that, in the words of one headmaster, "everything in the curriculum is built on the Koran, even in mathematics." An example from the official curriculum illustrated the point: "There are five prayers in the day [for Muslims]. Ahmad has already prayed twice. How many more times does he have to pray that day? In this way, the student learns that five minus two equals three. And instead of saying something in the abstract, we have a practical example."[15]

There is always a danger that those in power may resort to patronage or oppression. Indeed, the Organisation for Economic Co-operation and Development (OECD) reports that education appears to be one of the services most prone to "polarisation and manipulation."[16] So the second proposition is clear: if the government's power over education can be reduced, then the potential to use it for harm can be minimized.

With this historical context in mind, another interpretation of the rise of educational entrepreneurs running schools suggests itself. We are focusing on Liberia, but the same story also could be told about Sierra Leone, South Sudan, and so many other countries. In Liberia, to many in the slums—who have typically come in from the hinterlands and who would most definitely be classified as "African Liberians"—the public schools historically have been about stifling their freedom and opportunity. These people have come to the capital city to improve their lives and opportunities, and they are using private education, not public, as a way of doing this.

Ordinary Liberians whom I met in Monrovia appeared not to trust the power of the state over education. This seems to be one important reason why they use low-cost private schools instead of public education. They know that governments historically have withheld education from them or provided it indifferent to quality. They know that, historically, what governments can give, governments can take away. They'd rather have control over their children's education than be subject to the whims of those in government.

Liberia, the land of emancipated slaves, is undergoing another process of emancipation. Arguably, the people themselves are slowly freeing themselves from the power of the state over education by using private schools instead of those provided by government. It's the same process that is taking place across the developing world. One could call this process "educational emancipation."

How far can we take this argument? We've used it here as an argument about government controlling education—both provision and funding, but also control of the curriculum—in war-torn countries such as Liberia, Sierra

Leone, and South Sudan. But then without much extension, it would seem to be applicable to any other country in the developing world where the temptation could be strong to use education as a means of oppression or control of different ethnic or religious groups.

There are many examples of this at work. Here's one that might be surprising to readers: India.

The Hindu nationalist party, the Bharatiya Janata Party (BJP), has been in power in India at the federal level since 2014. It is promoting the "Hindutva" agenda, the "Hindu blood" movement that prioritizes Hinduism in all areas of life. The BJP also governs many states. At least three of these state governments—Rajasthan, Maharashtra, and Gujarat—have recently updated their social studies and history school textbooks, in a way described as emphasizing "Hindu triumphalism and Islamophobia."[7] Parallel, if subtler, changes appear to have been made at the federal level too.

Before the BJP, the Indian National Congress was in power, and for decades "India's textbooks were a stronghold of the country's left-wing ruling class."[18] In the schools I managed in Hyderabad, Andhra Pradesh, I recall the social studies textbooks, from which we had to teach, glorifying socialism and denouncing capitalism. So, it's not a new phenomenon for the government in power to seek to influence school textbooks. Now it is reported that the new textbooks "promote the BJP's political program and ideology."[19] They glorify Hindu warriors, claim the veracity of the Hindu myths, demonize Muslim rulers and by implication Muslims more generally, and, in at least one case, appear to praise Hitler. In a twelfth-grade history textbook, Hitler is recognized for his moves

> to release Germany from the Great Depression. He promised every person bread and job [*sic*]. … Hitler made a strong German organization with the help of [the] Nazi party and attained great honour for this. By favouring German civilians and by opposing Jews and by his new economic policies, he made Germany a prosperous country. … He *transformed* the lives of the people of Germany within a very short period by taking *strict measures*. He safe guarded [*sic*] the country from hardships and accomplished many things.[20]

One commentator has written that "it is not an accident or eccentricity" that textbooks are "exalting Hitler," because a "positive view of fascism enables a government eager for more power to tell its citizens about the potential of 'strict measures' to 'transform' society."[21]

Mention of Hitler brings us squarely to the West and this question: Is this argument also applicable to the rest of the world, including America, Britain, and Europe? Crucially, this seems to have been a key sentiment behind the writing of Article 26 of the Universal Declaration of Human Rights.

Article 26 is the famous "right to education." Most people only know its first paragraph: "Everyone has the right to education. Education shall be free, at least in the elementary and fundamental stages. Elementary education shall be compulsory." This, in fact, is only one of three paragraphs of Article 26; two other paragraphs were introduced because of fears raised by delegates about giving the state too much power over education through this first paragraph by making education "compulsory."[22]

Underpinning the discussions was what had happened in Germany, and the rise of Hitler and the Nazi Party. Several representatives argued against including the word compulsory because "it was essential to *guarantee freedom to choose education*, a principle flagrantly violated by the Nazis."[23] This was lurking behind all the considerations: The Nazis had had a very efficient and effective state education system. But look at the horrors that this led to, horrors that had to be prevented from ever happening again by ensuring that states were not given too much power over education. Count Carton de Wiart (representing Belgium) agreed with the Netherlands' representative about "the horror which the Nazi-occupied countries still felt at the thought that the State could compel children to be deformed morally and intellectually by the doctrine of the party in power."[24] Likewise, delegates from the UK, India, and Australia agreed that "it was dangerous to include the word 'compulsory' ... because it could be interpreted as acceptance of the concept of State education."

On the other side of the argument was a Mr. Pavlov, representing the Union of Soviet Socialist Republics (USSR), who argued *for* including the word *compulsory*. The word should not be feared, he said, for it would work "to the advantage of the child whose parents might not understand his vital interests and to the improvement of society."[25]

Representing UNESCO, Mr. Lebar agreed. Using the word *compulsory*, he soothingly reassured delegates, "did not mean that the state exercised a monopoly over education, nor did it infringe [on] the rights of parents to choose the schooling facilities they wished to offer their children."[26]

Consensus could not be reached, so in the end, it came down to a vote. Should the word *compulsory* be deleted from the phrase "This right includes free, compulsory …"? The vote was as narrow as it could be: "A vote on the proposal to delete the word 'compulsory' was narrowly defeated by eight votes to seven."[27]

It's salutary to recall this fact: when people glibly talk about the importance of compulsory education, they should remember that it was carried by only one vote in the deliberations of the United Nations' committees. And we should recall that, in that vote, three of the votes cast in favor were from the USSR—the Union itself, plus the Byelorussian and Ukrainian Soviet Socialist Republics. Had they been allowed only one vote—they were, after all, just one country—the vote would not have carried.

Other delegates were not reassured. Representing Lebanon, Mr. Malik said that his delegation had voted against the word *compulsory* "lest it be interpreted as making it imperative for children to be sent to schools designated by the State." So, Lebanon proposed an amendment that would "guarantee the right of the family to determine the education of its children." The Lebanese amendment would add the following third paragraph to Article 23: "Parents have the prior right to choose the kind of education that shall be given to their children." This amendment was adopted by seventeen votes to thirteen, with seven abstentions.[28]

Certainly in the middle of the last century, countries all over the world were worried about giving too much power to the state in education; the framers of Article 26 rather shrewdly saw the dangers in *any* state taking too much control over education, and that's why the paragraph on parental rights was inserted as a counter to this threat. In other words, our proposition that reducing the involvement of government in education can reduce the potential for governments to use education as a means of domination would seem to have universal applicability—it certainly lay behind the deliberations of the Universal Declaration of Human Rights.

This discussion has been about state control of education, but most significantly it brings in discussion of state control over the curriculum itself. In part 2 of this book, I explore this issue, focusing on government control of *the framework of education*, the curriculum and assessment framework, and the structure and organizations of schools. This is a critical area that currently inhibits educational entrepreneurship and is ripe for educational emancipation.

PART TWO

Reclaiming the Framework of Education

THE FIRST PART of this book has pointed to the way that the grassroots revolution of private schooling is challenging the role of government in the *provision* and *funding* of schooling. However, there is another area of government intervention, *regulation* of schooling. Regulation can be in terms of inputs, such as classroom size, size of playground, and teachers' pay and conditions. I wrote about this at length in *The Beautiful Tree*, where I raised three basic points: First, the inputs normally regulated have little to do with improving children's education and more to do with bureaucratic convenience. Second, in the countries I looked at, these kinds of regulations fall afoul of corruption: the inspector calls and demands a bribe to get around the regulations; the more regulations there are, the higher the bribes demanded. Third, development commentators usually overlook the accountability that private schools have to parents, which can obviate the need for these kinds of regulations altogether.

But there is a far more insidious and overlooked area of government regulation. This is government control of the "framework" of education—that is, the systems of curriculum and assessment, compulsory schooling, and the organization of schooling, imposed by governments and monitored by governments and international agencies. This is the focus of part 2.

6

Great Expectations

THE FIRST FIVE chapters of this book highlighted the re-markable revolution of low-cost private schools that is burgeoning across the developing world. While there are many critics of this revolution, we have suggested that their criticisms are not compelling. Low-cost private schools are clearly scalable—they are already ubiquitous, serving communities even in the most difficult parts of the most difficult countries. They are affordable to the poor—and the overall cost of sending a child to a low-cost private school is not much more than the cost of sending a child to a public school, once all costs of schooling are considered. Low-cost private schools exhibit higher edu-cational standards than public schools, even after taking relevant background variables into account. They certainly provide better value for money than public schools. Low-cost private schools are equitable—for instance, they're fair to girls, in many countries serving a majority of girls, in other places having the effect of reducing gender inequality. They're the preferred choice of the poor. All in all, educational entrepreneurs within these countries have created something worthy of celebration. Others are coming into the market and creating chains of schools, investing in R&D and realizing economies of scale, with the potential to improve academic quality even further. We've looked explicitly at some of the criticisms of low-cost private schools and shown them not to hold up under scrutiny; other similar criticisms are subject to the same kinds of responses that we've given here.

There are two additional criticisms that merit further investigation. Both lead us to focus on government control of the framework of education. We'll approach the problems here by tackling some arguments in two widely acclaimed books—*Poor Economics*, by Abhijit Banerjee and Esther Duflo, and Bryan Caplan's *The Case against Education*.

The Curse of Expectations

In the much-admired book *Poor Economics*, at first it seems that the authors, Duflo and Banerjee, are in favor of the low-cost private schools revolution, what they call "the surprising phenomenon of cut-price private schools."[1] In common with most informed commentators, Duflo and Banerjee are also damning about the quality of government schools for low-income families. They point to a range of evidence that shows that private schools, including low-cost private schools, do much better. Overall, they conclude, "children in private school learn more than children in public schools."[2] However, for the authors of *Poor Economics*, this is not enough. The authors agree, private schools are better than public. However, private schools be damned: they are not "as efficient as they could be."[3]

Now, many things are not "as efficient as they could be," but we still prefer them to the alternatives. Why wouldn't the same be true of private education, and especially those low-cost private schools that everyone agrees are already better serving the poor? For the authors of *Poor Economics*, there is "one key issue ... unique to education" that leads to their attack on low-cost private education.[4] It is, I believe, an important argument with profound implications. But far from supporting the role of government in education, the purpose for which they use it does, in fact, the opposite.

The crux of the argument in *Poor Economics* is the "peculiar way in which *expectations about what education is supposed to deliver distorts* what parents demand, what both public and private schools deliver, and what children achieve—and the colossal waste that ensues."[5]

They call this problem "the Curse of Expectations," which means that poor parents "see education as a lottery ticket, not as a safe investment." This is partly because the stakes are so high: poor parents "seem to see education primarily as a way for their children to acquire (considerable) wealth."[6]

In most developing countries, the ministry of education within the government either sets or regulates examinations that children must take at the end of a specified period of schooling. These examinations are the sole gatekeepers that decide if a child can continue with higher levels of schooling or further education: without passing these examinations, the better-paid and secure government jobs will be out of reach. In many developing countries, it is precisely this kind of employment that poor parents aspire to for their children. But the government-imposed exams might be taken nine, ten, or even twelve years after a child is enrolled in a school. So how can parents know that their school is helping their children achieve that goal? It's a huge problem, and one that clearly complicates accountability in the private school market—Banerjee and Duflo are surely correct in that.

There *are* informal methods that help with accountability that parents use to assess private schools. A while back, I was walking around poor communities in Ghana, West Africa, talking to parents about their choice of schools, particularly if they were interested in attending an Omega school, the chain that I had helped cofound. In that neighborhood, a year before, one of the Omega schools had not been doing very well, and—the only time we were ever forced to do this—we had closed it down. There was another Omega school nearby, so many of the families were willing to transfer to that; other parents took their children to other private schools.

Parents—both mothers and fathers—told me how they would never send their children to an Omega school again, because of the erstwhile school manager. They listed many complaints against him, all concerning low academic standards and lack of discipline. How did they know these things? Perhaps it was because they looked at their children's notebooks and saw how infrequently they were marked. Or they compared the way their children spoke English with how children from other schools spoke English. Or perhaps they simply asked their children what they had done in class that day and were dissatisfied with the results. Come to any parent-teacher association meeting of private schools anywhere in the developing world, and you'll hear parents similarly talking about the pros and cons of the school in question. So, parents do talk to each other about how well their children appear to be doing at school, and the community has a wealth of information at its disposal about the comparative standards in different public and private schools.

These things are important. However, as Banerjee and Duflo point out in general, parents won't necessarily be able to judge how well the child is going to do in public examinations, which are so crucial to his or her success in life.

So, in nine, ten, or even twelve years' time, when the child takes the public examinations and fails, there is not much the parent can do. There's little point in blaming the school; the parents have paid their dues and given as much attention as they could to the school, so it can't be the school's fault. Just as I can play the lottery for many years and, if I don't win, blame my choice of numbers rather than the lottery, so parents blame the child, not the school. Provided that the private school gets some children through the public exams, the school is absolved of blame.

This, I agree with the authors of *Poor Economics*, is a huge problem with the current accountability system under which low-cost private schools find themselves. Banerjee and Duflo are correct in pointing out that, under this system, private schools, especially those serving the poor, don't have to be as efficient as they could be. It is unfortunate, as they write, that even in low-cost private schools, there are still children who cannot read in fifth grade.

If, rather than a distant exam to be taken many years hence, there were more proximate pressure from the examination system, then perhaps private schools would try harder and perform better. But that is not the system that governments currently impose. The current system allows low-cost private schools (and, of course, public schools too) sometimes to get away with being less efficient than they might otherwise be.

Banerjee and Duflo are right about this. But then they place the blame for this situation with the private schools. That surely is incorrect.

They write, "Parents are not alone in focusing their expectations on success at the graduation exam: *The whole education system* colludes with them."[7] But what is the "whole education system"? It's the system that sets the curriculum and examinations, the framework of education. This is a *government-imposed* framework of education. The whole education system is the *public* education system. Banerjee and Duflo apparently seem to agree with this, but then miss its crucial implications:

> The curriculum and organization of schools often date back to a co-lonial past, when schools were meant to train a local elite to be the effective allies of the colonial state, and the goal was to maximize the distance between them and the rest of the populace. Despite the influx of new learners, teachers still start from the premise that their

mandate remains to prepare the best students for the difficult exams that, in most developing countries, act as a gateway either to the last years of school or to college.[8]

So, for private schools, "their entire point is to prepare the best-performing children for some difficult public exam that is the stepping-stone toward greater things, which requires powering ahead and covering a broad syllabus. The fact that most children are getting left behind is unfortunate, but inevitable."[9]

It's important to remind ourselves—and the critics—that private schools are doing better at this task than public schools. But they're not good enough. It is this realization that leads the authors of *Poor Economics* to disregard all the evidence they have accumulated about the superiority of private over public education. Private schools are not good enough, so therefore their argument unaccountably turns back to favoring public schools instead. We won't follow their argument anymore.[10] For us, it leads in another direction. We will probe deeper into government control over the framework of education.

Let's spell out carefully how *government policy*, particularly the government near-monopoly over curriculum and examinations, works to undermine the effectiveness of private schools, especially low-cost private schools serving the poor. It is normal for private schools to have to follow a government-approved curriculum and for their children to take government-approved examinations, in order to be officially recognized by government.

In the matter of assessment, typically a developing country will approve its own ministry of education's national curriculum and examinations, plus some examinations set by foreign bodies—for example, the International Baccalaureate (set by an organization based in Switzerland) or International General Certificate of Secondary Education (IGCSE, set by British organizations). High-end, expensive, elite private schools generally opt out of the government curriculum and exams and go for the international options. This, however, is too expensive for low-cost private schools, which are stuck with the government curriculum and exams—that is, low-cost private schools, in part because they can't afford any other option, must, if they want to be recognized by the government, follow the government-set curriculum, and their children must take the government-set exams.

What if schools decline to be recognized by government? Can they then follow any system they want? In many countries, being an unrecognized school brings a host of problems, including the threat of closure, so many private-school proprietors want to become recognized as soon as they can afford to do so.

This means that parents exert pressures on low-cost private schools. Poor parents know that the only show in town is the government curriculum and examination. The signaling benefit from the official certificate—awarded to children who have passed the government examinations—matters much more to poorer parents than it does to richer parents, who will have additional ways, such as extensive networks, to help their children along. Poor children are much more dependent on this government certificate to signal that they have passed the government-set examinations, this being the gateway to further schooling, higher education, and government jobs.

So, of course, poor parents will exert pressure on private schools to prepare their children for the government examinations. Sometimes private schools can get around the need to be recognized by linking with other private schools that are recognized by the government to allow students to take their exams in those schools. But whatever method is used, the pressure from poor parents works to ensure that low-cost private schools follow the government curriculum-and-assessment route rather than experiment or innovate with other systems that might overcome the severe problems correctly identified by Banerjee and Duflo.

It's wrong to blame these private schools for this, as Banerjee and Duflo do, rather than the government framework under which they operate. There should be no justification for faulting the private sector for successfully helping people navigate a baneful framework imposed by government. We'll come to alternatives to this baneful framework in the next chapter.

A Waste of Time and Money

A second critical argument that needs to be addressed is raised in another acclaimed book, *The Case against Education*, by economics professor Bryan Caplan. Here the criticism isn't directed only at low-cost private schools, but against the whole schooling system in general. So, it strikes me as being essential to explore, because if the "education system" *is* "a waste of time and money," then it wouldn't be unreasonable to think that this might apply to the low-cost private-school ecosystem too.

In this section, first, I aim to give a brief outline of Caplan's main arguments to show their appeal. Second, I want to explore, assuming that Caplan is correct, what implications this has for the private education sector, and low-cost private education in particular—that is, we're to going engage in a hypothetical argument: if Caplan is right, then does this mean that low-cost private education is also a "waste of time and money"?

In the introduction, I specified that there are two definitions of education—education as preparation for adult life and education as intrinsically valuable. Caplan addresses both, although it is mostly about the former. He summarizes his argument thusly: "*There's way too much education.* Typical students burn thousands of hours studying material that neither raises their productivity nor enriches their lives."[11]

Caplan challenges the "human capital theory" that many educators and commentators hold about education—that it develops useful knowledge and skills that are valuable for employment and thereby benefits the economy. On the contrary, Caplan says, education clearly *doesn't* develop human capital in this way, or at least not in large part. Instead, it functions as a "signaling" device to employers.

Education—and its certificates—signal to employers that people already have a set of attributes that are valuable for employment. Caplan doesn't dispute that schools "teach some broadly useful skills—especially literacy and numeracy."[12] A large proportion—his "best guess" is around 80 percent[13]—of what goes on in schools and colleges doesn't teach anything useful at all (nor does it enrich students' lives). But employers don't mind: "Even if what a student learned in school is utterly useless, employers will happily pay extra if their scholastic achievement provides *information about their productivity.*"[14]

There are three elements that education signals, what I call "the three Cs": cognitive ability ("intelligence"), conscientiousness, and conformity. These elements are the trinity that employers seek when they look to our educational certificates for information. In Caplan's neat phrase, "The road to academic success and the road to job success are paved with the same materials"—that is, "If you lack the right stuff to succeed in school, you probably lack the right stuff to succeed in the labor market."[15]

Caplan's demonstration of why the signaling approach fits the facts better than the human capital approach goes along the following lines: First, he notes the conundrum that most college or university degrees have very little, if anything, to do with knowledge and skills that are required in work, but this doesn't seem to matter to employers. Someone who obtains a degree in, say, history of art (classified as of "low usefulness") is still attractive to employers, even though absolutely nothing in the content of the degree will be used in the employment. Even a degree like mathematics, which he classifies as "high usefulness," contains areas such as geometry and trigonometry that are of low usefulness and seldom, if ever, get used in employment.

Second, of importance in any case is not how much content students learn but what they eventually retain. Those who support the human capital theory have to defend that the labor market "pays you for what you know *now*—not what you knew on graduation day."[16] However, they are confronted with the puzzle of "the coexistence of a high education premium and low learning/retention."[17] Learning retention is disturbingly low, Caplan points out, giving findings from a range of surveys of adult knowledge in America (which, of course, indicate an *upper bound* on knowledge learned at school, as adults could have learned stuff outside of formal schooling). The results are disconcerting:

> Basic literacy and numeracy are virtually the only book learning most American adults possess. While the average American spends years and years studying other subjects, they recall next to nothing about them. If schools teach us everything we know about history, civics, science and foreign languages, their achievement is pitiful.[18]

Not only is this "staggering ignorance" an "awkward fact" for human capital theorists,[19] it's also sobering for those who believe that education should be about human flourishing. It shows the dismal way in which (predominantly public) schooling brings learning to the population, which we'll return to later.

Nor can human capital theorists hide behind the notion that schooling should not be about teaching facts but rather should teach children critical thinking and transferable skills. These are "comforting claims," says Caplan, but unfortunately, they're not true. Transferable thinking skills just can't be located by psychologists: "As a rule, students learn only the material you specifically teach them."[20] Studies show that "people commonly fail to marshal what they know effectively in situations outside the classroom or in other classes in different disciplines. The bridge from school to beyond or from this subject to that other is a bridge too far." In conclusion, "The clash between teachers' grand claims about 'learning how to learn' and a century of careful research is jarring."[21]

If schooling doesn't lead to learning useful knowledge and skills for employment, or to retaining pretty much anything that is learned (useful or otherwise), and it doesn't lead to improved transferable knowledge and thinking skills, then what's left for the human capital supporters? There is one area: perhaps schooling could be about learning discipline and socialization—a slightly different form of human capital for sure, but still one that might be acquired through schooling.

Schools teach children the importance of getting to school on time, moving between lessons on time, sitting still, and obeying orders (however daft and illogical they sometimes may seem), as well as the extremely important skill of deferred gratification.[22] I remember, when I was helping create new schools in Sierra Leone, how extraordinarily difficult it was to get the kids to sit still and be quiet, things they just had not been accustomed to doing before. These skills are essential for any form of socialization. In addition, schools socialize the children by insisting that they cooperate (as well as compete), dress smartly in their uniforms, and defer appropriately to authority figures: "The typical worker spends the day doing boring work in a hierarchical organization. Perhaps education acclimates children to their future role."[23]

Caplan thinks there may be some truth in this. But is schooling any better at inculcating these disciplines than the world of work itself? He suggests it is not. Schooling may be beneficial for socialization, but it's not clearly better than young people being socialized in the real world instead.

So, the picture doesn't look good for those who support the human capital theory. Clearly education pays, but that doesn't seem to be because it brings many useful work skills. On the contrary, education pays, says Caplan, because it signals the qualities that holders of certificates already possess (or at least possess by the time they are in high school), especially their levels of cognitive ability, conscientiousness, and conformity.

But if the signaling view of education is preferred over the human capital view, this leads to a huge problem: a certification "arms race." Caplan explains it this way: Suppose you're at a concert, and you want a better view of the musicians. You can stand up. That works—if you stand up, you can get a better view. But what if everyone else stands up too? "Can *everyone* see better by standing? No way."[24]

Education works the same way. Someone with a better education can get a better job, true. But if everyone gets more education, that doesn't mean that everyone can get a better job (unless the country's economy is growing faster than the education system is turning out graduates, which is not happening in most of the countries I'm describing here): "In the signaling model, subsidizing everyone's schooling to improve our jobs is like urging everyone to stand up at a concert to improve our views."[25] In technical parlance, we can say that signaling "implies *negative* externalities: when students stay in school to impress employers, they hurt bystanders in the labor market who look worse by comparison."[26]

Caplan gives a playful example: If *everyone* has a college degree, then "an aspiring janitor might need a master's in Janitorial Studies to land a job scrubbing toilets."[27] Some forty years ago, Ronald Dore gave the example of librarianship in the UK to illustrate graphically the same problem.

As the twentieth century began, says Dore, a potential librarian had to have only a "love of books" in order to get employment as a librarian—they had, in other words, "actually to be able to do [their] job."[28] From the 1930s to the 1950s, by which time a majority of young people had a school certificate, the school certificate became "the minimal requirement."[29] By the 1970s, the minimum requirements had increased to two A levels—requiring schooling until age eighteen (the equivalent of American high school). By 1976, Dore noted that the Library Association—the professional body for librarians—was looking forward to the day when a degree was required of all librarians. Of course, that day has more than arrived now—with 50 percent of each age cohort now getting a degree, it's compulsory for librarians to have one. The

Chartered Institute of Library and Information Professionals, the successor to the Library Association, would now like all its members to have a master's degree in information sciences.[30]

Let's be clear: none of this has to do with the skills and knowledge required to be a librarian. If anything, information technology has made the job easier. No, it's because of credential inflation, the "diploma disease."

At the turn of the twentieth century, those who were "bright enough to be good librarians" often left school before they were fifteen; conversely, those who stayed in school and went to college after they were fifteen could access better-paid, more prestigious work than being librarians.[31] So employers of librarians focused on those who had left school before they were fifteen, for those were the people who were likely to seek work as librarians and would not be tempted to apply for more highly paid work elsewhere. By the 1970s, however, most youngsters who had what it took to be a librarian were now in school until age eighteen. Moreover, because large numbers of children were now staying in school until they were eighteen, they couldn't now expect jobs "*more* rewarding ... than librarianship," even though fifty years earlier, many more rewarding jobs would have been available to high school graduates.[32]

Dore describes exactly the "arms race" that Caplan also describes. They both are explicit—society and individuals would be better off if we had less of this certification: "A college degree now puts you in the top third of the education distribution, so employers who seek a top-third worker require this credential. Now imagine everyone with *one fewer degree.* In this world, employers in need of a top-third worker would require only a high school diploma. The quality of labor would be certified about as accurately as now—at a cost savings of four years of school per person."[33]

Let's assume Caplan's argument is correct. What follows from it? Does it mean we must accept that the education system—notably, the private low-cost part of it—is a waste of time and money?

No, there are hints first in Dore's work. Writing about the problems besetting countries such as Tanzania, Kenya, China, Cuba, and Sri Lanka, Dore concludes that it's when *governments* get involved in the educational process that credentialism becomes pathological: "It is not a bad generalisation that the almightiness of the certificate varies in direct proportion to the predominance of the state in the development process."[34]

Caplan seems to have a similar perspective from America.[35] It turns out that it's not the education system that is a "waste of time and money," but the *public* education system. The argument of this book, for a fully private education system, does appear to be largely immune from his argument.

Why is credentialism happening? Because, says Caplan, government (in America and England) makes schooling compulsory and provides it free of cost until you are eighteen, and then heavily subsidizes it (through loans to individuals and grants to universities) thereafter. It even subsidizes private education in many countries.

Caplan's proposed solution is to move toward "no education policy at all: the separation of school and state."[36] The crux of the matter is this: "We would be better off if education were *less affordable*. If subsidies for education were drastically reduced, many could no longer afford the education they now plan to get." But wouldn't this be harmful to social justice? Wouldn't it make social inequality worse? Caplan thinks not: "It is precisely because education is so affordable that the labor market expects us to possess so much. Without the subsidies, you would no longer *need* the education you can no longer afford."[37]

The underlying premise of my book is that if a solution doesn't work for the less-fortunate members of society, then it is not worth considering; Caplan seems to agree that this is important. But does cutting government funding of education make that impossible? For a start, as we've seen earlier, government education is eschewed by a large majority of poor urban parents in developing countries in any case—and there, low-cost private schools take up the slack, which even poor parents can afford. Does this stop degree inflation? Not quite, not on its own—but this is precisely the argument that we've already discussed with the critique of *Poor Economics*: Private schools are not as effective as they could be in this way too, because they are constrained by the government control of the framework of education, including compulsory attendance, curriculum, and assessment. (We'll be exploring later how the private sector can break into these arenas.) Caplan now provides us with another set of reasons to support the move away from education funded and provided by the government and says that this also can make the system fairer to the poor in terms of undermining pernicious signaling.

Says Caplan, "If education were largely about teaching useful job skills," then raising its cost would amplify "the *inequality* of skill: the poorer you are, the less you learn and the less you earn."[38] But if education is mostly about signaling, this doesn't apply. Of course, if free schooling is given to "one poor youth," then that helps that individual, who can now "send a fine signal to the labor market." But if you give free schooling to "all poor youths," then the meaning of that signaling changes. Now "more affluent competitors" have to get higher certificates in order "to keep their edge." So, all get sucked into the credential arms race. But the crux is this—now the poor who have free schooling have no advantage: "As education rises, workers—including the poor—*need* more education to get the same job." Just as we saw with the example of becoming a librarian, as education levels rise, the job you could get previously without any certificates at all now requires a bachelor's or master's degree. "Where's the social justice in that?"[39]

It would be rather like if the government, seeing the inequality of only a few people being able to give their fiancées expensive diamond engagement rings, decided to give everyone free diamond engagement rings. With government intervening for the sake of social justice, anyone can now go to a jewelry store, "knowing—whatever their income—they can buy a diamond ring."[40] Of course, this would then defeat the object of diamond rings, which is to signal wealth and commitment. The rich will see that diamond engagement rings don't signal their wealth in the way that they used to, so they'll go for something that will separate them from everyone else—whether that's a bigger diamond or something completely different. And so, the inequality that the government sought to eliminate—by providing diamond rings to the poor—will simply reappear.

Caplan argues that this is what has happened in schooling. Basic schooling—for literacy and numeracy—was probably affordable for all, or nearly all, in developing countries, as we've seen in the research outlined in part 1, and as we'll see when it comes to historical evidence from America and England later. As more advanced education, high school and university, was affordable for only a few, this meant that young people with only basic schooling could still be much in demand for employment—just as we saw in early-twentieth-century England, people could become librarians without any school certificate. But then higher levels of schooling are made possible for all by governments making it free and compulsory. Now everyone needs to go to high school, whether it is desired or not—and not to improve valuable human capital but simply because it has become a necessary signal to have in order to get a good job. But if you're poor, then it's more difficult to compete with this. For even if fees are eliminated, there are opportunity costs of going to school in terms of loss of income (income that is now possible only in less-well-paid jobs). And crucially, if you've got any money, now you move on to signal your position with university education, and soon that becomes required by all.[41]

Caplan argues that the signaling critique "highlights two desirable forms of educational austerity." The first is "cutting fat from the curriculum." The second is "cutting subsidies for tuition."[42]

First, cutting fat from the curriculum: "Anyone who scrutinizes modern schools with a mildly cynical eye witnesses piles of material students are laughably unlikely to use in adulthood. The fat emerges in kindergarten: history, social studies, art, music, foreign language. ... By high school ... students spend at least half their time on fat. In college, many majors are made of fat, think history, communications, or 'interdisciplinary studies.'" The school day should be ended "the minute useful learning is done." There should be no public subsidies for "impractical departments" at college level.[43]

However, Caplan realizes that he won't be able to get any of this through the system: "Curriculum reform has one big drawback: education officials have little incentive to cut fat. As long their funding holds steady, why should they confess that many subjects and majors are undeserving of taxpayer support? They've already opted for the status quo, so trusting them to pare down the very system they've built is naïve."[44] We'll have more to say about this in the next chapter, where we look at the incentives for public officials to change anything in education. So, with these changes unlikely to ever come about, he then turns to cutting subsidies for tuition. But won't that come up against precisely the same problem? Will the educational turkeys vote for Christmas (or Thanksgiving)? Presumably not. In his conclusion, Caplan largely admits this: his own job in public education is secure, he says. "I expect no vindication by future events."[45]

So, reducing (or eliminating altogether) government funding of education will reduce signaling. But Caplan doesn't think it will eliminate it altogether. He says, "If government spent zero on education, education spending wouldn't disappear—and neither would wasteful signaling."[46]

Why is this? "As fat disappears from the curriculum, students will inevitably find other ways to signal excellence to the labor market," but this doesn't matter so much, "because some forms of signaling are less socially wasteful than others."[47] Indeed, working harder on literacy and numeracy, English and mathematics, could bring real progress. Still signaling, he says, but on useful subjects. I'm not sure that there would be any point in calling this "signaling" anymore—it's certainly not *pathological* signaling if potential employees show that they have gained valuable human capital. In any case, it helps us see that what is going on in the schools that we've been talking about in part 1 of this book, where improving literacy and numeracy is paramount, is not to be underestimated.

Although Caplan does argue that his preferred education policy is the separation of state and school, he doesn't agree with his libertarian friends who argue that "free markets will make education even better." He says in response, "I've attended both public and private schools. They're cut from the same cloth."[48] This is an odd, and oddly unimaginative, response from Caplan. It appears to imply that if we really did succeed in separating school and state, everything else, particularly the framework of education, would remain the same as it is today. But, as I argue later in the book, "everything else"—government control of the framework of education—can also change.

We wouldn't need to have the kinds of compulsion, curriculum, and assessment systems that we see today in the public education system in a system of educational freedom. A new type of assessment system—possible under conditions of educational freedom, as I shall argue—would make it far less likely that wasteful signaling rather than valuable human capital development would be the outcome of a private education assessment market. Of course, writing about conditions today, Caplan agrees with the authors of *Poor Economics* that private schools are not as efficient as they could be. But that's not the end of the story.

There are hints elsewhere that Caplan could probably agree with this conclusion. He does agree that "without government support, modern education would be unrecognizable. Like a rich uncle, government *helps us waste*. Whenever we can't or won't waste our *own* money on schooling, federal, state and local governments are standing by to waste taxpayers' money on our behalf."[49] In his final chapter, which takes the form of an imagined conversation between him and others, he has himself saying, "Federal, state and local governments massively tilt the scales toward the status quo. Without hundreds of billions of annual subsidies, who knows what alternative worker certification systems would have arisen?"[50]

We've looked at two sets of criticisms that could be used against low-cost private schools in this chapter. The first, from the authors of *Poor Economics*, was really a critique of the government framework of education. Private schools were not as efficient as they could be, because government-imposed curriculum and assessment structures made them less so. But could we have alternative ways of doing curriculum and assessment, outside of government control, that didn't fall into these problems? That's the subject of the next chapter, where we suggest it is possible.

Second, we looked at the critique of *The Case against Education*, which was about schooling systems in general. We did this in a hypothetical way: if the arguments are correct, what does this imply for private schooling? Once addressed in detail, it seems that the case against education is in reality the case against *public* education. Low-cost private schools would be largely immune from this critique—except when they come under, again, the government framework of education, the curriculum, and assessment systems imposed by government. So again, there is a problem, but it's caused by the government-imposed framework of education.

These are not the only difficulties brought about by government intervention. Before we begin our consideration of viable solutions, there are several other problems brought about by the government framework that we need to explore.

7

The Unbearable Burden of Learning

A COUPLE OF years ago, I was stuck in Hyderabad, India, for a few months.[1] Unable to do much else, I went most days to a bookshop in a Banjara Hills mall. I gravitated to their philosophy, religion, and science sections. One day, I bumped into a young woman who was also interested in the same book categories. After a few days of greeting each other, we sat together in the coffee shop outlet that was part of the bookshop.

Her name was Amal. She was twenty-five years old, living at home in a Muslim family, with a very protective mother. Whenever possible, she escaped to the bookshop to absorb and read as much as she could. She was wearing a light blue shirt, and I noticed some carelessly applied makeup. She was particularly interested in science books, and she told me the story of how she had gotten hooked; it had, in fact, to do with personal appearance, which is the only reason I've mentioned hers.

When she was thirteen, she saw an article in the *Times of India* about Einstein. There was an accompanying photograph. What she noticed immediately was his "crazy hair." She thought, why is someone so unconcerned about his appearance? Everyone around her, at home and at school, was very focused on their appearance, as well as policing her own. So, the baffling question for her was, how did he manage to get away with it?

With her interest thus piqued, she downloaded a video on YouTube called "Einstein's Unfinished Symphony." This got her completely hooked, and it's why today you can find her reading popular science in the Crossword bookshop. She quoted to me what Einstein had said: "The most beautiful thing we can experience is the mysterious. It is the source of all true art and science."

But there was nothing mysterious about science at her school, she told me—unless you counted the mystery of how something so beautiful could be made so tediously boring. The contrast between school science and what she was discovering about Einstein was absolute.

In secondary school, she had been completely unhappy. Partly this was because it was an all-girls school, and she didn't fit in at all with the other girls' interests. All her fellow students, she told me, were "desperate to meet boys … sorry, desperate is probably not the nicest word, but it was true." She wasn't particularly interested in the opposite sex. But mostly her unhappiness arose because the school seemed to make everything as boring as it could.

School science, she said, was simply "burdensome, … there is no other word to describe it, there was nothing interesting or exciting or motivating about it."

From watching the YouTube video, she had gone on to read further about Einstein and had realized how fascinating and mysterious the concept of time was. "But there was nothing remotely fascinating or mysterious about the way anything was taught in science in school," she told me. Instead, all was subordinated to the "tyranny" of preparing for the government-controlled end-of-school examinations. Quite a bit of this was done through rote learning. But even when it wasn't, no one tried to motivate anyone about any of the topics. They could have been plowing their way through the Hyderabad telephone directory, for all anyone cared about fascination or intrinsic interest in any of the subjects.

Reflecting on her primary education, up to the age of ten or eleven, the method of learning probably wasn't so different, but it seemed that when you are small, you don't mind those strictures. You can have fun rote learning and pleasing the teacher, and, in any case, you do need to learn some self-discipline, such as the ability to sit still and listen, and, of course, you need to learn deferred gratification. These are all important. When you're young, you don't mind; as you grow older, everything becomes joyless.

She even thought that this could explain why there is so much rubbish on TV rather than inspiring stuff about science and the universe. "It must have to do with demand," she said. "The population demands pap, and so they get pap. But why don't they demand higher things? Because schooling has knocked out any love of learning, crushed their curiosity. If there weren't schools like we know them now, then there would be less pap on TV.

"At least," she said, "the good news is that you don't need school to be inspired to learn; you can learn by yourself," as she was doing through You-Tube, the internet, and the bookshop. But what a crying shame that schooling knocks this love out of most people. What a waste!

Talking to her, I realized that this was an educational injustice being perpetrated, beyond the one I normally think about. My work normally focused—as in the first four chapters of this book—on the injustice of the poor being denied access to quality educational opportunities. The low-cost private school revolution challenges that injustice.

Amal was highlighting a second injustice, something that I had difficulty articulating at first. It seemed to be something like this: The gatekeepers of education somehow deprive inquiring minds of access to the ideas and questions that could inspire them. Those who control the framework of education—the curriculum, the assessment, the teaching methods—must know that there are wonderful concepts, like the idea of "time" that so engaged Amal, that can be captivating, enlightening, mysterious even. They—those in control of the framework of education—know this, but instead of delighting young people with "the best that has been thought and said," as Matthew Arnold put it in his book *Culture and Anarchy*, they seem to delight in appearing to offer only "the most tedious that has been thought and said."[2] At least so it seemed to Amal.

"Those in control of education"—we're back again to government's framework for education. A framework for education seems to have been created that is often completely unattractive to young people. If this is true, then this is a further reason to explore an additional type of educational emancipation: emancipation from governments' framework of education, not just from the provision and funding of schooling.

Of course, those in American and British schools may not have it quite so bad as poor Amal in Indian schools. Or maybe they do. In American and British schools, they've moved away from a strong emphasis on rote learning, but looking through textbooks that my friends' children use, there's nothing there to show the excitement that these topics can convey. Indeed, text writers seem convinced that the topics aren't particularly interesting in a compulsory school setting, so they try to liven everything up with gaudy colors and cartoons. These only seem to convey the miserable message that "we know the subject matter is not engaging, so here are some bright colors and flashy graphics to at least alleviate your boredom." They don't succeed.

Amal's mother would let her stay out only until 8:30 each evening. Her mother called many times while we were talking to ask her why she was not home yet. As 8:15 p.m. approached, Amal reluctantly made her apologies and left. As she was leaving, she asked if I had ever read Tagore's story about the parrot. I hadn't. The next time we met, she brought in a small, handsome, bound copy of a book of Tagore's writing, and I read it out loud while we sat over coffee.

Tagore's Parrot

Rabindranath Tagore, one of India's great novelists and educationalists, who won the Nobel Prize in Literature, wrote a short piece titled "The Parrot's Training."[3] It seemed to highlight for Amal all the injustices that the framework of the curriculum had imposed on her, and on us all.

"Once upon a time there was a bird," it begins. This bird could sing and hop but couldn't do things like recite the scriptures; it was also somewhat lacking in manners. So, the prince sought to do something about this; he called his nephews and instructed them to give the bird "a sound schooling." In turn, they summoned the educational experts, who figured that the root of the problem was the low standard of the bird's nest. They fixed this, building a "golden cage with gorgeous decorations" that drew crowds from all around the world, exclaiming "How fortunate for the bird!" The goldsmith who had made the cage was paid handsomely and went happily home. (Already a parallel for me, this is precisely one of the often-made criticisms of low-cost private schools—that their buildings are not good enough. Governments come along and provide much better buildings.)

One of the experts then got ready to educate the parrot, with the claim that "textbooks can never be too many for our purpose!" An enormous team was assembled, who "copied from books, and copied from copies, till the manuscripts were piled up to an unreachable height." Again, crowds gathered in wonder at the "tower of culture." These scribes, too, filled their pockets with money, happy to go home.

The nephews were all the time working on keeping the golden cage looking neat and tidy, employing great numbers of people to do so. They, too, flourished. In fact, everyone seemed to be flourishing except, as some skeptical onlookers put it, the poor parrot.

One day, the prince wanted to see for himself how the bird was being educated. A grand ceremony was organized to welcome him, and he was accompanied by a grand procession featuring numerous percussion and musical instruments. It was all very impressive, and the prince commented on how sound the bird's education seemed. He was just about to leave when someone asked, had he seen the bird?

"Indeed I have not," said the prince, "I completely forgot about the bird."

So, he asked the experts how they were instructing the bird. "The method was so stupendous that the bird looked ridiculously unimportant in comparison." The bird itself was so "completely choked with leaves from the books" that it couldn't utter any comment, let alone complaint. Still, "Nature occasionally triumphed over training," and occasionally the bird was wont to flutter its wings "in a reprehensible manner" and even more occasionally peck at the golden bars.

This caused the goldsmith to go to the Department of Education, where he clipped the bird's wings and made a chain to stop it from being able to peck at the golden bars. He, too, was handsomely rewarded.

Then the bird died. Nobody knew when it happened. It was a rumor at first, which spread around the palace; the prince picked up the rumor and inquired of his nephews. In a scene uncannily reminiscent of Monty Python's "Dead Parrot" sketch, the nephew told him, "Sire, the bird's education has been completed."

"Does it hop?" inquired the prince.

No, the nephew said.

"Does it fly?"

Not that either.

Eventually, the prince wanted the bird brought to him. He poked it with his finger: "Only its inner stuffing of book-leaves rustled."

He didn't say, but you could hear him: This parrot is no more! He has ceased to be! He's shuffled off his mortal coil. This is an ex-parrot.

Tagore concludes, in a tone suggestive of Monty Python's "pining for the Fjords": "Outside the window, the murmur of the spring breeze among the newly budded asoka leaves made the April morning wistful."

Tagore's parrot was most definitely dead.

Amal said that that was what she felt like under the education system, in terms of her imagination and creativity and wonder.

Amal's experience is, unfortunately, all too common. But education doesn't have to be mindless drudgery. During the COVID-19 school closures, for example, some parents were able to witness firsthand how exciting learning could be again for their children once they were free to devise learning activities that both stimulated and challenged them. An education can be joyful and enriching, but to avoid the pitfalls Amal experienced, we need consider the ways schools stimulate curiosity or quash it. Like Amal, we need to think differently about education.

Sir Ken Robinson's Theory of Change

One of the inspirations for Amal to think differently about education was Sir Ken Robinson, knighted by Queen Elizabeth II in 2003. Amal watched his first TED Talk and had been extremely impressed by the way he articulated how schools quash curiosity and creativity. This chapter from now on focuses on his ideas. As in the previous chapter, I aim to engage in a hypothetical discussion: Suppose Sir Ken is right about the importance of creativity and curiosity for motivating learning, ideas for which he has achieved an extraordinarily large following. What follows for our discussion of the role of government in education?

This is particularly pertinent to Sir Ken's argument, because he is sure that what we call the "framework of education" is wrong—the curriculum and assessment systems and culture and ethos of schools all militate against motivating young people and arousing their curiosity and creativity. He has an explicit "theory of change" about how to mitigate this.

For those convinced by Sir Ken's ideas, this chapter explores how someone like him could best get his or her ideas from the page, or TED Talk, into practice. For those less convinced, staying on for the ride will still be satisfying, I hope, because the principles we explore will be applicable to anyone wanting to get from ideas to practice in an educational system.

This chapter begins to move us away from developing countries to the situation in the West, in America and Britain and elsewhere. The issue of bringing change to the framework of education is one that crosses continents.

Sir Ken Robinson is a personable, charismatic presenter. He has a mild Liverpool accent, reminiscent of the Beatles', and a dry, self-deprecatory sense of humor. His vision is a humanitarian one, of liberating people from the drudgery of schooling, something many in his audiences clearly appreciate. Sir Ken is not unduly modest about his first TED Talk: "It has proven to be the most watched talk in the history of TED. It has been viewed online more than thirty million times and has been seen by an estimated three hundred million people worldwide."[4] While accepting that this is not quite up there with the American singer and actress Miley Cyrus, he concedes, "I don't twerk." Indeed not; but he does do a very effective stand-up routine. He has a range of nice one-liners, which find their way into his books too. Apparently, he gets about the same number of laughs per minute for his TED Talks as do the actors in *The Hangover* and *Naked Gun*.[5]

Sir Ken argues that public education systems are bust. (He only writes about public education; his view of the world appears to be one of public education systems only, except when he unwittingly points to some powerful innovations in private education.) Public education systems are the wrong, outdated model. They are wrong in terms of organization of schools, and wrong in terms of curriculum and assessment (both national and international).

Current public education systems in countries across the world were "designed, conceived and structured for a different age."[6] Students, he says, "are educated in batches, according to age, as if the most important thing they have in common is their date of manufacture."[7] Some students "inevitably … grasp some material more quickly than others, but the class is intended to get through the material at the same rate and over the same amount of time."[8] The material they cover—the curriculum—is not of the right kind, either, and the way it is assessed is completely wrong.

He asks, "Why are schools so often run this way?" and suggests that it's because "the organizational culture of mass education is rooted in the manufacturing processes of industrialism."[9]

"Public schools," he argues, "were created in the image of industrialism"— that is, "they reflect the factory culture they were designed to support." He points out that "school systems base education on the principles of the assembly line and the efficient division of labor." The curriculum is divided into "specialist segments: some teachers install math in the students, and others install history." The day is arranged into "standard units of time, marked out by the ringing of bells, much like a factory announcing the beginning of the workday and the end of breaks."[10]

Why is it still thus rooted? Even the manufacturing process itself has changed beyond recognition since the nineteenth century; and, of course, what gets manufactured has changed still further. Yet public systems of schooling are largely unchanged. What's so distinctive about public education systems that has made them immune to the change? We'll come to, and challenge, Sir Ken's answers in a moment.

Most importantly for Sir Ken, this outdated model means that public education systems throughout the world stifle desirable qualities like creativity, curiosity, and divergent thinking. So, we need a "changed paradigm" for education that "transforms" all aspects of public schooling, including curriculum and assessment systems. We need, he says, to focus on three principles to change the system:

- Human beings are naturally different and diverse.

- Curiosity is a principle that drives human learning: "If you can light the spark of curiosity in a child, they will learn without any further assistance, very often. Children are natural learners. It's a real achievement to put that particular ability out, or to stifle it. Curiosity is the engine of achievement."

- Human life is inherently creative: "One of the roles of education is to awaken and develop powers of creativity. Instead, what we have is a culture of standardization."[11]

Robinson finished his first TED Talk by saying, these are the three principles, so let's do them—making it sound easy and obvious. However, he was aware that some of his listeners were frustrated by this approach because he didn't give more details on "what they can do to change the system."[12] His first response was flippant: "It was an eighteen-minute talk; give me a break."[13] But his considered response is found in his latest book, *Creative Schools*, which features his "theory of change."

Robinson's theory of change concerns *two* aspects: first, change through grassroots initiatives; second, change through the political process.

Change through Grassroots Initiatives

Robinson writes, "Revolutions don't wait for legislation. They emerge from what people do at the ground level"; it is a "grassroots process."[14] He cites Gandhi as saying, "If you want to change the world, you must be the change you want to see. Because when enough people move, that is a movement. And if the movement has enough energy, that is a revolution."[15] The revolution in education is not "to fix" the current public system, "but to change it; not to *re*form it but to *trans*form it." The "great irony" is that "we actually know what works. We just don't do it on a wide enough scale."[16]

In *Creative Schools*, he gives examples of how schooling is changing in America and elsewhere. They're often inspiring stories, but they're usually about how a few teachers or, occasionally, a whole school or even several schools together are doing worthwhile and interesting things.

I could list some of these examples, but one danger is that today's interesting examples may not seem so important tomorrow. For instance, Robinson illustrates how "flipped classrooms"—I'll define this below—are changing educational practices: in 2013, he writes, "Four dozen Idaho public schools began a pilot program to flip some of their classrooms using Khan Academy."[17] This is based on the work of another inspiring educator and TED Talker, Salman Khan, the creator of his eponymous academy, an online learning platform, where children can watch concise videos prepared by dynamic and inspiring teachers, outlining topics in mathematics and other subjects, and then work through questions on these topics using an adaptive-learning program.

One of Salman Khan's great ideas is that children can watch his videos in the comfort of their home. In the classroom, teachers can help them with their problems rather than waste time in exposition of topics that can better be explained by experienced teachers on video. This is what is called "flipped classrooms." But if you do an online search for the project that so excited Robinson, you won't find any references to it dating *after* the announcement that it was going to happen in 2013.[18] Apparently there was a grant of $1.5 million from a foundation to introduce the flipped classrooms, much fanfare, and then ... nothing. Does that mean that when the grant ran out, all the schools and teachers reverted to their normal ways? The web silence on the matter is hard to interpret.

Another danger of listing these small-scale innovations now is the problem of burnout.[19] Great teachers who try interesting innovations won't usually get rewarded for their efforts; they will have to spend their free time doing it, not paid school time. More important, what they do will not usually spread far. In the public education system, there aren't really any incentives for others to take what one amazing teacher did and replicate it in other classrooms, let alone in other schools and school systems. So, innovations often die out unless the teacher is resourceful and finds a backer. Listing significant innovations now runs the risk that they will no longer be there by the time readers get around to reading this book.

In any case, however great these small-scale initiatives are, Sir Ken wants to see system-wide change—he is not content with seeing only these modest programs—and recognizes that the wider public education system, far from supporting these kinds of initiatives, actively gets in the way of them. In his 2013 TED Talk, for instance, he says there is "wonderful work happening" in education: "But I have to say it's happening in spite of the *dominant culture* of education, not because of it. It's like people are sailing into a *headwind* all the time."[20] Crucially, he observes, "it's not because teachers want it this way. It's just because it happens that way." Why? In his second TED Talk, he says, "Because it's in the gene pool of education."[21]

All this brings us to the *second* aspect of Sir Ken Robinson's theory of change, bringing about system-wide change through the political process.

Change through the Political Process

Robinson uses three metaphors to describe the obstacle facing those who seek system-wide change: the dominant culture; sailing into the headwind; and the gene pool. But what is he really describing? His metaphors alert us to the key problem of *political vested interests*.

Education reform, he notes, is being driven by "political ... interests that misunderstand how real people learn and how great schools actually work. As a result, they are damaging the prospects of countless young people."[22] Politicians want to do something about education, and so they start reforms of one kind or another: "But the problems persist and in many ways they're getting worse. The reason is that many of these problems are being caused by *the system itself*."[23] The public education system causes the problems. There are vested interests that impede change in education: "There are political agendas, national priorities, union bargaining positions, building codes, job descriptions, parental ambitions, peer pressures. The list goes on."[24]

So, if the political culture impedes change, how can we get from individuals in schools doing innovative things (such as flipped classrooms) to systemic change in education more broadly?

Robinson doesn't have an answer: "However much schools do to transform themselves, their cultures are critically affected by the political climate that envelops them,"[25] he says. The political climate brings "many obstacles" to the kind of transformation he wants to see. "Some have to do with the inherent conservatism of institutions, including schools themselves, some with conflicting views about the sort of changes that are needed, some with culture and ideology, and some with political self-interest."[26]

Moreover, "education policy," he says, "is inevitably enmeshed in other cultural interests."[27] There are motives driving politicians and educational bureaucrats that will hinder the arrival of the public good of education: "Not all policymakers in education actually care about education," he writes. "Some are career politicians or administrators who are using education as a platform for professional advancement. Their own ambitions in education may be tied up with other political interests and motives."[28]

Policy makers in education have their own vested interests; these mean that the educational reforms brought in are not going to be the sort of policies that Robinson prefers:

> For all the rhetoric of promoting individual fulfilment and the public good, there is a well-documented history in education of social control, conformity, and mass compliance. In some respects, mass education is, and always was, a process of social engineering. Sometimes the political intentions have been benign and sometimes not. ... No amount of debate on strategy will result in consensus if the purposes we have in mind are opposed.[29]

All this seems entirely apposite. Sir Ken Robinson has hit upon the central problem of using the political process to bring about favorable change. Those with influence and power over education have interests different from "the public good." By his own admission, the second—most fundamental—aspect of his theory of change seems unlikely to succeed. Yes, there can be individual changes happening within the system, but if you want to transform schooling and change the framework of education, you're not going to be able to move forward through the political process.

The Difficulties and Risks of Political Change

It may be worth spelling out in more detail just how destructive the political process is for Robinson's preferred reform, nay "transformation," of the public education framework. There are three risks that need to be highlighted: arising from public opinion, the political process, and vested interests. Let's take each in turn.

First, public opinion. To get his ideas accepted, and then championed, by any political party, Robinson will need strong public opinion behind him. But Robinson himself is candid that his ideas often *go against* public opinion. Many policy makers, he says, "really believe that the current systems of education are basically sound; they're just not working as well as they should because standards have fallen"; most poignantly, his readers, he realizes, "may believe this story too and wonder what's wrong with it."[30]

And this is so, even though he tries to avoid some of the most controversial aspects, which are likely to frighten the horses of public opinion. (For example, "Some of the fiercest debates in education are about what should be taught and who should decide. It's not my intention here to go into the details of the content of the curriculum. ... Every such attempt courts controversy."[31]) If public opinion is not behind him, then this drastically reduces his chances of getting his ideas adopted by any political figure or party to bring through the political process.

Part of the problem here concerns the *contested* nature of education, contested because any definition of education embodies values, either explicitly or implicitly. If we say that education is preparation for adult life, then we are committed, if only implicitly, to a definition of valuable adult ways of living. There will always be different views about what education should be like, because there will be different views about what society should be like. There will always be people with different *but sincerely held* beliefs about education that can be independently, logically justified. People will legitimately hold different views about it because of their different premises about what human society should and can be like. Some philosophers even call education an *essentially* contested concept,[32] to indicate that there can never be any undisputed way of formulating even a definition of what "education" is, let alone what its content and organization should be like.

Second, the political process. Let's assume that through his tireless advocacy work, Sir Ken and other great educators like him can get a groundswell of public opinion on their side so that some politicians think it is worthwhile to adopt their ideas. Now, they must get these ideas formulated as policies and move them through the political process. Here lie dragons.

Sir Ken won't be sympathetic to her views, but he is likely to be sympathetic to Margaret Thatcher's plight. Back in the early 1980s, in the early years of her Conservative government, she became convinced of the merits of a national curriculum. Here's how she sketched out what she wanted: "I wanted ... a basic syllabus for English, Mathematics and Science with simple tests to show what pupils knew. It always seemed to me that a small committee of good teachers ought to be able to pool their experience and write down a list of the topics and sources to be covered without too much difficulty. There ought then to be plenty of scope left for the individual teacher to concentrate with children on the particular aspects of the subject in which he or she felt a special enthusiasm or interest."[33]

Public opinion was generally behind her on these modest ambitions, but the process wasn't going to be the way she imagined. She had to get someone to put her idea into practice, so in 1988 she appointed Kenneth Baker as secretary of state for education. He soon met with the simplest of problems: who to put on the curriculum subject committees and subcommittees? Baker knew that if he was going to get this through Parliament, he would have to have people with whom the vested interests—like the teachers' unions and educational bureaucrats—would be compatible. So, he appointed quite a few like that, as well as others with opinions that might be closer to Margaret Thatcher's. However, the problem then was that Baker couldn't get the committees to agree on anything.

This was "rectified" by one of his successors, Kenneth Clarke, who bulldozed decisions through the committees, but they then produced an extraordinarily complex, monolithic national curriculum and system of national testing. This could have been foreseen: political scientists John Chubb and Terry Moe, who shot to fame with their 1990 book, *Politics, Markets, and America's Schools*, pointed out that committees in a democracy are likely to produce excessive prescription, because of the combined problems of political uncertainty and the need for compromise.[34] The emerging national curriculum provided a master class for their theoretical arguments.

Mrs. Thatcher herself bemoaned the excessive detail that emerged from her national curriculum committees as well as the eye-watering expense incurred.[35] The national curriculum began to be taught in 1989, but by 1994, there was tremendous dissatisfaction from all quarters with the overly prescriptive nature of it. ("The National Curriculum is a National Disaster," I wrote in a polemical piece back then; I don't think many would have disagreed with me.) So, a review committee was established, which recommended a slimmed-down version.

And on it went. The new Labour government of Tony Blair came into power in 1997. Again, there was a national curriculum review. What prompted it this time was an example of the law of unintended consequences: the "broad and balanced" curriculum that had emerged from the committees included so many different curriculum subjects and topics that this may have led to a decline in literacy and numeracy. Every committee member's pet projects—which no one had been willing to concede—had crowded out the basics of reading, writing, and arithmetic.

Another revised national curriculum, which had more emphasis on the basics at the expense of other subjects, came out in 2000. But this didn't satisfy those who still craved a "broad and balanced" curriculum. Another prime minister resulted in another national curriculum review. And so it has been to the present date.

It was a long way from the simple proposal put forward by Margaret Thatcher. With the benefit of hindsight, her proposal has a touching political naïveté to it. But we don't have to be as naïve as her; we should by now have learned the lessons of educational reform through the political process.

The example of the national curriculum, of course, shows that it is *possible* to get change through, with a strong enough political champion and public opinion behind you. But the experience suggests that it may not be at all *desirable* to do so. The bureaucratic monstrosity that emerged was nothing like what was intended in the first place, and it satisfied nobody. It's now a political football that parties with different priorities try to put their stamp on. Why can they do this? Because it has now been conceded that political power can be wielded over the curriculum. Immense and potentially dangerous powers have been entrusted to the secretary of state for education, of whatever political persuasion. Is this really what visionaries like Sir Ken Robinson want to happen through their proposed educational reforms?

Getting something through is hard—in education, you may need someone with the political clout and stature of Margaret Thatcher. More often than not, however, it is likely that you won't be able to get educational reform through the system at all, because of the problem of vested interests, the third risk in attempting political change.

Let's focus on one of the vested interest groups, the teachers' unions, and spell out more closely how they can work to impede change—even when change may be of the desirable kind that Sir Ken Robinson seeks. Terry Moe and John Chubb have analyzed some of the difficulties in bringing educational change through the political system, difficulties that rest on the abilities of powerful interest groups to resist change, and we can use their argument to illustrate the risks inherent in Sir Ken's approach.

Teachers' unions are powerful all over the world, extraordinarily so in America. The National Education Association (NEA) and the American Federation of Teachers (AFT) are the two major unions, with more than four million members combined. With huge financial resources at their disposal, they can "contribute generously to electoral campaigns at all levels of government."[36] They are largely affiliated with Democrats in American politics, and their influence is immense. The teachers' unions were found to be "the single most powerful interest group in the entire country through the 1990s."[37]

How do teachers' unions—in common with other vested interests in education—pursue their interests through the political process, and how could this block reforms like those put forward by Sir Ken Robinson? Interest groups can do it in two ways: first, they can put pressure on politicians and bureaucrats for the kinds of policies they want enacted. Or they can try to block policies they don't agree with.

The first approach is fraught with difficulties, like those we've outlined for the national curriculum. In the United States, as in the UK, and in any parliamentary democracy, such as India, there are numerous checks and balances that inhibit policy making. Any bill has to go through various "subcommittees, committees, and floor votes in each house," and any piece of legislation has to be passed, in "identical form," in each place. In each setting, however, legislation is threatened by parliamentary obstructions, such as "filibusters, holds, and voting rules." Even if the legislation gets through, the executive can veto it. And even if the president signs it into law, it can still be "challenged and overturned in the courts."[38]

The second approach is much more straightforward—to block a policy is the simplest route. You only need to succeed "at just *one* of the many veto points along the way." In America, "blocking" is "far easier than taking positive action." So, any interest group that wants to maintain the status quo has the advantage.[39] If you want radical, constructive change, as does Sir Ken Robinson, you can be blocked at every stage on the way.

The teachers' unions have been "stunningly effective" at blocking reforms of which they disapprove: "Not only do all blockers have a decided advantage, but the unions' massive power magnifies that advantage many times over, making it quite likely that they can stop or water down *any reforms* that threaten their interests." Changes that they have blocked and will continue to block include "virtually all reforms that attempt to make fundamental changes to the system, for any major reform is likely to unsettle the jobs, security, autonomy, or working conditions of teachers—and to be threatening."[40]

Now, it must be clear that the kinds of reforms desired by Sir Ken Robinson are likely to be precisely the kinds of reforms that will offend teachers' unions, as well as other vested interest groups, threatening to unsettle them, threatening their members' working conditions. For instance, he says, "The role of a teacher is to facilitate learning. That's it."[41] The teachers' unions will resist this, because it undermines their professionalism. Or, Sir Ken says that teachers have to continually "light the spark of creativity."[42] That sounds like it's going to increase demands on teachers—not least because if new legislation is passed, this is likely to mean that the new requirements will get piled on top of the old—and on top of all the existing workload. Unions know that these new things will come in and simply add to the burdens of the job, instead of being substituted for something that is already there. And what is already there will also have its share of supporters, who will resist any move to replace it.

Then it's better to block it. It's simpler to give unmotivating classes as you've always done and have your students tanked up on Ritalin, one of Sir Ken's bugbears, than plan new and interesting lessons that might light that spark. Some teachers won't ever be able to do that, so their job security will be threatened. And some teachers will want to do it, but it will come at the expense of their workloads. Better block it.

Discussion of these three risks shows the potential impasse that Sir Ken Robinson and any educational reformers like him encounter when they try to use the political process to bring about their desired change. We've suggested that his "theory of change" may not in fact be able to change much.

Desirable change best comes from the grassroots, Sir Ken implies. However, the grassroots changes that he heralds affect only a few children at most. And they run the risk of teacher burnout, or at least teacher innovation fatigue. So, Robinson needs to bring his desired changes through the political system. But it will be hard for him to get any political figure to endorse them, because they're controversial. And even if he does manage to persuade the public of their worth and get a politician or party to endorse them, it's not certain that his ideas will be translated into policy. They might get through the political process but be nothing like what he intended—indeed, they might become the opposite of what he intended, just as Margaret Thatcher saw with her national curriculum proposals. But more likely, they wouldn't get through at all—they're too radical; so they'd be blocked at every turn. The political system in education is designed to thwart change.

We've not gone any further than Robinson has conceded himself—this section has just been putting flesh on the bones of the argument he himself has made. But his argument powerfully shows why desirable change not only does *not* happen in practice, but also is unlikely to happen in theory too. So, what is he left with?

He has no way out of this impasse. Except, there's a small glimmer, but it arises only accidentally. In two places, he comes tantalizingly close to endorsing the kind of position we're espousing in this book—that the way forward is for grassroots innovation *entirely outside of the state*.

First, in the introduction to *Creative Schools*, Robinson points to two ways of bringing educational change—from "within the system" by people pressing "for changes to the system," or "you can take initiatives outside the system."[43] He gives brief examples of this happening—where people go for educational improvements *by exiting public schooling*: "As disaffection spreads with the numbing effects of standardized testing, schools and their communities are starting to push back against it. Parents who are anxious about the effects of the industrial education of their children are increasingly taking matters into their own hands. There is a still small but significant movement in homeschooling and un-schooling."[44]

He's being a bit disingenuous here—homeschooling (where children learn at home with their parents) is driven by many things apart from the "numbing effects of standardized testing." It is, indeed, growing at an extraordinary clip—we'll be looking at some data in part 3. But homeschooling and "unschooling" (a modification of homeschooling, where children decide their own curriculum) are grassroots changes happening entirely outside of the state.

Second, in the afterword to the same book, he gives examples of people who have revolutionized education. The only examples he spells out, however, are the following three: Maria Montessori, Rudolf Steiner, and A. S. Neill.

"The list goes on," he says.[45] But there's something curious—and revealing—about the actual innovators he chose to highlight; they were all innovators *in the private sector, outside of the state.*

Maria Montessori created her first Casa dei Bambini in Rome in 1906. It was a private school; she continued to open other private schools. It was true that her ideas were adopted in some public systems for a while, but they were developed in the private sector and are common only in private schools to this day, having been found controversial in the public sector.

Rudolf Steiner's philosophical ideas inspired the Waldorf schools, the first of which opened in Stuttgart, Germany, in 1919. This was a private school, which has led to more than 1,000 private Waldorf schools in around sixty countries. It is true that there have been some publicly funded Waldorf schools in later years, including charter schools in the United States and academies or free schools in the UK. The first in America was the Yuba River Charter School in Grass Valley, California, 1994, and the first in the UK was the Steiner Academy in Hereford, 2008. Each has attracted controversy over the use of state funds to promote the philosophical ideas of Rudolf Steiner. Steiner schools still flourish, most readily as fully private schools.

Finally, A. S. Neill famously created one school, Summerhill, in Suffolk, England, in 1921. It was—you guessed it—a purely private school, renowned for its ideas on giving children freedom to learn as they wanted to. We'll be discussing this aspect of educational freedom in our closing chapter, where we look at Sugata Mitra's work. Apart from his earlier teaching experiences before he created Summerhill, A. S. Neill had nothing to do with public education.

Sir Ken Robinson didn't appear to notice that his key innovators were only innovating outside of the state, in the private sector. Or did he, and decide not to explicitly express this, for fear of frightening the horses? *Private schools* is a term not even found in the index to his book. It's very odd that these key innovators were introduced without comment on this important dimension to their work.

Many, including Amal, whom I met in that Hyderabad bookshop, admire Sir Ken Robinson's ideas on education, on how to foster curiosity and creativity. Sir Ken points to some small-scale experiments, taken up by individual teachers or sometimes whole schools, that help improve learning and opportunity. But he is aware that these minor changes are not going to change the system in general, because of the political incentives working against this. He wants to see educational reform across the board, but he thinks that the only way to do this is through public education. However, it's highly unlikely that the state will ever let reforms like his through.

On the other hand, in a situation where there are private schools that are free to adopt whichever curriculum they choose, someone like Sir Ken could easily bring his passion and enthusiasm to bear on promoting his desired curriculum ideas so that schools and school chains could adopt them and compete in the marketplace of ideas. Sir Ken Robinson is aware of the appeal of doing things outside of the state but can't see that his own ideas would have more success in the market than under state provision.

Rather than some messy battle of ideas where the winner takes all—where the winner gets to impose his or her ideas of what education should be like on everyone, even those with sincerely held views about how education should be different—the beauty of educational freedom is that you don't have to force your ideas on anyone! As some American parents experienced first-hand during the COVID-19 school closures, there are near endless learning opportunities once someone else's ideas of education are not imposed on their children. Children can learn at their own pace and in their own way. All can have prizes in the marketplace of educational freedom. To take one of Sir Ken's bugbears, there will likely always be parents and children who don't want to be part of a schooling system that puts them through standardized tests. Their preferences can be honored under a system of educational freedom—that is, if the visionaries/entrepreneurs can get takers (customers) for their ideas and offerings. *And they likely will.* Because education is contested, there will always be takers for entirely contrasting views of what education should be like.

So, we are left with Sir Ken's dilemma. The only way to change things, he thinks, is through the state. But gatekeepers within the state act within their own interests, which are only by accident coincident with the interests of learners.

I have had one or two conversations along these lines with Sir Ken Robinson—we were both involved with the committee for the $1 million TED Prize when it was awarded to Sugata Mitra. He, of course, wouldn't concede that I had any point in my favor.

For some reason, I'm reminded of a scene involving another knight of the realm, the Black Knight from *Monty Python and the Holy Grail*. King Arthur comes across this tall, silent knight defending a bridge across a stream. Impressed by his fighting ability, King Arthur first asks him to join his Knights of the Round Table, and when he declines the offer, King Arthur sets off to cross the bridge. The Black Knight refuses him entry, and there's a bit of a fight, in which King Arthur first cuts off the Black Knight's arms, then his legs. As he lies there, unable to do anything, he says, "'Tis but a scratch," vigorously denying that the fight is over.

When I think of Sir Ken Robinson's solutions to the problems of schooling and the challenges I've outlined, I can hear him shrugging them off: "'Tis but a scratch." On the contrary, I think his ideas are as wounded as the Black Knight.[46]

8

Five Problems in Search of a Solution

THE DISCUSSION IN previous chapters has given us five major problems that the government-imposed "framework of education" imposes on private (as well as, of course, public) education, which appear to be seriously deleterious to desired educational aims and goals. The five problems are typical in developing countries but seem to have application to countries in the West too.

1. National examinations measure children's performance only after ten years or more of schooling. Schools, including low-cost private schools, can get away with being complacent, because there are no *proximate* exams. This leads to a huge waste of talent.

2. Children who drop out of school before the end-of-school examinations leave with nothing. But they may have developed useful human capital.

3. National end-of-school examinations and curricula (as well as higher-education degrees) are mostly (if not entirely) about "signaling." Human capital development gets neglected.

4. Schools are structured so that children learn only or mainly in age-related classes—"batches." This does not reflect the potential of how children could learn.

5. The framework of education imposed by government can be demotivating for young people. There is no attempt to justify the curriculum content or learning outcomes to them; the structure and organization of schooling can be equally demotivating to many potential learners.

Let's look at each in turn.

1. National examinations measure children's performance only after ten years or more of schooling. Schools, including low-cost private schools, can get away with being complacent, because there are no *proximate* exams. This leads to a huge waste of talent.

This first problem was the argument of *Poor Economics*, which we discussed in chapter 6.

2. Children who drop out of school before the end-of-school examinations leave with nothing. But they may have developed useful human capital.

The second problem was also implied by the argument of *Poor Economics*. Talent is wasted for the poorest children, who are more likely to drop out before they have completed the specified years of schooling: 42 percent of pupils in sub-Saharan Africa will leave school early, with about one in six leaving before second grade. These children leave with no certification at all, which may lead to difficulties finding employment. This is the case even though their years of schooling may have led them to acquire knowledge, skills, and dispositions that would be valuable to employers, if there was a way of measuring and acknowledging what has been acquired.

3. National end-of-school examinations and curricula (as well as higher-education degrees) are mostly (if not entirely) about "signaling." Human capital development gets neglected.

The third problem was the major argument in *The Case against Education*, also outlined in chapter 6. It was suggested that most of what is learned in the curriculum is not about knowledge and skills that will be useful in future work. Learning for its own sake is, in any case, undermined with high-stakes examinations, where the only way children can perform to expectations is by cramming their short-term memories; knowledge and skills are immediately forgotten afterward. The examinations instead are used by employers and further education to signal the student's cognitive ability, conscientiousness, and conformity. This is wasteful enough in the West, but it is extremely wasteful for countries that urgently need to develop human capital for development.

Poor parents recognize that the only show in town is the government curriculum and certification. The signaling benefit from the official certificate matters even more to poorer parents than it does to richer parents, who may have additional ways, such as extensive networks, to help their children along. Poor children are much more dependent on this government certificate to signal that they can move on to further schooling, higher education, and government jobs.

4. Schools are structured so that children learn only or mainly in age-related classes—"batches." This does not reflect the potential of how children could learn.

The fourth problem was one of the concerns raised by Sir Ken Robinson. Another notable TED Talker, Salman Khan, also has pointed to this problem. The schooling system in developing (as well as in developed) countries makes children move together in their age group. Even though children learn at different rates, in classrooms "a single tempo" is "tapped out" by the teacher: "Bound to this lockstep beat, the students who catch on quickest will soon become bored and zone out. ... The students who need the most time will still be left behind. The tempo will be perfectly suited only for some hypothetical student in the middle of the curve. It's a case of one-size-fits-few."[1]

5. The framework of education imposed by government can be demotivating for young people. There is no attempt to justify the curriculum content or learning outcomes to them; the structure and organization of schooling can be equally demotivating to many potential learners.

The fifth problem was the issue raised by Amal. Governments typically impose the framework of education on compulsory schooling, and those responsible for it don't seem to have much interest in making it appealing to those who have to go through it. Most students find school "painfully" boring: this could be as much an issue for students who find that the curriculum is "dumbed down," not academically demanding enough, as for those who find that schooling appears not to be aimed at them. In the United States, one study reports that two-thirds of high school students are "bored in class *every day*," and nearly a fifth are bored "in *every* class *every* day."[2]

Why are they bored? For the vast majority (82 percent), it's because the content "isn't interesting." And boredom is the number one reason for dropping out of high school.[3] (Work is also boring for most people, but research shows that it is slightly less boring than high school or college.) Does schooling really have to be so deadly dull? Or is this another area where thinking radically about educational freedom could transform the reality of education?

Usefully, the last three problems are clearly not confined to developing countries but are issues in common with systems of education anywhere in the world. As we move through this and the next chapters, we will increasingly see that discussion of low-cost private education is raising issues that have purchase on education anywhere, including in America and England. The next couple of chapters address the five problems. We've seen how trying to solve these problems through government is not ever likely to be the solution—our discussion of Sir Ken Robinson's ideas has led us to that impasse. But can different ways of doing things come from the private sector? Could educational freedom solve these five problems in search of a solution?

Of Martial Arts and Music

The five problems all occur because of the government-imposed framework of education, national curricula, and assessment systems, and the structure and organization of schooling.

Are these problems inevitable? Could a private assessment system—where fully private organizations take control of this part of the framework of learning—be any different? Even radical thinkers—such as Bryan Caplan, the author of *The Case against Education*—seem stuck in the idea that a free market in education would leave everything pretty much as it is now. It's hard to break out of this way of thinking, given how used to governments' hold on education we all are. But let's try to disrupt our normal ways of thinking about education: Suppose the private education revolution that we outlined in the first four chapters of this book could extend beyond the *supply* of schooling, to the framework of education itself. Could what evolves be any different from the systems we take for granted from government?

I am not asking what happens when private companies conduct the school-leaving exams or publish the national curriculum books, as happens in England, for instance (where a small number of companies are licensed by government to publish the national tests). This only happens within the strict framework set for them by government. They are certainly not following what the private sector might think should be a desirable way forward, but only following what government tells them to do. What I am interested in is where the private sector is involved in curriculum and assessment *without* any direction from government. Could a private solution to curriculum and assessment be any different from those that are typically imposed by governments?

Indeed, educational freedom clearly can bring about completely different solutions. To find out how, we must look outside of government-imposed compulsory schooling. Only there can we see how, once left to its own devices, private initiative *already* easily solves *all* the problems that have been highlighted above. When private initiative is concerned with curriculum and assessment, it already easily navigates its way around the apparently intractable issues we've looked at. My examples begin with music, followed by martial arts.

In music performance and theory, competing private organizations have evolved over 150 years to create a functioning system of curriculum and assessment that is internationally standardized and completely outside of government control. If you are learning piano, or flute or trombone, or any of thirty-five other musical instruments, you are likely to take part in this private curriculum and assessment system.

There are several examination boards that operate internationally. The first was Trinity College London, which opened in 1877. In addition to music exams, they also now offer drama and language, and have more than 850,000 candidates a year in more than 60 countries, including Nigeria, South Africa, Brazil, Chile, the United States, the UK, Australia, and New Zealand.[4]

The second, which is now the largest deliverer of music examinations internationally, is the Associated Board of the Royal Schools of Music (ABRSM), founded in 1889. These Royal Schools are the Royal Academy of Music (founded in 1822; famous alumni include Sir Elton John), the Royal

College of Music (founded in 1883, based on the college founded by Sir Arthur Sullivan, of Gilbert and Sullivan fame), the Royal Conservatoire of Scotland (founded in 1845; the current president is Sir Cameron Mackintosh, producer of musicals such as *Les Misérables, The Phantom of the Opera, Miss Saigon,* and *Hamilton*), and the Royal Northern College of Music (founded in 1893; famous alumni include Sir Harrison Birtwistle). In other words, the ABRSM exams, which can be taken by anyone at any level around the world, connect the novice with the scholarship and musicianship of some of the most notable figures in musical performance in the United Kingdom. The ABRSM now delivers over 650,000 exams per year in 93 countries (including the UK, Australia, Aruba, Oman, and Sierra Leone, although apparently not in the United States in large numbers[5]).

The various boards have settled on examinations at eight levels (called "grades"), plus a preliminary grade (called the "prep-test" in ABRSM). These nine levels give "a series of realistic goals" for students and "tangible rewards for their achievements." The framework is one of "life-long learning"; there are no restrictions on "age, length of study, or the requirements that candidates are taught in schools or other centres." In other words, they are entirely flexible and open to peer learning and self-learning. A learner can be *any* age to take *any grade: only readiness matters.*[6] Moreover, no set pattern is imposed on learners, so learners not only take examinations when they are ready but also can jump grades if they feel they can advance more quickly or, of course, repeat grades if they didn't do well. It all evolved entirely outside of any government framework of education.

The examinations are internationally standardized, with examining panels bringing in more than seven hundred highly skilled musicians, who are trained both before and during service on the panels and regularly monitored and moderated to ensure international consistency of standards. Fees to take the exams and use the curriculum range from US$36 to US$91, depending on grade. You can be an autodidact or engage a music teacher of any shape or form. No one minds, as long as you pay your fee and present yourself for examination.

This privately evolved system is completely different from the government-imposed systems we see in compulsory schooling. Let's emphasize some of the differences: In music, you can take grade 3 piano, say, whether you're eight, eighteen, or fifty-eight years old, and you don't even have to have the grade 2 certificate in order to take it. You take the grade you want *when you are ready* and can progress through the levels *as quickly or as slowly as you need to.*

The contrast with what happens in compulsory schooling is clear—and rather puzzling once put in this context. In schooling, our system says something like this: assuming you started school at age five, by the time you're eight years old, you must be learning at a third-grade level. It doesn't matter if you are actually at a different level. If you're eight years old, you learn at a third-grade level—that's (typically) the way the system works.

In fact, it's even worse than that.

First, you might be put in third grade when you are eight years old, but in government-imposed systems around the developing world, you are not tested to see if you really are at that level; you're only tested externally once you've reached the equivalent of grade 8 level, the school-leaving age.

Second, once you're nine years old, usually you'll get promoted to the next level, in this case grade 4, whether or not you're ready for it. (Exceptionally, you might be considered by the school to be so far from ready that you're made to repeat grade 3 level, in full, again.) But if you're far more advanced than grade 4, that's a pity; it's very unusual for you to be put in anything other than grade 4 level.

This makes no sense at all. It is absurd—that is not too strong a word to use. Curriculum and assessment methods imposed by government systems the world over appear absurdly primitive and unscientific when compared with the system that has naturally arisen in a setting that allows educational freedom—the setting of music curriculum and examinations.

We can see how the music curriculum and assessment system solves at least four of the five problems that we noted arise with government-imposed assessment systems in compulsory schooling.

Regarding the first problem ("National examinations measure children's performance only after ten years or more of schooling"), we can see that, without any prodding from government, music bodies have created a system of nine (eight plus one) grades, which provides proximate testing of whether or not children and young people have reached the required standards. So, the problem of having to wait until you've gotten to the highest level before you're publicly assessed is simply and neatly avoided.

This approach could clearly solve the second problem too ("Children who drop out of school before the end-of-school examinations leave with nothing; but they may have developed useful human capital"). Obviously, anyone can leave the music examinations system at the level they have reached, and with certification to prove it. No one has to wait only until the final grade in order to get certified.

But these certificates are also clearly about human capital development and thus overcome the third problem ("National end-of-school examinations and curricula are mostly [if not entirely] about 'signaling'; human capital development gets neglected"). Indeed, the problem of signaling doesn't emerge in any harmful way at all. In fact, if it emerges, then its effects can be positively beneficial.

Suppose, up to now, standards in concert halls and on radio broadcasts had allowed those with, say, grade 5 in musical instruments to perform publicly and be appreciated for their talents. Musicians with this standard may also only be able to play a reduced repertoire, but if this standard and selection is all that's available, people are likely to appreciate it. Suppose there is an influx of performers who have achieved grade 8. In order to perform publicly, the current musicians would have to raise their game—and, because there is an easy and formal way of doing so, *signal* that they had raised their game by taking and passing the appropriate level music examinations. Does this signaling bring in the pathological consequences we discussed earlier? Not at all. Raising their game means they would genuinely improve their knowledge and skills in their chosen musical instrument, or, as we can put it, improve their human capital. In this purely private system, there is no danger of signaling being "a waste of time and money," as it leads to an improvement in the quality of musical performance.

I saw something like this in action once when I was traveling through Zambia and arrived in a small town. The small European population there aspired to stage cultural events that they may have recalled from long ago back home, and so they put on a classical music evening. Their individual level of musical ability was rather low, likewise the overall standard of performance. But it was much appreciated by all who attended—there was nothing much else to compare it with, and, in any case, live music is always a pleasure to listen to, so there was much gratitude. Imagine, however, if suddenly there had been an influx of highly talented classical musical performers to this remote corner of Africa. Then the current performers would have to raise their game in order to perform in public. And that would be of public benefit.

Clearly, the fourth problem ("Schools are structured so that children learn only in age-related classes") is also completely solved. Children, young people, and young or old adults learn at their own pace, not in an age-defined cohort.

Finally, what about the fifth problem, of motivation? ("The framework of education imposed by government is demotivating for young people. There is no attempt to justify the curriculum content or learning outcomes.") Perhaps it's not fair to compare this carefully circumscribed area, like learning the piano, with larger curriculum areas such as those found in schools. It should be much easier to motivate children or young people to progress through the grades. If you're learning the piano, then the motivation for moving through the grades is to improve your talent at piano and increase the pleasure of performance, both for you and for the listeners. It is agreed that this is a much smaller issue than that which arises for schooling in general.

Thus, in music, educational freedom has flourished, unconstrained by governments, and private initiative has evolved and emerged to produce curriculum and assessment—the framework of education. This has clearly solved at least four of the five problems associated with government frameworks.

From music, we can go to martial arts, where again private initiative has solved the same problems. In various martial arts, learners progress through a system of *belts* to demonstrate their level of expertise (that is, their human capital). The World Martial Arts Center gives the following nine belts: white, yellow, orange, green, blue, purple, red, brown, and black.[7] These colors go from lighter to darker, apparently because Korea and Japan were poor countries when these belts were developed, and so this progression meant that users only had to buy one belt. You started with a white belt, which was then dyed in progressively darker colors. Or so the story goes.

Karate uses exactly these same nine belts. In judo, the situation varies slightly from country to country, with typically seven or eight belts. For instance, in the United States, the entry-level judo belt is white, followed by yellow, orange, green, blue, purple, brown, and finally black.

Just as in music, in judo, with some age restrictions (for the very sensible reason that you may have to demonstrate how well you are doing by fighting others), you take these belts *when you are ready* and progress through them *as quickly or as slowly as you need to*. The belts also obviously signify acquired human capital—skills and knowledge about martial arts.

Again, we can see the contrast with what happens in compulsory schooling. If the martial arts system were like formal schooling, then it would compel children who were, say, seven years old to learn at the orange-belt level, no matter what belt level they could attain. Then the next year, they'd have to progress to the green-belt level, whether or not they were ready for it, or even if they were indeed ready for blue or higher belt levels. But here's the rub—in compulsory schooling, you wouldn't be tested, objectively and externally, to determine if you were at the right grade until you reached black-belt level, the final exams. There would be no proximate tests to guide you through the system. It makes no sense when you consider the availability and wide acceptance of these other learning approaches.

Again, we can see how the martial arts assessment system solves all the problems that we noted with government-imposed assessment systems in compulsory schooling. Regarding the first problem ("National examinations measure children's performance only after ten years or more of schooling"), again we find that, without any prodding from government, the sport has created a system of seven to nine levels, which provides proximate testing of whether or not children have reached the required standards. So, the problem of having to wait until you've gotten to the highest level before you're publicly assessed is simply nonexistent.

Concerning the second problem, if you drop out of advancement through the martial arts levels, there is no issue—you leave with whatever belt you've achieved. You can proudly be a green belt in judo, taking that wherever you go. In the government-imposed framework of education, if you drop out before the final exams, you've had it, you leave with nothing.

The third problem is also solved. The belts measure actual knowledge and skills that can be applied, human capital achieved—they are not about wasteful signaling at all. Just as we saw in the music example, any signaling that could arise would not be harmful: you might have previously been content and able to do all you wanted to do in the world of judo (martial arts) with, say, a green belt. But if many more people are coming forward with blue or black belts, then in order to compete with them, you'll need to raise your game to signal that you're also of a high standard. But notice that this signaling is not wasteful at all in the respect that you move forward and gain precisely the knowledge and skills that improve your judo as well as enable you to compete better with others. You do improve your human capital. This is completely unlike the negative signaling we see in publicly funded and subsidized education.

The fourth problem is also clearly overcome in martial arts assessments. You take the level of belt you are ready for and move to the group that is at your level; you are not stuck in some imposed system where you learn with your own age "batch" at all.

And again, the fifth problem of motivation is easily solved here, but perhaps again it's not fair to see this as a downside of government intervention, as it's clearly harder to solve this problem for a much broader curriculum than it is for extracurricular activities. (A bit later, we'll see how private initiative could solve this problem even in the broader area.)

We've looked at music and martial arts to show how purely private initiative can, in assessment and curriculum in areas as disparate as judo and piano, solve the problems that we take for granted in the schooling system. I believe it shows much about the ingrained nature of the schooling system that we simply assume that we have to take it all for granted and can't think of anything better.

As soon as you get out of school and into the world of work, the same phenomenon emerges, this time with professional associations. Banerjee and Duflo in *Poor Economics* come tantalizingly close to a similar realization. Focusing on the "huge waste of talent" that the government-imposed framework of education brings to education, they point to one private-sector initiative, run by the giant Indian technology company Infosys, that "has set up testing centers where people, including those without much formal qualification, can walk in and take a test that focuses on intelligence and analytical skills rather than textbook learning. ... This alternative route is a source of hope for those who fell through the gaping holes in the education system." This private-sector company is "doing what the [*public*] education system should have been doing," the authors suggest.[8] Indeed.

The key point is that in the private, civil-society sector, the problem of signaling removed from human capital doesn't appear to be an issue—we are continually inventing and reinventing new areas of assessment that genuinely measure human capital. Perhaps it is only in compulsory schooling that one is stuck in the bizarre world of credentials that act mainly as signals, not as developers of human capital.

Now the question arises: Could we imagine that educational freedom could lead to similar approaches even in mainstream schooling itself? (Of course, it may be that, under educational freedom, "mainstream schooling" might itself become an outdated concept, and instead you might see discrete organizations emerging in numerous areas of important human capital development. In what follows, we are sticking with the idea of mainstream schooling to show that even here, educational freedom can lead to different outcomes than we are used to at present. We'll have more to say about the other possibilities in our final chapter.) This question takes on special significance for those parents who've been educating their children during the COVID-19 school closures. Rigid curricula, course sequencing, and seat-time will likely make little sense to parents who've witnessed first-hand how their children progress through subject material at different speeds. They should not be rushed ahead, nor should they be held back. Their education should be at their own pace, not someone else's arbitrary timetable.

If educational entrepreneurs were able to come into mainstream schooling, there is no reason why they couldn't develop something that was similarly imaginative and flexible, and which would overcome the five problems listed above.

It's worthwhile outlining a possible system that could emerge in a private system of education. I am not saying this is the most desirable possible model, only pointing to the kind of model that could emerge if allowed to. It is important to stress that this kind of system has not emerged under government systems of education. But what if there were freedom to allow it to do so?

Here is an opportunity for an educational entrepreneur to start something like this. We've noted in the first five chapters that there is a grassroots privatization revolution taking place, which is arising because entrepreneurs are just doing it. No one is waiting for government reform to change the way education is delivered. They are simply getting on with it. There is a similar opportunity for an educational entrepreneur to emerge in this space too.

An Alternative Framework of Education

One solution that could solve the five problems is to create an alternative internationally recognized assessment/certification system, based on the technology that is widely available now in developing countries, that would provide frequent assessments and certificates in separate subjects for bite-size chunks of the curriculum—a new and improved curriculum, focused on knowledge and skills that are useful, that raise the person's human capital, just as we've seen in the examples of martial arts and music.

In the short to medium term, schools would probably have to offer this new curriculum alongside the knowledge and skills required by government to take the final school examinations or receive the high school diploma. Perhaps the final grade in some of the subjects, such as mathematics and language, would have to correspond, at least in the medium term, to the content of the final school examinations. It is likely to be desirable to ensure that poor parents and their children still would have access to the state's signaling devices, so they would need some or all of this content. How to accommodate this in the timetable would be a problem for the entrepreneur to address, but I don't see it as insurmountable. But it is assumed, as the new system develops, that it could become the desired route for children entering schools.

A majority of the curriculum could be developed from the outset in conjunction with in-country employers, investors, entrepreneurs, and businesspeople, to enable the levels to reflect knowledge and skills that would be needed for work and adult life. There would need to be subjects that are traditionally taught in the school curriculum—even for Bryan Caplan, not all of it is a waste, so literacy and numeracy would still be important. But new subject areas could also be created: entrepreneurship and life skills, for instance, and economic awareness, which could also bring in important knowledge, skills, and dispositions that are important for work and adult life. And, of course, a key range of vocational education options, from plumbing to agriculture to dressmaking, could also be included.

It is interesting that for both martial arts and music assessments, seven to nine levels emerged, and it may be that this is where the desirable number lies for this alternative assessment system too. With this number of levels, of course, there could be many sublevels, which you could attain in order to build up the levels that are recognized outside.

It would be crucial to delink these levels/grades from existing school levels/grades, so a suitable vocabulary must be invented to describe them. An obvious solution would be to use the language of martial arts and to describe students as attaining different-colored "belts" in their subjects: A student could describe herself thus: "I'm a green belt in dressmaking, yellow belt in English, blue belt in entrepreneurship, and brown belt in mathematics."

Finally, to ensure that the signaling needs, especially of poor parents, were met, the "black belt" in at least some of the relevant subjects would have to correspond initially to the level and content required for the national examinations. At first, students would probably have to take their national as well as their black-belt exams, but preparation for the latter would ensure preparation for the former.

In due course, it may be possible to convince national governments that the black belts were equivalent to the national examinations, and so didn't require students to additionally take those exams. Ultimately, of course, the aim would be to make the new system so widely acceptable that black belts could be modified to reflect the true needs of children in the country and globally and to be the assessment system of choice, irrespective of what government examinations there still were.

It would be essential for the widespread acceptance of the alternative system that certification be objective, above corruption. It would also be highly desirable that assessment results be very quickly conveyed to students (as they are in the judo and music examples) and that they be standardized both nationally and internationally. None of these problems are beyond the ability of a suitably motivated entrepreneur to solve.

I must stress, too, that none of this is like the standardized assessments, currently imposed in America and England by the government, that are used primarily to evaluate teachers and schools, and thereby lead to teachers teaching to the test. The assessments proposed here are about children gaining recognition for making genuine progress through a satisfying curriculum that genuinely develops desired human capital.

None of this is entirely an act of faith. It is possible for genuinely new curriculum and assessment systems to emerge through private entrepreneurship. I give two examples. The first is the case of NIIT (formerly the National Institute of Information Technology, India), followed by the International Baccalaureate (IB).

NIIT was conceived in 1979 by Rajendra Pawar, then a development officer for a computer company in Mumbai. He realized that the government curriculum in computing was completely unsatisfactory for the development potential of India—graduates of Indian universities in computer science were unemployable in the burgeoning software industry in India. So, what did he do? He didn't try to change the government university curriculum from within—he recognized that would be a thankless task. Instead, he created an entirely new curriculum and certificate, something that would run completely parallel to the official government system. The new company, cofounded by Pawar and Vijay Thadani, started with one learning center in a leased room in an office building in downtown Mumbai in 1982, was listed on the Mumbai and Delhi (National) Stock Exchanges in 1993, and has expanded globally ever since.

I chuckled once when interviewing the director of the All India Council for Technical Education (AICTE), the body that could have recognized NIIT certificates but wouldn't: "They're not worth the paper they're written on," the director told me in his dreary, dirty office—so dirty, in fact, that a rat came running in (I had to lift my feet to let it pass under my chair). The AICTE wouldn't recognize NIIT for various reasons, but perhaps the most significant was that it was given statutory powers in the 1987 AICTE Act to "take all necessary steps to prevent commercialisation of technical education."[9] Clearly, a for-profit, listed company such as NIIT wouldn't court favor with an organization with that as one of its aims.

But although the government wouldn't recognize NIIT certificates, the market thinks otherwise. NIIT is now the largest provider of computer education and training in India—with 54 percent of the market share of computer education and quarterly revenues of around INR 27.9 billion (US$55 million). Indeed, the market so much favors NIIT that it has become one of those rare brand names that serve to signify the field in general: when people say they are "doing an NIIT," they could mean they're doing any computer software course, not necessarily one by NIIT itself, just as "doing the hoovering" in the UK doesn't necessarily mean you're using that particular brand of vacuum cleaner.

NIIT created an alternative curriculum and assessment system that has led to genuine human capital development outside of the state—indeed, that is reviled by the regulatory body of government. It's a model for those who seek to do the same within the schooling curriculum.

My second example of a new curriculum and assessment system created outside of government is one that is almost universally held in high esteem, the International Baccalaureate (IB), the certificate issued by the organization of the same name, a not-for-profit educational foundation based in Switzerland. The organization was founded in 1965 as the International Schools Examination Syndicate (ISES), becoming the International Baccalaureate Organization (IBO) in 1967.

Interestingly, the International Baccalaureate grew out of a genuine market need. In (private) international schools around the world, this question was continually being raised: What satisfactory school-leaving examination can we offer our students, many of whom will be geographically mobile and wishing to have a credential that has currency across the world in all of the major educational systems? National examinations were usually unacceptable, often being of uncertain quality and certainly not of international durability. True, there were some certificates that had international credibility, such as the British A levels, but this was mainly restricted to the Anglo-Saxon world; and, in any case, there were severe doubts about their independence from government, with widespread accusations that grades were inflated for political ends. So, could a common curriculum and university entry qualification be created that could serve the widest possible range of linguistic and cultural communities?

The IB Diploma was the result. This is explicitly designed to meet the needs of highly motivated secondary school students between the ages of sixteen and nineteen. To support the program, the IB has provided an extensive global assessment infrastructure. The director general is based in Geneva, while assessment is governed from the IB Global Center based in Cardiff, Wales. To complement these, there is a large network of regional offices in New York, Geneva, Buenos Aires, and Singapore, with representatives in Stockholm, Sydney, Mumbai, Yokohama, Amman, Mexico City, and Moscow. In total, curriculum and assessment development, teacher training, and other educational services are offered to more than one hundred countries, with more than nine hundred participating schools. Globally, more than thirty thousand students complete the IB each year.

As only schools that are authorized by the IB are eligible to teach the curriculum and to register candidates for the examination, there is also a global quality control and inspection regime. Buttressed by extensive quality control mechanisms, the IB Diploma has achieved recognition by universities around the world, including prestigious institutions such as Oxford, Yale, and the Sorbonne. There are also formal agreements between the IB and ministries of education around the world, with some colleges and universities offering course credit to students with strong IB results.

Certainly, it has been a success measured in terms of practicality. But it was not just a practical need that inspired the IB's creators. They also had a more idealistic vision: through creating a common curriculum and certificate, they hoped that they could also create a shared academic experience that would foster tolerance and intercultural understanding. So, the IB program has several unique characteristics, including the "theory of knowledge" and the "creativity, action, and service" programs.[10]

Schools running the program ensure that the young people who emerge from the program not only excel academically but also are imbued with social concern. These factors, too, could counter criticisms that a private-sector approach to certification would lead only to a grim, utilitarian outcome. This is far from the truth in the case of the IB.

The IB is rather unusual, but it does show that it is possible to create an internationally recognized curriculum and assessment system that is available outside of the state. It is expensive, far too expensive for low-cost private schools, as it is aimed at the elite end of the private-school spectrum. But it gives us a taste for what is possible. (I did have discussions once with IB about creating an "IB-lite," something that would be possible to bring into the low-cost private schools. The discussions didn't proceed far, but I still believe it is a terrific idea and would love to see it—and competing ideas too—emerge.) So, it is possible to create new curriculum and assessment systems that challenge government monopoly of the framework of education.

Returning to the alternative system I outlined above, based on the idea of nine "belts" in a range of different curriculum subjects: it may be helpful to outline how this alternative system could solve the five problems outlined above.

Regarding number one ("National examinations measure children's performance only after around ten years of schooling; schools can get away with being complacent"), clearly this system could bring in a more proximate and frequent method of assessing how children are doing. Children and their parents would know about their own human capital development (achievement). Schools, too, would be judged, on a frequent basis, by objective measures of how well they were doing: comparing schools by the percentage of their children at blue-belt mathematics and green-belt English, say, would be a very effective way for parents to judge quality, and it would provide standards by which schools could compete with each other, improving the working of the low-cost private school market.

Concerning number two ("Children who drop out of school before the examination year leave with nothing; but they may have developed useful human capital"), if children have to drop out of school before they are able to reach black-belt levels (the equivalent of the national end-of-school examinations), under this proposed system they can leave with other belts that show achievement at various levels in various subjects. Because employers have been involved with developing the assessments, it's not only black-belt level that will signify a potentially valuable employee.

For number three ("National end-of-school examinations and curricula are mostly [if not entirely] about 'signaling'; human capital development gets neglected"), because employers, entrepreneurs, and colleges and universities would have been involved throughout in the development of the standards, all levels (apart from the black belt, which is likely to relate to the national examinations, at least in the short and medium term) will develop desired knowledge and skills that will be useful in relevant employment (as well as, where possible, building a love of learning for its own sake too).

Concerning number four ("Schools are structured so that children are in age-related classes; this does not reflect the reality of how children learn"), under the new system, children will learn precisely at the level they are at in different subjects and will be able to progress as quickly as they want or as slowly as they need. This will require imaginative work on creating timetables that consider the existing parameters of staffing levels and skills within current low-cost private schools. However, again, it is not envisaged that this would create insurmountable problems. No longer will the system be a "one size fits few" but instead a "multitude of sizes fit all."

It is interesting that a somewhat similar system was proposed by the TGAT, the Task Group on Assessment and Testing, in England and Wales during the 1980s.[11] A national curriculum was being introduced, and top education professors were able to think through precisely the sort of considerations introduced above. They proposed a somewhat parallel solution for government schools, with ten levels of assessment. I remember as a young education researcher at the time that I found it all rather intoxicating. However, within a year or two, the system had been completely modified. Yes, there were still levels, but these were now subsumed into the normal way of doing schooling—the levels allowed for a small amount of differentiation within normal classrooms.

How this came about is an interesting story, and like so much concerning the national curriculum in England, it is a story of how noble expectations got distorted by the actions of those charged with developing and implementing them. Again, as we've noted, vested interests, including teachers' unions, rallied to block anything that was too disruptive of the status quo ante. It's true that some new, more proximate assessments were introduced; but the teachers' unions have fought these tooth and nail, and watered them down, so that they are not widely perceived as adding much value.

I suggest that introducing radical change in the curriculum and assessment system is likely to be thwarted in the same way that it was in the British case. Resistance to it would simply be too great. It would appear too disruptive. However, within a system of educational freedom, the incentives would be completely different. Private schools would be engaged in a very competitive market, continually looking at ways to differentiate themselves within that market. There would be an opportunity for entrepreneurs to enter this area and create an assessment system that solved the very real problems noted above. If, when introduced in some low-cost private schools, it was seen to be successful and worthwhile, then it would be widely adopted across other low-cost private schools, hungry for innovation but crucially not worried about whether the innovation was disruptive. The only important thing would be that it was shown to be effective in raising standards and attracting students and their parents. This is crucial—my argument is that not only could an alternative curriculum and assessment system arise in a predominantly private system, but also, *it is only* in a predominantly private system that this sort of change could emerge.

This is one idea on how to challenge the government framework of education. Better ideas could emerge once entrepreneurs started thinking about this. The key point I'm trying to make here is that the current system raises so many problems that can be overcome if entrepreneurs are able to think imaginatively about them. Things could get quite exciting.

Nothing in this chapter has adequately addressed the fifth problem, "The framework of education imposed by government is demotivating for young people." Yet, this too can be challenged within a system of educational freedom.

9

A Thought Experiment in Educational Freedom

AMAL HAD A real thirst and appetite for learning about science. But not in school. School science was completely boring. Indeed, school in general killed any curiosity and creativity. Why? Because the gatekeepers of education appeared to contrive to make it so. These gatekeepers are those in charge of the framework of education—the curriculum, assessment, and ethos of schools. Can they be challenged? Can schools be made to encourage, rather than stifle, curiosity and creativity?

One of Amal's key inspirations, once she'd started thinking about how education thwarts curiosity and creativity, was Sir Ken Robinson. With his hugely entertaining TED Talks, he's inspired many millions to think about education differently, changed public opinion, and, most important to him, inspired individual teachers and school principals to bring informed changes to their schools. To do things on a larger scale in a public education system, to reach a far greater number of children, as Sir Ken wants to do, requires more.

Here he comes up against a roadblock. He'll find it very hard, if not impossible, to persuade politicians or parties to seek to impose his ideas through the public education system. Even if he could, these ideas, once made into policies, are unlikely to bear much resemblance to his original desires. Once they're out there in the political arena, too much has been conceded—they're now fair game as political fodder, subject to the whims of any political party. They can be adapted, changed, pushed in whatever way politicians of whichever party in power wish them to be.

That must be heartbreaking to a visionary like Sir Ken; in his writings, he accepts the problem as real. Meeting this impasse, he falls back on hoping that the small-scale changes he sees will slowly bring systemic change, one teacher, one school at a time. But you get the sense that deep down, ultimately, he knows that this will disappoint.

Change can indeed come from the grassroots, but it can't change a political system of education. The vested interests are simply too strong and resistant to change. However, is bringing change through the political system the only way to bring ideas to the widest possible audience? And I don't mean audience in the sense of TED Talk listeners—I mean the largest possible number of children learning in the ways that Sir Ken Robinson believes they can and should be learning.

Could it happen under educational freedom? I believe it can, as the following thought experiment will show.

This term *educational freedom* has been used throughout the book, but let's now spell out directly what I have in mind. Suppose there are no public, government-funded schools or other educational "outlets." (Educational outlets are an important addition, because in a system of educational freedom, schools may not be the desired place of learning for some or even many. We'll discuss this further in the closing chapter.) Parents use their own funding to send their children to the schools or educational outlets of their choice. (In cases of severe hardship, there could be targeted funding from state and/or philanthropy, but only in the way that we typically step in to help those in hardship for food and clothing too, by giving funds to allow people to use exactly the same outlets as everyone else.)

Why can I even suggest the possibility of a system of educational freedom? *Because it's very nearly the situation one sees in urban areas across sub-Saharan Africa and South Asia, and elsewhere.* That's what the first part of the book showed—the burgeoning of educational freedom in this respect, and its desirability on so many levels. In countries as diverse as Liberia, Nigeria, Kenya, India, and Pakistan, you will find most urban children in private education, including low-cost private schools. It's making substantial inroads into rural areas too.

So, we know it's possible for such a situation to emerge, through grassroots initiatives—exactly the kind of initiative that Sir Ken Robinson understands and commends; it has nothing to do with top-down reform. For the purposes of our thought experiment here, that's enough—we know that it can happen, because it has happened in many places around the world.

To adapt a Marxist phrase: the state has not been abolished, it has withered away. The "interference of state power" in education has become "superfluous."[1]

But not yet. This is the key. In those countries named above, while educational freedom has to a great extent emerged at the levels of funding and provision, state power in regulating the framework of education is maintained. The state largely controls the regulation of curriculum and assessment; it operates compulsory schooling systems. Even though it's not running or even funding schools, it still controls the framework.

But this is where further change can happen. In a system of government-provided and government-funded schools, it is *impossible* to see how governments would give up on the framework of education. With government controlling the purse strings, it can legitimately control what goes on in schools. But where a vast majority (and eventually, all) of the provision and funding is outside of the state, it is possible for the private, grassroots movement to resist government control of the framework of education and ultimately to replace it.

How do we bring about a "change of ownership" of the framework of education? Through precisely the same way that a change of ownership of funding and provision came about—through educational entrepreneurship. People didn't first decide they wanted to change educational provision and funding, and then set about convincing politicians and political parties that this was a good thing. They just did it. A self-organized system, a spontaneous order, emerged through the individual actions of educational entrepreneurs creating schools and through individual parents choosing to send their children to these schools. And so, slowly, imperceptibly at first, these grassroots initiatives replaced state provision and funding.

For some parents, educating their children during the COVID-19 school closures has brought some tentative first steps toward this movement's realization. Prior to the COVID-19 school closures, these parents may have worried that they lacked the expertise to educate their children. But having done so, some parents have felt more empowered than ever to direct the education of their children, including choosing private providers they deem better than the public-school status quo.

In the same way, government control of the framework of education can be replaced. Individual educational entrepreneurs can establish new assessment systems—like the ones I outlined in chapter 8—that respond more closely to the needs of children and their parents. Individual entrepreneurs can introduce systems of curriculum that respond more closely to the needs of children and their parents, and better motivate them for learning—and here I don't just mean providing curriculum experiences within schools that are following the government framework of education. What I mean is (as I discuss below) ultimately educational entrepreneurs creating curriculum that *replaces* the government framework of education.

Compulsory schooling may be the hardest part for governments to relinquish. But if educational freedom is emerging in terms of curriculum and the framework of education, then it may be that compulsion becomes increasingly less intrusive, as the options for education become more desirable—until it's no longer necessary.

How would a system of educational freedom work for individual educational entrepreneurs, like Sir Ken Robinson or those inspired by him? In educational freedom, Sir Ken Robinson doesn't have to convince politicians of the virtue of his ideas and then watch as these become distorted as they are taken through the political process before they—or, more likely, warped and twisted versions of them—come into effect. In a system of educational freedom, entrepreneurs inspired by Sir Ken can create curriculum and assessment systems, with Sir Ken closely involved to make sure they correspond to the intricacies of his educational ideas and desires. They can take these to the educational marketplace of the hundreds of thousands of entrepreneurs running schools, and to the managers of the chains and other groupings of schools that have emerged within these.

They will need to generate investment to create their curriculum, but this should not be difficult at all. Perhaps someone like Sir Ken can begin by putting some of his own money in, just as I did when I first cocreated chains of schools around the world. I can imagine there would be nothing more satisfying to a thought leader like him than seeing your thoughts put into practice. In any case, major investors will love a curriculum and assessment system designed by Sir Ken, because clearly his ideas and passions have been able to animate millions of people worldwide; market demand does not seem to be in any doubt.

This is one of the key points: whereas politicians might not be convinced that Sir Ken has adequately inspired the *political* constituencies that need to be convinced (for example, majorities of people in voting constituencies, majorities of teachers and teachers' unions, key people in the educational bureaucracies), educational investors will be easily persuaded that he has inspired the required *market demand*. Investors don't have to see majorities convinced anywhere; they need to be convinced that there is a *market* for the product. And given Sir Ken's global best-selling, iconic status, that would hardly be in any doubt.

So, under conditions of educational freedom, Sir Ken could bring to market his desired curriculum and assessment system, and bring to life his passion for and commitment to educational improvement. Many schools and educational systems outside of the state will adopt them and test their efficacy to see how they work to foster creativity and curiosity.

In a system of educational freedom, moreover, he would not need to worry that the only way of figuring out if they had "worked" was to see if students did better at government-imposed standardized national and international tests—something he opposes, which, again, we agree about. (We'll be exploring this more in the next chapter.) Under a system of educational freedom, performance in such tests would certainly not be compulsory to demonstrate success if this kind of testing existed at all. The only test would be whether sufficient numbers of individual parents and students, making choices based on what they perceive to be in their own and their families' best interests (not the interests of politicians, teachers' unions, and educational bureaucrats), choose schools (or other educational outlets) that offer Sir Ken's curriculum and assessment systems. That's it. Sir Ken is a master of persuasion. He should find this easy.

That's how educational freedom could work. What about the objection that governments will not, in the end, relinquish control of the framework of education, even if they can be persuaded (clearly, they can) to let go of funding and provision of schooling?

In the end, I must concede that this is the most uncertain part of my argument. I don't *know* that governments will do this. But we've seen several examples, including that of the International Baccalaureate and NIIT diplomas, where grassroots initiatives have been able to take back control, at least for certain areas and constituencies. And if enough entrepreneurs will come into the space of the framework of education too, into curriculum and assessment and the organization and ethos of school, and enough entrepreneurs running schools desire what they offer, then it is hard for me to see how ultimately such a movement could be resisted.

The timing may be uniquely ripe for a movement toward educational freedom. With the defaulting of the public education system brought about by the COVID-19 school closures during 2020, some parents had the opportunity to craft an education designed to help their children flourish. Such parents may be unlikely to settle for anything less and will be open as never before to the idea of educational entrepreneurs who will help them achieve that goal for their children.

It is, in any case, our only hope. If we want the Sir Kens of this world to be able to bring their ideas into education in order to transform the system, then we, the people, have got to regain control of the framework of education.

What kind of entrepreneurial initiatives do I envisage coming into the system? Let's focus on the issue of motivation here, the issue raised in the last chapter. Here, I want to outline *one possible way* in which educational entrepreneurs could start to solve the problem of motivation, or the lack of it, that suffocates children's desire for learning in the state system. It's just one idea, just one of many possibilities that entrepreneurs could come up with to transform the framework of education. I make no greater claims to it than that.

I wrote an earlier book, *From Village School to Global Brand*, about the Lebanon-based education company SABIS, which operates private and charter schools in many countries across the world, including in the United States and Iraq. I was impressed with all they had achieved. However, there was one area where I wish they had been able to go further—and this is something I've felt ever since with all education providers, such as Bridge International Academies. SABIS's approach to the curriculum is focused on their chosen *end point*—British A levels, American Advanced Placement (AP) exams, and various national baccalaureates. They worked backward from this end point to provide the curriculum that would adequately prepare children and young people for the final assessments that they would eventually reach—a very rational and systematic approach. It's the process also used by Bridge International Academies. At first glance, it all sounds sensible and good.

This approach, however, elevates these end points of education to a place of huge importance. Two issues are raised here.

First, who decides these end points? In general, the government decides what these end-point certificates or qualifications are— that is, they are the end points of the government-imposed framework of education. But why are big independent education companies, which have created wonderful educational opportunities outside of the state, accepting these government-provided end points? Why do they accept that governments have got it right about these end points when everything else they do shows how they doubt governments' abilities to manage and fund schools? As educational entrepreneurs, couldn't they imagine better end points to prepare children and young people for?

Second, how do we get children motivated, excited, and enthused to work toward these end points? At present, all over the world, there appears to be little effort made to motivate children and young people with any bigger picture as to why these particular end points are important, except for the answer—always disappointing to a young person—that you need your A levels or AP scores, or baccalaureate, because that's the only way you can get into university or get a job. The end points appear only to be described in this utilitarian, instrumental fashion.

The serial educational entrepreneur Chris Whittle writes about the problem of student motivation in this way: "Motivation is not part of our standard curriculum. Very simply, our schools do an absolutely miserable job of showing students *why* education is important."[2] He continues:

> The problem here is palpable and easy to see. ... Visit a school that serves students from kindergarten through twelfth grade. It is a study in contrasts. Visit the younger grades first. At that level, schools don't have to worry about the motivational issue. School is new, an adventure for children. As educators, we're still surfing on the natural desire of these kids to explore, to find out. But then go directly to a middle school or high school class and you can literally see a drop in the level

of energy and engagement. The children are leaning back, not forward. There is a tactile listlessness to classes. You can feel it. Participation is limited, awkward. It is easy to say this is just adolescence, yet adolescence is not always so—a fact made very clear by a trip to the lunchroom in the same school. There, energy abounds.[3]

I identify with this description completely—in my field notes of trips to schools around the world, I often reflect on precisely the same phenomenon. Why do schools seem fine for young children, but so unpleasant, so boring, for older ones? It's the same issue that Amal picked up on in the earlier chapter—yes, schooling seems fine for younger kids, who don't mind pleasing the teacher, but for older kids, typically it's dire.

One of the areas we need to explore to understand why motivation may be so hard to foster is in the *content* of the curriculum itself. Chris Whittle says, "When something we are teaching is just mindless, we should stop doing it. Or if we must teach children something so that they can pass some equally mindless exam, then it's best that we admit it. Better that students know we know." His own life demonstrates what he means:

> I run a reasonably complex $400+ million company, and I cannot recall needing most of the higher-math material that I learned. I know that statement is heresy, but ask yourself: if 99 percent of children are not going to use it, why is it, again, that we're teaching it? (If the answer is that it helps them to learn in a more general sense or identifies those with particular aptitudes, let's let them know that.)[4]

Whittle is right—we never go through this process with children and young people. We never explain why what they're learning is important, or the context into which it fits. The question "Why are we doing this?" is never satisfactorily answered in current government frameworks of education.

Could an emancipated education system do better? If entrepreneurs were encouraged to explore this area too, could they produce both the content and ways of motivating young people to engage with it? To lay the groundwork for my suggestion, let me share what may seem like a digression.

The Knowledge

I am not alone in having thoughts, from time to time, about the end of the world, what form it might take, and whether one could survive it. Sometimes I find myself browsing YouTube using keywords like "end of the world," "last days," and "apocalypse." Judging by the amount of material out there, I know I'm not the only one. For decades, there have been many films featuring post-apocalyptic worlds, from the 1950s' *The Day the Earth Stood Still* and *The War of the Worlds* through to this century's *The Day after Tomorrow*, *The Road*, and *10 Cloverfield Lane*. Some of these are based on novels, and there are many more novels not made into films. There are numerous postapocalyptic video games, including the *Fallout* series, *Darksiders*, and *Metro 2023*.

Of course, it goes back much further than these recent works of fiction. Where does the word *apocalypse* come from? It's the original Greek name for the end-of-the-world story incorporated as the last book of the Christian Bible, translated into English as "Revelation."[5] The other "religions of the book" have their own end-of-the-world stories too. In Islam, the Great Judgment and the Great Resurrection are described in the Quran, and the Great Tribulation in the Hadith. Judaism, of course, has its end-of-days transition from the old to the new era, when the Messiah will come.

Clearly, apocalypses strike a deep chord in the human psyche. Apocalypses connect with our deep angst about our place in the universe. They connect with fears about the harm we are doing to our planet, to each other, and to ourselves. They highlight terror about what lies outside of humanity's control. But apocalypses also connect with hope, about what might be achieved afterward, once so much of what is wrong with humanity has been wiped clean. They can nurture our hopes as to how we would be able to rise above adversity to become a hero in the strange, new postapocalyptic world.

Young people find these apocalyptic scenarios especially stimulating, as evidenced by the market for films, novels, and computer games aimed at young people. One writer explained it as follows: postapocalyptic novels are "essentially heroes' journeys … set in an imagined future world." When something catastrophic happens, "the teenage protagonist is catapulted out of their normal existence into the unknown." Their journey begins, along which they are tested, and as they survive these tests, they realize their destiny to change the world: "the stakes are high. ... It's heady stuff, far removed from the routine of everyday life."[6]

Young people are particularly interested in the hopes and fears excited by postapocalyptic scenarios. This idea set me thinking. Could the idea of apocalypse and postapocalyptic survival somehow be incorporated into *the end point* of the curriculum, framing children's motivation to engage with it?

An end point must satisfy three criteria: First, it must provide motivation for children and young people to learn the content. Second, it must also go some way *itself* to provide a justification for the content to be learned. We could describe this as a "transcendental justification," following the great philosopher of education R. S. Peters, who created a "transcendental justification" for education that didn't depend on anything outside of education itself.[7] Third, linking in with the arguments of earlier chapters, the end point must encompass the knowledge and skills, character and dispositions, that will enable students to live fulfilling adult lives.

Now, arriving at a high school today means finding our classroom and then being introduced to each of our teachers, who teach different subjects without any indication of how each fits into anything we'd be interested in learning and without any attempt to motivate or engage us. We learn mathematics of this kind in our first year of high school because that's what we do for first-year mathematics, and that's the end of the story. No explanation required. There's no road map. At best, we eventually are told we are doing this because it fits into the school-leaving examination or graduation requirements. Even that's a stretch for most schools. Certainly, no one feels any obligation or responsibility to say more than that.

But imagine a scene where arriving at our new high school is a very different experience from the way it is today (for, along with Chris Whittle and Amal, I agree that elementary schools might not need changing too much—smaller children are happy to please their teachers and to engage with learning in a way that older children are not).

In my imagined scene, this isn't what happens at all: It's our first day of high school. We're led into a huge auditorium. There are students like us from all over the district, region, state, country, even nations of the world. The venue is alive with an expectant buzz, like when you're waiting for the famous headline event after the supporting warm-up act at a music festival. We know that something amazing is going to happen—everyone knows this about the first day at high school. But our elder siblings and older friends have all been sworn to secrecy (as we have also been sworn to secrecy as we entered the auditorium). None of us know precisely what we are in for.

Suddenly, there's a blinding flash, then a crashing explosion, and people all around start screaming. It's the beginning of our initiation into why we are here and what we're going to do for the next few years. So unfolds a dramatic, multimedia spectacular. We shall remember it forever.

The apocalypse has begun. An asteroid has struck planet Earth, out of the blue. The special effects and (we learn later) actors mingling among us convince us of the reality of the catastrophe that has befallen our planet. After a while, there is only darkness. Most people have been wiped out. But there are a tiny number of us left, those of us in the auditorium, and slowly we begin to emerge from our hiding places. At first, there is chaos, anarchy. Some start hoarding food and attack those of us who are defenseless. For a while, this terrifying episode unfolds, as some take on the roles of marauders, while others of us are forced to hide in fear for our lives. But eventually, when we've had enough of all this, we pull ourselves together: putative leaders emerge from among us, building support for creating order out of chaos.

Our predicament is stark. The technological and scientific infrastructure that previously supported us has gone. The whole social and cultural fabric has gone too. So, what to do?

Our task begins to emerge. We must build a new human civilization from scratch, rebuilding the best of the past and forging it together with new elements for a future, better society.

Could this be an *end point* for a curriculum that excites and motivates students to learn? We've seen that apocalypses excite interest in many young people. Could it be an end point that begins to justify the content of the curriculum itself and the purposes of assessment? It is, after all, a real fear *but also a real possibility* that in our lifetimes we might be faced with the same, real predicament. Would we be able to survive? Very doubtful. Would it be desirable to survive? I think most young people, when push comes to shove, have a survival instinct. Being initiated into a curriculum that serves the end point of surviving an apocalypse could justify content that needs to be learned.

What would the structure of this curriculum end point be? As luck would have it, I came across a book in the same bookshop where I met Amal, in Hyderabad, India, that provided at least part of the curriculum structure I was looking for. The book was *The Knowledge: How to Rebuild Our World from Scratch*, by Lewis Dartnell. Dartnell had been thinking along lines somewhat similar to mine. He begins with this scenario: "The world as we know it has ended."[8] It doesn't really matter how; perhaps it was through disease, bioterrorism, nuclear war, or something "entirely beyond human control," like the earth being hit by a huge asteroid.[9] So we want to rebuild our world. How? This is what Dartnell's book is all about, at least the technological and scientific side of it.

We will need to recover as quickly as possible. What knowledge do we need to do so? None of us, or our parents or anyone else, will have the required knowledge: "The most profound problem facing survivors is that human knowledge is collective, distributed across the population."[10] In the developed world, we are completely "disconnected" from all the processes that give us the life we are used to:

> Individually, we are astoundingly ignorant of even the basics of the production of food, shelter, clothes, medicine, materials, or vital substances. Our survival skills have atrophied to the point that much of humanity would be incapable of sustaining itself if the life-support system of modern civilization failed, if food no longer magically appeared on shop shelves, or clothes on hangers.[11]

We're surrounded by gadgets of modern technology, each of which "requires an enormous support network of other technologies." Could we make a smartphone? It would be impossible to make it, let alone the infrastructure to support it.[12] Could we even make a device as simple as a pencil? The great classical liberal economist Leonard E. Read, founder of the Foundation for Economic Education, showed in his beautiful story "I, Pencil" that even that would be beyond our reach. As Dartnell put it, "Because the sourcing of raw materials and production methods are so dispersed, there is not a single person on the face of the Earth who has the ability and resources to make even this simplest of implements."[13]

There might be information in books, which we could find if there were any libraries remaining undamaged; perhaps we could scour the homes of intellectuals in the hope of finding some helpful books. But this knowledge won't be presented in a way that we, random survivors, without specialist knowledge or training, would be able to understand. Most of the academic literature, of course, would be completely lost—because most of the knowledge produced today is recorded only digitally, and everything digital has been wiped out. Bookshops for general readers won't help much either. How far would we get in trying to rebuild civilization "from the wisdom contained in the pages of self-help guides on how to succeed in business management, think yourself thin, or read the body language of the opposite sex? The most absurd nightmare would be a postapocalyptic society discovering a few yellowed and crumbly books and, thinking them the scientific wisdom of the ancients, trying to apply homeopathy to curb a plague or astrology to forecast harvests."[14]

In short, there won't be a huge amount left to help us. What we survivors need is a guidebook, a "reboot manual." This is what Dartnell's book is. Reading it, I became convinced that this reboot manual could be a model for a satisfying curriculum for high school. His reboot manual "provides enough of a grounding in the fundamentals to help survivors in the early years, and broad directions for tracing the best route through the web of science and technology for a greatly accelerated recovery."[15] The reboot manual allows us to understand how to rebuild the infrastructure for a civilized lifestyle.

Couldn't this provide a framework for a curriculum that could be practical for humanity as well as provide the motivation that keeps alive "the fire of curiosity, of enquiry and exploration?"[16]

Dartnell focuses only on technology and science, so we'd have to extend his ideas to other areas that also would need to be rebuilt. A complete curriculum end point might need the writing of two parallel books:

The Knowledge 2: How to Rebuild Society and Culture from Scratch
The Knowledge 3: How to Rebuild the Economy from Scratch

These three books, Dartnell's plus those two, could then provide the complete end point for a new curriculum.

I don't want to take this idea too much further here—the aim is to point out how entrepreneurs might think about how to create a suitable end point for education and how to motivate children and young people to work toward it. The apocalypse scenario seems to me one that could do that. A memorable, unforgettable initiation, over a day or a week, into why and what we will be learning provides the basis for the curriculum and forges the desire to learn in the minds of the young people involved. The immense value of what we are going to learn, which will give us the ability to rebuild the scientific, technological, economic, and cultural bases of civilization if ever it should be destroyed or threatened, will be hard to miss by anyone. Every young person involved can become a hero in that quest, a desire among the young that is usually hard to satisfy and that now will be brought into the very heart of their curriculum.

The curriculum end point can also dictate how we set about learning. Some of it will obviously involve getting together in teams to solve problems and to build the models. But some of it will require us to work on our own, to understand the theory and mathematics behind the models that we will build. There can be extended projects, where people plan for the moral, political, and economic structures of society. But there can also be traditional-style lessons. Students with practical skills can focus on the very practical projects where they can shine, while others with academic skills can tease out some of the theoretical issues.

Curriculum developers working under a government framework don't have any pressure or obligation to make the framework inspire or motivate young people. And they don't have any pressure or obligation to link with employers, civil society, or other individuals or groups to ensure that the curriculum will give children and young people what is required for adult life (or will lead to love of learning for its own sake). They *do* link in with what universities require in certain subjects, but this exacerbates the main problem, precisely because universities only think about what is required for the subject itself, not what is required for adult living.

The creators of what might be dubbed the "Apocalypse Now framework" will only be interested in these three principles of curriculum development:

- Does this content motivate young people?

- Does the content itself provide, at least in part, a justification for learning that content?

- Does the content provide young people with useful knowledge, skills, dispositions, and values for moving on to adult life?

How long could something like this motivate students? Perhaps the effect could last five years or more. Or perhaps it would motivate for only one year or less. This is a practical question that our entrepreneurs can explore. Perhaps we'd need to have a similar initiation into each year of learning to show how far we've gotten, but also to reveal what problems we still have left to solve. Or perhaps we could throw in some events to keep the children and young people on their toes. Perhaps all is going well, and then a smaller asteroid hits us. Or perhaps some of the survivors might revolt, so we must devise ways of protecting ourselves from them. Aliens might invade. The diseases that we thought we'd conquered might come back. So, each year, some further complications are thrown in, to keep us thinking, motivated, and inspired.

None of these details have to be answered to anyone's satisfaction by me now. They will be the R&D questions for those developing this new framework—and wouldn't it be wonderful if those involved were the brightest and most creative from around the world? How much more satisfying it would be to be part of this development and marketing team, developing ways to initiate young people into the best that has been thought and said as well as to help them become productive and flourishing adults, rather than creating marketing campaigns for a new soap powder or computer game?

Once you've reached an end point like our "how to rebuild our world from scratch," it might be hard for students to resist. Under our proposed system, moreover, with our end point, you'd have to be a pretty dull curriculum organizer to produce stuff that is not imaginative, creative, and curiosity enhancing. *The Knowledge 1: How to Rebuild Science and Technology from Scratch* leads to so many ideas on building working models of things that will excite and motivate children. *The Knowledge 2: How to Rebuild Society and Culture from Scratch* obviously lends itself to thinking of the school itself as a functioning community, where we can explore the importance of creating the rule of law, a vibrant civil society, and a functioning democracy, as well as explore how the arts emerge. *The Knowledge 3: How to Rebuild the Economy from Scratch* lends itself so easily to thinking of how we can nourish business opportunities and entrepreneurship for students, staff, parents, and community alike.

For each of these routes, it's likely that you will still want young people to be initiated into areas like mathematics, languages, history, and science. But the reasons why they are being initiated into these areas will be clear to all—to enhance survival. And the curriculum designers will be certain that everything that is learned will also be helpful for adult life. (This, of course, can also be told to students who particularly and forcefully question the point of it all.)

Of course, there will have to be alternatives and competition to make educational freedom work properly. That's just one idea above, but it would best work if parents and children were able to choose from competing frameworks. Some children might be extremely practical and happy with a curriculum framework that is simply and expressly about developing into adult life and might not need any of the complexities about apocalypses and the like to motivate them. When I was a schoolboy, going through deep teenage angst about existential matters, I was deeply struck that a couple of my contemporaries had no such anxieties about the meaning of life at all. One of these guys wanted to be a dentist. On the face of it, the guy seemed to have the potential for all the rebellious streaks that normal teenagers had. He was handsome and tall, and a hit with all his classmates too, quite the showman. But he wasn't remotely interested in existential questions. He wanted to be a dentist, and that was it. That was why he was doing the required courses, and he needed no further justification.

For children and young people like him, you might not need to couch the experience in any other form than saying, "This is what you'll need to do dentistry and other vocational areas." But at least, if we arrive at true educational freedom, and the curriculum developers work in the ways described above, then the curriculum won't be about wasteful signaling but instead will be about gaining the actual human capital required to be a dentist or whatever is desired. Of course, this option doesn't need a "transcendental justification," contained within the premise itself, as to why it's worthwhile—not transcendental, just dental will be enough!

The same is true for those who are champions of learning through the literary canon of the "best that has been thought and said."[17] If these champions can be given the liberty, under conditions of educational freedom, to present their case and to show the worthwhileness of what they offer, then they, too, will find parents and children wanting to engage with what they are offering.

Mention of existential doubt brings me to another possible curriculum outline. For those children and young people who are deeply interested in these questions, what curriculum do you need to answer the question "What is the meaning of life"? I find it's a lot of science and mathematics, to be able to at least understand some of the debates about science and atheism, obviously supplemented with some understanding of the arts and philosophy.

Again, the curriculum entrepreneurs would have to bear in mind the three principles of curriculum development mentioned above. For some, at least, this curriculum end point idea would provide motivation—just as many young people are interested in apocalypses, so many are interested in the question of the meaning of life. It also has a transcendental answer to the Chris Whittle question of "Why are we doing this?" If you're interested in exploring the question of the meaning of life, these are the things you'll probably need to understand to get there.

Does this curriculum feasibly provide some way of getting the knowledge and skills for adult life, and does it motivate the child and young person in achieving those? I am limited by my imagination here; I believe that once this area is open to entrepreneurial thinkers, more imaginative people than I can get involved and come up with a range of stimulating ideas.

Crucially, none of this is about saying we want this kind of system brought about by governments. This is where my position differs from what people like Sir Ken Robinson favor. They write and speak in their brilliant TED Talks about bringing in a new system, but then they ask for this to be brought in by governments. But there are strong reasons why these innovations won't be brought in by the state, as I've outlined earlier in this chapter. *Even if they could*, that would be precisely the wrong approach, because then the new system would be set in stone and quickly become old and stale. Even if it could be brought into the state system, it would then become the status quo against which no change would be possible. The whole point of suggesting ideas like this is to put them forward as possibilities that can be tested and honed in the marketplace of ideas. They need continual reinvigoration through trial and error, choice, and competition, so that they never become stale.

In five years, the ideas I've outlined above might become tired and excite no one. If so, then the curriculum designers will have to produce something just as exciting and newly meaningful to the next generation of scholars. The key is that they'll change it if they need to, but it'll stay the same if they don't need to.

We're starting to build up a picture of what the framework of education could be like if there were freedom for educational entrepreneurs to engage with it—and readers can start fitting together the different ideas we've outlined to make a coherent whole. So, for instance, the carefully calibrated belt system of assessment outlined in the previous chapter could become the preferred assessment system for the kind of curriculum framework described in this chapter. Or it might be something completely different.

In a condition of educational freedom, no more would we need to see children muddling along in age batches, following a curriculum that suited only some imagined child in the middle. No more would we need to see schools getting away with being complacent because objective testing was many years away. No more would we need to see children studying stuff that no one had explained the reasons for doing. Instead, as education becomes emancipated, we can see how individuals can flourish, learning a curriculum with a relevance that people have gone out of their way to explain. We can see how children could learn at their own level and pace, not bored out of their minds when things are going too slowly or lost forever because their teachers are constrained by a schooling structure that allows them no time to help children who need more time.

And all this can come through the actions of entrepreneurs, creating opportunities outside of government that can be taken up by individual schools.

We've looked at the "five problems in search of a solution" and suggested that educational freedom could lead to each being solved through the actions of educational entrepreneurs. There is another, sixth problem, which many authors, including Sir Ken Robinson, argue is a major impediment to educational innovation. National governments, they say, obsess over their countries' positions in international league tables—those league tables of academic performance based on results from international assessments. This leads to further constraining pressures on the framework of education within each country. Schools can spend their time inculcating desirable features like creativity and curiosity among children, but pretty soon they have to be assessed with some form of standardized testing in mathematics and English, which may not have been their focus, and so they may not perform well, even though they have done amazing things outside of these subjects.

It's to these international assessments that we turn in the next chapter. Can entrepreneurs also "just do it"—that is, create something that undermines the grip that these international assessments have on the education systems of the world? It turns out, perhaps surprisingly, that they can. This could be another nail in the coffin of government control of the framework of education.

10

A New Measure of Education

ENJOYING ELK MEATBALLS with black currant sauce on Finnair from London to Helsinki, I, like many concerned with education, was on my way to pay homage to Finland. In my case, the pretext was being invited to the Helsinki Book Fair to launch the Finnish translation of *The Beautiful Tree*.

Others have gone to Finland simply to champion the success of its school system—Michael Moore, for one. In his film *Where to Invade Next* (2015), the award-winning documentary filmmaker "playfully invad[ed] countries to explore different practices, attitudes and ideas that could help make America a better place."[1] One of his concerns was education, and one of the countries visited was Finland. Michael Moore is enamored with their system because it's egalitarian and free of standardized testing. He listens to teacher after teacher telling him how they are totally against the kind of standardized tests that are crippling American education.

Tony Wagner and Ted Dintersmith are two educational reformers who have also been on the pilgrimage to Finland, "a country that has developed what most people consider the best education system in the world." Finland's "education system ... is an inspiring model for preparing kids for a world that values creativity and innovation." It certainly isn't exposed to the explosion of standardized tests under which the American system suffers.[2]

Sir Ken Robinson is another. The Finnish educational system, he says, "is so successful that visitors from around the world make pilgrimages to Finland to understand the education miracle that seems to have happened there." Robinson likes its noncompetitive nature: "Finland encourages schools and teachers to collaborate rather than compete by sharing resources, ideas, and expertise with each other." He holds it up as a country with an egalitarian model that really works, and against which the United States and UK draw only negative comparisons. As do all the others, he heralds its lack of standardized testing— "there is no standardized testing apart from a single examination at the end of high school."[3]

These people love the education system in Finland because of its lack of standardized testing. But how did they all learn about Finland's "education miracle"? Ahem. Because of standardized testing.

Finland has done well on one set of international tests, PISA (Programme for International Student Assessment). Says Robinson, "Finland regularly appears at or close to the top of the PISA rankings for mathematics, reading, and science, and it has done so since the tests were first administered in 2000."[4] That's the *only* reason why anyone thinks that Finland is an educational miracle. It's done well on one set of international tests. Period.

PISA and the Flexing of Political Biceps

Interest in international studies to compare educational achievement across nations had begun as early as the 1950s, when the International Association for the Evaluation of Educational Achievement (known as the "IEA," not to be confused with the London-based classical liberal think tank, the Institute of Economic Affairs) was founded. However, these international studies didn't really become mainstream until the mid-1990s. The IEA itself rolled out two international assessments, the Trends in International Mathematics and Science Study (TIMSS), beginning in 1995, and the Progress in International Reading Literacy Study (PIRLS), beginning in 2001.

The best known and most influential of all the studies was launched by the Organisation for Economic Co-operation and Development (OECD), the intergovernmental agency of mainly rich countries, in 2000. This is PISA, whose tests are repeated every three years. PISA assesses fifteen-year-olds' performance in mathematics, science, and reading (but not always all three at the same time).

These international tests, especially PISA, have become very influential with national governments. Sir Ken Robinson notes how its political impact has increased, at first attracting little attention but by 2013 making "headlines around the world," sending "tremors through governments everywhere. Ministers of education now compare their respective rankings like bodybuilders flexing their biceps. Like the press, they seem to treat the rankings as an absolute measure of their success."[5]

This "flexing of biceps" leads to increased government control, pushing education in certain directions. Governments all over the world are "yanking firmly on the reins of public education, telling schools what to teach, imposing systems of testing to hold them accountable, and levying penalties if they don't make the grade."[6]

This is the reason why these international assessments are seen as negative inhibitors to bringing innovation into educational provision. Politicians who might otherwise be keen on introducing the kinds of educational changes favored by visionaries such as Sir Ken Robinson will be afraid of the impact of any experimental reform on PISA results. So, it makes them even less motivated to attempt to introduce any reforms.

Steve Hilton, a former adviser to British prime minister David Cameron, concurs with the negative assessment of tests like PISA. He argues that the league tables for PISA and other international tests not only get "all the attention" and "drive headlines" but also put "pressure on policymakers." These league tables are "the GDP of the education world, the metric that drives all yet includes just a fraction of what matters." Of course, he agrees, "maths is important. But because of PISA, we focus on maths excessively. ... The culture of tests is a fitting symbol for schools as factories, complete with bells, separate facilities, and batches of children."[7]

In this chapter, I agree, in large part, with these commentators. I agree that the way politicians (and commentators and critics) tend to use PISA, and similar international tests, is restrictive. It is plausible that they dictate to some extent what is taught in schools nationally. It is true that some, perhaps many, politicians (and commentators and critics) have become obsessed with these league tables and draw comparisons from them about the quality of their education systems. What I aim to do in this chapter is suggest that there might be an alternative, more appropriate, way of looking at the quality of education systems than by consulting league tables of school performance.

However, I also suggest that there might be a danger in throwing out the baby with the bathwater. I can see some profitable use for competing systems of international assessments even under conditions of educational freedom. But this would only be when school providers chose to use them because they were deemed worthwhile *to their market*. I'll say more about this later.

So, Sir Ken Robinson is right to catalog the extent to which politicians worry about their countries' standings in these tables, as if it really matters to education. Since he is right, we can forgive his (and Michael Moore's) hypocrisy, where he uses the international test rankings when it suits him, even though he thinks they are wrong and harmful. For the way *he* uses the test rankings is precisely the way *politicians, the media, and the general public* tend to use them: Finland is (or was, as we'll see) doing very well in the rankings; therefore, it is getting its education system right. If we want to do better at education, we should follow Finland's education system model.

Vietnam is doing better than the United States in PISA; therefore, it is getting its education system right in a way that the United States is not, and we should learn from what they are doing. There's something odd about this, isn't there? Steve Hilton thinks so. "Politicians trumpet PISA scores as if they were a key factor in economic success, yet Germany and the United States, two leading global economies, lag behind countries like Vietnam and Poland."[8]

If you looked at results in the individual PISA subjects for 2015, out of 72 participating countries, you would have found the United States ranked only 40th in mathematics, with Vietnam (22nd) and Poland (17th) well ahead. In science, Vietnam is 8th, well ahead of Germany (16th) and the United States (25th). Combining all three subjects in one grade, we find the United States scraping in at 30th, well behind Vietnam and Poland (18th and 19th, respectively). The United Kingdom doesn't do much better, at 23rd. But what does this all mean? Does it really show which countries are doing better at education?

We'll explore this in a moment. But before we do that, I want to clarify the position on Finland.

Table 10.1. Finland's Declining Performance on PISA, Ranking All
Countries Taking Part

	2000	2003	2006	2009	2012	2015
Math literacy	4	2	1	3	12	13
Reading literacy	1	1	2	6	6	4
Scientific literacy	3	1	2	2	5	5

Source: Adapted from Ministry of Education and Culture (Finland), 2018, 2015, 2012.

The Luck of the Finnish

Sir Ken Robinson and Michael Moore, and many other left-leaning educational commentators, praise Finland for its educational egalitarianism and are excited by its international success. But they're wrong on both counts.

First, this international success story has been rather overdone. Table 10.1 shows Finland's performance over the years on PISA from 2000. We can see that the enthusiastic commentators are stuck in a time warp. In the first decade of the twenty-first century, it was true, Finland led the world, academically speaking. The 2006 results were outstanding, with Finland ranking 1st, 2nd, and 2nd out of all countries taking part in mathematical literacy, reading literacy, and scientific literacy, respectively. The 2009 results were still good.

But by 2012 and 2015, Finland's place had rapidly declined. Finland was 12th and 13th in 2012 and 2015, respectively. That's way behind Denmark, the Netherlands, Canada, Estonia, and Switzerland, as well as the Asian high performers such as Singapore, Japan, China, and South Korea. Importantly, the Finnish Ministry of Education and Culture says that 2012 was "the first time it [was] possible to assess developments in proficiency in mathematics in a reliable way."[9]

We don't see the Michael Moores of this world paying homage to the Netherlands or Switzerland, or Singapore and Japan, countries where they won't find particularly egalitarian systems at all.[10] Or indeed paying homage to America, Northern Ireland, or England. Finland did well in the past on PISA, but it's not done so well on another international test of mathematics,

TIMSS, the Trends in International Mathematics and Science Study. The 2015 study showed Finland coming in at 17th in mathematics for nine- and ten-year-olds. That's behind Northern Ireland (6th)—which has a traditional "selective" (nonegalitarian) education model—England (10th), and the United States (14th). The Asian high performers were at the top, as usual.

It's odd that education commentators focus only on the early PISA results for Finland rather than updating their statistics or looking to other tests that tell a different story. There would be no homage to Finland if later or different tests had been their source of information.

In any case, Finland's egalitarian educational model has probably been overblown a bit too. On my trip to Finland, I visited schools in various parts of Helsinki, and I was immediately struck by how some did seem better than others, in terms of facilities, student and teacher application, and so on. I wondered: Did these subjective impressions carry over into objective academic performance, and was there any pressure from parents to send their children to schools that seemed better than others? A school principal told me that, as Finland had an egalitarian system, there were no official data published to assist parents, so they didn't do this. Later, his deputy quietly took me to one side as he guided me through his school and told me that, while the Finnish government won't publish league tables of schools to highlight differential performance, national and local newspapers have filled this gap. They publish league tables to show which are the better schools to get your children into, and parents respond accordingly. Some schools have high demand and waiting lists, and others have surplus places. He even showed me how his school used its position in these league tables in its publicity materials. There's a guilty little secret that Michael Moore didn't notice in his visits to Finland's schools.

And then it turns out that, in this supposedly egalitarian system, the schools are only "comprehensive"—that is, nonselective—*until the age of sixteen*, when children have to choose between selective schools, in academic and vocational streams, based on their academic performance.[11] Earlier schooling reflects the choice of these destinations, so streaming in preparation for this selective schooling starts much earlier.

Perhaps it's safest not to try to compare education systems across different countries using the results of international assessments in the first place. Finland is a tiny country of 5.5 million, with a hugely homogeneous population:

three-quarters of the population belongs to the Evangelical Lutheran Church, and the largest non-European ethnic community is Somalis, who make up a tiny 0.3 percent of the population. Contrast this with the United States, with its population of 326 million and huge ethnic and religious diversity. It seems to be odd indeed to try to compare these vastly different countries on one simple indicator that doesn't consider any other variables.

However, we will come back later to one issue that has been raised here— it's good to see that there is competition among international assessments. In this case, it has enabled us to get a better perspective on the Finnish miracle. As we go through this chapter, I'll try to bring another potential competitor into the ring to disrupt the whole thing a bit more.

Comparing Countries

International tests like PISA and TIMSS are used by politicians and social commentators to make comparisons between countries in terms of education. It might be tempting to think that these tests are similar to international "tests" like the Olympics, which are used to make comparisons between countries in terms of sporting achievements. Indeed, an internet search finds commentators making precisely this connection.[12] So the UK, ranked third in the 2012 Olympics, "only ranked 21 in PISA terms." Coming out at the top in the Olympics, the United States "lies at 26 in PISA terms."[13] And so on.

There's one obvious difference between the way PISA tests and the Olympics are conducted: while the Olympics measure a nation's sporting *excellence*, tests like PISA measure a nation's *average* educational achievement. If the Olympics were organized similarly to how we measure a country's education system, we would first select an age cohort, then we'd randomly select participants from this age cohort, certainly not looking for the elite. Without knowing anything about the interests of these participants, we'd then test them in the same three events—ones that are the easiest to measure, such as the 100-, 200-, and 400-meter track events. Moreover, you wouldn't be told that you were selected until the last minute, so you wouldn't have any time to train for the events. You wouldn't be informed about the forthcoming event and its significance, so you wouldn't have any incentive to do well in it.

This wouldn't give us the same information as the real Olympics, which look at the cutting edge of human accomplishment in a country. It would only tell us what the average person of a certain age was like at preselected sports. So, it's worth mentioning that international tests like PISA have an *egalitarian* assumption behind them. They randomly select children, so they are not testing how well a country's education system performs to create academic excellence or foster human accomplishment. Instead they are saying that a country's education system must be measured by how it creates academic achievement across the board, for everyone—hence the random selection.

There is another, much more significant difference between the Olympics (and other international sporting events) and international tests such as PISA. Highlighting it may help us realize how illegitimate it is to think of tests such as PISA as a measure of a country's *education*.

It has to do with the *goals* or *aims* of competitive sports. Each competitive sport is *an end in itself*. People don't typically take part in a competitive sport to achieve some end other than winning or performing better.

Of course, we can say that sports foster health and fitness, and sometimes (depending on whether the sport is an individual or team event) teamwork and cooperation. However, we could promote these goals in many ways without competitive sports.

Now, because each competitive sport is an end in itself, a sensible way of comparing how well our country is doing internationally is to get our country to compete against other countries in the sports themselves, like running, swimming, and shot put. The Olympic-style measurement of gold, silver, and bronze medals in competitive sports seems, then, to be a sensible way of measuring comparative achievement in competitive sports.

But is education like that?

To answer that question, we need to ask what the goals or aims of education are, in the same way that we've just done for competitive sport.

Most commentators today would say that the aim or goal of education is the preparation of children and young adults for adult life, including for the world of work (the economy), the family (social), and society (political), through developing knowledge, skills, disposition, character, and values. The development economist Lant Pritchett, for instance, writes, "The goal of education is to equip children to flourish as adults—as parents and caregivers to the next generation of youth, as participants in their communities and societies, as active citizens in their polity, and as productive workers in their economy."[14]

Sir Ken Robinson is somewhat in agreement. He writes that "the aims of education are to *enable students to understand the world around them and develop the talents within them so that they can become fulfilled individuals and active, compassionate citizens*."[15]

The crucial point here is that education is not normally considered by such commentators as an end in itself. It is a means to other ends, not its own end. This is different from the case of competitive sports and should have huge implications for the way in which we measure the success of schooling systems.

Countries compare their sporting systems by comparing their scores (number of medals) on international tests (such as the Olympics) in a range of sports, such as track-and-field events, swimming, and gymnastics. This precisely matches the goals or aims of the sport, which is to increase speed or distance, or whatever appropriate measure is used in a sport.

But in education, it starts to look a little odd: Countries compare their education (schooling) systems by comparing their scores on international tests (PISA, TIMSS, and so on) in mathematics, reading, and science. But the aims or goals of education, as noted above by Pritchett and Robinson, do not mention achievement scores in mathematics, reading, or science.

If we padded the definitions, of course, we might come across mathematics, reading, and science somewhere. For instance, some—but certainly not all—might need mathematics for their roles as productive workers in society (but, as Chris Whittle and Bryan Caplan pointed out in previous chapters, perhaps the vast majority might not need very much of it). Perhaps everyone would need some (but again, probably not much) mathematics in their role in democracy. But for all these aspects, so many other things are required too, such as values and disposition, and aspects of character, as well as knowledge and skills in so many other areas. Others look at the importance of creativity and curiosity as being crucial to the educational endeavor.

One route might be then to say that international assessments like PISA are not up to measuring the goals of education (in a way that the Olympics is up to measuring the goals of competitive sports), because they only measure achievement in mathematics, reading, and science. But the goals of education include far more. Shouldn't we, then, also be measuring all these other areas to know how well our country's education system is doing compared with other countries?

Some people have gone that route, looking for more inclusive international assessments; several influential groups were formed to lobby precisely for this. These include the Collaborative for Academic, Social, and Emotional Learning (CASEL) and the National Commission on Social, Emotional, and Academic Development (NCSEAD) at the Aspen Institute. Prompted by these efforts, the OECD has created a supplement to its PISA regime, an additional test, the Study on Social and Emotional Skills (SSES), which will focus precisely on the "noncognitive" side of learning.[16] So we should begin to see a broader range of knowledge, skills, and dispositions tested, and international comparisons made.

That's one route—this ship has already left the port, so if you feel uneasy about this as I do, it may be too late to stop it now.

However, before we are tempted to go down this route, to find measurable outcomes in so many different areas, including the noncognitive, let's consider another analogy, a journey between two places—let's call them A and Z. We are at point A and want to go to point Z.

Now, there is much in the way of skills and knowledge, values, and disposition that I need in order to travel from A to Z.

Regarding skills and knowledge, if I didn't have a global positioning system (GPS), I'd need map-reading skills. I would also need knowledge of the different ways of getting from A to Z—for example, by walking, driving, or taking a train, plane, or bus. If I decided to take a train, plane, or bus, then I would need the knowledge and skill of being able to understand timetables and/or make reservations. If driving was the best way of getting to Z, then I would need knowledge and skill to drive safely. It doesn't take a lot of imagination to list further skills, knowledge, and dispositions that I would need: Clearly I have to want to get to Z from A. I have to want it enough that I arrive early enough to be in time to catch my "plane, train, or automobile." If I'm driving, I have to want to be able to learn to drive, have the motivation and perseverance to take my lessons, and pass my test, and so on and so forth.

Now suppose someone says he wants to measure whether I went from A to Z. Further suppose that he singles out for testing some of the skills and types of knowledge required to make the trip. Would these enable him to measure whether I'd gone from A to Z? Clearly not. The straightforward way of measuring whether I have traveled from A to Z is to check whether I am indeed at Z.

What we do in our international assessments is the equivalent of seeing if children have their map-reading and timetable skills and not whether they made it to point Z. Many people have criticized this, saying it's not what education is about. They've been campaigning for further tests, such as tests of creativity or personality, and it looks like they've gotten their way with the new tests from the OECD. But surely the most appropriate measure of whether we've gotten to Z remains to look at Z itself. Do we have a society that is flourishing in desirable ways (point Z)? If so, then *this should be enough.* Instead of measuring the journey, what is taught in schooling, we could measure the destination, the goal of education.

A major problem is that international measures like PISA serve to restrict and constrain to a very narrow band the kinds of innovations and experimentation that can be allowed within any public education system. A visionary innovator like Sir Ken Robinson knows that any politicians interested in his approach to transforming education must continually look over their shoulder at their educational system's PISA performance. Can they risk allowing any innovation that might not lead to improvement in their standing on PISA? Can they risk encouraging any innovation that could lead to a decline, heaven forbid? No, because the media and social media will be on their government like a shot if stagnation or decline is the result. Far better to focus on classroom reform that, in effect, teaches to the test. That way, you'll gain accolades and acclaim for your educational progress on PISA.

Look at this from the perspective of an educational visionary *who believes that what he has to offer can change society for the better.* Many educational visionaries believe this. They want to improve employability or economic productivity; they want a better democracy, to strengthen the rule of law, to improve family life, or to focus on other ways that will lead to greater human happiness and flourishing. These are all possible goals of education. But the question that will be asked is this: Will they lead to improvements in mathematical literacy scores on international assessments? If they're not sure, then politicians are unlikely to adopt their ideas.

Do we want to inhibit those who want education to improve society by imposing this constraint on them? What would it matter if their educational transformations *did not* lead to an improvement in mathematics scores but if they *did* lead to improvements in society at large? The goals of education are about human flourishing in adult life, not about classroom mathematics scores.

Let's be clear, I'm not saying that this is the greatest obstacle to an educational visionary/entrepreneur. But it's an additional constraint added to all the obstacles already listed in the previous chapters. It's a further nail—not necessarily the largest or most significant—in the coffin of educational innovation.

It's also clear to me that, under a system of educational freedom, where governments were not in control of the framework of education, there could be some use for standardized assessments. Under a system of educational freedom, it could be that testing agencies emerged to show how well individual school chains or groupings were doing, on carefully defined metrics, in the same way that we outlined the value for a proximate measurement model for individual students along the lines of judo belts or piano grades.

Presumably, schools following the methods and ideas of someone like Sir Ken Robinson would *not* be convinced of the value of these international assessments, and so wouldn't seek to apply them. Some of the systems like Montessori or Steiner schools, or schools like Summerhill, or schools using project-based learning (or, as we will later see, self-organized learning environments) may not want to subject their children to international standardized assessments. They might not worry if mathematical literacy stagnates. They can legitimately argue that this is not their purpose. They are about improving society and so can eschew these narrow measures of progress. On the other hand, another type of chain—for instance, Bridge International Academies— might find them worthwhile, to show how they were doing compared with similar school chains in other parts of the world. The key is that there would be choice and competition in this area too.

Toward a New Measure of Education

In *Most Likely to Succeed*, Tony Wagner and Ted Dintersmith express their skepticism of international standardized testing: "Let Singapore, Shanghai, and South Korea drill the hell out of their kids and deal with off-the-chart dysfunction and the workforce of robotic clones that ensues. In a world that increasingly values the core innovative strengths of our nation, it is pure folly to obsess about the global standardized test race."[17] America, they say, is far ahead of other countries in so many ways, it's not sensible to focus on mathematics scores on international assessments. The authors give a chart showing the number of Nobel Prizes; one hundred most innovative companies and patents (over the last five years); and how the United States, China, Japan, India, and Korea fare on these measures. In each case, the United States is far ahead. It's far ahead on these measures but far behind most of the other countries on PISA.

I want to take this idea further. Here, I will explore how a measure could be constructed that reflected the aims or goals of education. I'm sketching out one possible approach here; others can take it and refine it (or find some better approach altogether). I am following Ian Morris's method in *Why the West Rules—for Now*, where he proposes a new measure of social development, to effect comparisons between nations. I am using his method to propose a new measure of education, based on the aims of education, that will enable comparisons to be made between nations in terms of the efficacy of their educational systems, and that will not fall down the rabbit hole of thinking that this means comparing how well kids do on international mathematics tests.

Morris suggests six criteria for each dimension or trait to be included in the measure. Traits must be:

1. Relevant.
2. Culture independent.
3. Independent of one another.
4. Adequately documented—there must be existing independent databases available on them.
5. Reliable.
6. Convenient—"the harder it is to get evidence for something or the longer it takes to calculate the results, the less useful that trait is."[18]

These seem to be reasonable criteria that I've followed here. Adapting the definitions of Lant Pritchett and Sir Ken Robinson given above, I suggest that a new measure of education could have four dimensions or traits that could adequately summarize and articulate the goals of education. These involve equipping children to flourish in the following:

- The economy
- Democracy
- Communities and societies
- Family life

My aim is extremely modest here: to construct a simple one-off index to compare countries in a single moment of time, so I've used data as close as possible to 2015. A more sophisticated version could offer data over time, to enable one to compare countries longitudinally, and it would of course consider the variables and indicators more carefully than I've been able to do here.

Let's take each of these dimensions in turn. The idea of education for enhancing economic growth is a basic ideal that is widely accepted by politicians and policy makers, although the discussion of signaling in an earlier chapter suggests that what is important is economic productivity. So I've used GDP (at purchasing power parity) *per hour worked*, a standard measure of worker productivity.[19] The data available on this are more limited than on other standard measures such as GDP per capita, which is a slight disadvantage, but there are enough countries included to explore interesting comparisons.

Second, we have the notion of one of education's goals as a flourishing democracy. This again is widely accepted as an aim of education. For some philosophers of education, such as John Dewey, it was a major goal; for most others it is seen as something important. There are widely accepted measures of democracy that we can use. Here I use the Economist Intelligence Unit's democracy index.[20]

Third, education should lead to flourishing communities and societies. It's harder to find a measure that will satisfy Morris's six conditions here. But it might be easier if we flip it over and ask, what would be indicators of societies that are *not* flourishing? Presumably, high rates of crime would be one strong measure. If there is crime in society, particularly violent crime, then it is hard to see how individuals can be flourishing in society. Reduction of crime was also held up to be one of the earliest externalities of education by economists,[21] and it was certainly seen by many of the promoters of a more educated society as an important reason for its promotion. There are various indicators available; I've used the crowdsourced global database Numbeo on crime rankings by country for our point of reference here.[22]

Fourth, education should lead to flourishing family life. We could take a measure of family breakdown here, but this could be controversial—many argue that families are changing and that new types of families are emerging (including through the breakdown of the traditional family) that are just as capable of supplying flourishing families as the ones of old. Rather than get into any of this controversy here, perhaps it would be much simpler to note that for families to flourish, they need flourishing individuals, and one strong measure of flourishing is human happiness. Conversely, people's satisfaction in their family relationships is one of the key inputs into their awareness of their own happiness. There are several measures of happiness that we could use. Alternatively, we could ask, what would be a key indicator of individuals who are not flourishing (and so not flourishing families)? One measure could be suicide. Using either of these indicators, happiness or suicide, leads to remarkably similar results (obviously one is a positive indicator, the other negative). Below, I use the age-standardized indicator of suicide from the World Health Organization.[23]

These four could be enough, but there is one goal of education that seems to be missing from this list—that is, the way that education can lead to new discoveries, creativity, and so on. There are many indicators that one could use here. Initially I thought that the Nobel Prizes would be an obvious measure. However, after doing calculations of Nobel Prizes awarded per capita, I realized that Sweden is awarded a higher number of Nobel Prizes per capita than any other country, closely followed by its neighbors Norway and Denmark. Far be it from me to say this, but there might be some Scandinavian bias in this indicator.

Another indicator could be citations of scientific papers published. However, this brings in two problems. First, people could be included in a country's output if they've been schooled somewhere else but are currently employed by, say, an American or British university. So, it would be unfair to include citations to their publications as a measure of the output of American or British education. A second shortcoming might be the advantage that the English language gives to certain countries, which, again, could bias the results. Instead, I've gone with a measure that has some, albeit limited, potential to reflect creativity and scientific and technological understanding—the applications for patents. Usefully, data from the World Bank Development Indicators show application for patents by *residents* of a country,[24] which may help mitigate in part the problem noted above for scientific paper citations and universities (residents too could have been educated elsewhere, so this is of course not a foolproof indicator).

From these five measures, I have constructed a new measure of education. These five indicators can be used to rank societies in terms of the success or lack thereof of their education systems at meeting the *goals* of education. I make no grand claims for it, apart from putting it forward to show an alternative way of thinking about the efficacy or lack thereof of a country's education system. It's designed to show how countries fare in terms of realizing the goals of education, the destination of education, rather than focusing on the journey to get there.

I weight each of these five criteria equally—as did Morris, as "no obvious reason appeared for giving one any more weight than another."[25] Following Morris's method, I set 1,000 points as the highest possible educational achievement for that year, and divide that equally between the five traits, so each is marked out of a possible 200 points.

Take the suicide index. Jamaica ranks highest, in that it has the lowest recorded number of suicides, with 1.4 suicides per 100,000 people. So, Jamaica gets the full 200 points. This gives the calculation that 1 point is 1.4 divided by 200. For every other nation's score, then (as this is an inverse measure), its score is 1.4 divided by the nation's suicide rate, multiplied by 200. This gives the points in the suicide column of Table 10.2.

The labor productivity index is in the next pair of columns. Here Norway had the highest labor productivity, with a GDP per hour of US$75.18 (at purchasing power parity). Norway thus gets 200 points here. For every other country, we divide their GDP per hour by 75.18, and multiply by 200, to give the country points as in the table.

For the patents index, South Korea ranked highest, so gains 200 points. Scores for each other country are divided by 3.2811 and multiplied by 200 to give the points in the table.

Norway ranked highest for democracy, with 9.93 points on the *Economist*'s democracy index. Norway gets the full 200 points. Every other country score is divided by 9.93 and multiplied by 200 to give the points in the table.

Finally, for crime, Japan had the lowest crime rate, with 13.1 on the index. Japan gets the full 200 points, and other countries' points are calculated in the same way as for suicides, as this also is an inverse indicator.

The results are shown in Table 10.2.

The underlying point of this new measure of education key is this: If we want to measure a country's success at education, then we should look at outcomes concerning the goals and aims of education, not some part of the schooling process (such as learning of mathematics, language, science) that may or may not be relevant to these goals of education.

What does our table show? Our new top ten features the following countries:

1. Japan
2. South Korea
3. Norway
4. Luxembourg
5. Denmark
6. Austria
7. Switzerland
8. United States
9. Netherlands
10. Canada

For what it's worth, this feels to me more intuitively satisfactory than the PISA rankings. In PISA, the United States is lagging down in 40th place, despite being the world's most successful and vibrant economy. Now, it's firmly in the top 10, alongside countries one might expect to be there. Singapore is no longer on top as it is in the PISA rankings, but it is in the top 20, alongside the United Kingdom and Finland. And Poland, which we saw earlier was easily beating the United States in the PISA rankings, is now down near the bottom of the top 40.

What difference does this alternative measure of education make? Now, with PISA and other rankings, politicians are keen to improve their country's

Table 10.2. A New Measure of Education, Top Forty Places

Country	Suicides per 100,000 people	Points (Jamaica = 200)	GDP (PPP) per hour	Points (Norway = 200)	Patents (residents) per capita	Points (S. Korea = 200)
Japan	15.4	18.18	43.77	116.44	2.0226	123.29
South Korea	24.1	11.62	32.31	85.95	3.2811	200.00
Norway	9.3	30.11	75.18	200.00	0.2217	13.52
Luxembourg	8.5	32.94	73.22	194.79	0.2259	13.77
Denmark	9.1	30.77	55.75	148.31	0.2570	15.67
Austria	11.7	23.93	54.83	145.86	0.2541	15.49
Switzerland	10.7	26.17	49.88	132.69	0.1775	10.82
United States	12.6	22.22	67.32	179.09	0.9012	54.94
Netherlands	9.4	29.79	60.06	159.78	0.1303	7.94
Germany	9.1	30.77	57.36	152.59	0.5799	35.35
Iceland	11.8	23.73	50.01	133.04	0.1211	7.38
Finland	14.2	19.72	48.79	129.80	0.2351	14.33
Singapore	8.6	32.56	41.46	110.30	0.2654	16.18
Australia	10.4	26.92	55.87	148.63	0.0963	5.87
Sweden	12.7	22.05	55.28	147.06	0.2087	12.72
Jamaica	1.4	200.00	12.95	34.45	0.0024	0.15
Ireland	11.1	25.23	56.05	149.11	0.0532	3.24
Spain	6.0	46.67	49.59	131.92	0.0603	3.68
United Kingdom	7.4	37.84	51.38	136.69	0.2273	13.86
Canada	10.4	26.92	50.29	133.79	0.1190	7.25
France	12.3	22.76	59.24	157.60	0.2219	13.53
Malta	5.0	56.00	36.02	95.82	0.0210	1.28
Italy	5.4	51.85	45.04	119.82	0.1445	8.81
Cyprus	3.9	71.79	31.18	82.95	0.0052	0.32
Israel	5.4	51.85	38.99	103.72	0.1593	9.71
Belgium	16.1	17.39	60.98	162.22	0.0841	5.12
Greece	3.2	87.50	32.77	87.18	0.0490	2.99
New Zealand	12.3	22.76	36.83	97.98	0.2566	15.64
Hong Kong SAR, China	12.3	22.76	41.30	109.87	0.0330	2.01
Slovenia	15.0	18.67	39.78	105.83	0.0000	0.00
Estonia	14.9	18.79	23.50	62.52	0.0228	1.39
Czech Republic	10.6	26.42	31.23	83.08	0.0830	5.06
Slovakia	9.9	28.28	33.44	88.96	0.0419	2.56
Portugal	8.5	32.94	27.23	72.44	0.0888	5.41
Trinidad and Tobago	13.2	21.21	40.04	106.52	0.0022	0.13
Lithuania	26.1	10.73	27.53	73.24	0.0344	2.10
Poland	18.5	15.14	25.81	68.66	0.1222	7.45
Romania	9.2	30.43	15.46	41.13	0.0491	2.99
Chile	9.1	30.77	19.55	52.01	0.0249	1.52
Latvia	17.4	16.09	21.15	56.26	0.0683	4.16

Source: Author's team analysis.

Country	Democracy Index (Economist)	Points (Norway = 200)	Crime Index	Points (Japan = 200)	Measure of Education	Rank
Japan	7.99	160.93	13.10	200.00	618.84	1
South Korea	7.92	159.52	35.83	73.12	530.21	2
Norway	9.93	200.00	43.33	60.47	504.09	3
Luxembourg	8.81	177.44	32.12	81.57	500.51	4
Denmark	9.20	185.30	22.02	118.98	499.03	5
Austria	8.41	169.39	20.41	128.37	483.04	6
Switzerland	9.09	183.08	21.76	120.40	473.17	7
United States	7.98	160.73	49.58	52.84	469.82	8
Netherlands	8.80	177.24	28.94	90.53	465.28	9
Germany	8.63	173.82	36.65	71.49	464.02	10
Iceland	9.50	191.34	24.49	106.98	462.47	11
Finland	9.03	181.87	23.70	110.55	456.27	12
Singapore	6.38	128.50	16.23	161.43	448.96	13
Australia	9.01	181.47	42.55	61.57	424.47	14
Sweden	9.39	189.12	49.26	53.19	424.14	15
Jamaica	7.39	148.84	66.87	39.18	422.62	16
Ireland	9.15	184.29	43.82	59.79	421.66	17
Spain	8.30	167.17	36.74	71.31	420.75	18
United Kingdom	8.36	168.38	41.20	63.59	420.35	19
Canada	9.15	184.29	39.28	66.70	418.95	20
France	7.92	159.52	45.29	57.85	411.25	21
Malta	8.39	168.98	31.93	82.05	404.14	22
Italy	7.98	160.73	44.53	58.84	400.04	23
Cyprus	7.65	154.08	30.18	86.81	395.95	24
Israel	7.85	158.11	36.90	71.00	394.40	25
Belgium	7.77	156.50	42.17	62.13	390.97	26
Greece	7.23	145.62	39.07	67.06	390.34	27
New Zealand	9.26	186.51	39.15	66.92	389.81	28
Hong Kong SAR, China	6.42	129.31	20.90	125.36	389.31	29
Slovenia	7.51	151.26	24.71	106.03	381.78	30
Estonia	7.85	158.11	20.83	125.78	366.59	31
Czech Republic	7.82	157.50	28.81	90.94	363.00	32
Slovakia	7.29	146.83	30.15	86.90	353.52	33
Portugal	7.86	158.31	34.54	75.85	344.95	34
Trinidad and Tobago	7.10	143.00	72.22	36.28	307.14	35
Lithuania	7.47	150.45	37.59	69.70	306.22	36
Poland	6.83	137.56	36.23	72.32	301.12	37
Romania	6.62	133.33	29.04	90.22	298.11	38
Chile	7.78	156.70	46.48	56.37	297.36	39
Latvia	7.31	147.23	36.89	71.02	294.77	40

rankings, because these are thought important. But the temptation is to teach to the test, to improve students' math or reading scores; educational innovation is thus likely to be severely curtailed. Governments try to follow one of the best-performing countries (like Finland or Singapore) and think they have to have an egalitarian system with no homework (like Finland) or perhaps a fully selective system (like Singapore—although curiously, commentators such as those at the BBC tend to ignore this fact, as it goes against their egalitarian assumptions[26]). Whatever they do, they aim to do something within schooling that looks at ways of improving their scores in mathematics, science, and language. The framework of education that we find ourselves in—the framework created by PISA—constrains us to move in certain directions.

But improving scores in mathematics, science, and language is not what education is for. It's for human flourishing, in all the ways we've outlined. What do scores in mathematics, science, and language contribute to human flourishing? The simple fact is, *we don't know*. They might have a lot to do with it, or they might have remarkably little. Given the current situation, where politicians obsess about these international scores, we can't experiment and innovate to find out, because it's just taken as a given that school mathematics and science are important.

That's where any strengths of this new measure of education come in. Whereas the PISA-type model constrains us to seek educational improvements within the narrow confines of improving math, science, and language scores, the new measure of education liberates us to ask: *In what ways can the education system be improved to enhance human flourishing?* The new measure of education allows us to think rationally about what it is that will lead to enhanced human flourishing, and to think of ways in which the education system could be improved to encourage this.

Government frameworks of education compel us to think of schooling in very narrow terms: schooling should be about mathematics and science. Any innovation in education has to fit into that narrow framework. But, to state the obvious, the curriculum and assessment systems we have were not scientifically created as the best ways to achieve human flourishing. They came about because of many incidental reasons, typically during the nineteenth century, mixing the desire for a classical education with the needs of a civil service engaged in subduing native populations, combining it somehow with the needs of the mass of the population that was typically going to work in factories.

This curriculum and assessment system initially emerged through a self-organizing system, at least in part, but was then set in stone by government, as governments took control of the framework of education. This, then, made it largely impossible to change, because of the types of reasons given in a previous chapter when we looked at the difficulties facing Sir Ken Robinson's desired changes. So, what we're left with today is a system of curriculum and assessment that may have little to do with human flourishing in the twenty-first century.

We simply don't know. We don't know because it's too hard for anyone, any visionary or entrepreneur, to try out new ways of learning, as the government will measure any innovation against the standards it has already set in stone—writ large in the international assessments. By using alternative ways of measuring educational systems, we can be free to think of educational alternatives that can really improve the aims of education—that is, can improve human flourishing.

PART THREE

Off to America

IN PART I, we explored the extraordinary revolution of low-cost private schools taking place across developing countries, in sub-Saharan Africa, Asia, and Latin America. Low-cost private schools are a grassroots movement, delivering education for the people outside of state funding or provision. This emancipated education we saw to be ubiquitous, serving even the most difficult nations and the most difficult places within them. It is affordable, even to those in poverty, and not much more expensive to parents than sending children to public schools. It is of higher quality and better value for money. It is fair to girls and other disadvantaged groups, and is the clear preference for parents, who make informed choices about it.

But this emancipated education still has one shortcoming. This is where we began part 2. The shortcoming was because of government control of the framework of education. With governments in control of the framework—especially the curriculum and assessment systems—there was a limit to how far private initiatives could go. Yes, private schools could deliver what was required much more efficiently and effectively than the state. But government control of the framework of education meant that private schools were not free to innovate and explore new ways of motivating children and young people. In part 2, we suggested ways of prying government control away, through the individual actions of entrepreneurs and investors.

While part 1 was firmly rooted in evidence, part 2 was more speculative about what could be achieved if we were able to emancipate education from government control of the framework of education. Next, in part 3, we want to explore what implications the discussion of part 1, tempered by our observations of part 2, has for America and Britain (these two countries as proxies for other Western countries, such as Canada, Australia, New Zealand, and most European countries). We'll be taking as assumptions here the observations made about the desirability of moving away from state intervention in education and ask: If we want to move away from public education, how might we best go about doing that?[1]

In part 3, there will be four approaches. First, we'll squarely address the criticism by the influential social scientist Charles Murray, who appears unsympathetic to the notion that education, especially for the most disadvantaged, can be substantially improved. The argument will be used to illustrate what I call the "absurd" and "illogical" approaches we have in education systems today. Implicit is that these approaches have arisen because of state education; if we want to move toward emancipated education, these difficulties will have to be dealt with, and *can* be dealt with. These absurd and illogical approaches are linked to some of the issues we've raised in part 2 about motivation and differentiation.

Second, we'll look at the possibility that some sympathetic readers might have in mind, that if we want to move toward the kind of educational emancipation proposed, then we need educational reforms like school vouchers to get there. I suggest that this approach may be mistaken. But exploring it does bring in some helpful discussion of the argument of the great economist Milton Friedman for vouchers and, crucially, how and why he changed his mind. This will take us on an excursion back in time, to look at the secret history of education without the state.

Third, we'll explore whether the kind of revolution in education away from the state that we've seen happening in developing countries could possibly occur in America too. This leads us to sketch a potential business model for a chain of low-cost private schools for America.

Finally, as the argument set up at the beginning of the book concerned education as a self-organizing system, we'll focus on one of the foremost proponents of this idea, Sugata Mitra. We'll use his work to reinforce our notion of education as a spontaneous order, and to understand exactly what implications this will have for the way it develops in the future of learning.

11

Some Problems with American Education

IF CHARLES MURRAY were to read any of this book, he would dismiss it as naïve educational romanticism. Murray is one of the most important social scientists in America today, so I feel obliged to address the criticisms that he'd likely level against this work. Best known for his works of incisive social commentary, including *Losing Ground*, *The Bell Curve*, and *Coming Apart*, Murray made his most significant contribution to the education debate with his treatise *Real Education*.

I agree with much of what Murray writes on education. For instance, I believe he is correct about the responsibilities of the liberal elite and the appropriate education for them. I think he's correct when he writes about the way we overrate college education and neglect opportunities for those who would benefit better from alternatives. I have little problem with his discussion of IQ or cognitive ability, which many do find a stumbling block.

I disagree with him, however, on his understanding of how bad things are, in general, in public education, especially the way it caters to children and young people of lower cognitive ability. He thinks public education can't be much improved in this regard; it's almost as good as it can be. On the contrary, I believe that we are stuck in the dark ages of educational provision—because governments set in stone what was on offer when they took over a century or more ago. What was provided then may have been appropriate for the time. But it is singularly inappropriate for the present. Great improvements are possible, including for those of lower cognitive ability too.

Murray is disdainful of people who are bedeviled by a destructive "educational romanticism."[1] He writes, "One source of the romanticism is the belief that American schools are so bad that there's lots of room for improvement for all students, including those in the lower half of the distribution."[2] On the contrary, he says, "The silence about differences in intellectual ability on educational topics that scream for their discussion is astonishing. It amounts to living a lie."[3] People like me, educational romantics, are living a lie, says Murray, because we ignore the fact that "low intellectual ability" is "the reason why some students don't perform at grade level."[4]

I, for one, certainly do not ignore the possibility that intellectual ability is important for educational success. Indeed, I had my first dalliance with public controversy when I wrote in support of Murray's *The Bell Curve* back in 1994, defending the idea that children's cognitive ability can affect so many things in their lives, and that to ignore this is to ignore an important dimension of education.[5]

But this belief does not stop me from thinking that Murray is missing something important about the state of American schools—and schools of most every nation. They *are* "so bad that there's room for improvement" for all. But perhaps their faults are fundamental, affecting all they try to do, as I shall try to explain in this chapter.

Half of the Children Are Below Average

Murray argues that educational romantics refuse to accept that differences in educationally relevant abilities between children lead to differences in outcomes in schools. Murray's is a clever argument, skillfully building on Harvard professor Howard Gardner's classification of seven or eight "multiple intelligences." Murray would normally find Gardner's approach unpalatable, but instead of making this explicit, he shows that only a couple of Gardner's multiple intelligences are relevant to academic and job performance. These are the areas that we would normally have called "cognitive ability" or "intelligence," as measurable by IQ tests.

Many educationalists find Murray's position here controversial; I'm going to sidestep this controversy, because whatever your views on the argument, in the end the practical implications remain the same: not many would dispute that academic ability varies and that half of the children are below average. We don't live in an educational Lake Wobegon. The key question, then, is whether it is, as Murray claims, educational romanticism to suppose that schools can do better, much better, for those children who are currently left behind.

Murray gives two key examples to illustrate the "devastating" effect that educational romantics have on schooling. He is fundamentally mistaken on both.

> Example 1: "The nine-year-old who has trouble sounding out simple words and his classmate who is reading *A Tale of Two Cities* for fun sit in the same classroom day after miserable day, the one so frustrated by tasks he cannot do and the other so bored that both are near tears."
>
> Example 2: "The fifteen-year-old who cannot make sense of algebra but has an almost mystical knack with machines is told to stick with the college prep track, because to be a success in life he must go to college and get a BA."[6]

These two examples clearly have something to do with two of the "problems in search of a solution" that we discussed in part 2. The first is about differentiation, the second about motivation. So, the discussion here will supplement the earlier discussion and take it further. We must also be aware that we have discussed how the curriculum, structure, and organization of education could change under conditions of educational freedom.

Murray's argument depends on an important distinction. There are two types of differences in abilities within a random selection of the population, he says, "differences in degree, and differences in kind."[7] In other areas of our lives, he thinks this should be obvious. For example, while most of us can manage a basic forward roll or cartwheel, the ability to do a "somersault with a full twist off a pommel horse" is simply out of reach for most of us, no matter how much practice we might put in.[8] Thus, there is a difference *in kind* between the abilities of the advanced gymnast and ordinary people.

In areas like gymnastics, we take this distinction for granted, Murray says. But for those abilities learned at school, particularly mathematics and language, we somehow become blinkered. Again, says Murray, the differences that emerge between children are differences *in kind*, not degree—and to think otherwise is part of the trap that educational romantics fall into. For mathematics, getting children to do a set of calculus questions would be an effective way of showing this: "The resulting scores would not look like a bell curve. For a sizeable proportion of children, the scores ... would be zero. Grasping calculus requires a certain level of logical-mathematical ability. Children below that level will never learn calculus, no matter how hard they study."[9] This is a difference in kind, just like in the gymnastics example.

The same is true of linguistic ability. Everyone *can* be taught to read, Murray agrees. But think of how various levels—say the 90th and 20th percentiles—of a high school class would react to a discussion of *Macbeth*. Again, this would show a "difference in kind" rather than a "difference in degree": "Those at the 20th percentile will completely fail to understand the text in the same way that someone at the 20th percentile of bodily-kinesthetic ability will completely fail to do a somersault with a full twist." Those at the 90th percentile, on the other hand, will be able to engage fluently with the text. In short, "Many of the things that high-ability students can do are different in kind from the things that low-ability students can do. *That's a fact*, and the design of every aspect of education needs to keep it in mind."[10]

To illustrate these "facts," Murray gives several examples from the National Assessment of Educational Progress (NAEP), the US national testing system, which incidentally was influential on international tests such as PISA. I think it's worth looking at these examples in greater detail, for they reveal the shortcomings of Murray's argument; he believes they show deficiencies in educational ability. For me, they show real deficiencies in American schooling, deficiencies that are unlikely to be addressed until the framework of education is emancipated from government.

For Murray, the answers to NAEP questions demonstrate that "children in the lower half of the distribution are just not smart enough to read or calculate at a level of fluency that most of the rest of us take for granted." Even worse, those in the "bottom third ... are just not smart enough to become literate or numerate in more than a rudimentary sense."[11]

Let's look at one of the English questions first. Children have to read a short passage and answer a question on it. Here is the passage:

The Anasazi made beautiful pottery, turquoise jewelry, fine sashes of woven hair, and baskets woven tightly enough to hold water. They lived by hunting and by growing corn and squash. Their way of life went on peacefully for several hundred years. Then around 1200 AD something strange happened, for which the reasons are not clear.[12]

The question is, "The Anasazi's life before 1200 AD was portrayed by the author as being:

A. dangerous and warlike

B. busy and exciting

C. difficult and dreary

D. productive and peaceful."[13]

Murray tells us that 41 percent of eighth graders did not choose *D*, the correct answer, so around 55 percent didn't know what the correct answer was.[14] (This higher percentage he derives from the assumption that some may have guessed, so we need to adjust the actual percentage answering incorrectly.[15])

This, for Murray, shows how dire is the lack of ability of American eighth graders: "Why weren't students able to answer the question about the Anasazi?" he asks. All the hints and clues are there—the word *peaceful* is used in the sentence before the one mentioning "1200 AD," and the previous sentence "talks about the Anasazi making things, obviously related to the meaning of *productive.*"[16] The problem is, he says, this is an example of needing logical-mathematic understanding as well as linguistic understanding and making "inferential leaps" about the words read.[17]

He asks us to put ourselves "in the position of the teacher. How does one teach a child to make inferential leaps? Drilling in vocabulary will not help. Diagramming sentences will not help. The skills that the child must master do not involve learning words or the mechanics of reading but putting two and two together in novel settings."[18]

So, it is inappropriate to blame public schools and public-school teachers for the low level of language ability as revealed by the answers to this question. Don't blame public schools and their teachers because the "wrong answers reflect nothing more complicated than low academic ability."[19]

I have two problems with this example. First, I must admit that I sympathize with the students who got this question "wrong." Examiners at the NAEP, English teachers, and Charles Murray all think that *D* is the only correct answer here. But is it really? Yes, the first sentence about making pottery, and so on, might signify productivity, and, yes, the word *peacefully* is used in the third sentence. But what about hunting? Hunting, by my definition, is not a peaceful activity, neither to the animals hunted nor to those engaged in the hunting; it is, on the other hand, one fraught with danger and could also be described in some ways as "warlike." So not only does the hunting part seem to undermine the possibility of *D* as the correct answer, but also it would suggest answer *A* (dangerous and warlike) as fitting the bill, at least if you take into account the hunting activity, for which I see no reason not to.

For, importantly, the question is not asking us for the *best fit*, for the closest approximation, of what life for the Anasazi was like according to the author (however one could measure that, I'm not sure), but simply asking how Anasazi life is portrayed. Inter alia, a student answering *A* could legitimately say, the author portrays the life of the Anasazi as being dangerous and warlike. *A* is a correct answer.

What about *B*? Some might find the idea of making pottery and the like "busy and exciting," while I would describe the same activities as "difficult and dreary." So, in my view both *B* and *C* are also possible correct answers.

In other words, *each* of the given answers is conceivably correct.

The only way in my view that *D* could be seen as the only correct answer is if the question had asked, "The Anasazi's life before 1200 AD was portrayed *most closely* by the author as being …" Even then, it all depends how one weights the different activities, which is not clear from the text. If hunting occupied most men's time, say, then clearly *D* would not be the correct answer, even with this more closely constrained question.

Rather than showing low achievement, for me this question illustrates something about the misuse of the authority of educators. It's relevant to the discussion that we had in chapter 7 about the gatekeepers of education. A common problem that I've often come across when conducting teacher training in settings as varied as England, Honduras, Ghana, and India is that when questioning pupils, teachers often have a particular answer in mind, and students have to spend time guessing which answer the teacher has in mind. I've done the same myself as a teacher. The teacher believes that the answer he has in mind is the only correct answer, but it might not be. Murray's NAEP example seems to be a painful illustration of precisely the same problem.

The teachers setting the exam knew that the answer was *D* and wanted the children to guess what was in their heads. But, unfortunately, their question had many other possible answers.

Motivation, Motivation, Motivation

This is *one* problem with the Anasazi example given. But it is not the most important objection to challenge Murray's conclusion that this is all to do with low ability. This next consideration is generalizable to *all* questions in the NAEP and similar tests.

Ever since John Locke first wrote about this in the late seventeenth century, we've known that motivation is important for learning, and compulsion can hinder it: "Where there is no desire, there will be no industry," Locke writes. "None of the things they are to learn should ever be made a burden to them, or imposed on them as a task."[20] This consideration builds on the discussion we had concerning Sir Ken Robinson's ideas, where we looked at ways in which children and young people could be motivated to learn but that are not within the current public educational framework.

What is the motivation for eighth-grade students (that is, for thirteen-to-fourteen-year-old children) to do their best to answer NAEP test questions? (And, of course, then we must ask what motivates these children to learn anything in school in the first place, something we discussed earlier.)

First, these thirteen- and fourteen-year-olds may not want to be in school; it is compulsory after all, and compulsory schooling is likely to be a turnoff to many young adolescents, who are more interested in other areas of life. Second, their school has been selected to take part in these tests, so they've been given this extra burden of work. They might want to work hard to show themselves, their teachers, and their school in the best possible light. Alternatively, having heard that their answer sheets are anonymized, they might want to show their teachers and school in a bad light, just for a laugh.

Children might not want to put much effort into this extra, unwanted work. It's not, after all, showing how well they are doing as individuals. Indeed, a recent *Economist* article even suggested that the reason for differences for the achievement gap between American and Chinese pupils might be precisely because American children can't be bothered to make the effort on international or national tests like this, whereas Chinese students just get on with what's demanded of them. (The *Economist* had a playful homophonic way of expressing the American kids' approach: "Can't Be Asked" was its headline.[21])

Indeed, the Anasazi question itself raises doubts about motivation: some youngsters might see this decontextualized question about the Anasazi and think that they are not interested in them, whoever they are. They might have other things on their mind, as thirteen- and fourteen-year-olds, and so not be particularly interested in pursuing silly questions like this, deducing what answer the teacher/examiner wants them to guess.

Conversely, someone who had heard of the Anasazi might think the question so trivial that, again, it was not worth answering. Some of these youngsters may have read Erich von Däniken's *Chariots of the Gods?*, which explicitly mentions the Anasazi and suggests that something very strange did happen to them around 1200 AD—that they completely vanished off the face of the earth.[22] The point is, even for someone who was interested in the Anasazi, why would one want to answer this dreary question about how they lived? Surely, there are many other things of greater interest to discuss about them.

Now we come back to Murray's two examples highlighted at the beginning of this chapter. Might it be the issue of motivation that is raised in his example of "the fifteen-year-old who cannot make sense of algebra but has an almost mystical knack with machines"?

What Murray overlooks is that this person's "mystical knack" may be nothing more than his fascination with machines. Such motivation, even for the youngster that Murray is focusing on, could perhaps be equally applied to schoolwork, if only it was made more motivating and engaging, or if the curriculum had been presented to the young man as something relevant, rewarding, or appropriate for him to learn. We simply don't know. Murray wants to say that the child's lack of interest in schoolwork shows his lack of intelligence; equally, it could show the way the public schooling system has failed to engage him.

As a teenager, I went to a British comprehensive (that is, nonselective) school in east Bristol. I was one of the kids who excelled at mathematics, at least until I got so bored with the teaching that did not distinguish between various levels of ability that I, too, dropped out. There were boys in the class who were totally left behind. But I was struck by how, during recess, these same boys had an "almost mystical knack" for calculating betting odds on soccer matches and horse racing, which involved concepts of probability that we'd never been taught—and were never going to be taught. It was also striking that the boys who couldn't learn any facts from history or geography for their school tests and therefore failed them could recite whole teams of soccer players, present and past, and knew all their clubs' standings and positions over the years. I couldn't recite any of these things, lacking motivation to do so. I don't think my failure to do so revealed my lack of intelligence, only my lack of motivation. Could the students' failure at history and geography be put down to the same lack of motivation?

In other words, far from showing differences in cognitive ability that can't be overcome, the shortcomings in answers to these questions could equally show that there is something wrong with public schooling. Those creating the framework of public schooling don't feel responsible for motivating children to learn or to focus learning on the various learning needs of the student—what educators call *differentiating learning.* In any case, the questions given are sometimes no more than the tiresome guessing of what a teacher wants to hear from you, inane and uninteresting to boot. (I had a similar response when I read all of Caplan's depressing examples in *The Case against Education,* listed in chapter 6, where he shows how the American public retains so little knowledge and understanding of practically everything, from history and civics to science and languages. Is it because people simply can't retain this stuff from school? Or is it more likely that the way we learn in school is so unmotivating that we never engage in the first place?)

The issue of motivation is not just about the curriculum. It also concerns the very structure and organization of compulsory schooling, which often can seem more like a demotivating prison to children than a place of liberating learning. A recent BBC documentary series illustrated this well.[23] One of the schools was what in America might seem a typical middle-of-the-road middle and high school. It was not in a bad area. There was no serious crime happening, no knife crime, no guns, no violence. But every lesson that was observed was marred by petty, low-level disruption. You could almost call it petty bickering between the teachers and a small number of the students. There was continuous sniping from the teachers at extremely minor behavioral infringements from some of the students. One eleven-year-old white working-class boy was quietly making faces at other students. These misdemeanors were not allowed to go on. The teacher, who was trying to teach his group *Hamlet*, constantly interrupted his teaching flow to reprimand this boy. This meant that there was no teaching flowing for anyone. The school had an escalation chart for misbehavior, so first the teacher gave a verbal warning, then he put the boy's name on the chart; and before we knew it, the boy was being punished *with one week away from school*. How odd it is that the punishment for misbehaving in school is one week's holiday from it.

Then there was a black girl, fifteen or sixteen years old, who had been suspended from school for three weeks and was now finding it difficult to get back into the flow of things. She had a detention after school for, again, causing low-level disruption. But her detention clashed with exam preparation classes. She was understandably upset by this and "talked back" to the teacher—and so was threatened with expulsion.

These small examples illustrate that the issue of motivation is not just about the curriculum itself—it's all about the way schools and classes are structured. The school I saw on the BBC was exactly like the school that I attended as a boy, which was why it resonated so much with me: continuous low-level disruption, which meant that those who wanted to learn couldn't. In the end, I took to cutting class to go sit in the library, where I could learn to my heart's content.

This low-level (and, of course, higher-level) disruption is a norm in schools for ordinary people. It's bound to impact motivation. It's bound to impact their performance on tests like the ones Murray is asking us to believe show that children can't learn. I repeat, I don't know that they can learn. What I do know is that it's far too early to give up on them, with what goes on in schools today as our only evidence. We need a much better counterfactual than that.

It also reveals some of the absurdity of structuring schools the way we do today, in America and Britain and elsewhere. We know there is this low level and higher level of disruption taking place. We know that it is widespread. We know that it leads to loss of learning, both for the disrupter and for the rest of the class. And yet, all our attempts at doing something about it are at best like rearranging the deck chairs on the *Titanic* as she sinks. We adopt these disciplinary measures that suspend students—like the boy described above being suspended for a week and the girl being suspended for three weeks—so, as a punishment, they miss out on the learning that is supposed to be so valuable!

But still schools are the same—high schools are often massive buildings with a thousand or more alienated students getting lost in them. It's clear that kids like the disruptive ones above preferred a smaller school setting, so why aren't these set up as a matter of course? Why the big monstrosities that are so alienating? Small schools could easily be set up. The cost of required specialized teaching (which is the reason often given for large schools) could easily be reduced through technology or through experienced teachers being peripatetic between schools.

The larger point is that today's schools are not the answer for providing motivating learning environments for ordinary students. In a normal market, that would mean we try to adjust what is going on to cater to the needs and interests of our customers. Nothing like that happens under government provision, where the solution is simply to ban kids temporarily who are disruptive. Since they miss more learning and get further behind, this guarantees their future disruptiveness too.

So, we go back to Murray's accusation that there are educational romantics living a lie that public schools "are so bad that there's lots of room for improvement for all students." I think these are far more serious problems with schools today than Murray acknowledges. They go to the root of the framework of education imposed by government—the compulsory attendance, the structure and organization of schools, the curriculum, and the national and international assessment systems that constrain and compel schools.

Incorporeal Punishment

Charles Murray also has some mathematics examples. Usefully, his first example here is precisely one of those problems that need a bit of "putting two and two together in a novel context" to be able to solve, the difficulty that he said was at the root of children not being able to answer the question about the Anasazi above:

There were 90 employees in a company last year. This year the number of employees increased by 10 percent. How many employees are in the company this year? The possible answers are: A: 9, B: 81, C: 91, D: 99, E: 100.[24]

Murray writes, "By eighth grade, it would seem that almost everyone should be able to handle a question like this. Children are taught to divide and to calculate percentages in elementary school. Dividing by ten is the easiest form of division. Dividing a whole number by ten is easier yet. Adding a one-digit number (9) to a two-digit number (90) is elementary."[25]

But 62 percent didn't get it right, so correcting for those who may have guessed, 78 percent "did not know the right answer." For Murray, this shows something patently and pitifully obvious about children's lack of ability. Children, even if they know these basic concepts, lack the "logical-mathematical ability," the putting two and two together in a novel context, and so they cannot do questions like this. For Murray, this lack of ability illustrates the differences in *kind* of ability rather than the differences in *degree*, as we noted above.

But can he jump to that conclusion so quickly? There are many reasons why children could get the wrong answer here—reasons that could have nothing to do with their *ability*:

First, children may not be motivated to answer questions like this, for the kind of reasons already provided.

Second, some children may have answered it incorrectly because they have never been taught how to break down a word problem like this. Murray implies that once you've been taught the constituent parts of the problem, then children can simply put these together and teachers don't need to teach the particularity of the word problem. That certainly seems to be the assumption that teachers and textbook writers have. A textbook from a well-known company used across Africa has a section on these kinds of word problems and gives absolutely no guidance to pupils or teachers about how to solve them. Presumably, this is because the textbook writers held the same kind of reasoning that Murray holds: children have been taught to do the constituent parts, so therefore why do they need additional explanation to do the whole?

But, on the contrary, it *is* possible to break down this kind of question and to teach the logical steps required so that those who don't get the method immediately have more of a chance of solving these problems as they go along. As a young mathematics teacher, I thought it was my responsibility and my challenge to do so, and I spent a lot of time breaking down questions like this and making them accessible to children. As someone engaged in teacher training now, in a variety of countries across the world, I see it as my responsibility again to help teachers to do this.

So maybe one reason children can't answer this type of question is simply because they have never been taught how. With some explicit teaching on the method, they could get started.

Third, and now we start to get on to the more generalizable critique of Murray's position: even if approaches to this kind of question *had* been taught in schools, think what that might mean in the context of schooling as we know it today.

What happens typically in schooling today is that a teacher teaches a topic—such as solving word problems like this—for, say, a week. Similarly, the constituent parts (fractions, decimals, and so on) will also have been taught for, again, a week or so, perhaps earlier in the year or earlier in previous years. But what if you are one of the children who, for whatever reason, has been absent during some or all of that time allotted to teaching this topic? The way that learning in schools is structured, you've probably missed your opportunity to learn that topic *forever*.

Some teachers might try to help children catch up when they've missed time, but this is typically done, if done at all, in only a perfunctory manner, so it doesn't really make much impact. And, of course, this would happen only if you'd been physically absent when the topic was taught. But suppose you were *physically* present but *emotionally* or psychologically absent, unengaged. Perhaps your parents were going through a rough patch and your mind was full of their distress. Perhaps you were falling in love, and your mind was focused only on the object of your desire. The way schooling is structured today, if you're emotionally absent, you'll never get that topic taught to you again.

Even more painfully, children who are slow, medium, and fast learners are typically taught together—precisely Murray's point raised in his first key example above, where he highlighted the problem of the nine-year-old who can't read sitting alongside someone who reads advanced texts for pleasure. Murray seems to accept that this is inevitable in public schooling, so he uses it to illustrate the problem of differentiated ability in children. It shows the *absurd* reality of public schooling, which we simply should *not* accept.

Teachers in this normal situation may be aware of fast learners getting bored and slow learners getting lost. If they are conscientious, they'll offer additional help during the lessons to those who have difficulty, and they may give some learning extension activities to the fast learners. But most teachers, let's be honest, don't do much of either. In any case, time is severely limited in the few hours during the week they are teaching the topic. So, typically they pitch their lessons somewhere in the middle and hope for the best. Crucially, once the time allocated—a few days or a week—for teaching this topic is over, *that is the end of it*. If you didn't get the topic then, you've had it. Yes, children may meet the topic again in review periods later in the year to prepare for exams, and sometimes there may be a review of topics learned in earlier years, but typically the topic will be taught in precisely the same way as before, but this time more quickly. Again, learners who didn't get it the first time are highly unlikely to be able to understand it the next time they meet it.

So, what happens to slower-learning children who don't get the topic in the week allotted to it? They never get the topic. And because mathematics is hierarchical, they *never get much of anything else in that subject either*. In a hierarchical subject like mathematics, the way that learning in schools is structured, it is completely hopeless. Had the children managed to get that topic, learning it at their own pace, perhaps other areas in mathematics would become clear too. As it is, the way it is taught, you can quickly become a loser in mathematics, simply because of the way schooling deals with you. And what subject, to some degree, is not hierarchical in the same way that mathematics is?

Instead of criticizing the children for not understanding, these considerations suggest that we criticize, resolutely and strongly, the *absurdity* of the *unscientific way* in which we approach learning. It is simply *absurd*, if learning for all is our goal, that children are put together in the same age-determined class, as Murray describes, without any way of tailoring the learning to the individual's needs.

I saw a recent example of this absurdity in another excellent and revealing documentary for British television, *Indian Summer School*.[26] It was an educational reality TV show where five boys who had done badly in school in England and Wales were sent to an academic boarding school in India, run by a traditional British headmaster, and featuring high standards of behavior and application for the boys there. One boy didn't get involved and was sent home. The other four, to different degrees, wanted to study. But one boy was completely out of his depth in the English class he was assigned to. He explicitly told the teacher this, that what he was given to learn was completely incomprehensible to him. And this started making him angry, to the extent that he even beat up one of the other boys. The school's solution to this? To give him some anger management classes—*not* to change the level at which he was being taught English.

This example shows how rigid our thinking is about what schooling should be like. The teacher, bless her, made heroic efforts to help the boy, who clearly wanted very much to learn, but everything was simply set at the wrong level for him. Surely, wouldn't it have been easy enough to move him down a class to where he was comfortable with the level? Or, given the time constraints on when they had to take their exams, couldn't they have let him follow a digital program that would find his level and help him rapidly progress to the required level? The fact that we don't think along these lines shows how the mindset of public education has captured us all. The school could respond sensibly when it came to the boy's anger, because there it was not constrained by normal conformist thinking about education. But when it came to differentiating academic ability, the school was completely stumped.

The point is that it should be obvious to schools, but it doesn't appear to be obvious at all, that many children will get lost going through hierarchical subjects. Perhaps they've been physically absent even for a brief period and never caught up with work missed. In a hierarchical subject, this means they will never get to grips with it. Or perhaps it's because they've been emotionally absent, with the same repercussions. Or perhaps it's because they're slower learners who, however conscientious they are, simply cannot get the topic in the time span allowed *but may have been able to do so if given more time.*

As Murray would say, that won't be true for everyone; some kids won't be bright enough to grasp all aspects of the curriculum. But we simply don't know how many kids that would apply to, because of the stupidity of the only system from which we have any evidence.

The Harvard development economist Lant Pritchett writes about the same problem in an Indian context, which again helps us get a sense of the absurdity. Pritchett is commenting on the appallingly low standards in public schools in the state of Uttar Pradesh (standards that are, incidentally, higher in the private schools). After five years of compulsory schooling, only one in five children enrolled can read even simple words. This lack of literacy "means that everything else that is happening in school for these children is unlikely to make sense, as nearly all schoolwork in grade five involves some reading."[27] For "adept and intellectually brilliant" researchers from outside, like him, it is easy to "lose sight of what a miserable and alienating experience school can be." He asks us to imagine that we are "one of the half of the fifth-grade class that still cannot read. The teacher's writing on the board, textbooks, and workbook exercises on any subject mean nothing to you. *You realize you are falling further and further behind but do not know what to do about it, nor does anyone seem to care.*"[28] This dramatic example is from India. But the sentiment applies equally to those children stuck in undifferentiated learning classes—as Murray observes happens—in America too. Children in India are also subject to corporal punishment and receive frequent beatings for lagging behind. Fortunately, we don't do this in America. But it is every bit as brutal—albeit in an emotional or psychological, rather than physical, way—to organize schooling that doesn't differentiate—that forces the child who can't read to sit alongside and supposedly learn at the same pace as the child who can read well—as it is to have corporal punishment. An antonym of *corporal* is *incorporeal*. Perhaps we can describe the schooling system as constituting "incorporeal punishment" for those who are made to endure it.

We can all see the absurdity. But no one appears able to challenge it within the public system. Private schools may go along with the same absurd system because they can be complacent, or because they are subject to the same government framework that constrains their approach as that found in schools in Asia and Africa. But the contention of this book is that as education becomes truly emancipated, then private education can and must start to seriously address this issue. It will have to address it, and it will have the freedom to do so.

Murray believes that test results like NAEP show that such children can never learn, and we should stop romanticizing about what schools can deliver for such children. On the contrary, probing into what the schools are like reveals that it's the schooling system that is clearly guilty, not the children involved.

Children are of differing abilities—on this much we can agree with Murray. But instead of thinking this means that we can do nothing for slower children, it should be our call to arms to focus on how to organize schooling differently—radically differently, not tinkering at the edges—to make sure it can help those who are slower as well as stimulate those who are faster.

Murray doesn't see any of this. He says, "The schools are the usual scapegoats for results like these. But how much can they be blamed that three-quarters of eighth-graders did not know the answer?"[29]

He's referring to the mathematics example above and means it as a rhetorical question. But it shouldn't be left at the level of rhetoric. Given the way schooling is structured, it seems extremely easy to say that the schools—that is, the schooling system—should be blamed. Murray suggests that we should "talk to elementary and middle school teachers about their experiences trying to teach children who are well below average in logical-mathematical ability."[30] He clearly believes that the teachers are the ones who will tell you the truth of the matter. On the contrary, it is possible that some teachers might be the worst people to talk to about the failings of the schooling system. Some might not be able to think of an alternative way of approaching teaching and learning, such as through proper differentiation. This is the way they were taught, and they are blind to other possibilities. It might also be that teachers despise the "dull" children.

Reading Murray on this topic, I was reminded of Pritchett's description of the incident that, he said, motivated him to write his book. It was in Uttar Pradesh, India, where the fifth graders couldn't read or do simple arithmetic. You can, as Murray says, (wrongly) blame the schools for these failings. One middle-aged father did precisely that. In a public meeting at the school, he stood up and described how the public school had betrayed them: "I have worked like a brute my whole life because, without school, I had no skills other than those of a donkey. But you told us that if I sent my son to school, his life would be different from mine. For five years I have kept him from the field and work and sent him to your school. Only now I find out that he is thirteen years old and he doesn't know anything. His life won't be different. He will labor like a brute, just like me."[31]

Murray's approach is to turn the criticism back on the children themselves. He does it more politely, but nonetheless Murray's approach doesn't really differ in kind from the Indian school principal's response: "It is not our fault," says that school principal. "We do what we can with your children. But you [are] right, you are brutes and donkeys. The children of donkeys are also donkeys. We cannot expect to teach your children. They come from your homes to school stupid and you cannot expect that they will come home from school anything other than stupid."[32]

Perhaps in the Indian case, it is easier to side with the parent than the principal, given what we know about the appalling laxity with which Indian public-school teachers do their teaching—in common with other developing countries, data show that less than half of public-school teachers are present and engaged in teaching when they should be on any school day. One household survey showed that around one-fifth of children reported being "beaten or pinched" by teachers in school during the previous month. Another study showed that for 1,700 classrooms in five states of India, in around 40 percent of the classes there were no "child-friendly" practices at all (that is, things like students being allowed to ask teachers questions, or teachers smiling, laughing, or joking with students).[33]

I think most people, even Murray, would side with the poor parent against the head teacher calling his children "donkeys" here. But my contention is, even when teachers are present in American schools, and however good they are, in general they might as well not be there, for all the good it does for children who are the lowest in academic ability. This is because of the absurd way that schooling is structured.

Instead of asking the teachers, as Murray wants us to do, you could ask the children of "low ability" and see what they say about their teachers or about the structure of schooling. Perhaps they might say: The teachers ignored me; they told me to keep quiet. When I asked for help, they simply instructed me in the way they had instructed the class already, which I already hadn't understood, so why would I understand this time? When I asked for help again, they were impatient with me. They ridiculed me in front of the class; they'd rather concentrate on the attentive and pretty children at the front than on kids like me.

Murray does not countenance such possibilities. His sympathies lie with the teachers. Yes, they might agree, "given time, you may be able to get such a child to understand … the concept of decimal notation … for the duration of the tutoring."[34] But they simply can't retain it: "A few days later, given a fresh exercise using decimal notation, the student will miss every question because the concept of decimal notation is beyond the capacity of that child to absorb and retain."[35]

We've suggested that this may be simply an indictment of the current way schooling is organized. Murray continues, "Could such a child absorb and retain the concept of decimal notation if the teacher *is given unlimited time and resources*? Sometimes yes, sometimes no, but the *investment of time must be so large* that it cannot possibly be generalized to the whole curriculum. *Limits on logical-mathematical ability translate into limits on how much math a large number of children can learn no matter what the school system does.*"[36]

Note here that Murray's crucial distinction between differences *in degree* and differences *in kind* seems to take a battering. He's conceding that, at least in many circumstances, there's just not sufficient time to get a child to understand what earlier he had implied was a matter of degree of understanding, things that some children simply couldn't possibly ever understand. What Murray is saying is that his concept of differences *in degree* is not actually about children's abilities, but about *time limits within the current schooling system.*

Moreover, Murray seems to think that the current system—where you have a teacher in front of the class teaching a topic for a few days or a week—is the only possible way forward. Interestingly, when he talks about homeschooling, he is much more open to there being interesting alternative technologies for teaching. He writes that "when parents can purchase an excellent curriculum off the shelf, including books, lesson plans, and lectures on DVD, homeschooling suddenly becomes easier."[37] Can't he see that these kinds of technologies and their extensions—particularly the ones used by Salman Khan or Sugata Mitra (authors we encounter elsewhere in this book)—could help overcome the problems he describes about limited teacher time and (implied) limited teacher patience?

Sophisticated educational software and interactive videos can be *infinitely* patient, not minding how many times a child must do a problem over again to understand. Because their use is not restricted to the likely three hours a week that the school typically gives to mathematics, the child can spend as much time as required to get the answers right.

If people think this requires technology, then the example of what happened under the Madras System in India, transported to England and across the world in the late eighteenth and early nineteenth centuries by the Reverend Dr. Andrew Bell, shows that you can work at the level that children are at without any complex technology, simply by taking into account the different learning needs of children. Put simply, this was a system of what we would today call "peer learning." A school was administered by a teacher superintendent, who selected children by their abilities into those who would do the teaching (the pupil-teachers) and those who would be taught (the pupils). The superintendent would typically begin a day, or week, by teaching the pupil-teachers what needed to be taught; once they'd grasped it, they would then teach the remainder of the pupils, either singly or in pairs, depending on the size of the group assigned to them. Importantly, the pupils were divided into groups based on their attainment in the particular subtopic being taught, and they could move between groups as soon as they had mastered the content being taught: "The school is arranged into forms, or classes, each composed of members, who have made a similar proficiency. ... The scholar ever finds his level, by a constant competition with his fellows, and rises and falls in his place in the class, and in the forms of the school, according to his relative proficiency."[38]

Murray is right that in public schools today, it is unlikely that these different approaches will happen, at least in large numbers. But to suppose that this is a limit on educational ability rather than a contrived limit brought about because of the irrational and bizarre processes that schooling uses today is completely wrong.

Murray has a section titled "Schools Have No Choice but to Leave Many Children Behind." He writes, "The changes we can expect in academic achievement in the lower half of the ability distribution are marginal, *no matter what educational reforms are introduced.*"[39] He points to multibillion-dollar programs, like No Child Left Behind and Title I, to show how throwing money at the problem is simply wasting money. But if nothing much changes about the way schooling is structured, because of the way vested interests prevent radical change, this is less of a surprise. It would rather be like saying that if our transportation system involved only horses and carts, no matter how much money we invested to upgrade our carts, our horse-and-cart combination would still travel at only around 10 to 15 miles per hour. To prove the speed of travel, clearly money invested in only upgrading carts would be wasted. Instead, we could think of replacing the horse and cart with a vehicle powered by an internal combustion engine, or, even better, an exciting hybrid electric engine. Billions invested there would likely make an enormous difference to transportation, in a way that working so hard to improve a cart could not.

Moving Away from Educational Malpractice

Murray's work does touch on differentiation; he has two major things to say about it. One section is titled "Find Out What Each Child's Abilities Are." Here, he notes that a "good teacher can size up most students accurately after a few weeks," but "not all teachers are good." So, therefore, "every child should receive a professional assessment of his or her palette of abilities during first grade, with periodic follow-ups to guard against diagnostic errors and to identify developmental changes."[40] He concludes, "Not doing such assessments now, despite the availability of the tools to do them, amounts to *educational malpractice.*"[41]

I've described what goes on in schools today as absurd and unscientific. Murray says it's educational malpractice. That is precisely the right term to use to describe what goes on in schooling systems today. Giving children tests to find out where they fit, says Murray, would "give teachers a better chance to respond to their students' individual abilities and needs as they enter school and as they develop during school." But why would teachers respond to their students' individual abilities, even with this information? I've suggested that teachers would not do anything like this under the current system—they are too heavily constrained to have this kind of flexibility. It's nearly impossible to imagine how teachers could adequately differentiate learning under normal age-related classroom situations.

The second point Murray makes about differentiation is in his section titled "Let Gifted Children Go as Fast as They Can." He writes, "If a third-grader is reading at the sixth-grade level, give that child sixth-grade reading. If a third-grader can do math at the sixth-grade level, give that child sixth-grade mathematics." This is because the literature shows that "academically gifted children do well when they are given a curriculum that is complex, acceler-ated, and challenging, and when they have teachers with lofty expectations. Academically gifted children do best when they are with peers who share their interests and who do not tease them for being nerds."[42]

But why does he stop the argument with gifted children? Surely his argu-ment here applies equally to all abilities. Using an analogy to the principle of mathematical induction, we can see that this should apply to everyone: once we've removed the (arbitrarily) defined "gifted" group, then there will be a new group who are also more advanced than the others, and they too should be able to go at their own pace. The same principle could then apply all the way down the range of abilities.

I began this chapter by saying that Murray would classify certain people as "educational romantics." *Merriam-Webster's Dictionary* has two relevant definitions of *romantic*: having no basis in fact, or impractical in conception or plan.

I guess Murray would use these definitions to describe people like me. We seek educational change with no basis in fact. We do so with impractical plans of action and, in the process, do untold harm to schooling by pretending it can be better than it is, especially for lower-ability children.

I don't accept the charge. In this chapter, I've tried to show that my ap-proach is very much based on facts and logical arguments. I've also argued that educational freedom would help break us away from current harmful constraints. But what about the suggestion that I've no practical plan for its conception? In the next chapter, I turn to look at some ways in which people have planned to move toward educational freedom, and I suggest that there is a better plan, for which I provide a sketch.

I'm not against the epithet "romantic" entirely, however. *Merriam-Web-ster's Dictionary* also provides a third definition: "marked by the imaginative or emotional appeal of what is heroic, adventurous." I think the next few chapters can help us imagine a heroic and adventurous way forward to educational emancipation, in America as much as it is happening in the developing world.

12

The Theory and Practice of School Vouchers

EDUCATIONAL REFORMERS IN America who are sympathetic to ideas in this book may think of school vouchers as a way of reaching the desired goal of educational freedom.[1] In its ideal form, instead of funding schools directly as governments do now, the government works out the total funding *per child* that is spent in the public education system and allocates this to individual parents instead. Parents choose a school for their child, and the funding goes with the child to the school of their choice. In the competitive market for schools that results, popular schools attract more children. Because this means more funding, these schools flourish and even expand. Schools that are not popular lose money as a result, and they either improve or are eventually forced to close. Importantly, schools become accountable to parents: parents feel they are responsible for funding schools because they carry the voucher to the school of their choice.

In this chapter, we will look at some of the pros and cons of this idea, and especially the justification for introducing school vouchers in the first place. We examine voucher proposals in the same way that we have already looked at proposals of visionaries like Sir Ken Robinson: will anyone be able to get vouchers through the political process in practice (even if they appear justified in theory)?

School vouchers have a considerable vintage in the educational reform movement. First mooted by Milton Friedman in his seminal 1955 article "The Role of Government in Education," they are now routinely mentioned by sympathetic school reformers in America as the way forward.[2] Charles Murray mentioned school vouchers along with charter schools as two possible routes that could improve educational opportunities.[3] Lant Pritchett says that the case for educational vouchers as set out by Milton Friedman is "totally persuasive." He adds, "No one susceptible to economic reasoning can read the clarion call for vouchers in Milton Friedman's classic *Capitalism and Freedom* and not be persuaded."[4]

While some see school vouchers as the *end* of reform—once vouchers are introduced, this will spur competition and innovation in education, leading to great improvements—another school of thought sees vouchers as a *means* to the more radical option of educational freedom, an education system outside of government, along the lines explored throughout this book.

John A. Allison, a former president of the Cato Institute, takes the second approach: The public school system "has failed," he writes; in particular, it has failed low-income and minority families.[5] The solution is "a private educational system driven by competition and innovation."[6] In order to get there, we need "to privatize education initially by subsidizing the students (through tax credits or vouchers), not the schools."[7] These reforms "would lead to intense competition in existing education," eventually bringing about the "ultimate goal" of "truly private schools with no subsidies."[8]

A similar approach, seeing educational vouchers as a means to reaching purely private educational provision, was advocated in England in the 1970s and early '80s when it appeared that the government of Margaret Thatcher would opt for a voucher system. "Impressive academic studies" by the London-based Institute of Economic Affairs (IEA) convinced Dr. (later Sir) Rhodes Boyson, who was to become education minister in Thatcher's government, of the need for "an extension of fee-paying private education." This required "*either* a cutback in taxation and generous scholarships for poorer families, *or* a state-sponsored voucher system for all." While Boyson preferred the first approach, the universal voucher was more politically feasible; in any case, it would be a "steppingstone" to private education for all.[9]

Whichever approach is taken, vouchers as end or means, voucher reforms first must be implemented. How has that implementation taken off in America?

The American film producer Samuel Goldwyn is alleged to have said in 1934 about his failed blockbuster *We Live Again*, "The public stayed away in droves." I don't think it's being unkind to say that that also appears to have been the fate of voucher systems in America: "Every time a voucher scheme has been put before the voters in the United States," says Pritchett, "it has been defeated."[10] Pritchett was using Utah as an example.

The focus in this chapter is on vouchers and associated reforms such as tax credits or tax deductions, tax-credit scholarships, and education savings accounts. These are "demand side" reforms, mobilizing parents to effect educational improvements. There are also "supply side" reforms, notably charter schools, which focus on changing the nature of the supply of schools to improve education. Although these are only briefly mentioned, I believe a parallel argument can be made about charter school reforms too.[11]

The Justifications for School Vouchers

In 1962, Milton Friedman published *Capitalism and Freedom*, his classic defense of capitalism and free markets. One chapter was a reprint of his 1955 article "The Role of Government in Education," the definitive statement in favor of vouchers, a key inspiration for the current school choice movement in America.[12] The key argument built on Friedman's economic treatment of cases where government intervention is required, the two relevant ones for education being where there are "externalities," or "neighborhood effects," and where the "protection of minors" principle was invoked.

The protection of minors principle holds that government is justified in intervening in education to protect children from "the incompetent decisions of their parents,"[13] because of the harm that such decisions could cause the children. This was a fundamental principle of classical economists such as John Stuart Mill. They disliked "over-interfering government" but were prepared to make "exceptions to their general principle of freedom of contract" for the protection of children.[14]

Friedman agreed that the protection of minors principle led to the need for government intervention, because not all parents could be trusted to provide an education for their children that satisfied the second principle, the "neighborhood effects" or "externalities."

"Neighborhood effects" or "externalities" are an economic concept to describe the situation when "the costs (or benefits) of private transactions do not take into account spill-over costs (or benefits) to other individuals who do not participate in the transactions in question."[15] For instance, whether I get myself or my children inoculated against dangerous diseases can have an impact more widely in the community on whether or not these diseases are spread. If I don't get inoculated, this could cause widespread damage to the community. As Friedman put it, in the case of neighborhood effects, "strictly voluntary exchange is impossible," as "actions of individuals have effects on other individuals for which it is not feasible to charge or recompense them."[16]

A major neighborhood effect of education, Friedman argued, concerns democracy. "A stable and democratic society is impossible without a minimum degree of literacy and knowledge on the part of most citizens and without widespread acceptance of some common set of values." Education contributes to both, and "the gain from the education of a child accrues not only to the child or to his parents but to other members of the society"—that is, "the education of my child contributes to other people's welfare by promoting a stable and democratic society." For Friedman, this is a genuine neighborhood effect, in that "the action of one individual imposes significant costs on other individuals for which it is not feasible to make him compensate them or yields significant gains to them for which it is not feasible to make them compensate him."[17]

This neighborhood effect, says Friedman, justifies state intervention in two areas of schooling: compulsion and funding that is for "the imposition of a minimum required level of schooling and the financing of this schooling by the state."[18] Together, these requirements lead Friedman to propose giving *vouchers* to parents as a means of enhancing the educational market, within the twin constraints of public compulsion and funding: "Governments could require a minimum level of schooling financed by giving parents vouchers redeemable for a specified maximum sum per child per year if spent on 'approved' educational services."[19]

Friedman's proposed voucher system creates many freedoms. Schools should be allowed to be for profit or nonprofit; clearly there should be no objection to for-profit schools, as the profit motive is a major source of incentive for innovation and growth. Parents should have no restriction on their choice of school. They should be allowed to supplement the amount given to them by government—there should be no egalitarian restrictions against parents "topping up" vouchers to increase the funding available to expand educational innovation even further (for the same reason given below concerning universality).

The voucher system should also be universal, rather than aimed at only specifically targeted groups, such as the poor. In part, this is because compulsory schooling is required to bring about the desired neighborhood effect of education for democracy; compulsion implies the need for *universal* government funding. Moreover, it has to be universal because everyone, the rich and middle classes alike, needs to be involved, in order to stimulate the kind of innovation in education that is required: "One function of the rich is to finance innovation. They bought the initial cars and TVs at high prices and thereby supported production while the cost was being brought down, until what started out as a luxury good for the rich became a necessity for the poor."[20]

Regulations, finally, should be kept to a minimum: government's role "*would be limited to* insuring that the schools met certain minimum standards, such as the inclusion of a minimum common content in their programs, much as it now inspects restaurants to ensure that they maintain minimum sanitary standards."[21]

Friedman's argument has been widely accepted as the justification for both education vouchers and compulsory schooling by classical liberals. Notably, Friedrich Hayek's proposals for education are entirely based on Milton Friedman. In *The Constitution of Liberty*, published in 1960, some five years after Friedman's proposals, Hayek argues that the case for compulsory education, at least "up to a certain minimum standard," rests on two arguments. The first "is the general argument that all of us will be exposed to less risks and will receive more benefits from our fellows if they share with us certain basic knowledge and beliefs." The second is that "in a country with democratic institutions, there is the further important consideration that democracy is not likely to work, except on the smallest local scale, with a partly illiterate people." For both, what is required are enforced "certain common standards of values."[22]

Hayek does warn of the dangers of instituting these standards through public education, echoing John Stuart Mill: "The very magnitude of the power over men's minds that a highly centralized and government-dominated system of education places in the hands of the authorities ought to make one hesitate before accepting it too readily." Moreover, "the more highly one rates the power that education can have over men's minds, the more convinced one should be of the danger of placing this power in the hands of any single authority."[23]

Hayek supported "the greatest variety of educational opportunities."[24] One of his reasons is similar to what I've been arguing in earlier chapters: we know "so little about what educational techniques may achieve." We don't know what the best and worst educational approaches are, because educational research is in its infancy, and there are very few, if any, counterfactual situations to explore alternative approaches, so better a hundred flowers bloom. But Hayek also points out something else: "The argument for variety would be *even stronger* if we knew more about the methods of producing certain types of results."[25] If we ever do know the best ways of educating young people, then we certainly don't want those methods in the hands of governments, who could be tempted to use them for their own ends, usually political power, against those of their citizens. (We've discussed these kinds of possibilities in the earlier chapters on war-torn countries, but they appear to be applicable more widely too.)

Hayek also points out, like Friedman: "It would now be entirely practicable to defray the costs of general education out of the public purse without maintaining government schools, by giving the parents vouchers covering the cost of education of each child."[26] Again, following Friedman, he says the reason *for* public finance is the need for *compulsory schooling*: "It is probably a necessary consequence of the adoption of compulsory education that for those families to whom the cost would be a severe burden it should be defrayed out of public funds."[27]

Milton Friedman's writings are the major inspiration for the school choice movement in America. How has the movement fared since 1955?

They Stayed Away in Droves

As part of their advocacy work, Friedman and his wife, Rose, created a foundation in 1996 focused on promoting school choice in America (originally the Friedman Foundation for Educational Choice, it is now known as Ed-Choice). The foundation publishes a comprehensive annual survey of school choice programs in America. This publication, *The ABCs of School Choice*, is an extremely thorough source for voucher and related programs.

Table 12.1. School Choice Programs in America

	Number of children (2015)		Number of children (2011)	
Children enrolled in US	49,839,400		49,521,669	
"School choice" programs— demand-side reforms	2017	% of children enrolled US	2013	% of children enrolled US
Voucher programs	177,393	0.36%	104,919	0.21%
Tax-credit scholarship programs	256,784	0.52%	151,165	0.31%
Education savings accounts	11,024	0.02%	362	0.00%
Total demand-side reforms	*445,201*	*0.89%*	*256,446*	*0.52%*
"School choice" programs— supply-side reforms				
Charter schools	3,100,000	6.22%	2,300,000	4.64%
Total "school choice" programs	3,545,201	7.11%	2,556,446	5.16%

Source: Collated from Friedman Foundation for Educational Choice (now EdChoice), (2017, 2013).

I previously reviewed the 2013 report;[28] here I update this by looking at the 2017 report, making comparisons over this four-year period (Table 12.1). The table does not make great reading for voucher (or other school choice program) advocates.

America has only 0.36 percent of enrolled children using vouchers. A further 0.52 percent are on tax-credit scholarship programs, and 0.02 percent use education savings accounts. That is, less than 1 percent of enrolled children (0.89 percent) in America are using any kind of demand-side school choice reform. In other words, only 1 in 300 children in America uses an educational voucher, and fewer than 1 in 100 children in America has experience of any kind of voucher-like reform.

This is higher than it was in 2013, true. But once we look at the detail of the figures below, we can see that this rate of growth is highly unlikely to be able to continue for much longer—because the largest voucher programs will become saturated.

For the sake of completeness, I've also added charter schools in the table. More children are using these: 3.1 million students attend charter schools, adding a further 6.22 percent of children in America using some form of government school choice programs. However, elsewhere I've cataloged the political roller coaster of charter school reform, showing how politically fraught the entire process is. Charter schools bring in even more political instability than the voucher and tax-credit schemes. There are significant caps on the number of charter schools that can be created (even though an estimated six hundred thousand children are on waiting lists for charter schools), so the percentage of children in America having access to them may not increase much more than this.[29]

Including all these figures, we arrive at a total of 7.11 percent of enrolled children involved in school choice programs, or around 3.5 million children. To put it another way, around 1 in 15 children is touched by school choice programs in America. I'm all for looking at a glass and seeing it half-full rather than half-empty, but it is hard to see this glass other than being very nearly *empty*.

For those readers who are interested, I'll give more detail behind these summary figures. Those who would rather go straight to a discussion of the implications of these data can jump to the section "What Goes Wrong? The Problem of Vested Interests Again."

What do the data show in detail? First, vouchers.[30] Table 12.2 shows some of the relevant figures. In the 2017 report, 177,393 children are using vouchers in America. The good news is that this is up from the 104,919 children using vouchers in 2013, an increase of 69 percent over the four-year period. The less good news is that this figure is still only a tiny proportion of the total children enrolled in the United States—only 0.36 percent (up from 0.21 percent in 2013). That is, only 1 in every 300 children in America is enrolled in a voucher program. This is up from 1 in every 500 in 2013, but it's still a very tiny number. If we look in more detail at the kind of voucher programs operating, this number is put into an even less optimistic perspective.

Let's consider first Milton Friedman's desire that voucher programs should be universal. Without this, the *benefits* of vouchers would not arise (because there would be less innovation in education), and the *economic justification* for vouchers would be undermined (universal funding is required because of universal compulsion).

It turns out that not one of the twenty-five voucher programs operating in sixteen states aspires to universality. First, twelve of these programs are for "special educational needs" children only, so there is not even any intention of universality. Eliminating these would leave only thirteen programs in nine states. This would bring us down to only 0.26 percent of US total enrollment. None of the remaining programs has universality as an aim, let alone a reality.

The largest of all the programs by proportion of state population is that found in Vermont, serving (only) 3.8 percent of the state's enrolled population (3,350 students out of 87,800). However, this program, like that in Maine (5,727 students out of 185,900, or 3.1 percent), is an unusual one, called "town tuitioning," which "allows students who live in towns that don't have district public schools to receive their per pupil education tax dollars to pay tuition at a neighboring town's public school or a private school of their choice."[31] It thus has no pretense of being universal (or universal to a particular income group), applying only to those students whose home districts do not have public schools.

Putting Vermont to one side, the largest single program is in Indiana, with 3.4 percent of the state's enrollment (34,645 children out of 1,019,100 in total), while the four programs in Wisconsin (including one for special-needs children) serve 3.8 percent of the state's enrollment (32,961 children out of 867,200 total). No other program has 3 percent or more of the state enrollment population. Ohio has five programs (two for special-needs children), which together have 2.8 percent of the state's enrollment. After that, we have only Washington, DC; Florida; and Louisiana with more than 1 percent of children enrolled in voucher programs. That is, half of the states using vouchers (eight of the sixteen states) have programs that are *tiny*, serving less than 1 percent of state children enrolled.

Not one of the programs is aimed at universal provision—they are typically for low-income students, with only one (in Indiana) aimed at reaching low- and middle-income students.

In other words, there is nothing like a universal voucher system that Friedman proposed, not even within states, let alone across the country. But surely the growth in enrollment in voucher programs is a source of encouragement? Doesn't this growth challenge the "stayed away in droves" jibe?

Table 12.2. Voucher Programs by State and Washington, DC

State	Children served	State children enrolled	Children served, % state children population	Difference 2017–2013 reports	Voucher value
Arkansas	20	484,900	0.00%	20	$6,646
Colorado	0	888,600	0.00%	-494	$1,143
Washington, DC	1,166	73,000	1.60%	-418	$9,472
Florida	30,392	2,745,000	1.11%	7,381	$7,217
Georgia	4,185	1,712,200	0.24%	958	$5,614
Indiana	34,645	1,019,100	3.40%	25,321	$4,024
Louisiana	7,110	709,200	1.00%	2,166	$5,856
Louisiana	342	709,200	0.05%	320	$2,264
Maine	5,727	185,900	3.08%	-3,091	$8,482
Maryland	2,447	873,000	0.28%	2,447	$1,943
Mississippi	159	482,900	0.03%	117	$4,980
North Carolina	828	1,537,900	0.05%	828	$7,421
North Carolina	5,317	1,537,900	0.35%	5,317	$4,024
Ohio	8,594	1,704,200	0.50%	2,593	$3,101
Ohio	3,325	1,704,200	0.20%	3,325	$20,279
Ohio	22,892	1,704,200	1.34%	21,550	$4,257
Ohio	4,635	1,704,200	0.27%	2,394	$9,794
Ohio	7,840	1,704,200	0.46%	7,840	$3,761
Oklahoma	553	679,600	0.08%	384	$6,285
Utah	905	643,500	0.14%	191	$4,938
Vermont	3,350	87,800	3.82%	849	$13,152
Wisconsin	27,302	867,200	3.15%	3,275	$7,384
Wisconsin	2,464	867,200	0.28%	1,965	$7,337
Wisconsin	2,993	867,200	0.35%	2,993	$7,399
Wisconsin	202	867,200	0.02%	202	$12,000
Totals	177,393	16,046,000	1.11%	88,433	$6,089
% of US enrollment	0.36%				

Source: Collated from Friedman Foundation for Educational Choice (2017, 2013).

State spending per child	Value of voucher/state spending per child	Is the program universal?
$9,616	69.1%	Special needs only
$8,985	12.7%	Permanent injunction against this program
$18,485	51.2%	Low-income students
$8,755	82.4%	Special needs only
$9,202	61.0%	Special needs only
$9,548	42.1%	Low- and middle-income families
$10,749	54.5%	Low income students
$10,749	21.1%	Special needs only
$12,707	66.8%	Town tuitioning program
$14,003	13.9%	Low-income students
$8,263	60.3%	Special needs only
$8,512	87.2%	Special needs only
$8,512	47.3%	Low-income students
$11,354	27.3%	Low-income students
$11,354	178.6%	Special needs only
$11,354	37.5%	Low-income and low-performing public schools
$11,354	86.3%	Special needs only
$11,354	33.1%	Low-income students
$7,829	80.3%	Special needs only
$6,500	76.0%	Special needs only
$16,988	77.4%	Town tuitioning program
$11,186	66.0%	Income-qualified
$11,186	65.6%	Income-qualified
$11,186	66.1%	Income-qualified
$11,186	107.3%	Special needs only

Let's look first only at the programs that are not specifically targeted at special-needs children. These showed an increase in enrollment of 74,149 between 2013 and 2017. However, fully 79 percent of this increase came from two states only—Ohio (45 percent) and Indiana (34 percent).

Without these two states, there would have been far less to celebrate about any increase in the number of children using vouchers in America. Importantly, further growth in these two states is limited. The Indiana voucher program is restricted to the "largest eligible voucher population," of 530,000 students. This is around 54 percent of the total student population. If the program should continue at its current strong rate of growth, then it would reach this limit shortly after 2025. The Ohio programs would likely stop growing at about the same time, as they also are constrained in terms of who they can serve—special-needs children and low-income families, and children in low-performing public schools. So even if the growth of all voucher programs continued at their current rate, with Ohio and Indiana the drivers of that growth, by around 2025, that growth would peak at just over 1 percent of the American school population. Thereafter, growth would be roughly halved, because the two biggest programs could expand no further.

I estimate what realistic growth might look like in Table 12.3. If all programs grew at their current rate (that is, from 0.21 percent of enrollment to 0.36 percent of enrollment, an increase of 71 percent per annum) until 2025, then we'd have about 1.1 percent of American children enrolled in voucher programs. If growth after that halved, roughly—because the two major programs were by then at capacity—then by 2033, we still would not have reached 2 percent of the American school population using vouchers.

Certainly, there is limited success. But it is not enough to convey optimism about moving toward anything approaching a universal voucher system, as proposed by Friedman.

What about funding levels? Friedman had in mind that per-pupil voucher funding would be *nearly* equivalent to that in public schools. The largest (and most universal in aspiration) voucher program, in Indiana, falls short of this: "The average voucher amount [US$4,024] is below half of what public school students receive."[32]

So not only is this program nowhere near being universal, but also it provides funding of less than half of what public school students receive.

Table 12.3. Actual (2013–17) and Estimated (2021–33) Voucher Enrollment as Percentage of US Enrollment

Year	2013	2017	2021	2025	2029	2033
Enrollment as percentage of US enrollment	0.21%	0.36%	0.62%	1.10%	1.40%	1.90%

Source: Author's extrapolations using data from Friedman Foundation for Educational Choice (now EdChoice), (2017, 2013).

What about other voucher programs in terms of funding? How do they fit in with what Friedman desired? If we exclude the vouchers for special-needs children, which are typically better financed, the highest percentage values of vouchers are in the town tuitioning programs in Maine and Vermont, at 66.8 percent and 77.4 percent, respectively, of the total government spending (recurrent, not including capital and other costs) in those states. If we exclude these unusual and nonreplicable systems, we have the voucher programs in Wisconsin at around 66 percent, followed by 56 percent in Louisiana and 51 percent in Washington, DC. All other programs are less than 50 percent. The large ones in Indiana and Ohio are 42 percent and between 27 percent and 36 percent, respectively.

So, the voucher programs in existence neither remotely aspire to universality, nor typically bring amounts close to per-child public spending in schools. And none of the voucher programs allow top-up spending by parents, nor do they typically allow all kinds of providers, including for-profit school providers, to enter the market. Vouchers currently in existence do not remotely come close to the proposal set out clearly by Milton Friedman. Why not? We'll turn to this in the next section, where we will show again how vested interests in education come together either to block reforms completely or to water them down so that they have very little impact. In other words, all the difficulties that we suggested would emerge with desired educational reforms, like those proposed by Sir Ken Robinson, conspire to undermine the introduction of school vouchers. Before we do that, we'll look at other similar school choice reforms advocated by the Friedmans to measure their impact.

The second type of school choice reform explored by the Friedman Foundation for Educational Choice (now known as EdChoice) is education savings accounts. These "allow parents to withdraw their children from public district or charter schools and receive a deposit of public funds into government-authorized savings accounts with restricted, but multiple, uses." These funds could cover "private school tuition and fees, online learning programs, private tutoring, community college costs, higher education expenses and other approved customized learning services and materials."[33]

This does sound promising. Yet in the 2013 EdChoice report, there were *only* 362 children using these, in one state (Arizona). It was envisaged that the program would expand from being restricted to only those with special needs, to include "students from the foster care system, children of active military members, and students in public schools or districts graded D or F."[34] This appears to have happened. After expansion, however, only around 22 percent of Arizona's children are eligible,[35] so it's still far from being a universal program.

It has certainly expanded since 2013—it now includes 3,357 children, with savings accounts set at $4,645 (grades K through 8) and $4,904 (grades 9 to 12). The average per-student funding in Arizona schools is $7,528, so this figure is around 60 percent of that figure; again, this appears rather lower than what Milton Friedman might have reasonably anticipated.

Now, 3,357 children may sound like a start, but it's only 0.30 percent of Arizona's school population. There are two other educational savings account programs running—in Florida and Mississippi; both are for special-needs pupils only. Two other programs were due to start in 2016–17, but the one in Nevada was stopped due to litigation,[36] and there were no data available for the program in Tennessee—in any case, the maximum percentage of Tennessee children allowed would be 2 percent, confined to special needs only.

Altogether, there are 11,024 children with educational savings accounts, that is, 0.25 percent of the children in those states and 0.02 percent of children in America. If we take out the special-needs programs, we are left only with Arizona, at less than 0.01 percent of America's children.

So far, this doesn't seem a program that fits with Friedman's aspirations for universal vouchers. Given that one of the newer programs is subject to litigation, it's unlikely that other states will eagerly take them up.

Third, tax-credit scholarships "allow taxpayers to receive full or partial tax credits when they donate to nonprofits that provide private school scholarships."[37] It seems slightly odd including these in a summary of school choice programs, as it appears to be more of a charitable tax-relief program: The nonprofit organizations giving scholarships don't really have anything to do with the state. The law simply allows individuals and corporations to claim tax relief on their donations to these scholarship organizations.

Again, the numbers are not large.

There are 21 programs in 17 states, up from 14 programs in 11 states in 2013. The estimated number of recipients is 256,784, which is 1.77 percent of all schoolchildren enrolled in these states, and about 0.52 percent of schoolchildren enrolled in America. This has increased from 151,165 recipients in 2013, just over 1 percent of the children in the states that had these programs. Programs in just three states (Arizona, Florida, and Pennsylvania) make up 84 percent of all children in the programs, so the rest are small.

The Florida program is projected to provide 62.5 percent of the per capita government funding and is the most generous. Other programs are far less generous: the two largest programs in Arizona and Pennsylvania provide scholarships of 24.5 percent and 11.4 percent, respectively.

Finally, there are individual tax credits and tax deductions. These allow parents to "receive state income tax relief for approved educational expenses," including "private school tuition, books, supplies, computers, tutors, and transportation."[38]

Of the eight programs for which data are available (up from five in 2013), while the number of taxpayer beneficiaries at least is now beginning to look more impressive, 879,655, this is only marginally different from the 847,874 found in 2013 and only 2.36 percent of the adult population in those states. For America at large, it is only 0.35 percent of the adult population.

Moreover, the average credit/deduction amount allowed, as a percentage of the total per-student spending in public schools, is tiny—on average, a tax credit of $206 is allowed, a tiny proportion of any likely private-school tuition, let alone all other costs of private schooling (books, supplies, computers, and so on). The largest program is that in Illinois, with 285,972 taxpayers participating. The average tax credit is $280, or 2.1 percent of the per capita government funding for public schools. The next-largest program is in Minnesota, with 209,963 taxpayers participating, with a tax credit of $1,154, or 14 percent of the per capita state funding for public schooling. Smaller programs are slightly more generous but obviously serve fewer taxpayers.

As these figures show the number of taxpayers rather than the number of students, they can't strictly be included in the summary table. However, given that the amounts for students are so low, it seems reasonable to discount these programs from our overview of school choice programs in America as being too small to be of any significance.

In summary, as EdChoice points out, there have been 150 years of voucher systems (the earliest began in Vermont in 1869), over sixty years of high-level advocacy (since Friedman's paper in 1955), and thirty years since the introduction of vouchers in America's "modern" era (in 1990). What is there to show for it? The figures are not exactly mind-blowing.

What Goes Wrong? The Problem of Vested Interests Again

Fifty years after Friedman's seminal 1955 essay, the Cato Institute published a volume celebrating Friedman's influence, titled *Liberty and Learning: Milton Friedman's Voucher Idea at Fifty*. Friedman wrote both the prologue and the epilogue.

In the prologue, taking all of the school choice reform programs in America together, he noted that "they cover only a small fraction of all children in the country."[39]

Friedman also expresses how he has been "repeatedly frustrated" over the last fifty years of advocating vouchers by the "adamant and effective opposition of trade union leaders and educational administrators to any change that would in any way reduce their control of the educational system."[40] In California, he and his wife had been involved twice, in 1993 and 2000, in attempts to bring in a "statewide," *universal* voucher program through a ballot initiative. In both cases, he writes, "the initiatives were carefully drawn up and the voucher sums moderate." Friedman had accepted a smaller voucher in terms of funding than he would otherwise have wanted for political reasons. Budgets had been carefully worked out to show the advantages. Public opinion polls only nine months or so before the elections showed "a sizable majority in favor of the initiative," while "a sizable group of fervent supporters" were active in promotion. But then, on each occasion about six months before the election, "opponents of vouchers launched a well-financed and thoroughly unscrupulous campaign against the initiative. Television ads blared that vouchers would break the budget," even though the carefully worked-out sums clearly *showed a reduction in government spending*, given that the vouchers for private schools were "only a fraction of what government was spending per student." Most sinisterly, "Teachers were induced to send home with their students misleading propaganda against the initiative. Dirty tricks of every variety were financed from a very deep purse." In each case, these tactics won the day: "The result was to convert the initial majority into a landslide defeat."[41] The same thing occurred, Friedman says, in Washington State, Colorado, and Michigan. "Opposition like this explains why progress has been so slow in such a good cause."[42]

In his epilogue, Friedman was less confident in the way vouchers can bring competition, innovation, and experimentation into the education system, which is severely curtailed by the problem of "how to get from here to there."[43] The kind of voucher that has been tried in America—"limited, directly or indirectly, to low-income families" (or special-needs children)—is not the solution at all and does not allow parents to supplement them if they so desire. Progress toward Friedman's desired kind of educational voucher has been almost nonexistent, he writes. The reason is that "centralization, bureaucratization, and unionization have enabled teachers' union leaders and educational administrators to gain effective control of government elementary and secondary schools. The union leaders and educational administrators rightly regard extended parental choice through vouchers and tax-funded scholarships as the major threat to their monopolistic control. So far, they have been extremely successful in blocking any significant change."[44]

In other words, the kinds of factors that we discussed earlier in relation to getting reforms like those of Sir Ken Robinson's through the political process are acknowledged by Friedman to have fatally blocked his desired reforms too.

A decade ago, when I was writing an earlier book, I made my editor suffer last-minute changes because, as the book was going to press, my attention had been drawn to a new voucher program in Utah that was finally going to break the mold. Revising the book, I breathlessly wrote that "the state of Utah, in February 2007, passed a bill to sign into law *the first universal voucher scheme* in the United States ... [which mandates that] by 2020 every child in the state will be able to participate in the program."[45] Utah, you'll recall, was the state given as an example by Pritchett earlier, as showing how voucher programs in America always get turned down.

I looked with keen anticipation for the Utah voucher program in the Ed-Choice report of 2013, then again in 2017. It's nowhere to be found. Indeed, in Utah there is only one tiny voucher program, for special-needs students. It currently has 905 students (up from 714 in 2013)—that's 0.14 percent of the population of children in Utah. What went wrong?

Perhaps to keep myself covered, in my book revisions I had continued, "As this book is being finalized, a group called the Utahns for Public Schools, formed by, among others, the Utah Education Association, the state teachers' union, is trying to stop" the program.[46] This was happening even though to "soften the blow to government schools, if a student uses his or her voucher to transfer from a public to private school, the school district will continue to fund the school for a period of five years as if the student had not transferred."[47] Surely wouldn't that placate even the most ardent teacher unionist? I even reported the additional complexity that, procedurally, the Utahns for Public Schools had apparently challenged only half of the required bills: "Short of a court-ordered injunction," I reported the Senate majority leader as saying, "vouchers are going forward."[48]

Yet they didn't. The problem is that high-profile voucher programs are very susceptible to political blockage, as we discussed about transformative reforms in general in chapter 7 and as public choice theory would predict.[49] That was the fate of the Utah program. It was blocked—even though, as it passed through the legislation process, it was progressively watered down so that, even if it had gotten through, it would only have been a shadow of what was intended.

They stayed away in droves in the United Kingdom too; the vested interests successfully blocked any moves toward vouchers. When Margaret Thatcher's government came to power in 1979, all the "intellectual groundwork" for vouchers had been prepared, and the "prospect of political action on the voucher quickened." The secretary of state for education, Sir Keith Joseph, became convinced by the arguments, writing that he was "intellectually attracted to the idea of education vouchers."[50] A national petition demanding educational vouchers added to their armory, as the idea went through policy committees.

Yet, at the 1983 Conservative Party conference, Sir Keith Joseph announced that the voucher idea was "dead."[51] It was dead because all the vested interests—bureaucrats in the Department of Education and officials in the local education authorities and teachers' unions—saw no benefit in disrupting the status quo. Vouchers were a threat to them, and they killed them. One sentence from the Department of Education neatly summarizes the opposition: a voucher system "could lead to a situation in which parental choices and decisions undermined the character of the maintained school system."[52] Reading the opposition to vouchers, clearly no one had any understanding of how an educational market could operate. Ignoring the possibility that private enterprises, such as shops, hotels, and restaurants, deal with this every day, they argued that the "ebb and flow of pupils" would "create difficult management and organizational problems for schools."[53] They could not see how the supply side of private schools could expand, given that "starting a new independent school is a slow, expensive and risky business."[54]

Although a coterie of academics—economists and political scientists—supporting vouchers responded to this, they were faced with a fundamental problem: the academics could offer no real evidence of how an educational market might operate; because there was a near-state monopoly, both in the UK and overseas, no obvious evidence could be forthcoming. There was no counterfactual to show how educational freedom could work.

The voucher proposal died in the UK and has not been revived since.

I am not optimistic that voucher programs of the kind desired by Milton Friedman would ever get through the political system in the United States or the UK. Some readers might be rather impatient at this stage: What about where voucher systems *have been* brought in? Don't these tell us that it is at least possible to do so? Don't these at least show that getting reform through the political process, while difficult, may not be as impossible as I'm suggesting it is in this book?

There are two cases to examine where universal vouchers have been introduced—Chile and Sweden.

Chile is the easiest to dismiss. The Chilean voucher system was introduced in 1980 under the regime of dictator Augusto Pinochet. How did he solve the problem of teachers' union leaders' resistance to change that would impact their members? He locked them up and worse. The way Pinochet dealt with the teachers' unions in Chile is not open to any other country practicing democratic methods. Once democratic governments came into place in Chile, while they didn't get rid of the voucher, they began to impose ever-greater regulations on private providers, which some argue make them unlikely vehicles to push forward Friedman's vision.[55] So, Chile doesn't really provide a replicable model for getting change through the political system.

The Swedish case is more interesting. Here a universal voucher program was introduced in 1992, under a Social Democrat government. It is genuinely universal, it does allow parents some ability to top-up, and it embraces for-profit as well as nonprofit private-school providers. All schools taking part have to be approved by the National Agency for Education, which apparently has quite stringent requirements, and have to teach the national curriculum, so there are limits on the freedom of the system. Moreover, it's not quite a voucher system in Friedman's sense, in that parents are not actually given anything to take with them to the school of their choice. Instead, parents make their choice, and schools submit numbers of students and are funded accordingly by the government. This may reduce schools' accountability to an extent. Nevertheless, it certainly shows that it is possible to introduce a system that is somewhat along the lines of that proposed by Milton Friedman.

How likely is it to happen in any other country, though? Swedish commentators have noted how the political constellation was quite exceptional at the time and unlikely to reoccur, and it is hard to see how even in Sweden a similar system could be introduced again, even with the same political parties still active.[56] So, although it shows the possibility, it may be, to use that hackneyed phrase, the exception that proves the rule.

Sweden clearly *can* be held up as an example of how it is possible to achieve radical reform through the democratic process. The reforms have been watered down over the years, so the case doesn't totally undermine the argument that has been introduced throughout the book about this danger. Nevertheless, it did happen.

But does this make it more likely that it could happen in America? I think the situation is so different that it seems unlikely. If I were a betting man, I would stay with the predictions I gave earlier—that there won't be much more than 1 percent of American schoolchildren using vouchers by 2025.

Second Thoughts about Justifications for Vouchers

Twenty years after writing his seminal 1955 essay, Milton Friedman took part in a symposium organized around an essay by Professor E. G. West at the University of Chicago, financed by the Liberty Fund. Friedman's piece is very brief—a page and a half—but of huge significance, challenging the case that he had previously put forward in defense of vouchers. Recall that Friedman's case for both compulsory schooling and government finance through vouchers was based on the neighborhood effects, or externalities, of education. Now Friedman wrote, "Over the years, I have become increasingly persuaded that the case for (1) compulsory schooling and (2) government financing of schooling based on supposed externalities is seriously flawed. The flaw is present in my own treatment of these issues in *Capitalism and Freedom*."[57] He now sees that "private self-interest alone" would lead to *most parents* providing schooling for their children. We'll come shortly to where he got this idea from, but of course we already know that this idea is plausible given the evidence from developing countries. He continues:

> I have never found any plausible argument for net positive externalities from schooling that would not be satisfied if 90 percent, to take an arbitrary figure, received elementary schooling—the three R's. I have yet to see a plausible argument for any net positive marginal externality from additional schooling. But if this be so, *and if private interest alone could lead to at least this much schooling—as I believe it is overwhelmingly plausible that it would*—then there is no case from externalities for either compulsory schooling or the governmental financing of schooling. There may, of course, still be a case, on paternalistic or redistributive grounds, for government assistance to pay *for schooling children of indigent parents*, but not for increased government financing of schooling.[58]

In other words, there could be a case for targeted assistance to the most disadvantaged children to attend school, but the case for a universal voucher system was now eroded.

An even stronger restatement of this conclusion was made in 1980, when Milton Friedman, writing with his wife, Rose, observed how they were no longer convinced about the "justification for ... compulsory attendance."[59] As compulsory attendance provided the justification for public finance through vouchers, the intellectual edifice for vouchers was crumbling.

It is fitting that this admission was first made in a publication edited by Professor E. G. West, for it is West's writing that led to the Friedmans' changing their minds. Milton Friedman wrote to Professor West on the occasion of his winning the Alexis de Tocqueville Award for the Advancement of Educational Freedom: "I am only one of many who has had his views changed by your pathbreaking work. We want more!"[60]

So, what changed their minds? The Friedmans write that they had become aware of research on "the history of schooling in the United States, the United Kingdom, and other countries" that "has persuaded us that compulsory attendance at schools is not necessary to achieve that minimum standard of literacy and knowledge." This historical research has shown that schooling was "well-nigh universal in the United States before attendance was required," while in the United Kingdom, it was "well-nigh universal before either compulsory attendance or government financing of schooling existed."[61]

We turn to explore this secret history of education without the state in the next chapter.

13

Why Milton Friedman Changed His Mind

THROUGHOUT MY TWENTIES, I was committed to public education and would fight to defend it. When I returned to England after three years teaching high school in Zimbabwe and began to think about a topic for my PhD dissertation, I decided to focus on Margaret Thatcher's "market" reforms in education that were disturbing the political "left" at the time. Elements of parental choice were being introduced into education. Funding would follow students to the (public) school of their choice. New types of schools could emerge within the state sector. Even though, as we saw in the earlier chapter, school vouchers had been on the agenda and abandoned, they could easily, we thought then, be brought back onto it. My focus was on Margaret Thatcher's reforms, the better to attack them and defend public education. But then something happened that changed the life perspective of my younger self forever.

I worked on my doctoral thesis at what is now the University College London Institute of Education. In 1990, at the library, I came across E. G. West's *Education and the State*. It certainly wasn't on any reading list that I'd been given, and no one had recommended it. The book hadn't been borrowed for a while, as I could see from the lack of stamps on the front page. Picking it up, I began to read. Borrowing it, I couldn't put it down when I got it home, for I realized that the book challenged everything that up to that point I had believed.

Until then, the fact that governments intervened in education was, for me, a taken-for-granted norm. Any deviation from the status quo—such as Thatcher's moves toward "markets" in education—needed to be justified, not state intervention itself.

West's argument made me realize that it was possible I had *gotten it all wrong*. West pointed to evidence showing that state intervention was not required to ensure almost universal school attendance and literacy in England, Wales, Scotland, and New York. When government got involved with education, it was, in his memorable phrase, "as if it jumped into the saddle of a horse that was already galloping." Crucially, education was provided by church and philanthropy, yes, but also by what were explicitly called "for-profit" private schools, in effect low-cost private schools set up in slums and poor neighborhoods by people from those communities themselves.

If West was right, then it appeared crystal clear to me that the lion's share of justification had to lie with those (like me at the time) who wanted to support government intervention, not with those like the market reformers who wanted to move away from it. If the poor had historically managed without the state, and government intervention eliminated their cost-effective means of gaining education, and undermined their control and responsibility for it, then there could be no easy acceptance of the statist status quo.

If West was right ... but, of course, he must be wrong. His arguments about concepts like equality, social justice, democracy, and public goods had to be challenged. And I dug deep into the historical arguments that he had presented. Far from proving him wrong, however, I eventually had to conclude that in all its essentials, his argument was correct.

West's work completely changed my life. It was because of what he had described happening in Victorian England—the burgeoning of low-cost private schools in the slums—that I went searching in the slums of Hyderabad, India, on that fateful day in 2000 with a hunch about what I might find *because* of what I'd read in West's work.

E. G. West changed the course of my work. But more importantly, he also changed the way Milton Friedman thought about the role of government in education.

The Amazing Newcastle Commission Report of 1861

What was the evidence given by West that changed Friedman's views? It was the history of education *without the state* in Victorian England and Wales, and in New York.[1]

In England and Wales, beginning in 1833, there had been modest sub-sidies to schools, and government got involved in teacher training. Government first became properly involved in schooling itself in 1870, when the Elementary Education Act (commonly known as Forster's Education Act) led to funding and provision of some "board schools" (so I am writing this in the 150th anniversary of state education in England and Wales). Universal compulsion came only in 1880 (between the ages of five and ten), and elementary school fees were not abolished until 1918.

The key question is: Did we need state intervention to bring about universal schooling? That's the accepted wisdom, as put forward by numerous historians of education. It is commonly assumed that in nineteenth-century England, before state intervention in education, provision for the working classes was inadequate, in terms of both quantity and quality of provision. In the classic *British History in the Nineteenth Century*, G. M. Trevelyan notes that on the eve of the 1870 act that laid the foundations for state education in England and Wales, "Only about half the children in the country were educated at all, and most of these very indifferently. England, for all her wealth, lagged far behind … several foreign countries."[2]

West was to turn this received wisdom completely on its head. In fact, he showed that, before state intervention in education, there was an extensive system of private education, educating most of the working class. Before 1870, there was almost universal provision of schooling, without any state compulsion and with parents funding around two-thirds of all the costs. In other words, there was a spontaneous order of education—education as a self-organizing system—emerging in England and Wales without the state.

West looked at an extensive list of sources, but if we only were to look at one of them, it would be the Newcastle Commission Report of 1861. This is the definitive and comprehensive source on nineteenth-century private education for the poor. To understand the nature of the spontaneous order, the self-organizing system of education that emerged during the nineteenth century, we need to answer three questions:

1. How much schooling?

2. What quality schooling?

3. Who paid?

Each of these areas is addressed in the Newcastle Commission Report, and we'll look at each in turn, supplemented by other evidence illuminated by E. G. West.

How Much Schooling?

Assistant commissioners assigned to each district first collected all the available data on the number of "public" schools for the whole of England and Wales. They then took a sample of one-eighth of the districts and asked the assistant commissioners responsible for these areas to ascertain what proportion of scholars there were in "for-profit" schools compared with those in public schools. They made their final estimates "assuming this proportion to hold good for the country at large."[3] Using these data, they estimated the numbers of private schools for the whole of England and Wales.

We must be very careful about what the commission meant here by "public" and "private."[4] It turns out that the distinction is actually between what today we would call "nonprofit" and "for-profit" private schools. The "nonprofit" schools were mainly church and philanthropic schools: "They are the National Society for the Education of the Poor in the principles of the Established Church … ; the British and Foreign School Society; the United Committees of Privileges and Education of the Wesleyan Conference; the Roman Catholic Poor School Committee; the Congregational Board, which is connected with the Independents and the Voluntary School Association, constituted on a nonsectarian basis (these two are opposed on principle to State aid of or interference with education), and the London Committee of the British Jews."[5] Certainly some of these schools, but not all, received small government subsidies, but these were marginal, as we shall see, to their functioning.

The commission gives data on the small number of schools that were "wholly or mostly" financed by government. There were 999 such schools, with 47,748 children—that is, 1.7 percent of schools serving 1.9 percent of children. In other words, a vast majority (over 98 percent) of the so-called public schools in the Newcastle Commission Report are what we'd call fully private schools today, nonprofit ones. There were also for-profit private schools:

Table 13.1. "Nonprofit" and "for-Profit" Schools, and Students by Sex, 1858

School type	Schools	Students	% Total schools	% Total students	Boys	Girls	% Girls
Nonprofit private	24,563	1,675,158	42%	66%	911,152	764,006	46%
For-profit private	34,412	860,304	58%	34%	389,607	470,697	55%
Total	58,975	2,535,462	100%	100%	1,300,759	1,234,703	49%
of which: Nonprofit private financed mainly or wholly by the state	999	47,748	1.7%	1.9%			

Source: Compiled from data in Education Commission (1861), 79.

"Private day schools are kept entirely for profit, and their character and arrangements depend entirely upon their respective proprietors."[6]

Rather than have confusion in what follows, where the Newcastle Commission refers to the distinction between public and private schools, I will instead use the contemporary terminology of *nonprofit private* and *for-profit private* schools. The Newcastle Commission data are shown in Table 13.1. The commission estimated that there was a total of 2,535,462 children in schools, of which 1,675,158 (66 percent) were in nonprofit private schools and the remainder 860,304 (34 percent) in for-profit private schools. It may also be interesting to note that while the population of male and female students in the schooling system was roughly equal, there was a higher proportion of female students in the for-profit than in the nonprofit private schools.

From their findings, the commission was able to estimate the proportion of children who were not in school, in the following way. First, their evidence showed that the average length of school attendance was six years, and children were not in school after the age of fifteen. Hence, they assumed that *half* of the total number of children aged from three up to fifteen years (that is, *half* of this twelve-year interval) would be in school. Half of the official figure (supplied by the registrar general) of this age group was 2,655,767. This is the number (assuming equal distribution of children in each age year) that the commissioners suggested *should* be in school. But the "number actually on the books of all schools was 2,535,462. This falls short of the number required by 120,805."[7]

This is a *tiny* deficiency, and the Newcastle Commission was fully aware of this. The figures show the extraordinary success of the private education system before the state started running schools.

Even this percentage of 4.5 percent out of school may be too large, because "against this deficiency we have to set off children permanently incapacitated by bodily or mental infirmities, of whose number we have no certain estimate, and children, educated at home, the number of whom must be small, except in the wealthier classes." So, the actual figure out of school is likely to be smaller than 4.5 percent. The Newcastle Commission summarized the position by saying that "almost all the children in the country capable of going to school receive some instruction."[8]

This statistical conclusion is reaffirmed by many of the descriptive reports of the assistant commissioners: "Wherever the Assistant Commissioners went, they found schools of some sort, and failed to discover any considerable number of children who did not attend school for some time, at some period of their lives." The commission concluded that "there is no large district entirely destitute of schools and requiring to be supplied with them on a large scale, nor is there any large section of the population sharply marked off from the rest, and capable of being separately dealt with, as requiring some special and stringent system of treatment. The means of obtaining education are diffused pretty generally and pretty equally over the whole face of the country, and the great mass of the population recognizes its importance sufficiently to take advantage to some extent of the opportunities thus afforded to their children."[9]

The Newcastle Commission was also able to make international comparisons. The proportion of scholars to the population *as a whole* was 1:7.7. This compared reasonably favorable with Prussia, where schooling was compulsory (1:6.27), Holland (1:8.11), and France (1:9.0).[10]

Let all these quite extraordinary conclusions sink in: a government committee (often biased, as we shall see, against for-profit private education in particular) conducts an extremely thorough and comprehensive survey of schooling provision across England and Wales and finds that all but a tiny percentage of students were in school for around six years—all of this with only small government subsidies to some of the schools, and well before there was any compulsion. This compares very favorably with countries that do have compulsory schooling. Anyone still thinking that we need government to ensure enough schooling in the developed world absolutely must think again.

When I first encountered this conclusion, it took me a while to recover my balance—I suppose I never did, because it changed my perspective forever, as it did for Milton Friedman. The evidence from the Newcastle Commission was part of the evidence that E. G. West presents in *Education and the State*.

E. G. West also supplied other evidence to show that the Newcastle Commission Report was not an outlier but entirely in the mainstream of what had been consistently found. First, he suggested that in the early part of the nineteenth century, the activity of the state was more to hinder the development of working-class literacy, not to encourage education of the masses. The government was concerned about the ability of the "lower orders" to read seditious material and levied high taxes on newspapers and other print material. But this didn't stop ordinary reading well before the state got involved in education. Thomas Paine's Rights of Man sold one and a half million copies, and William Cobbett's *Address to the Journeymen and Labourers* sold two hundred thousand copies in only two months.

Widespread literacy was noted by many in officialdom: a report from 1838, for instance, showed that 87 percent of *pauper* children aged nine to sixteen years, living in the workhouses of Norfolk and Suffolk, could read to some extent.[11] For "shoploom" weavers in Gloucestershire, an inspector's report of 1839 showed that only 8 percent could neither read nor write, while a special survey of people over the age of twenty-one in Hull (also in 1839) found that 92 percent could read, and indeed that 97 percent had attended day or evening school.[12] Research from the historian R. K. Webb estimated that around 1840, "at least two-thirds of the working classes were literate," a proportion that increased to around 90 percent by the middle of the 1860s.[13]

There were also extensive anecdotal observations about the role of private schools in meeting the educational needs of the poor that show how the findings of the Newcastle Commission were very consistent with the general perception at the time. Writing in 1813, James Mill, father of John Stuart Mill, noted,

> From observation and inquiry ... we can ourselves speak decidedly
> as to the rapid progress which the love of education is making among

the lower orders in England. Even around London, in a circle of fifty miles radius, which is far from the most instructed and virtuous part of the kingdom, there is hardly a village that has not something of a school; and not many children of either sex who are not taught more or less, reading and writing.[14]

This "love of education" was being demonstrated by the working classes a full fifty-seven years before the 1870 act, and twenty years *before any subsidies at all* were provided by the state, beginning in 1833.

Similarly, in 1816, the third report of the select parliamentary committee of inquiry into the "education of the lower orders" noted "unquestionable evidence that the anxiety of the poor for education continues not only unabated but daily increasing; that it extends to every part of the country, and is to be found equally prevalent in those smaller towns and country districts, where no means of gratifying it are provided by the charitable efforts of the richer classes."[15]

Henry Brougham's parliamentary select committee of 1820 provided the first official statistics on schooling. It established that, in 1818, between one in fourteen and one in fifteen of the population was being schooled, showing "the increasing willingness of parents to send their children" to school and "to pay the fees which were nearly always asked."[16] In 1828, Brougham conducted another survey and was astonished to find a doubling of the number of children in schools.

Parliament authorized a further survey of schooling across the whole country in 1833 (the "Kerry report"). The 1833 figures showed 1,294,000 children in school, an increase from the 1818 figure of 478,000.[17] As Lord Brougham in the House of Lords observed, these children attended schools "without any imposition of the Government or public authorities."[18]

Brougham was so impressed by this growth in schooling that he spoke of the "irresistible conclusion" that, given "such a number of schools and such means of education furnished *by the parents themselves from their own earnings*, and by the contributions of well-disposed individuals in aid of those whose earnings were insufficient, it behoves us to take the greatest care how we interfere with a system which prospers so well of itself."[19]

So why do we persist in thinking that government was needed to ensure enough quantity of education?

It may have something to do with the architect of the 1870 Education Act, who started the process of changing a fully private system of schooling—as found by the Newcastle Commission—into the almost fully state schooling system we know today. When W. E. Forster introduced his education bill into Parliament (later the Education Act of 1870), very strangely he made hardly any reference to the Newcastle Commission's findings. Instead, he relied on evidence from a small-scale survey conducted by two inspectors over a brief period in 1869, in four industrial towns—Liverpool, Manchester, Leeds, and Birmingham. This survey found that in Liverpool, for example, out of an estimated 80,000 children of school age, "20,000 of them attend no school whatever, while at least another 20,000 attend schools where they get an education not worth having."[20] In other words, here we have at least 25 percent and, if the quality judgment is believed, up to 50 percent of the relevant population not in schooling at all, or not in schooling of any suitable quality—hence, the figures used by historians like Trevelyan quoted above.

We'll be looking at quality in schools later. But concerning the quantity of schooling, how did this major discrepancy come about? If these were two pieces of educational research published in academic journals today, we'd be far more inclined to take seriously the research of the Newcastle Commission—national in scope; taking three years to conduct its research; using a team of fifteen (five commissioners and ten assistant commissioners) rather than a small-scale survey conducted by two researchers over a period of months, possibly with a political agenda (the introduction of state intervention in education). But we don't even have to raise these kinds of doubts, for the discrepancy is easily spotted and was spotted by a contemporary member of Parliament.[21]

The Newcastle Commission had found that the average length of schooling was about six years. But, in calculating his figures, Forster said that average schooling should be *eight years*. He said that in the fully private system he was observing, schooling should be between the ages of five and thirteen—and yet under the state system he created, the school-leaving age was not even raised to *twelve* until 1899, some thirty years later!

Table 13.2. Data Compared: Forster versus Newcastle Commission

	Forster		Using Newcastle Commission findings	
	Total number of children of school age (eight-year range)	% of total	Total number of children of school age (six-year range)	% of total
Total	80,000		60,000	
of which:				
Out of school	20,000	25%	0	0%
School of low quality	20,000	25%	?	?

Sources: West (1965) and Education Commission (1861).

This assumption alone clearly leads to the discrepancy between the two sets of data. For instead of Forster's estimated eighty thousand children of school age, we are likely to find a reduced figure of sixty thousand who were *actually* of school age, as found by the Newcastle Commission—that is, six-eighths of eighty thousand, again assuming that the proportion of children in each year group is proportional to the whole (see Table 13.2). But this was exactly the figure that Forster's survey *did* find in school!

So, the source of the popular misapprehension about the quantity of schooling in England and Wales is easily found—and just as easily dismissed. We could do the same trick today if we wanted to make a political point, as did Forster, about the need for more state intervention in education. We could look at the American population up to, say, age twenty-one and observe that there is a significant percentage of them not in school. That would be cheating, as we know the age of schooling is only up to eighteen, not twenty-one. Forster did *precisely the same cheating* when he brought his bill to the British Parliament in 1870.

West politely calls this "erroneous calculations" (and points to numerous instances from around the world when politicians desired to bring in state education), when politicians put forward data to justify their case. Forster was on the winning side, and so the rest is history: people believe his data, not the Newcastle Commission's, which seemed to decline into oblivion, or at least it did until E. G. West picked it up. In any case, people have paid attention to Forster's comments about the quality of schooling—that 25 percent of children were in schooling that was not of a good quality—and observed that this didn't seem far removed from comments about quality by the Newcastle Commission (which we'll come to shortly); perhaps people in the end felt all parties were arguing for and against much the same thing.

Before turning to quality, however, we can note that Forster's proposals didn't make much of a difference from those of the Newcastle Commission's: Forster introduced his 1870 bill *explicitly* as a measure to cater to those children who were not being served by existing voluntary measures. It was not designed to cater universally to all children, but only to fill in the gaps in the current private system. Moreover, under the Education Act of 1870, the country was divided into school districts, a survey of the educational needs of each district conducted, and voluntary sources given six months to rectify the deficiencies.[22] Clearly, Forster was aware that voluntary private provision was a very valuable resource and simply needed to be supplemented by his new board schools as required, but not replaced.

What Quality Schooling?

The Newcastle Commission, in line with most other available sources, shows that most children of school age were in school before the state got involved in education in 1870. The schools were almost completely private. But what about the quality of provision? Says the Newcastle Commission concerning for-profit private schools, "No doubt many of the schools are exceedingly bad."[23]

First, there was worry about the quality of the buildings. In developing countries today, critics of low-cost private schools there describe them as "mushroom" or "mushrooming" schools.[24] Interestingly, the same adjective was used to describe the burgeoning private schools of Victorian England and Wales: "The majority of these private schools," reported assistant commissioner Mr. Fraser, "are of very mushroom growth, by far the larger proportion of the existing ones having sprung up since the census of 1851." The report reflects that "most of the private schools which came under the notice of the character of Assistant Commissioners were institutions of the most temporary kind, set up and afterwards laid aside, apparently without any notion on the part of those who conducted them, that they were either intended or suited for permanence, a conclusive proof that they were mere makeshifts for the purpose of obtaining a precarious livelihood."[25] I've written elsewhere about this criticism of low-cost private schools in developing countries today and suggest that it's best to separate the buildings from the educational experience—you can have buildings that seem to outsiders as inadequate but that house excellent education.[26] Those who criticize the quality of the buildings often ignore the fact that the schools are much better than the children's homes in the slums, so it may be that we can take the criticisms of the buildings with a pinch of salt.

One assistant commissioner, Dr. Hodgson, concurred. He reported of one school: "Males 60. Females 71.—A gentle, tidy, intelligent young person, who seems to maintain a good tone and spirit among her pupils. I have had occasion to visit this school three times, and I have been always pleased with the conduct, intelligence, and neatness of the girls, *in spite of the very bad neighbourhood and unsuitable premises*. They sing also remarkably well, and are permitted to sing at intervals during needlework, which, I think, has a very good effect."[27]

In other words, in an "extremely poor" slum neighborhood, the school premises were, unsurprisingly, not good, but the inspector could still determine that the education offered was of a different standard. (Notice, too, that the school had more girls than boys, as we observed in general for the private for-profit schools.)

So, ignoring premises, what about the quality of the education itself? The commission says there are the good, the bad, and the ugly. The school above was classified as one of the good schools. One of the "very bad indeed" schools does sound grim: "Male 1. Females 6.—Widow: age about 70. Her husband died 12 years ago, through intemperance. She receives 2s. 6d. a week from the Union;[28] 7 pupils at 3d. each make 1s. 9d., and this is her income! She was very grateful for the small donation of 1s. She complains of inability to buy meat, and without meat her strength fails. She is very weary of life, and hopes that her time on earth will not be long."

One wouldn't want to be a student in her school, which may be why there were only seven children left. Seven was too many. But the Newcastle Commission suggests that a school so bad was unusual. The associate commissioner reports that "the great majority of the private schools … are kept by most respectable people, some of them by very admirable men and women," and this is taken as a "unanimous" appraisal. The problem, however, for *all* the for-profit schools was that the teachers were not trained as teachers, so the consensus continued. "The teachers have often no special fitness, or, at least, no fitness that is the fruit of preparation or training for their work but have taken up the occupation in default of or after the failure of other trades."[30]

Teachers were not trained, but "picked up their knowledge *promiscuously*; several combined the trade of school-keeping with another." The schoolteachers had been (some still were) barbers, sailors, soldiers, millers, ship owners, accountants, blacksmiths, journeymen tanners, excise men, solicitors, dockyard laborers, and seamen, among others. Moreover, and this appears to be a common source of complaint, many of the teachers suffered "from some bodily infirmity." One assistant commissioner called "without design, on five masters successively, all of whom were more or less deformed; one, who taught in a cellar, being paralytic and horribly distorted." "A cripple," we are informed, "may not usually make a good teacher."[31]

Prejudices like this informed those commissioners' judgments about inferior quality. Indeed, one of the stories about a "crippled" teacher from an assistant commissioner is extraordinary in what it reveals, both about the prejudices of the commissioners and of the likely reality of the quality of schooling itself.

The story is of "a poor cripple, without legs from infancy," who was himself schooled in a national school (a Church of England school), where at about age fourteen and "possessing good abilities and teaching power," he was employed as what we would call today a teaching assistant (a "monitor"). Eventually, he was "dismissed for misconduct. ... [F]or some years he lived on alms, wheeling himself about the streets." Ultimately, "through the help of friends," he opened a school, which was "two rooms in a small court." Significantly, this was close to a government-subsidized national school, one "in high repute, under an excellent certificated master, an assistant, and five pupil-teachers." This school charged fees of 2d. a week, but was undersubscribed: "there are 150 boys, and there is room for 50 more." In contrast, the commissioner is pained to point out that "the private school under the cripple is crowded to excess; the rooms being about 20 feet by 10, and 8 high, the children have scarcely room to sit." Not only that, but the fees are more expensive at the cripple's school—at 3d. and 6d. per week, depending on grades and subjects. But, and here's the most surprising observation, "boys are sometimes taken from the 1st, 2nd, and 3rd classes of the National school to be FINISHED AT THIS PRIVATE SCHOOL."[32]

Let's go through this remarkable story in detail. First, it's obviously assumed that the reader will think that having a cripple in charge of a private school is not a good thing. Second, the capitals at the end indicate that the commission is surprised by what has been observed: there is an excellent school next door—one, moreover, that is only three-quarters full and less expensive than the private school—and yet not only does the cripple's school attract students to the extent that it is "crowded to excess," but some parents clearly think the education offered in the private school is more desirable than the national school, so they move their children to it for the most critical "finishing" years.

What's going on here? Parents who can afford it prefer the education that this cripple gives to that of the certified teachers in the reputable national school. I've seen the same story countless times in South Asia and sub-Saharan Africa, where the modern-day equivalent of the assistant commissioners puzzle over why parents prefer the low-cost private schools with their untrained teachers and inadequate buildings (some, indeed, run by people with physical disabilities) to the government schools, where the teachers are trained and the buildings substantial. My guess is that the answer to why this is happening is the same in both contexts.

It is a recurring puzzle to the commissioners throughout their report: "Notwithstanding the inefficiencies of many of the private schools, they appear to maintain their ground against the public schools, on account of the preference which exists for them in the minds of the parents." Similarly, "the great popularity of private schools affords another reason for supporting them. The parents … often prefer them, because they think that the pupils are more respectable, that the teachers are more inclined to comply with their wishes, that the children are better cared for, and that they themselves, in choosing such schools for their children, stand in an independent position, and are not accepting a favour from their social superiors. These are natural grounds of preference, and it would be rash to say that they are always unfounded."[33]

It is not hard to imagine why some had this preference. The route to becoming a teacher was being formalized: start out as an apprentice ("pupil") teacher, get a scholarship to training college, and after two years come out as a fully trained teacher. The best young people were typically not selected as pupil-teachers, as young people could make a much better living even as laborers or mechanics. Those who could, did, whereas those who could not, went into teaching.[34] The apprentice teachers were "often too pedantic and too mechanical ... they are apt to fall into the faults of meagreness, dryness, and emptiness, or the opposite and not less mischievous evils of presumption and ostentation."[35]

Moreover, the apprentice teachers "were too much absorbed by preparation for their own examinations to attend properly to the children."[36] Their preparation was overwhelmingly one of "mechanical" rote learning: "The constant repetition of the same routine must always tend to cramp and formalize the mind," reported the schools' inspector, Matthew Arnold.[37]

An overwhelming majority (87 percent) of these pupil-teachers passed the apprenticeship, and most went on to teacher training college. Here they were taught the academic curriculum that is so familiar today: in the first year, "the first four books of Euclid, algebra, as far as quadratic equations, or, instead, that part of the Latin grammar which relates to accidence, concords, genders of nouns, perfect tenses and supines of verbs."[38] In the second year, students chose from physical science, mechanics, mathematics, English literature, and Latin. Everyone also studied religion, "which comprises in the first year the history, chronology, and geography of the Bible, with the text of some one gospel; the text of the Catechism, and of the Morning and Evening Services and Litany, and the scriptural authorities on which they rest. In the second year the Acts of the Apostles and one of the epistles are added. In Church history, the outlines of the history of the Reformation, and of general church history in the fifteenth and sixteenth centuries are learned in the first, and the history of the Book of Common Prayer in the second year."[39]

They learned all this by rote. When they were back in schools, as certified teachers, they then taught it all again by rote, in a "routine and mechanical" fashion,[40] teaching to the tests. As one critic observed, "The manner in which the teaching of elementary subjects, religious knowledge, English history, and geography is conducted is, however, open to grave objection. These subjects, or some of them, are probably indispensable, but the teaching of all of them is liable to degenerate into a mere exercise of verbal memory, and there is strong evidence to show that in point of fact it does so, and that this is attended with bad results on the minds of the students."[41]

It is worth noting that the government was largely in control of the funding of teacher training and its curriculum by this stage. While many of the colleges were set up by private benefactors, only one, Homerton Training College, Cambridge, was supported entirely by voluntary contributions.[42] The Newcastle Commission report notes that "the regulation of the syllabus has produced a degree of uniformity in their management which could hardly have been expected a priori, and by altering it as occasion may require the Committee of Council can modify the character of the instruction given to all the certificated teachers in the kingdom in every point."[43]

Put yourself in the place of a student. Would you like to be taught by someone who has picked up knowledge "promiscuously" through working in varied and exciting professions and can teach you through real-world applications of that knowledge? Or would you prefer to be taught by someone who may be less able to start with, who has learned knowledge by rote and is set to regurgitate it all so that you will do the same?

And what if you are a parent? Would you prefer the young trained teachers, who even the Newcastle Commission points out are often too young and inexperienced to control the class, or would you prefer teachers who are older and more experienced, with "self-knowledge," "discernment in child-nature, and sympathy with childlife"?[44] And would you prefer a school that is obsessed with teaching religion, by rote, or would you prefer schooling to be concerned with practical knowledge and skills, content to leave religion to Sunday school or church itself?

It seems likely that the criticisms of the for-profit private schools by the commissioners assume that a standardized formal curriculum is always better than an informal one grown out of practice. They assume that the certified teacher is always better than the experienced, and that a religious curriculum is superior to a practical one. But poor parents did not seem to share these prejudices. They were criticized for this by the Newcastle Commission: "The anxiety of the parents for the education of their children is, however, limited in its objects. The result which they wish to secure is that which they can themselves appreciate, namely, a knowledge of reading, writing, and arithmetic, of the elements of religion and of the principles of good conduct."[45]

By contrast, the private nonprofit subsidized schools "are almost universally religious in their character, and are to a great extent under the influence and care of ministers of religion of various denominations." These schools had as their leading objective "the improvement of the poorer classes in a moral, and, above all, in a religious point of view."[46] The "general principle" upon which they were based was "that a large portion of the poorer classes of the population were in a condition injurious to their own interests, and dangerous and discreditable to the rest of the community; that it was the duty and the interest of the nation at large to raise them to a higher level, and that religious education was the most powerful instrument for the promotion of this object."[47]

With attitudes like this, poor parents were perhaps justified in not wanting to send their children to such schools. The Newcastle Commission is critical of the parents for preferring the for-profit private schools, but it keeps giving us evidence to show why parents' inhibitions may be justifiable. One assistant commissioner says that parents, rather than acting for the moral betterment of their class, "act individually for the advantage of their respective children."[48] They might, of course, want their children to be "imbued with religious principles," but this is of secondary importance to being taught *"the specific knowledge which will be profitable to the child in life*. It is of some importance in estimating the conduct of the parents to keep this difference of sentiment in view."[49]

Another opines: Poor parents' choice of schools for their children seems "rather to be determined more by the efficiency with which such things as tend to the advancement in life of their children are taught in it, and by its general tone and discipline. The evidence upon this head is conclusive."[50]

From another: "I have been asked whether the poor show a preference for one system of education over another, whether they neglect the education of their children because of religious differences, and whether in short there is anything in the present schools which indisposes parents to send their children to school. I made the most diligent inquiry into these matters, and found no difference of opinion. Schoolmasters, clergymen, ministers, city missionaries, all told me that the poor, in selecting a school, *looked entirely to whether the school supplied good reading, writing, and arithmetic.*"[51]

Of course, none of this is to say that some of the for-profit schools would not have been below par. Some charlatans could have come into the market, or some people remained running schools long after they should have given up—like the widow, noted above, who wanted to die. But it's unlikely that such people could last long in the market. One of the assistant commissioners argues that his district is remarkable for the bad state of its education, yet he says,

> It is a subject of wonder how people so destitute of education as labouring parents commonly are, can be such just judges as they also commonly are of the effective qualifications of a teacher. Good school buildings and the apparatus of education are found for years to be practically useless and deserted, when, if a master chance to be appointed who understands his work, a few weeks suffice to make the fact known, and his school is soon filled, and perhaps found inadequate to the demand of the neighbourhood, and a separate girls' school or infants' school is soon found to be necessary.[52]

This commissioner gives several instances of this happening: In one case, "a schoolmaster began with three pupils, and raised the number in 15 months to 180."[53]

E. G. West reviews all of this evidence and more to conclude that not only was the quantity of schooling in Victorian England maintained without the state intervening, but also quality was maintained, especially in the for-profit private schools that were outside of government control of the curriculum (through teacher training).[54] The inspectors criticized these private schools, but they were criticizing them because they weren't inculcating the preferred religious knowledge and weren't utilizing the formally educated teachers. But once we probe these criticisms, we can see that poor parents appeared to have been making rather shrewd choices. A very practical knowledge base was being taught by teachers with a wide range of practical experience, and parents preferred this to the mechanical learning of abstruse subjects by immature teachers who couldn't even control some classes and who knew nothing else of life apart from being teachers.

Who Paid?

The government began giving some grants to the major school organizations in 1833, and these slowly increased over the years. By the time of the major state intervention of 1870, what proportion of funding was being provided by the state?

The Newcastle Commission notes that school income came from five sources:

1. The government grant
2. School fees paid by parents
3. Subscriptions
4. Endowments
5. Other sources, such as collections in churches and chapels, and occasional gifts[55]

It must be observed that the first is funding from government, while all the rest come from private funds. "Subscriptions" may not be as clear as they might sound. They can be involuntary subscriptions for the purpose of supporting education: sometimes employers who themselves are funding schools "compel the persons in their employment to contribute also, by means of weekly stoppages from their wages."[56] In rural areas, voluntary contributions come from clergymen, landowners, householders, those renting property, and ordinary people. And "in some cases these subscriptions are given by the parents of the scholars"—that is, the subscriptions are given by the parents themselves.[57]

The Newcastle Commission provides detailed figures for the funding of diverse types of nonprofit private schools ("public" schools), which I've collated in Table 13.3.

We can see that in all school types except the "uninspected church" category, fees from parents make up the *biggest* contribution. For instance, in church inspected schools, parental fees make up 29 percent of income, compared with 23 percent from government grant and 27 percent from subscriptions. In the British inspected schools, parental fees make up 40 percent of total income, compared with 26 percent from both government grants and

Table 13.3. School Management Type, Nonprofit Private Schools, by Funding Source

	Gov't grant	School fees	Subscrip- tions	Endow- ments	Other	Public	Private
Church, inspected	23%	29%	27%	9%	12%	23%	77%
Church, uninspected	0%	24%	34%	31%	12%	0%	100%
British, inspected	26%	40%	26%	0%	8%	26%	74%
British, uninspected	0%	50%	33%	6%	12%	0%	100%
Denominational, inspected	26%	46%	22%	0%	5%	26%	74%
Denominational, uninspected	0%	61%	25%	7%	7%	0%	100%
Nondenominational, uninspected	0%	38%	9%	46%	8%	0%	100%

Source: Adapted from Education Commission (1861), 68.

subscriptions. In the denominational inspected schools, school fees make up 46 percent of income, compared with 26 percent from government grants and 22 percent from subscriptions. Overall, the Newcastle Commission reports that for schools that receive grants, government contributes about "a quarter to the income of the schools,"[58] so around 75 percent is from private sources.

In the uninspected schools (which don't get any government grants, so they are 100 percent privately funded), parental fees typically make up a larger proportion of income. So, in the British uninspected schools, it is 50 percent of total income, and in the denominational uninspected, it is 61 percent of all income. In the for-profit private schools, fee income makes up 100 percent of the school's total income.[59]

Overall, in all school types, private sources greatly outweigh public ones. The highest proportion of government funding for any school type is 26 percent.

The Newcastle Commission doesn't give overall figures for the proportion of government funding of the schooling system, but we can estimate an upper bound by combining the figures we've looked at so far. Table 13.1 shows that 66 percent of students were in nonprofit private schools. If government grants made up 25 percent of all income for *all* these schools (we know it is less, as Table 13.3 shows that many nonprofit schools didn't receive any grant at all), and assuming that government grants were distributed equally on a per-student basis, then we'd find that government income was a maximum of 17 percent of total income to schools (that is, 66 percent multiplied by 25). As the for-profit schools get no government income, this means 17 percent is an overestimate of the total income to schools from government sources. A maximum of one-sixth of all income came from government, five-sixths from the private sector.

E. G. West gave details of expenditure by parents, which confirmed that the "*biggest* part of the cost of day schooling … was covered neither by the church nor by philanthropy, but from direct payments (fees) from working families."[60] His figures also reveal that in 1841, the government's annual education subsidy to the *whole* of England and Wales was less than that contributed by the parents of one medium-size city, Bristol, alone!

Milton Friedman read West's work and realized that West's "galloping horse"—the private provision that was already there in education before the state got involved—showed that neither state compulsion nor funding had been needed to provide almost universal education in England and Wales.

No Need for Compulsion: Education in Nineteenth-Century New York State

Friedman also would have read that this wasn't just true of England and Wales. E. G. West demonstrates the same story from New York State. Here, West reports, schooling was nearly universal by 1821, well before compulsory schooling, and with only small state subsidies. In other words, just as for England and Wales, education emerged in large part as a self-organized system.

A New York legislative commissioners' report of 1812 suggested that while public education might not be necessary for a monarchical government like the United Kingdom, it was essential for a republic, because where government was of the people, the people had to be suitably enlightened. But the commissioners noted, just as in England and Wales in the early nineteenth century, that schooling was already widespread: "In a free government …

there is a natural stimulus to education; and accordingly *we find it generally resorted to, unless some great local impediments* interfere."[61]

These impediments were poverty and geography—in remote rural areas, schools were not being established, unlike in the cities, where, the commissioners noted, "schools are generally established by individual exertion. In these cases, the means of education are facilitated, as the expenses of schools are divided among a great many." However, in the remoter, thinly populated rural areas, "education stands greatly in need of encouragement," for the simple reason that families were living too far apart from each other to make (private) schooling economically viable: "Every family, therefore, must either educate its own children, or the children must forego the advantages of education."[62]

The commissioners' report informed the common school law of 1812, which can be interpreted as having similar intent to Forster's act in England fifty-eight years later, to "fill the gaps" in private educational provision. This could, of course, have been done by subsidizing poor families or providing subsidies to school owners to encourage them to open schools in neglected areas. This was not the way forward for the commissioners, who went straight to the solution of "the establishment of Common Schools, under the direction and patronage of the State,"[63] without discussing these other simpler alternatives.

Two points are of interest for our discussion about how Friedman was influenced by E. G. West. First, there was no intention within the 1812 common school act of providing *free* schooling. Yes, there were government subsidies, but as the commissioners in 1812 reported, "it is hardly to be imagined the Legislature intended that the State should support the whole expense of so great an establishment."[64] Far from schooling being free at the point of delivery, parents were required to supplement the government subsidies by paying rate bills (fees) "in proportion to the attendance of their children." These parental fees again made up a "substantial" part of the total schooling costs. In 1830, for instance, the fees contributed by parents made up 59 percent of the total required for teachers' wages ($346,807 out of the total sum of $586,520).

Second, there was not any intention to make schooling compulsory. This simply was not deemed necessary, as most parents were providing schooling for their children.

Schooling was neither free nor compulsory. Yet by 1821, the annual report of the Superintendent of Common Schools of the State of New York showed that schooling had become nearly universal: the total number of children in New York State between the ages of five and sixteen (that is, for eleven years) was 380,000; and the total number of all ages in school was 342,479 (90 percent of the total).[65] Bearing in mind the discussion concerning Foster's parallel estimates, children were likely to have been in school for fewer than eleven years, hence the claim of more or less universality.

In any case, by 1836, the superintendent was able to report that "the number of children actually receiving instruction is equal to the whole number between five and sixteen years of age," with children provided for in the common schools and private schools[66]—that is, universal schooling of the five-to-sixteen-year-old age group appeared without this schooling being free (although it was subsidized) and without compulsion. A sizable proportion of the schooling was provided through purely private schools: a census of New York City for 1829, cited in the superintendent's report of 1830, showed that 18,945 of 24,952 schoolchildren (76 percent) were attending private schools.

Schooling was not made compulsory in New York State until the Compulsory Education Act was passed in 1874. Schooling was not made free at the point of delivery until the Free Schools Act of 1867. Neither was required for universal schooling.

Self-organization worked in New York State during the early nineteenth century, just as it did in England and Wales, to provide education for almost everyone. All this evidence, painstakingly delineated by West, led Milton Friedman to change his mind about the desirability of vouchers.

Change of Mind, Change of Heart

Historically, just as in developing countries today, education emerged as a spontaneous order, a self-organizing system, long before governments got involved to any large degree. Certainly universal, or near-universal, schooling was made available to parents and their children long before there was compulsory schooling. And universal, or near-universal, schooling was made available to parents and their children without it being free but including a sizable proportion of school fees paid for by parents and other parental contributions.

So, the historical evidence is equal to the contemporary evidence from developing countries. The two sets of evidence reinforce each other. Importantly, note that this evidence not only challenges the justification for school vouchers—*the evidence challenges the very foundation of any argument for state funding and compulsion.*

Only the historical evidence was available to Milton Friedman—one can imagine his interest in the evidence now accumulating from developing countries!—but this was enough for him and his wife to change their minds. Although still viewing the education voucher as a useful *stepping-stone*, by 1980 the Friedmans were in favor of something more radical: "We regard the voucher plan as a *partial* solution because it affects neither the financing of schooling nor the compulsory attendance laws. *We favor going much farther.*"[67] Where they favored going instead might be characterized as a move away from the desirability of *universal* vouchers to an emphasis on, at most, *targeted assistance*: "Public financing of hardship cases might remain, but that is a far different matter than having the government finance a school system for 90 percent of the children going to school because 5 or 10 percent of them might be hardship cases."[68]

So, by 1980, they were in favor of government withdrawing from funding of education and compulsory schooling laws, except for, at most, a small minority of parents who were "hardship cases" (a justification based not on externalities but on the protection of minors principle).

Disappointingly, in *Free to Choose*, the Friedmans wrote that they would not elaborate on the more radical implications of their position, recognizing that their new views "on financing and attendance laws will appear to most readers to be extreme."[69] Instead, they returned "to the voucher plan—a much more moderate departure from present practice."[70] But implicit here is that vouchers are now seen, to go back to the beginning of this chapter, as a means, not an end, to a fully privatized education system—to full educational freedom.

The allure of the school voucher is fading fast: Friedman's justification for a system of universal vouchers lost its power after he reviewed the historical evidence accumulated by West. He had supposed that universal education (for democracy) required compulsion and state funding, but it was clear that it did not: universal schooling arose independently in both the United Kingdom and the United States long before there was state compulsion and significant state funding.

In any case, despite many decades of high-level advocacy, little progress has been made in terms of the take-up of voucher programs—with only one in three hundred children in America benefiting from them. Even including all kinds of school choice reforms, including charter schools, we still only get to fewer than one in fifteen children. Vested interests raised against changing education appear to be succeeding in thwarting any change as radical and threatening as this. So, neither the theoretical justification for these kinds of school choice reforms, nor much evidence of their successful application, remains. Fortunately, this isn't the end of the story.

14

Two Types of School Choice

IN THE 1950S, Milton Friedman put forward the argument that democracy required universal compulsion for schooling and universal funding too—for Friedman in the form of school vouchers. The Newcastle Commission report, however, makes clear that, in the nineteenth century at least, parents valued their independence. "In general," the report says, they didn't want schooling to be provided free of charge or made compulsory. "*The sentiment of independence* is strong, and it is wounded by the offer of an absolutely gratuitous education." Most parents, the inspectors and the assistant commissioners agreed, "mistrust the value of a purely gratuitous education"—that is, schooling free at the point of delivery. Nor would they want compulsion, the Newcastle Commission stressed: "An attempt to replace an *independent* system of education by a compulsory system, managed by the Government, would be met by objections   on the grounds of the feelings, both political, social, and religious, to which it would be opposed." In any case, "our education is advancing successfully without it," so "we have not thought that a scheme for compulsory education to be universally applied in this country can be entertained."[1]

Poor parents' wanting *independence* from the state regarding education is a valuable sentiment. It appears to have been lost. I think it's worth revisiting and reclaiming.

Friedman lost his faith in the argument but continued to promote school vouchers as a stepping-stone to a recovery of educational independence. But widespread success has been elusive. Only a tiny percentage of American children are using vouchers nationwide, and no state has more than about

3 percent of school-aged children enrolled with vouchers. The educational vested interests are against vouchers and have the power and desire to block them. That route to educational independence seems to be a dead end.

Some might argue that charter schools are a better way forward—a larger percentage (6 percent) is using them nationwide. And although they have their critics, they clearly are a tremendous source of innovation and improvement in America's schools: "Charter schools, by themselves, are not a strategy for improving education. … Nevertheless, the existence of charter legislation has enabled some truly outstanding school models to come into being. Collectively, they represent the very best educational R&D currently under way."[2]

The problem with charter schools is that they're still under political control and are tolerated only in certain states and districts, and then only up to a point. Previously, I've written about the problems of an extremely successful school chain being thwarted time and time again in its plans to open charter schools, or expand existing ones, because the vested interests in education don't appear to want this challenge. They could open some schools, but "thus far and no further."[3] That experience is not at all untypical. The cap on the number of charter schools means that there is *huge* unmet demand for them. The National Alliance for Public Charter Schools estimates that there were 1,043,311 student names on waiting lists for charter schools nationally in 2013–14. Some students may have their names on more than one charter school list, so, correcting for this, the National Alliance estimates that there were 586,511 "individual students … hoping to attend a public charter school" who were not able to realize their choice.[4]

Political control leading to unmet demand—doesn't this raise the question of why those with power and influence can thwart the desires of parents and students for a different, presumably better, schooling experience? Why are we letting those with power and influence preempt and override the educational desires of parents for their children—desires that we've seen historically led to education that seemed to offer better, more appropriate options for families, and that we see across the world today are leading to better educational outcomes? Why do we allow this to happen?

This leads me to my main objection to charter schools and school vouchers. Both are still part of a "supplicant model" that assumes that government *should oversee* education. We're allowed to approach government as supplicants and ask, beg even, to be allowed some small-scale, baby steps that embody some aspects of educational independence. The supplicant model allows some of us to be lucky and get through the convoluted processes to try some small-scale experimentation. But it also grants these exceptions only within strict parameters, and at governments' total discretion.

That's not what parents in Victorian England—and, by assumption, in nineteenth-century America—wanted. They cleaved to their educational *independence*. I believe we should be bold enough to rekindle that desire again today. How? A first step would be to see if the grassroots educational revolution of low-cost private schools that is taking place across much of the developing world could happen in the United States too.

Low-Cost Private Schools for America

It may be helpful to distinguish between two kinds of educational choice: School Choice (with capital letters, referring to that brought about through government reform) and school choice (in lowercase, denoting the free acts of individual parents and children, outside of government reform). Sixty years of School Choice has brought around 7 percent of American children into some form of heavily constrained independence, as we saw in chapter 12. How many children has school choice impacted?

There are around 5.4 million attending private schools in the United States (10.8 percent of America's children). There are also an estimated 1.8 million children being homeschooled (3.6 percent of America's children)—that is, more than twice as many children are getting these two types of provision—through school choice—than there are in all the different types of School Choice provision (7.2 million children compared with 3.5 million). Indeed, the number of children in the (voluntary) school choice movement is forty times greater than the number of children in School Choice voucher programs.

Children are going to private schools, paid for by parents who are not waiting for any government permission to be allowed to do so. There are regulations on private schools in some states, but these are, in America, typically easily satisfied. Likewise, children are being homeschooled, again without parents having to go through all the rigmarole we've witnessed in terms of

School Choice reform. (It's true that governments can get in the way and stop these kinds of freedoms. For example, in Germany, homeschooling is illegal, and in many countries, there are restrictions on private schools.)

So, a question naturally arises from this discussion: If you are someone like a Milton Friedman today, wanting to move toward educational freedom, toward educational independence, as was Friedman's desire later in life, what would reward your energies the most? Should you focus on School Choice, which, with considerable blood, sweat, and tears, has delivered x percentage of children? Or should you instead focus on school choice, the spontaneous-order, self-organizing educational system that, with minimal fuss and bother, has delivered $2x$?

I agree; the $2x$ is still small. It's 14.4 percent of America's children, not a huge percentage, only one in seven children. However, one purpose of this book has been to spell out that the self-organized, spontaneous order in education has considerably more potential than that.

We are brought full circle. In the first part of this book, we looked at the growing evidence from developing countries that shows the extraordinary revolution of low-cost private education taking place around the world. It serves a majority of urban schoolchildren, including those on the poverty line, and a large minority of rural children. There may be 450,000 of these low-cost private schools in India alone; one state of Nigeria, Lagos State, probably has 14,000. Children in the private schools outperform those in public schools, even after controlling for background variables and selectivity bias. The private schools are fair to girls, indeed sought out by parents as safe havens for their girls, a point not lost on terrorist organizations.

It was a great moment when Milton Friedman changed his mind after decades arguing for government intervention in education through compulsion and vouchers, after he saw that another spontaneous order in education had emerged in nineteenth-century England and America (and indeed elsewhere[5]). Friedman's conversion based on the evidence shows it isn't futile to investigate how we can break government's hold on schools, including government's control of assessment and curriculum, as well as its compulsory model of schooling. There are examples of private organizations, like the Indian software education company NIIT and International Baccalaureate, that are organizing assessment and curriculum outside of governments. The thought experiments in the earlier chapters suggest ways in which private organizations can increasingly take away government control. The right kind of educational entrepreneurs are needed to take areas such as assessment and curriculum away from government too, allowing the spontaneous order fully to flourish. In any case, under conditions of educational freedom, compulsion becomes less of a problem if educational institutions are clearly providing what customers and communities desire.

But the argument of the earlier chapters was predicated on the widespread existence and use of low-cost private schools. It doesn't take a genius to point out that there is no low-cost private school revolution in America, or Britain, or elsewhere. But could there be?

Will the First Entrepreneur Step Forward in America?

There are many hundreds of thousands of school entrepreneurs in Africa and Asia today, but there must have been a *first entrepreneur* somewhere who experimented with creating a low-cost private school, in some district of one country, who was the first to succeed and thus provide a model that others began to emulate. Or more likely there was a series of entrepreneurs, simultaneously discovering the same principle in various places across different countries. But in any case, it must have started on an exceedingly small scale. And look at the outcome today—a grassroots education revolution, education by the people, for the people. There is no reason (as we shall see) why the same process cannot happen in America and England today. All it requires is for that first entrepreneur to get started, and to succeed, and for others to come in and copy what he or she is doing.

If you're an entrepreneur, or aspire to be an entrepreneur, why not set out to create a stand-alone low-cost private school, or even a chain of low-cost private schools, to begin this disruption of the status quo, this educational revolution? If you're an investor or philanthropist, you can look for potential entrepreneurs to support or encourage in this endeavor. And if you're neither entrepreneur nor investor nor philanthropist but, say, a parent or grandparent with children, looking for something better than what the government offers you, then let your views be known in your community. Many of the low-cost schools we've seen in Africa and Asia emerged because potential entrepreneurs became aware of demand from within their communities. Indeed, sometimes they were pestered by the community until they opened a school.

But there can be niggling doubts—doubts that I've also had for years until recently. In Africa, Asia, and Latin America, low-cost private schools emerge readily and easily. Are there, perhaps, some crucial reasons why the same has not happened in America or England? We'll look at seven possible reasons later in this chapter and suggest that none of these are valid. But before we do that, let's set out some parameters for a possible business model for a chain of low-cost private schools for America. The following is based on a model devised with MBA students at the Wharton School of the University of Pennsylvania in Philadelphia.

Outline for a Business Model for Low-Cost Private Schools in America

Our goal is to build a high-quality, low-cost private school in the United States that is scalable. We need to ensure that the business is sustainable at the individual school level first—the school is our unit economic model. We'll focus on K–12 schools, with an initial focus on K–5 grades. We'll target families who do not have access to quality public schools and cannot afford traditional private schools.

How will our low-cost model find cost savings over a traditional private school? We will seek cost savings in four key areas:

1. Staffing
2. Facilities
3. Curriculum
4. Technology

Staffing

There are various ways of keeping staffing costs low. One is to employ teachers who have retired from the profession or who are no longer active in teaching, but who would be excited about coming back to teach in an innovative environment such as ours. Such teachers are likely to agree to lower compensation than others. Second, we can employ newly certified teachers who can come in at the lower end of the pay scale. As we are growing to be a chain of schools, these newly qualified teachers can grow with the organization, becoming teacher trainers or mentors, curriculum developers, lead teachers, school managers, regional managers, and so on. So, there would be an exciting career path for them that could encourage them to join, even if salaries were low to begin with. We can also employ teachers part-time or on a daily rate, which again can reduce costs.

Facilities

Facilities would typically be rented, so as not to tie up capital in buildings. In some American cities, declining enrollment in Catholic schools has led to major consolidation and school closings, leaving empty school buildings for lease or even purchase. Such schools are likely to be close to target populations and may not require too much refurbishment to make them suitable for students. But we can also look at leasing nontraditional spaces, as many charter schools across America are already doing, such as office suites or church and community buildings.

Curriculum

We can reduce costs on the curriculum as we go to scale, by developing a "school in a box" model. This process will create high-quality materials that can be used across all schools in the chain, focusing on common standards and curricula, teaching plans, lessons, and assessments that will streamline the processes for teachers. Technology can deliver these where appropriate (for example, assessments). How does this save money? With lesson plans, curriculum, and assessments developed centrally, this reduces the requirement for teacher-prep time and planning days, thus enabling more on-task teaching to take place. It should also be possible to have economies of scale in purchasing curriculum materials; technology can ensure the need for less printed material.

Technology

Our model envisages using some level of blended learning—that is, where the student learns at least part of the curriculum content through online (or indeed offline) delivery; assessments can also be delivered and assessed online. This approach has the possibility of allowing a slight increase in the student-teacher ratio (unqualified adults, for instance, can supervise students when they are in the learning labs, so qualified teachers during those times are not required). As there is a great deal of excellent and free content on the web, this can also reduce costs of curriculum and assessment content, although the cost of curating the material would have to be included in the start-up funding.

A Model Emerges

Using each of these assumptions, and using standard costs for staff, facilities, and so on, we developed eight models based on different permutations of full- or part-time staff, high or low levels of blended learning, and leasing or owning the buildings. These give a variety of outcomes of sustainable school models with fees of around $3,000 per annum. For instance, Table 14.1 shows the model with part-time staff, low blended learning, and leased buildings. This requires an annual fee per student of $3,000, or about $58 per week. The building is leased, but the budget includes infrastructural improvements, fixtures, furniture, and fittings of around $400,000, and a technology budget of $182,000, for a total of $582,000 amortized over ten years.

We can break down these costs to show the annual costs per student of each element of the school. In Table 14.2 we can see that teaching staff takes up 42 percent of the total, with the facility rent taking up 26 percent.

Table 14.3 shows how the per-pupil cost varies as a function of enrollment, student/teacher ratio, and total school costs. We can see that school can be made more affordable by keeping the total costs of the facilities as low as possible (such as by finding buildings with lower rents) and/or by increasing the number of students.

Table 14.1. Low-cost Private School for America,
Outline Model

Key assumptions	
Total enrollment	360
Pupils per class/lab	30
Active classrooms (two classes per grade, K–5, minus classes in labs)	10
Computer labs	2
Aides in classroom (grades K–2)	6
Number of grades (K–5)	6
Number of class equivalents (two per grade)	12
Estimated tuition	**$3,000.86**

Source: Author's team analysis.

Table 14.2. Breakdown of Costs per Student
per Annum

	Total	%
Instructional staff	$1,247.36	42%
Noninstructional staff	$159.03	5%
Other employee expenses	$175.53	6%
Instructional resources	$250.89	8%
Facilities	$777.78	26%
Administrative plus other	$228.61	8%
School capital costs	$161.87	5%
Total	**$3,000.86**	**100%**

Source: Author's team analysis.

Affordability

How affordable is this model of low-cost private education? The key here is to look at families' *discretionary* income—that is, the amount families have left over after spending on all the essentials, such as food, housing, and clothing. Typically, discretionary expenditure is what is left over for savings, Christmas and birthday presents, vacations, eating out, and movies, as well as fees for education. US household income is split into deciles, with the poorest decile

Table 14.3. Per-pupil Cost as a Function of Enrollment and Total Cost

		Total Enrollment / Students per Classroom			
	300 / 25	**360 / 30**	**420 / 35**	**540 / 45**	**720 / 60**
500,000	1,667	1,389	1,190	926	694
750,000	2,500	2,083	1,786	1,389	1,042
1,000,000	3,333	2,778	2,381	1,852	1,389
1,250,000	4,167	3,472	2,976	2,315	1,736
1,500,000	5,000	4,167	3,571	2,778	2,083
1,750,000	5,833	4,861	4,167	3,241	2,431
2,000,000	6,667	5,556	4,762	3,704	2,778

Total Annual Cost of School (USD)

☐ < $1,500 per year / $8.33 per day	▨ < $3,000 per year / $16.67 per day	▧ > $3,000 per year / $16.67 per day

Source: Author's team analysis.

earning up to $11,165 per annum, while the richest decile earns $140,197 or more.

The discretionary income of each of these deciles is shown in Figure 14.1. From this graph, we can see that the low-cost model we've constructed here begins to be just about affordable for those in the fourth-poorest decile (who earn between $26,785 and $35,682 per annum). Their average discretionary income is $6,040, which is enough to send one child to low-cost private school and would almost cover the costs of two children, assuming that all discretionary income is spent on school fees. The official US poverty threshold for a family of four with two school-age children is $24,339 per annum.[6] So, our low-cost private school begins to look affordable for families just above the official poverty line.

This should be compared with average private-school fees in the United States, which come in at $9,263 per annum at the elementary level (or three times higher than the fees in our model).[7] Again for two children, these average private-school fees begin to become affordable to families in the seventh-richest quintile (who earn $59,550 to $75,977 per annum), and more comfortably for those in the eighth-richest quintile (who earn $75,978 to

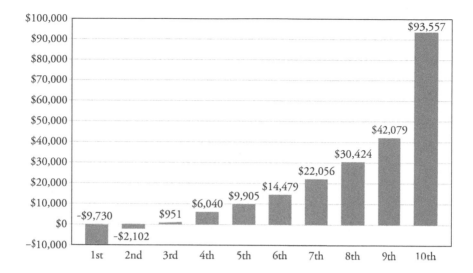

Source: Bureau of Labor Statistics, 2015. Graphic courtesy of Infogram: https://infogram.com/discretionary_income_by_income_decile.

Figure 14.1. Discretionary US Income by Decile

$99,623) and above. Our model clearly could make private school affordable to many more income levels than is currently the case.

So, the private-school model laid out here begins to be affordable to those just above the poverty line in America. In other industries, as they become embedded, costs fall dramatically, and the same would likely be true of education. Philanthropy or targeted funding could widen accessibility to these low-cost private schools further still. In combination, both factors could make this model accessible to all. But would it be desirable? Is there any market to send children to a school of this type? We conducted some opportunistic market research in poor suburbs of Philadelphia (see Figure 14.2). This shows that of those not currently using private schools, 90 percent of parents would consider private schools if there was something within their budget.

In interviews, it was clear that parents wanted their children to attend private school but struggled to imagine how they could pay, given typical assumptions about tuition costs—53 percent of survey respondents could not provide a "willingness to pay" number without prompting. But parents also said that they were willing to find a way to make private schools work,

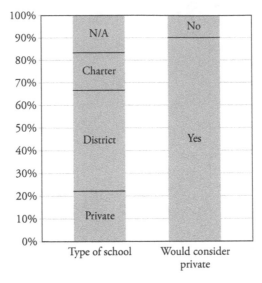

Source: Data from interviews conducted by students from Wharton School of the University of Pennsylvania in Philadelphia.

Figure 14.2. Parents' School Choices in Low-Income Neighborhoods of Philadelphia

especially at a tuition range of $1,500 to $3,000 spread over multiple payments. We were told that it would be "easier to pay tuition if monthly or daily." It is also worth noting that there are private voucher programs in the United States today, such as those provided by the Children's Scholarship Fund. A typical annual voucher of $1,500 apparently can attract a top-up of around $3,500 from poor parents. This reinforces the suggestion that the amount of tuition we're proposing could be affordable.

Where in America?

Finally, where would be a good place to start a chain of low-cost private schools in America? There's no definitive answer to this, of course—and the most preferable place for any entrepreneur is probably the entrepreneur's hometown, where he or she will have the desired contacts and familiarity to make it work. However, it may be worth setting out some criteria that one could use—say, if an outsider was coming in to start a chain of low-cost private schools in America, or one was looking to expand a stand-alone school to a chain.

The first hurdle to overcome is regulation, particularly in terms of teacher certification, curriculum, and school hours:

- Teacher certification: Most states researched (twenty-plus) do not require certified teachers; some may require a bachelor's degree, but even this requirement is limited.

- Curriculum: Requirements vary significantly from absolutely no curriculum oversight to strict rules; most common regulation requires a curriculum of similar quality to that required of the local public schools.

- School day/hours: Most (but not all) states regulate the number of days and/or hours that students must be in school to comply with compulsory attendance. This varies widely between strict limitations on days versus total hours of attendance.

Other regulatory factors, such as accreditation, health and safety, and tax exemption, are unlikely to be major factors in choosing locations.

In Table 14.4, to illustrate the kind of information considered, we've ranked a selection of states, as well as the District of Columbia, in the eastern half of the United States based on their "regulatory flexibility." We gave each state a 1–5 scale rating (where 1 is the most flexible, 5 the least flexible) for teacher certification requirements and curriculum flexibility. So, for teacher certification, 1 shows no requirements and 5 shows "must be certified" (usually by the state). For curriculum flexibility, 1 is no or limited requirements, while 5 shows the state-prescribed curriculum or requirements to be largely similar to those of public schools. Hence the lower the score, the better for our purposes.

Five other key determinants for attractive markets to enter are likely to include the following:

- Presence of low-performing traditional public schools: This may not be hard to find, as nearly every large American city in the United States has a public education system marked by underachieving schools.

- Inefficient supply of alternatives to traditional public schools: It may be that the most attractive cities are those that already have charter school

Table 14.4. Major Regulations by Selected States and Washington, DC

State	Teacher certification	Curriculum flexibility	Total flexibility
Arkansas	1	1	2
Virginia	1	1	2
North Carolina	1	1	2
South Carolina	1	1	2
Florida	1	1	2
Massachusetts	1	1	2
Missouri	1	2	3
Wisconsin	1	2	3
Kentucky	1	3	4
West Virginia	1	3	4
Georgia	1	3	4
New Jersey	1	4	5
Connecticut	1	4	5
Illinois	2	3	5
Mississippi	4	1	5
DC	3	3	6
Minnesota	3	4	7
Michigan	3	4	7
Tennessee	4	3	7
Indiana	5	2	7
New York	3	5	8
Louisiana	4	4	8
Ohio	4	4	8
Maryland	4	4	8
Rhode Island	4	5	9
Iowa	5	5	10
Alabama	5	5	10
Pennsylvania	5	5	10

Source: Data from interviews and library research conducted by students from Wharton School of the University of Pennsylvania in Philadelphia.

enrollments, as this suggests that a significant segment of the population is frustrated with the status quo and willing to experiment with new education models. Long waiting lists for charter schools would also be a signal that there could be a market for low-cost private schools.

- Large, growing child and youth population: Obviously, the larger this is, the more attractive the growth prospects.

- Large black population: In some places, black families have shown a greater willingness to enroll their children in charter schools than Latino (or Hispanic) families,[8] which suggests that these families may also be open to enrollment in low-cost private schools.

- Access to public-school alternatives, such as charter schools, as well as a friendly regulatory environment.

Housing, demographic, and educational data related to these criteria have been entered for the largest US cities in Table 14.5. From these data, certain cities jump out as being particularly desirable locations, other things being equal, to open a chain of low-cost private schools (see Figure 14.3). So Jacksonville, Florida, for instance, has on the positive side a friendly regulatory environment (with the highest score of 2), a low cost of living (which is likely to make staffing cheaper), a large population of black students (who may be more likely to try alternatives such as we are proposing), and a high poverty rate (so there is need for what we are offering). On the downside, it has a low charter school market share and a smaller population under age five.

All of this is, of course, an outline only. The aim has been to show that it should be possible to create a comprehensive, financially viable business model for a chain of low-cost private schools in America. We'd need to bring in the cost of living in different areas of the country to make this conclusion more robust, but I've illustrated the kind of steps needed to make the argument.

So, let's return to the question raised earlier: Are there reasons why low-cost private schools are commonplace in Africa and Asia but are unlikely to appear in America or England? There are seven reasons that could be given, seven objections as to why low-cost private education could not emerge here. I don't think any of the objections are substantial.

Table 14.5. Key housing, Demographic, and Educational
Indicators for Largest US Cities

City	State	Population	Per capita income	Median rent
New York	New York	8,244,910	$30,498	$1,071
Los Angeles	California	3,819,702	$27,620	$1,077
Chicago	Illinois	2,707,120	$27,148	$885
Houston	Texas	2,145,146	$25,927	$793
Philadelphia	Pennsylvania	1,536,471	$21,117	$819
Phoenix	Arizona	1,469,471	$24,460	$847
San Antonio	Texas	1,359,758	$21,812	$748
San Diego	California	1,326,179	$32,553	$1,259
Dallas	Texas	1,223,229	$26,716	$789
San Jose	California	967,487	$33,233	$1,339
Jacksonville	Florida	827,908	$25,227	$872
Indianapolis	Indiana	827,609	$24,334	$716
Austin	Texas	820,611	$30,286	$882
San Francisco	California	812,826	$45,478	$1,328
Columbus	Ohio	797,434	$23,144	$753
Fort Worth	Texas	758,738	$23,792	$803
Charlotte	N. Carolina	751,087	$30,984	$823
Detroit	Michigan	706,585	$15,062	$747
El Paso	Texas	665,568	$17,812	$620
Memphis	Tennessee	652,050	$21,007	$758
Boston	Massachusetts	625,087	$31,856	$1,199
Seattle	Washington	620,778	$40,868	$958
Denver	Colorado	619,968	$30,806	$798
Baltimore	Maryland	619,493	$23,333	$859
Washington	D.C.	617,996	$42,078	$1,063
Nashville	Tennessee	609,644	$26,550	$773
Louisville	Kentucky	602,011	$24,696	$647
Milwaukee	Wisconsin	597,867	$18,884	$736
Portland	Oregon	593,820	$29,797	$813
Oklahoma City	Oklahoma	591,967	$25,042	$669
Las Vegas	Nevada	589,317	$26,993	$999
Albuquerque	New Mexico	552,804	$25,819	$712
Tucson	Arizona	525,796	$20,243	$690
Fresno	California	501,362	$19,709	$832
Sacramento	California	472,178	$25,427	$959
Long Beach	California	465,576	$25,929	$1,033
Kansas City	Kansas	463,202	$25,683	$721
Mesa	Arizona	446,518	$24,647	$856
Virginia Beach	Virginia	442,707	$30,873	$1,143
Atlanta	Georgia	432,427	$35,453	$884
Miami	Florida	408,750	$19,745	$875
Tulsa	Oklahoma	396,466	$26,069	$676
Cleveland	Ohio	393,806	$16,302	$628
Minneapolis	Minnesota	387,753	$29,551	$774
St. Louis	Missouri	318,069	$21,406	$658

Sources: Data compiled by the author from the US Census Bureau; American
Community Survey; Council for Community and Economic
Research; National Alliance for Public Charter Schools.

Cost of living index	Population <5 years of age	% Black	Poverty rate	Charter market share	Regulation flexibility score
225	6.4%	25.2%	19.1%	5%	8
131	6.8%	9.7%	19.5%	15%	n/a
117	6.9%	34.0%	20.9%	11%	n/a
95	8.2%	24.4%	21.0%	18%	n/a
123	6.6%	44.0%	25.1%	23%	10
97	8.5%	6.2%	19.1%	22%	n/a
88	8.7%	6.8%	18.9%	26%	n/a
132	6.2%	6.7%	14.1%	10%	n/a
99	7.6%	24.6%	22.3%	12%	n/a
153	7.5%	3.0%	10.8%	n/a	n/a
97	7.1%	30.5%	14.3%	6%	2
94	7.6%	27.1%	17.9%	25%	7
96	7.4%	8.4%	18.4%	n/a	n/a
163	4.4%	6.2%	11.9%	n/a	n/a
90	7.5%	27.8%	21.4%	21%	8
91	9.1%	18.6%	17.0%	n/a	n/a
95	7.7%	34.5%	13.9%	n/a	2
97	7.0%	82.7%	34.5%	41%	7
93	8.2%	3.2%	24.1%	n/a	n/a
86	7.5%	62.6%	25.4%	6%	7
140	5.2%	25.0%	21.2%	10%	2
115	5.1%	7.8%	12.7%	n/a	n/a
105	7.4%	10.3%	19.2%	23%	n/a
116	6.6%	64.3%	21.3%	15%	8
145	5.5%	52.9%	18.5%	41%	n/a
89	7.1%	28.7%	17.8%	n/a	7
91	6.7%	22.5%	17.3%	No charters	4
101	8.0%	39.4%	26.3%	22%	3
116	6.1%	6.4%	16.3%	n/a	n/a
91	8.0%	14.4%	16.6%	11%	n/a
90	7.5%	10.8%	13.1%	24%	n/a
n/a	7.1%	3.2%	15.7%	10%	n/a
95	7.0%	4.6%	21.3%	18%	n/a
107	8.8%	7.7%	24.9%	n/a	n/a
118	7.6%	14.0%	17.3%	n/a	n/a
n/a	7.5%	13.2%	19.1%	n/a	n/a
100	7.5%	29.9%	18.1%	37%	n/a
n/a	7.6%	2.8%	11.9%	18%	n/a
n/a	6.7%	19.2%	6.8%	n/a	2
97	6.4%	54.3%	22.6%	10%	4
109	6.2%	21.2%	27.3%	12%	2
89	7.5%	15.5%	19.3%	n/a	n/a
102	6.7%	53.1%	31.2%	28%	8
109	6.9%	18.2%	22.7%	21%	7
92	6.7%	49.8%	26.0%	31%	3

St. Louis, MO

+ Friendly regulatory environment, low cost of living, large population of black students, high poverty rate, low charter school market share

− Small population under age five

Charlotte, NC

+ Friendly regulatory environment, low cost of living, large population of black students, large population under age five

− Low poverty rate

Atlanta, GA

+ Friendly regulatory environment, low cost of living, large population of black students, high poverty rate

− Small population under age five, low charter school market share (although numbers are increasing − 29% growth in enrollment between 2011 and 2012)

Jacksonville, FL

+ Friendly regulatory environment, low cost of living, large population of black students

− Low poverty rate, low charter school market share (although numbers are increasing − 43% growth in enrollment between 2011 and 2012)

Louisville, KY

+ Friendly regulatory environment, low cost of living, large population of black students

− Charter schools don't currently exist in KY; small population under age five, low poverty rate

Milwaukee, WI

+ Friendly regulatory environment, low cost of living, large population of black students, large population under age five, high poverty rate, large charter school market share

− Given prevalence of private school vouchers, model may not be deemed replicable if Milwaukee is initial launch spot

Source: Author's team analysis

Figure 14.3. Selected Attractive City Markets in the US to Launch Low-Cost Private Schools

Seven Objections, Dismissed

1. Public schools are not as bad as they are in the developing world.

The first objection is that public schools might not be as bad as they are in Nigeria or India, say, so there wouldn't be the same incentive for parents to find an alternative to the sector.

This objection is clearly true, but not as relevant as it might seem. It's been made clear to me many times, in many different countries, that the desire for private education is *not* simply a reflection of how bad the public schools are. Many parents have a genuine, deep-seated desire for schools that are accountable to them that only private schools can satisfy.

In any case, many parents do find public schools *undesirable enough* in many parts of America and Britain for parents to want to leave the sector. Charter schools are seen by many parents as a preferred alternative to public schools; there are six hundred thousand students on waiting lists, indicating a huge unmet demand to leave the public sector. Is it possible, perhaps, that enough of these aspirational parents would see that there is an alternative to the public schools they are keen for their children to exit? Is it possible, perhaps, that enough parents could be found to make the first one or two low-cost private schools sustainable, to enable investors to risk investing in a chain of schools?

Moreover, while the public schools may be tolerable to communities, I have found many parents (including public-school teachers) who argue that the public schools are not good enough *for their children*, even if they felt they were fine in general.

2. Public education alternatives will crowd out low-cost private schools.

The second objection is related to the first—yes, public schools can be bad, but governments allow certain freedoms for parents and others to set up alternatives *paid for by government*, such as charter schools, and these innovative schools will therefore crowd out any desire of parents for low-cost private schools (for which they'd have to pay fees themselves). Since I stated my desire to open a low-cost private school in England, quite a few people have asked why I'm doing that, when there's the option of creating a "free school" or "academy"—the nearest equivalent to charter schools in England—that will bring government funding. There's something in this objection. If excellent charter schools are available that overcome some of the problems in the state sector, then the demand for them may well meet the same demand that might have been there for low-cost private schools.

Two points can be raised in response, however. First, as we've already noted, there is a huge unmet demand for charter schools, whose places must be allocated using lotteries because of that demand. One excellent charter school, for instance, has a genuine waiting list of three thousand students, updated each year, twice the school's total enrollment. But charter schools are unable to expand to meet this demand—there are huge bureaucratic impediments to so doing. The same is true in England concerning free schools and academies. Since I've come out as someone interested in creating a wholly independent school, many have told me their horror stories of dealing with government bureaucracy while setting up free schools and suggested that if they could do it all over again, they'd go for full independence. So, there may be some crowding out for sure, but it may not be enough to eradicate all demand.

3. Regulations are onerous.

The third objection is that perhaps there is no burgeoning low-cost private school movement in America or Britain because regulations here are onerous, more onerous than they are overseas, or at least not as easy to get around. It's certainly not true in many states in America, which have absolutely no regulations for private education. Texas is one such state. And in England, while it's true that there are some regulations to meet, especially for building requirements, safeguarding of children, and so on, it is possible to meet them within reasonable budgets, so ensuring that a genuinely low-cost private education can still be offered. Crucially, there are no onerous regulations on who can be recruited as teachers and what they should be paid, so this can surely enable low-cost private schools to develop.

4. Costs are too high.

Low-cost private schools in Africa and Asia can afford to be low cost because everything there can be low cost, whether it's teacher salaries, cost of land and buildings, or textbooks and printing. This is true, so of course we can't afford to create educational opportunities that are proportionately as low cost as they are in Africa and Asia—that's agreed. But the costs in England and America are not so high that you can't create something that is affordable to families. You just must look at the business as a no-frills business. So, you should rent premises rather than purchase them, and building rents in low-income parts of town can be much cheaper than expected. And you don't look for the most expensive teachers, but this means you can target energetic young people who are keen to learn, or retired teachers who are eager to contribute more, or teachers who no longer wish to work in the public sector and would be willing to work for less if the satisfaction was greater in a low-cost private school.

5. Can private education ever truly be affordable?

The objection here is that we could never get fees low enough to be affordable for low-income families in the way that they are in Africa, South Asia, and many other places. Already I've given some indication of affordability for the American model above to suggest this might not be true. Let's additionally look at the United Kingdom here.

Currently, private schools are unaffordable except for the richest income quintile in the United Kingdom. School fees are reportedly an average of £15,500 per annum[9]—that is, around £298 per week (dividing £15,500 by 52). Data on UK family *discretionary* income show that this is affordable only for the richest quintile.[10]

The richest quintile has on average £688 per week discretionary income (see Table 14.6), so if two children are in school, even these families will use up *all* their discretionary income on fees.

But I've devised a business model rather like the one I described for America above, which has school fees of £52 per week. Table 14.6 again (fourth column) shows that £52 per week is affordable even for parents in the *second-poorest* quintile—for one child, at least (their discretionary income is

Table 14.6. Affordability of Private School in the UK Based on
Family Discretionary Income

Quintile	Discretionary income (per week)	How many children in private school can a family afford? (average fees)	How many children in private school can a family afford? (low cost)
Poorest income quintile	-£23	-0.1	-0.4
2nd quintile	£56	0.2	1.1
3rd quintile	£111	0.4	2.1
4th quintile	£264	0.9	5.1
Richest income quintile	£688	2.3	13.2

Source: Data on discretionary income from Centre for Economics and Business
Research (2017), 5–7.

£56 per week). Parents in the third quintile (discretionary income £111 per
week) can now afford to send two children to private school. With fees as
low as this, private education no longer needs to be the preserve of only the
richest. And, of course, we're not ruling out that there could be philanthropy
and/or targeted assistance to fund scholarships for the poorest of the poor,
thereby increasing the way in which the Western version of these low-cost
private schools could meet the needs of all low-income families. And as we
said earlier, prices are likely to fall as the model becomes established, just as
prices fall in other industries.

6. The lure of welfarism is strong.

A sixth objection is that in countries like the UK and the United States,
"welfarism" is too strong—that is, lower-income families might be very aware
of their welfare entitlements to, among other things, free public education.
Because they feel they have this entitlement, they would resist paying for
what they believe should be theirs by right for free. Low-income families in
America and Britain are not used to paying for education as families elsewhere
around the world are, so they would avoid doing so. I think there's something
in this objection; it's likely in my view to be the strongest impediment to
the public using low-cost private schools. But even here, I don't believe it is

insurmountable. I've had enough discussions over the last few months, as I've been opening a low-cost private school in England, with parents who *don't* feel this entitlement, and would be willing to pay, to make me realize that this may not be a serious impediment to getting the first few schools off the ground. Once enough families are using the first couple of schools, then the whole thing can take off, and those who may have felt this entitlement earlier could even lose it, if they saw a better education being provided to families similar to themselves, at a price they could afford.

7. No educational entrepreneurs or investors are interested.

The seventh objection is that there are no low-cost private schools in America and Britain because no educational entrepreneurs or investors are interested here. They've got better things to invest in. They've got no interest in low-cost private education. I don't believe this for a minute, but I must admit I've got little or no evidence to deny it yet. That's why I am issuing a challenge now. This chapter is a call to arms for those entrepreneurs and investors who might be interested to come forward and put their resources to work.

And why would we want to do it? Because we are dissatisfied with what government has done to education. We see the examples from around the developing world, of higher standards, greater access, and nonpoliticized educational provision, and we want that for ourselves. Charles Murray puts it well. He wants real school choice, including an expansion of private schooling, because of its "real advantages," such as the cultivation of "safe and orderly learning environments," curricula that "typically provide more substance ... than the curriculum offered by the typical public school," and "a supportive intellectual environment for hardworking students who, in public schools, are often subjected to peer pressures *not* to study."[11] But he realizes that "none of these good things will be implemented by a large, centrally administered public school system. All of them are too politically sensitive for one reason or another. ... Large school systems will dither, posture, and get nowhere."[12]

So many other commentators agree with him—the same sentiments are implicit in the writings of all the educational reformers we've referenced in earlier chapters. Government school systems "will dither, posture, and get nowhere." But we want to get somewhere. We can only do it outside of the state.

And it doesn't have to take too long. As was mentioned earlier, chains of low-cost private schools for developing countries were first mooted in my 2006 IFC/*Financial Times* prize-winning essay "Educating Amaretch." Within two years, the American entrepreneur Jay Kimmelman, after coming to visit me in Newcastle, had cofounded Bridge International Academies in Kenya, which opened its first schools in 2009 and reached one hundred thousand students within five years. Within five years, this one chain reached roughly 60 percent of the number of students using vouchers in America—and voucher proponents have had sixty years to get that far.

Clearly the idea of chains of schools has gone from being an idea to a proven concept at scale. The idea did not depend on getting any government reforms through: governments, of course, need to be persuaded not to make it all impossible, but that's far easier than getting School Choice (with capital *S* and *C*, to signify the top-down approach) reforms past the gatekeepers and vested interest groups that have resisted attempts so far in America.

So if the time and scale were to be the same in America as in the developing world, then possibly by five years after the publication of this book, say by 2025, there could be the American equivalent of Bridge International serving one hundred thousand students, serving them better than the public equivalent, and starting to make a huge impact on American education. In America, much more obviously than elsewhere, competitors would be entering the same market; it's easy to see how the first million children could quickly be served, a respectable 2 percent of total enrollment in America. And after that, growth would dramatically accelerate.

It only needs the first entrepreneur or entrepreneurs to dip their toe in the water and make a start. Is anyone up for it?

15

Education as Spontaneous Order

IN APRIL 2000, a few months after I'd discovered for myself low-cost private schools in the slums of Hyderabad, India, I went to Delhi and met Dr. Sugata Mitra for the first time. He was then head of research for NIIT, the software training company. The experiment that was to make him world famous, the "hole in the wall," had been going for only a year then, its results already receiving accolades. It's hard to take oneself back to the excitement and shock of his findings because use of the internet has progressed so rapidly, and we all know *now* how children can access it so readily. But then we didn't know, and Sugata helped us see some of its enormous potential for learning.

The NIIT headquarters bordered the slum area of Kalkaji, where there were many children who didn't attend school. Walking in that area one day, Sugata wondered, *can these children learn through the internet without any tuition?* He constructed an "internet kiosk" in the NIIT boundary wall, with the monitor visible through a glass plate built into the wall. The PC itself was on the other side of the brick enclosure, connected to the internet. Instead of a mouse, there was a touch pad, which was later modified to an unbreakable joystick. The kiosk was made operational, without any announcement or instruction, in January 1999. A video camera recorded activity near the kiosk, and activity was monitored from another PC on the network.

Young boys between ages six and twelve started to use the site first, and within a few minutes they had established, apparently by accident, that clicking on the touch pad was of significance. Within a few days, children of both sexes were learning the basics of working the computer and accessing the internet. All this was quite remarkable at the time. And through numerous other experiments, some of which we'll come to in a moment, Sugata showed how children could enhance their learning in many areas, without teachers, using the internet. As Sugata said to children when first introducing his learning technology into villages, "Well, there are things that you can learn by yourself and things that you need a teacher for, right?" He left open the question of how far this philosophy could go in relegating teachers to the fringes and placing learners at the heart of the educational process. It's this area that we will explore in this chapter.

On the plane leaving Delhi, I wrote in my diary, "This fellow is great. He's a wild academic, wild jet-black hair, on and below his shoulders. He has a huge personality, very open, very kind, very West Coast. ... He really inspired me."

He inspired millions. His work was the inspiration for the book Q&A, by Vikas Swarup, which in turn inspired the film *Slumdog Millionaire* (Sugata has been dubbed the "Slumdog professor"), his TED Talks have been watched by millions, and it was no surprise that he won the first million-dollar TED Prize in 2013. Today, Sugata Mitra is probably one of the world's best-known and best-loved educators, and his ideas have had, and are having, significant impact and influence. It's been an honor to be colleagues with him as professors at Newcastle University.

His ideas now focus on "self-organized learning environments," or SOLEs. This is the key link to my work, for throughout this book I have also written about education as being a spontaneous order, or a self-organizing system.

Self-Organizing Systems, or Spontaneous Orders

The terms *self-organizing system* and *spontaneous order* describe how social order can arise out of disorder without the need for any central planning, typically through the actions of self-interested individuals. Social order can arise spontaneously, without the need for any control by external agents. It was Adam Smith's great insight in *The Wealth of Nations* to show how individual self-interest can lead to the benefit of others. While we, of course, value benevolence, says Smith, "it is not from the benevolence of the butcher, the brewer, or the baker, that we expect our dinner, but from their regard to their own interest. We address ourselves, not to their humanity but to their self-love, and never talk to them of our own necessities but of their advantages."[1] The executive vice president of the Cato Institute, David Boaz, spells this out: as "people interact freely with each other," protecting "their rights to liberty and property," then social order "will emerge without central direction."[2]

One example of a social spontaneous order is the market economy: "Billions ... of people enter the marketplace or the business world every day wondering how they can produce more goods or get a better job or make more money for themselves and their families. They are not guided by any central authority, not by the biological instinct that drives bees to make honey, yet they produce wealth for themselves and others by producing and trading." Another example is language: "No one sat down to write the English language and then teach it to early Englishmen. It arose and changed naturally, spontaneously, in response to human needs." The law is also an example of a social spontaneous order: "The common law grew up long before any king or legislature sought to write it down. When two people had a dispute, they asked another to serve as a judge ... to 'find' the law, to ask what the customary practice was ... [and] in case after case the legal order developed." The system of money, too, "arose naturally when people needed something to facilitate trade."[3] The evidence and arguments adduced throughout this book suggest that education must be added to that list of self-organizing systems or spontaneous orders.

In the case of ensuring education for the next generation, we've seen dramatic instances of how this educational social order—the orderly provision of educational opportunities for all—arises in some of the world's most difficult places (as well as, of course, in richer communities). In the poorest slums in sub-Saharan Africa and South Asia, even in countries coming out of terrible civil wars, individual entrepreneurs, pursuing their own self-interest to create a modest income for themselves and their families, have created stand-alone schools. They've thought carefully about what their communities can afford and have offered school places at prices to suit the pockets of the people they want to serve. They've employed teachers, janitors, custodians, and cooks from the communities, creating employment opportunities. And many of the schools offer some free or subsidized places for the poorest of the poor.

The sum of all these individual actions has resulted in a system, a social order, that provides educational opportunities for nearly all. (It is important to stress that government-imposed systems also only cater to "nearly all"; we've accepted the principle throughout that there could be required some targeted financial assistance for the tiny percentage who cannot afford what the market offers. This is the same as in the market for food and clothing, so there is nothing exceptional about this.) Schools emerge to meet new demand in communities that are growing. Schools compete for students, and so keep standards high, and seek to innovate where possible to keep up with demand.

But there is no central planner. No committee in any government decides to provide these school places. Indeed, in many countries, government central planners are decidedly against these low-cost private schools. Instead, the order is all accomplished spontaneously. It genuinely is a self-organizing system.

Now some entrepreneurs are building chains of low-cost private schools—realizing that the market is ripe for consolidation, that there could be economies of scale to be made to improve educational efficiency. Those who are planning these are still part of the spontaneous order; no central planners in government have decided that these chains should be part of the educational picture. And because these chains are not monopolistic and will eventually compete, they don't experience any of the problems that monopolistic school districts come up against. The scale of the chains is growing but still only a tiny fraction of total provision by the private sector.

This is the picture in country after country across the developing world. In a couple of exceptions, governments are entering into public-private partnerships with private educational providers to take over parts of the public system. These are distortions in the spontaneous order, which continues to thrive in most places. And thrive it does: we have seen throughout this book how the low-cost private-school sector is serving a large majority of urban children, outperforming the government sector, and doing so in an affordable way.

Ironically, America, the land where most people think free enterprise is grounded, is outside of this spontaneous order in education. It is still largely stuck in what has been dubbed "educational communism."[4] Could a spontaneous order of education emerge in America too? We saw in the last chapter one way in which it could, if entrepreneurs are willing to learn the lessons from the rest of the world. And there's another reason that could lead to optimism for this outcome. The public-school system has been massively disrupted by the COVID-19 school closures. These school closures have been an opportunity for some parents to experience educational freedom and spontaneous educational orders that have been commonplace in developing countries for some time. Having experienced such freedom, flexibility, and innovation, such parents may not be so likely to return to the pre-COVID-19 "educational communism." The key is not to get sidetracked into the red herring of School Choice reforms such as vouchers and charter schools. They're not educational freedom. They're likely to distract us from moving toward the spontaneous order of education.

The way schools are structured can be completely rethought—and experiments can emerge in chains and individual provision. With the framework of education reclaimed from governments and international agencies, education could emerge as a genuine spontaneous order. American entrepreneurs, I believe, could be especially helpful in some of the challenges of wresting the framework of education from government control, given their potential global influence and reach.

Recently, I spoke at a student conference in Prague. The students were bright and enthusiastically embraced the evidence about education being a self-organizing system. But I realized many of them assumed that this meant a certain kind of learning would inevitably arise within this self-organized system—learning of a freewheeling kind, with children deciding their own curricula, exploring it in whatever ways they wanted, or sometimes not at all. Their model was close to the free school Summerhill, founded by A. S. Neill, which is famous for its educational anarchy, where "anything goes."[5] Education as a self-organizing system would inevitably and only lead to learning environments like—or even more radical than—Summerhill, they thought. They loved the ideas of Sugata Mitra, who had, as it happened, also visited them a week or so before my visit. His views on self-organized learning clearly reflected their understanding of what learning should be like. I found similar expectations about the way self-organized learning will develop from Sugata's students at Newcastle University.

In the rest of this chapter, I want to address this issue, because it is fundamental to understanding the idea of self-organization. The spontaneous order of education won't necessarily lead, or only lead, to a kind of free, anything-goes style of learning that the students in Prague and Sugata Mitra's class assumed would appear. It could be quite different, even accommodating conservative ideas about educational provision.

The SOLE of Sugata Mitra

Sugata Mitra's ideas have evolved from his "hole in the wall" experiments, beginning in the late 1990s, through to his work leading up to the $1 million TED Prize in 2013 and to the present. Mitra's ideas have enormous impact and influence—not the least on the students I met in Prague and his students in Newcastle. As I mentioned earlier, his key concept is that of self-organized learning environments, or SOLEs. How does he understand these, and how do they fit in with the ideas discussed throughout this book?

Mitra defines a "self-organizing system" as one with "a set of interconnected parts, each unpredictable, producing spontaneous order in an apparently chaotic situation."[6] In more detail, "a self-organising system consists of a set of entities that exhibit an emerging global system behaviour via local interactions without *centralised control*."[7] In this book, we've been focusing on this "self-organizing system" at the level of the school (or similar learning environment). The aggregation of these learning environments (schools) is the self-organizing system. Mitra starts from the level of the individual learner or groups of learners and looks at self-organization in the learning process itself. This seems to be a useful extension of the way I've been describing self-organization throughout this book—let's see how useful it is as we go through Mitra's work.

From 1999 to 2005, Mitra conducted the "hole in the wall" series of experiments, where (often internet-connected) computers "were embedded into walls in villages and urban slums in India."[8] The computers "had no specific learning software and children were given no instructions about what they were and what they were for."[9] Drawing data from "a random sample of children in 17 locations all over India," he was able to conclude that "the children had learned to use the computers by themselves."[10] In particular, this experiment found that children could, among other things, "learn how to use the computers to play games, download media, and search for information."[11] One of the experiments we conducted together, in the slums of Hyderabad, India, showed how children could improve their English pronunciation without any formal teaching—or teacher input—simply by using a newly available software program.[12]

It would, indeed, seem justified to term the processes emerging from these original "hole in the wall" experiments as largely "self-organized learning." The only thing that could remotely be called "centralized control" was that it was provided by Sugata Mitra, but he was deliberately giving children learning opportunities without stating or even planning how they should happen. Yet a "spontaneous order" of children learning did emerge from out of this "apparently chaotic situation." These experiments raised radical questions about the nature of education, the curriculum, teaching, and learning: If children can learn on their own without teachers, then what future is there for teachers and schools? What are the implications for curriculum and assessment?

It may be worth noting that, since these early experiments, Mitra has formalized the creation of what he calls SOLEs. These were first created under a project I directed with him in low-cost private schools in poverty-stricken areas of Hyderabad. However, they are increasingly used inside public schools, and the "self-organizing" dimension appears to be increasingly tenuous. For instance, rather than self-organizing, the children are compelled to learn in groups of four or five, whether they want to learn in that way or not: "*We make sure that* the number of children in the space is 4 or 5 times that of the number of computers."[13] Moreover, "each class should have at least one session of about 90 minutes in the SOLE, as part of the timetable every week."[14] Children are even told by the teacher what questions they have to pursue, and the teacher is there throughout, supervising the session: "During this time, a teacher will engage the children with a question that they answer using the SOLE. Examples of questions could be: 'Who built the pyramids and why?,' 'What are fractals?,' 'What are they looking for with the Large Hadron Collider at CERN, in Geneva?,' 'Who is Gandhi and what did he do?,'" and so on.[15] These timetabled lessons are even prescriptive down to what happens after the exploration: "About 30 minutes before the end of the session, the *groups should* produce a one-page report where they describe what they have found. The teacher can then expand on this in a later class."[16]

Mitra believes that the same fundamental questions mentioned above are raised by his new-style SOLEs as were raised by his earlier experiments; I'm not so sure. In any case, let's look at the radical questions that Mitra raises to see what implications they have for our understanding of education as a self-organizing system.

There are three sets of issues we'll address. The first concerns the role of groups versus individuals. For reasons I don't quite understand, Mitra appears largely fixated on learning by groups. This is misplaced; self-organized education can and should benefit from a focus on individual learning too. Second, we'll look at Mitra's views on assessment. He sees this as radically transformed under self-organized learning. Again, I'm not so sure. Third, Mitra raises questions about the future of learning under self-organization, and we'll explore the logic of his ideas.

The Red Herring of Emergent Learning

One of the findings that Mitra reports from SOLEs around the world is that groups of children working together "seem to be able to make sense of material at reading levels considerably above their own. *This anomalous result is intriguing* and may well be the key to understanding this form of learning."[17] Mitra and his team set out to explore this phenomenon: "We presented children with passages that are suitable for adults and tested their understanding when they read in groups, compared to when they read alone. Our results ... suggest that children can read and understand adult-level texts in groups if they are allowed to work in the SOLE style."[18]

He relates these findings to what he calls the "science of emergence," which he believes "offers a potential explanation of children's ability to read in groups above their individual capabilities. Emergence, a common phenomenon in nature, is the appearance of properties that are not evident in the parts of a system."[19]

Mitra thinks this is an important route to explore, with huge implications for how we see the role of groups in learning. I find this puzzling. Far from its being mysterious, on the contrary, I suggest that logic and first principles can easily explain how a group of children can "read" at reading levels above any individual member's capabilities or to read at adult levels when still children. But crucially, it doesn't change the desired focus of learning from the individual to the group; indeed, it reinforces it.

Suppose we've got a group of five individuals, Andrew to Elizabeth, with individually tested reading abilities on a numerical scale of, say, the number of words they know: Andrew (70), Beverly (60), Charles (50), David (40), and Elizabeth (30). If "the group," rather than the individuals, was asked to do the same reading test, it is trivial that the group can score higher than *all but one* of its members. That is, the group can score 70 on the test, because that is what one of the members (Andrew) can score. Therefore, "the group" can read at a higher level than all but one (Andrew) of its members.

However, it is also easy to show that the combined group *could* score higher than *every* member of the group, including Andrew. All we need for this to happen is for at least one other member of the group to know one or more words that Andrew doesn't know. So, suppose Beverly has 55 words in common with Andrew but knows 5 words that he doesn't know. Then the combined group can score 75 in the reading test, higher than every individual member's reading score.

Similarly, using the same example, we can show the plausibility of Mitra's other finding, of the group reading at adult level even though the individual members are all reading like children.

Suppose that reading at adult level requires a score on this test of 90, while a child typically scores 50. If we average our scores above, we see that the average score is indeed 50, so, on average, our group is reading at the level of a child, and not one is reading at the level of an adult.

However, if Beverly, Charles, David, and Elizabeth each know 5 unique words in the test unknown to Andrew (and to each other), then the combined score of "the group" will be 90. That is, "the group" would be reading at the level of an adult, even though not one of the individuals is reading at that level, and the average score of the individuals is the level of an average child.

There is nothing particularly remarkable about these findings—nothing that needs anything as mysterious as the "science of emergent systems" to explain. It is all to do with the logic of the way individual members of a group can contribute to a combined task. It's the same principle at work when individuals are selected to take part in a team for any general knowledge quiz, such as a pub quiz or BBC's University Challenge. In such competitions, it is assumed that bringing together individuals with different sets of knowledge can allow a team to score higher than any one individual.

It is certainly plausible, by the way, that within groups of children, individuals may know words different from each other. Even those with a very limited vocabulary (David and Elizabeth in the above example) could know words that the better readers don't know; children can pick up all sorts of unusual or specialist vocabulary from their particular environments, which others, including those with large vocabularies, would not necessarily share. When I was a child, for instance, I was an avid reader and could well have been the class member who had the most words in his vocabulary. But many of my classmates who were not keen readers would have had additional vocabulary because of their love of sports (which I didn't share), while one boy kept falcons and another came from a family that trained greyhounds, each of which may have given them specialist vocabulary unknown to me. You can see how a group of us put together could have had a higher reading age than any one of us alone, including the one with the largest vocabulary.

So, there is no great mystery as to how the group can have a higher reading level than each of the individual members. But—and this is the crucial educational question that we can pose back to Mitra—in our example above, while "the group" can read very well, some of its members cannot read at all well individually. This could be a severe handicap in a world where reading is important and where support from a group with readers of a higher standard is not readily available. Is this an educational problem that needs addressing or not?

It *is* an educational problem. While it may be useful to know that "the group" can read as well as it can, this in no way undermines the reality that there are individuals within it whose educational needs require addressing. In other words, group work through SOLEs has not addressed the problem of how to improve individuals' learning at all—unless it could be argued that the group could help with peer learning so that the abler members helped the less able ones. In which case, peer learning could lead to better outcomes for the group as *individuals*. If this is what Mitra is saying, then fair enough. But it's still the level of the individual that we're concerned about, not the group; the group then becomes a mechanism to help the individual learner, but it would still require learning—and testing—at the *level of the individual*, not the group. Self-organized learning certainly doesn't change the importance of the individual learning at all.

Because of the way Mitra has addressed the issue, however, it appears that the group's ability is what concerns him now, not that of individuals within it. For instance, he suggests that his arguments show the need for "considerable changes in education policy"; one of the areas that "policy-making bodies" need to consider is that "individual performance does not necessarily indicate the efficiency of an educational system."[20] What Mitra seems to be suggesting is that outcomes like those illustrated in our example above could be considered efficient because "the group" can read well. On the contrary, I suggest that all it would show is that the "system" has enabled one or two children to read well and that a group can hide behind these individuals. This is an inefficient educational system and would not obviate the need for learning and assessment directed at individuals.

Mitra's discussion of emergent learning detracts from the real need to focus on improving *individuals'* learning. Just because groups can do something doesn't mean that we have solved the problem of individuals' learning performance. Self-organized learning, the spontaneous order of education, doesn't change the need for that at all. The focus can be very much on the individual, not on some collective.

The New World of Assessment

Mitra raises further radical questions. One of his ideas is that it is "imaginable that, using the internet, a learner could 'pretend' to be educated."[21] By "pretend," he means that "the learner could claim to know a subject that he or she has not been taught in the traditional sense."[22] Indeed, he continues, this is precisely what children do when they use SOLEs. Crucially, however, "we must notice that the act of 'pretending' eventually results in their learning the subject. In other words, *when a learner practices a set of skills without being taught them* but uses the internet for support, she learns the subject, over a period of time. The learner becomes what she pretends to be."[23]

Again, we can ask, is there anything remarkable about this? The italicized passage can help here. Mitra agrees that practice of "skills," and presumably of knowledge, can lead to these being learned. He says that this can happen using the "internet for support," but isn't this simply the same as what happens with rote learning or whenever we take skills and knowledge from short-term to long-term memory? Even without the internet, we know we can look something up—in books, crib sheets, whatever—and "pretend" we know it. But if we pretend like that several times, then we might really learn the item: it will go from the crib sheet to short-term memory and then on to long-term memory. When it reaches long-term memory, then *we really do know it*. With this, Mitra agrees.

Mitra explores this further. He asks the reader to imagine a person who is "claiming to be an accountant" but "who has no knowledge of the subject." This person, using "search engines, websites, and web-based tools," can solve "accounting problems for his clients." Initially, "he may look up the words 'balance sheet.' The next time, he would not look up those words because he would know what they mean." Hence, for Mitra, the "internet makes it possible for people to become self-made professionals, just as in another age people became self-made mechanics, electricians, etc."[24]

Now, Mitra starts with someone who has *no knowledge* of accounting. At first, it seems as though he is magically able to *solve accounting problems* for his clients. That indeed would be extraordinary. But it's not that magical at all. Behind the scenes, the normal processes of learning are still going on. The person "claiming to be an accountant" is learning about accounting from the internet. He must look up things like "balance sheet" at first, and quickly learns what this means. Then he looks up other things and learns what they mean, and how they all fit together, perhaps through consulting experts in the field or by going on to specialized accounting websites. It doesn't seem that difficult to imagine that a person could learn accounting in this way.

So again, we can ask: Is there anything remarkable about this description, or is it just what autodidacts have always done? Coincidentally, in an earlier book, I gave an example from the 1950s about a young upstart teacher, Ralph, who wanted to take over the school's accounts. (The Ralph in question is Ralph Bistany, the cofounder of the global chain of schools SABIS.) The school owner, Charles, replied, "You don't know accounting." "Fine," said

Ralph, "when I know accounting, will you agree to let me take care of this issue?" Charles agreed.

A day or two later, Ralph went into Beirut and bought the latest accounting books. Every spare moment he got, he devoted himself to their study. After a month of this, he brought the subject up again at afternoon tea. Ralph said, "I'm an accountant now." Charles dismissed him: "You can't be, not so quickly." Charles had friends who were auditors. Ralph said, "Call your auditors—let them come and interview me. If they tell you I'm not a good accountant, then I'll forget it." This was done. "Yes," said the auditors, "he knows accounting."[25] So the experience of becoming an accountant through the autodidact route could—and did—happen in an age well before the internet.

But this discussion suggests that the way Mitra has framed the problem may be needlessly mystifying. He began, "Let us imagine a person claiming to be an accountant, *who has no knowledge of the subject.*" Surely, at that moment, because he has *no knowledge* of the subject, his claim to be an accountant would be *false.* He's in the same position as Ralph in my story before he bought and studied the accounting books: Charles is justified in saying he is *not* an accountant. It's only when the tools of accounting are learned—in Mitra's example, through the person's online learning; in my example, through studying key textbooks—that eventually he gains knowledge of the subject, and he can now call himself an accountant and solve accounting problems for his clients.

Building on this discussion, Mitra moves to an important question concerning assessment. In such a world where we can learn accounting and other areas by ourselves through the internet, Mitra asks, "What would happen to certification and qualifications in an Internet-immersive world?"[26]

Mitra doesn't answer the question in his paper, but he leaves it open with the suggestion that this and similar questions "challenge the fundamentals of traditional education," rendering the assessment system *"obsolete."*[27] But that isn't necessarily so.

I've spent quite a lot of time in earlier chapters arguing that the assessment system (as well as the curriculum system) has been taken over by government, has been set in stone and stagnated, and so is unlikely to be fit for purpose now. Some readers may have assumed that I would then be going the route of Mitra and seeing only challenges to the "fundamentals of traditional education." That might not be the case, however: the challenges may well come from different directions (perhaps the kinds of directions we've already encountered in part 2).

Let's see how far we can get with an answer here. Let's focus on the accounting example. It is enjoyable seeing Sugata Mitra give lectures where he vividly describes, in a very entertaining way, how our putative accountant could set up stall, saying he is an accountant even before he knows very much at all. Someone like me comes along with an accounting problem. He says he can solve it and that I should come back within a few hours. After some time, lo and behold, he has managed to solve the accounting problem I brought to him. That's great, so I will bring other problems to him, which he also manages to solve; eventually I recommend him to others, and all is well with Mitra's charming example. An accountant has emerged via the internet, and it all somehow shows for Mitra that the system of accounting qualifications is now obsolete.

But this is too fast. Suppose the putative accountant gives me a solution to the accounting problem I brought him, but it turns out to be incorrect. Perhaps through his internet searches, he gets "profit and loss account" muddled up with "cash flow statement." To a novice, these things might look somewhat similar. Or, dare we say it, the person might be a bit lazy, or not very good with numbers, or not very intelligent, or a combination of these things, and so, in the end, he is not able to satisfactorily solve the problem I brought him. In Mitra's example, the person who says he wants to be an accountant simply succeeds at mastering the necessary knowledge and skills. But there seems to be a good chance he won't. Perhaps accounting is not as easy as Mitra makes out.

So, what do we do with my internet-self-taught accountant who makes errors—perhaps such big mistakes that I lose money as a result? Obviously, I will not use him again, will not recommend him, and will actively warn people against this upstart who pretends to have skills and knowledge that he, in fact, doesn't. In a genuinely self-organizing system such as this, our self-taught but mistaken accountant is likely to quickly go out of business.

But other possibilities could also happen. First, within the self-organizing system of people learning in the way Mitra describes, people might get fed up with impostors setting up shop saying they are accountants when they don't understand the complexities, or they make silly mistakes. Putative customers like me—losing money because of getting involved with this impostor—would create market demand for some way of solving this problem. Moreover, those who are, like Mitra's version of the accountant, successfully self-taught, would also get fed up with charlatans coming in and pretending to be able to do the work. So, guilds or brands of self-taught accountants could emerge and create ways of showing that they know what they are doing, to distinguish them from those who don't.

Second, it might be that another entrepreneur in this self-organizing system sees the problem and decides to create a way of distinguishing between these two types of people. (This kind of entrepreneur is someone focusing on the *framework* of education.) In my example from the 1950s above, Ralph had asked to be examined by an ad hoc board of auditors. This might be a rather inefficient way of doing things, and a more replicable way would be to create a test or series of tests that the self-taught accountant could take. If he passed these tests, then he could advertise this fact, and so attract customers. Similarly, a guild could also decide that passing a test was required to gain admittance.

So, each of these genuinely self-organized learning ways leads to the creation of some form of assessment. Importantly, if using the internet allows you to bluff to a certain extent that you can do accounting, a skill that falls apart as problems become more difficult and more is demanded in terms of accounting knowledge, then it may well be that the self-organizing assessment system would go as far as to *prohibit* the use of the internet. In other words, contrary to what Mitra suggests, assessment in a self-organized learning environment might emerge to make sure that any self-professing accountant has the requisite knowledge in long-term memory rather than simply the skills to access it via the internet.

Elsewhere, Mitra suggests that as innovative technologies are introduced, these make the old ones educationally obsolete. He writes that "the introduction of logarithm tables into the classroom and examinations would change a teacher's emphasis from multiplying by hand and memorising tables to correctly and quickly using log tables."[28] I don't think that was historically true.

Instead of abandoning the first method, teachers wanted students to be able to demonstrate *both* techniques. The same might be true even of assessment in our self-organizing system. Sure, assess what you can do with the internet (or whatever invention comes next; the internet might seem like old hat to readers of this text even in the near future), but also demonstrate what you know and can do without any access to the internet at all, for having basic concepts in long-term memory is of great importance.[29]

Mitra appears to suggest that the answer to his rhetorical question— "What would happen to certification and qualifications in an Internet-immersive world?"—is that traditional ways of assessment will become "obsolete."[30] His example appears to show the opposite. Precisely because there are *self-taught* accountants, the self-organized system of which they are a part requires ways of assessing who really has grasped what is going on and discarding those who have not. Within this genuinely self-organized system, even quite traditional forms of assessments could emerge. But because they emerge through self-organization, they are likely to be fit for purpose, and not fall foul of the problem of signaling that we discussed in chapter 6.

Self-Organized Learning—the Future of Education

We can take this example further and try to imagine what a putative self-organizing education system might look like. Mitra focuses on a profession like accounting. But it might be that this and other professions have a wide range of skills and knowledge in common, and moreover that these are in common with skills and knowledge required for nonprofessionals and trades too. Things in common could include areas such as literacy, numeracy, communication skills, and an ability to defer gratification, say, or a disciplined approach to work. In a genuinely self-organized learning environment, we could see that it would be possible that some entrepreneurs might decide to set up organizations that would offer to get every child up to speed on these basics, without which none of the professions or trades is possible, so that not everyone trying to acquire a profession or trade has to start from scratch.

Terry Leahy, the former CEO of Tesco (the Walmart of the UK), has written that certain character traits are essential for managers to acquire—

for instance, "Picking up on small failures before they become big ones, and before an 'I can get away with it' culture begins to spread."[31] Can these traits perhaps be learned early on, by children, in environments that support their learning? Leahy quotes the Victorian self-help guru Samuel Smiles:

> Attention, application, accuracy, method, punctuality, and despatch are the principal qualities required for the efficient conduct of business of any sort. These, at first sight, may appear to be small matters; and yet they are of essential importance to human happiness, well-being, and usefulness. They are the small things it is true; but human life is made up of comparative trifles. It is the repetition of little acts which constitutes not only the sum of human character, but which determines the character of nations.[32]

One could take from this that these "trifles" of character need to be learned by children to become happy, useful, and fulfilled adults. Smiles may have had in mind the industrial factory requirements of the nineteenth century. But Leahy is writing about a very modern service industry—supermarkets—and pointing to comparable needs. If young children need to learn these things for human flourishing (happiness, well-being, and usefulness), where can they learn them? Of course, these things can be learned, say, in the family or religious community. But just as Tesco and Walmart offer customers the possibilities of getting food, clothing, and electrical goods all under one roof, so educational entrepreneurs could aim to offer "attention, application, accuracy, method, punctuality, and despatch," as well as academic learning, also under one roof; it may be that if parents see this as valuable, then these "generalist learning environments" will thrive.

Generalist learning environments—perhaps we could call them "schools." They could emerge in a genuinely self-organized way, as a response to the needs of all learners. Indeed, self-organized learning *did* lead to schools in the nineteenth century. This is important to stress again. In chapter 13, we witnessed systems of genuine self-organized learning emerging in England and Wales, and New York, before the state got involved in learning. Importantly, the purely private schools that emerged taught a curriculum that wasn't prescribed by the state, but that satisfied parents—with a heavy emphasis on literacy and numeracy and a practical but disciplined approach to learn-ing—and had learning methods that also emerged spontaneously without any state intervention.

So, we do have genuine, historical examples of self-organized learning environments emerging. They emerged through a spontaneous order of the people acting in their own perceived best interests.

What parents wanted in the nineteenth century led to the spontaneous or-der of *schooling* emerging. But then, in country after country, the spontaneous order of education, the genuinely self-organized learning environment, was taken over by governments and used for their own ends. And the state "set in stone" what was going on, stultifying it so that it became very hard to change and improve—something with which Mitra concurs: "Curricula around the world remained static: they assumed a top-down, hierarchical, predictable, and controllable world that progresses slowly."[33] Many of the educational reformers we've met throughout this book would agree too.

A key question, then, is this: What would emerge as a self-organized learning environment in the twenty-first century? Presumably, it would not be the same as that which emerged in the nineteenth century. The self-or-ganized learning environment of that time—schools of various shapes and sizes—might not be the appropriate self-organized learning environments of the twenty-first century. But the key is, we don't know what genuinely self-organized learning environments would be like in the twenty-first century, because all over the world, "centralized control"—for Mitra and for me, the nemesis of self-organized learning—has power over education. Governments have power over the provision and funding of education, and they impose the curricular and assessment frameworks on schools, as well as compulsory schooling.

All of this suggests that it is hard to see what a self-organized learning environment would be in today's world, but we know that what centralized planning delivers is likely to be completely different from what is desirable. We also know that what could emerge under the spontaneous order will converge on what is most desirable for the needs of children and their families rather than, at present, converging on what the state has set in stone, irrespective of the needs of children and their families.

Mitra concludes his paper with this: "A child who is 8 years old in 2014 will probably live for another 100 years. Self-organised learning environments (SOLEs) are a first faltering step toward preparing our children for a future we can barely imagine."[34]

Extending this, genuinely self-organized learning environments, away from centralized (government) control, are the route to preparing children for this barely imaginable future. In fact, there would seem to be no other way of doing this. The future is too unpredictable to rely on anything else.

Imagine going back one hundred years to 1918 and trying to predict what might emerge in the next century. Of course, it would have been impossible to predict the information technology revolution—that would have been inconceivable to predict even thirty or forty years ago: the first commercially available mobile phone, the brick-size Motorola DynaTAC 8000X, came on the market in 1984, costing around $10,000 in today's money, with thirty minutes' talk time after a ten-hour charge. Who could have predicted the ubiquity of the tiny and powerful smartphones of today?

But even the widespread adoption of more mundane innovations would have been impossible to predict: One hundred years ago, you could die from a scratch from a rosebush if it got infected. Alexander Fleming didn't isolate penicillin until 1928, and it was not until the late 1940s that antibiotics became available to anyone outside of the military. Doctors used to treat infections with bloodletting, either through an incision in a vein or artery or applying a juicy leech to the infected area.

Or what about household chores, such as doing the laundry? In 1918, it would take a housewife (or servant) more than eight hours to do the week's washing, and she would walk one mile in the process of doing it. It was back-breaking work. Now, anyone can put a load in the automatic washing machine and it virtually does itself.

Could people have predicted how even these small innovations—not part of great and applauded technological revolutions—would change the world? Likewise, we are in complete ignorance about what our future holds. But the good news is that humanity has developed a method for dealing with uncertainty and ignorance. It's called the market, itself a spontaneous order, a self-organizing system, as we saw earlier. Through the individual decisions of millions of people, we are able, in a process of trial and error, to arrive at solutions that work to satisfy the need for human flourishing, solutions that are versatile and fluid. Entrepreneurs search for solutions, and the ones that work survive and prosper, while the duds die. The market in education, the self-organizing system of education, rather than centralized *planning*, can enable that same discovery process to work for education.

So, what will education be like in the future? It all depends on whether we progress toward educational freedom or remain with the kind of government control of the framework of education that we have today. If educational freedom, then education will evolve through self-organization to cater to the needs of the community. If, on the other hand, education is left to the state, it will remain stuck in ways that may become increasingly irrelevant.

Who knows what riches the education system can bring to bear on change? One set of goals of education—one philosophy of education—is to prepare children for adult life. This is a forward-looking approach. Many important educational reformers have had a go at predicting what education could be like in the future. Sir Anthony Seldon, for instance, in his fine book *The Fourth Education Revolution*, looks at the impact that artificial intelligence (AI) will have on schooling: "Schools will change fundamentally in the next 15–25 years," he writes, "as will the jobs for which schools are preparing their young people."[35] The role of teachers will change "forever."[36] Even though the "application of AI places more responsibility for learning … in the hands of the student, for how their time is spent and on what, even from a young age," teachers will still be needed: "Learners take time and encouragement to become more autonomous. The job of teacher will thus increasingly become to structure students' learning, help them with confusion and difficulties, run whole-class learning discussions, look after students pastorally, and guide them through their wider personal, social, cultural, sporting and character development."[37] With AI taking its rightful place in the future of education, the "five inherent problems of the factory system"—the system condemned by, among others, Sir Ken Robinson, as we've seen earlier in this book—"will be swept away."[38]

There is also the philosophy of education that says education is initiation into the best that has been thought and said, a liberal education.[39] This is, in a sense, a backward-looking philosophy of education. It is looking at the best that has been thought and said *in the past*. It doesn't need to be able to predict what the world will be like in the future. Its premise is that for humanity and individual humans to flourish, we need to look backward as to how we have answered big questions in the past—big questions such as "Why are we here?" "What is it to be good?" "What is the nature of beauty and truth?" and so on.

It might be that as the spontaneous order develops, education focused on these aspects could become increasingly important, especially as society changes at a faster and ever more bewildering rate. The future may be best met by standing on the shoulders of humanity's giants. And, of course, this philosophy of education doesn't rule out the possibility that learning from the great thinkers of the past can be imbued through artificial intelligence as well as through traditional learning models.

I don't want to predict what will happen in the spontaneous order of education. The experiences around the world let us know that it will meet the needs of all the people. Our discussion suggests that it could help motivate learning and address variations in learning styles and speeds. Two of the key stories I've told in this book are those of Jennifer stuck in her mathematics class and Amal bored silly in her science classes. As I've shown, educational entrepreneurs can do something to address both issues raised.

The spontaneous order in education will also continue to reach out to the world's most difficult places. I warmed to hear that the chain of low-cost schools Bridge International Academies is managing a school in Borno State, northern Nigeria, where Boko Haram's influence is at its peak. Western education is forbidden, but being forbidden doesn't stop worthy educational entrepreneurs. The spirit of educational self-help is alive and well. I can't wait to see how it unfolds as we reclaim education from the state, to arrive at true educational emancipation.

None but Ourselves Can Free Our Minds

In chapter 1, we started in Liberia, the "land of the free," so let's finish there too. On the last evening of my first trip there, back in 2012, I was at my hotel bar by a lagoon on the outskirts of Monrovia. It was a pretty place to sit and wind down at the end of an exhilarating journey. There was a pianist-and-singer duo helping the evening along. The singer was a diminutive young man, with a beautiful, mellow baritone voice, sounding every bit like Nat King Cole.

The last song of the evening from the jazz duo was Bob Marley's "Redemption Song." The key lyric is taken from a 1937 speech by Marcus Garvey, the Jamaican-born black nationalist who inspired so many in the civil rights movement: "emancipate ourselves from mental slavery ... none but ourselves can free the mind."

I recalled what John Stuart Mill had written against bringing universal state education to bear in England and Wales: public education is "a mere contrivance for moulding people to be exactly like one another ... in proportion as it is efficient and successful, it establishes a despotism over the mind."[40]

"Despotism over the mind" sounds pretty much like "mental slavery." Mill would have agreed with the idea of emancipating ourselves from the mental slavery that is public education.

But "none but ourselves can free the mind." None but ourselves—that's what this book fundamentally has been about. None but ourselves—we don't need government, we don't need lobbying for School Choice reforms; we can just do it ourselves. Education for the people, by the people. We can be entrepreneurs who create the changes that are desirable. We can be investors or philanthropists who get behind them. We can be parents, grandparents, or students who are prepared to push for the kind of education we want, not what is doled out to us, we supplicants, by governments. Or we can be people like me whose task is simply to write it all up, in the hope of inspiring and motivating others to get involved.

I've witnessed something remarkable happening across the developing world in the last twenty years. A movement has been created around low-cost private education that has transformed the way we think about the role of government in education. I'm confident that in the next twenty years I will see something just as noteworthy happening in America and Britain too. Education, including the framework of education, can be reclaimed from government. It's not going to be easy, but I'm sure that if enough people join in, it's going to be an exciting ride.

Notes

Introduction

1. This first section adapts material from James Tooley, "Malala for Free Schools," *Spectator*, November 9, 2013, https://www.spectator.co.uk/article/malala-for-free-schools. I am using the term *education* loosely until I define it later in this introduction.

2. I will follow international usage in this book and refer to "public" schools as those run and managed by government; this is contrasted with private schools, which are not. (In the UK and India, there is an idiosyncratic usage that "public" schools are elite private schools. I will not follow this custom.)

3. BBC News, "Malala Yousafzai: 'Education for Every Child,'" July 12, 2013, https://www.bbc.com/news/av/world-asia-23274568/malala-yousafzai-education-for-every-child.

4. Malala Yousafzai and Christina Lamb, *I Am Malala: The Girl Who Stood Up for Education and Was Shot by the Taliban* (London: Weidenfeld & Nicolson, 2013), 34.

5. These are English-medium schools—that is, the language of instruction is English. Across the Indian subcontinent, schools are defined in this way: English-medium, Hindi-medium, Urdu-medium, etc. This does not refer to the grades.

6. Yousafzai and Lamb, *I Am Malala*, 38.

7. Yousafzai and Lamb, *I Am Malala*, 41.

8. I don't like this phrase, but I am not sure that any of its synonyms—such as "the Global South" or "the Rest" (as opposed to the West)—are any better.

9. *Businessmen* is the word that critics used to further damn them. In fact, it wasn't true, since many were women.

10. Free to Choose Network, "Victoria's Chance," YouTube, January 12 2011, https://www.youtube.com/watch?v=5Hew07jZQ_4.

11. Steve Hilton, Scott Bade, and Jason Bade, *More Human: Designing a World Where People Come First* (New York: PublicAffairs, 2016), 92.

12. See, for example, Laura Day Ashley et al., *The Role and Impact of Private Schools in Developing Countries: A Rigorous Review of the Evidence*, Final report, *Education Rigorous Literature Review* (London: Department for International Development, 2014); Gates Foundation, "Bill & Melinda Gates Foundation Request for Proposals: Self-Help Group

(SHG)," April 13, 2018, https://www.gatesfoundation.org/~/media/GFO/How-We-Work/RFP/SHG-Portfolio-Evaluation--RFP--online-version.docx?la=en.

13. K–12 is the American system; there are numerous variations of this around the world, including in England and Wales, where the grades are called "Reception" to "Upper Sixth Form" (actually K–13). Throughout this book, when I talk about K–12, I do not intend to exclude this or other systems around the world. All I want to convey is a focus on the years of state-imposed compulsory schooling.

14. William Cobbett, *Advice to Young Men* (London: n.p., 1829).

15. Milton Friedman, *Capitalism and Freedom* (Chicago: University of Chicago Press, 1962), 86.

16. Bryan Caplan, *The Case against Education: Why the Education System Is a Waste of Time and Money* (Princeton, NJ: Princeton University Press, 2018), 238.

Part 1: A Global Revolution

1. James Tooley, "Private Education: The Poor's Best Chance?," *UNESCO Courier*, November 2000; James Tooley, "Private Schools for the Poor," *Economic Affairs*, June 2000; James Tooley, *Reclaiming Education* (London: Continuum, 2000).

2. Kevin Watkins, "Private Education and Education for All—or How Not to Construct an Evidence-Based Argument: A Reply to Tooley," *Economic Affairs* 24, no. 4 (December 2004): 11.

3. For example, see Prachi Srivastava and Geoffrey Walford, eds., *Private Schooling in Less Economically Developed Countries: Asian and African Perspectives* (Oxford: Symposium Books, 2007); Prachi Srivastava, ed., *Low-Fee Private Schooling: Aggravating Equity or Mitigating Disadvantage?* (Oxford, UK: Symposium Books, 2013); Ian Macpherson, Susan Robertson, and Geoffrey Walford, eds., *Education, Privatization, and Social Justice: Case Studies from Africa, South Asia, and South East Asia* (Oxford: Symposium Books, 2014); Pauline Dixon, *International Aid and Private Schools for the Poor: Smiles, Miracles and Markets* (Cheltenham, UK: Edward Elgar, 2013); and James Tooley, *The Beautiful Tree: A Personal Journey into How the World's Poorest People Are Educating Themselves* (Washington, DC: Cato Institute, 2009).

Chapter 1: Ubiquity and Affordability

1. For example, Keith M. Lewin, *The Limits to Growth of Non-Government Private Schooling in Sub-Saharan Africa*, CREATE Pathways to Access, Research Monograph No. 5 (Brighton, UK: University of Sussex, Centre for International Education, June 2007).

2. For example, Joanna Härmä, "Access or Quality? Why Do Families Living in Slums Choose Low-Cost Private Schools in Lagos, Nigeria?," *Oxford Review of Education* 39, no. 4 (August 2013): 548–66.

3. For example, Day Ashley et al., *The Role and Impact of Private Schools in Developing Countries*; Gates Foundation, "Bill & Melinda Gates Foundation Request for Proposals."

4. Joanna Härmä and F. Adefisayo, "Scaling Up: Challenges Facing Low-Fee Private Schools in the Slums of Lagos, Nigeria," in *Low-Fee Private Schooling: Aggravating Equity or Mitigating Disadvantage?*, ed. Prachi Srivastava (Oxford: Symposium Books, 2013), 129.

5. *Banking on Education, Nairobi*, CapPlus, http://capplus.org/files/2016/12/Banking-on -Education-in-Nairobi-05.01.pdf; *Low Fee Private Schools in Low-Income Districts of Kampala, Uganda*, CapPlus, http://capplus.org/files/2017/04/Kampala-Private-Schools -Market-Study-2017-03-24.pdf; *Banking on Education, Accra*, CapPlus, http://capplus.org /files/2018/03/Banking-on-Education-in-Accra-2018-03-20.pdf.

6. James Tooley and David Longfield, *The Role and Impact of Low-Cost Private Schools in Developing Countries: A Response to the DFID-Commissioned Rigorous Literature Review* (London: Pearson, 2015).

7. Geeta Kingdon, *The Private Schooling Phenomenon in India: A Review*, CSAE Working Paper, IZA Institute of Labor Economics, London, March 2017, http://ftp.iza.org /dp10612.pdf.

8. Kingdon, *The Private Schooling Phenomenon in India: A Review*, 8.

9. David Pilling, "Liberia Is Outsourcing Education. Can It Work?" *Financial Times*, April 21, 2017; "A Report Card for Liberia's Charter Schools," *Economist*, September 7, 2017.

10. Karen McVeigh and Kate Lyons, "Beyond Justification: Teachers Decry UK Backing for Private Schools in Africa," *Guardian*, May 5, 2017 , https://www.theguardian.com/global -development/2017/may/05/beyond-justification-teachers-decry-uk-backing-private-schools -africa-bridge-international-academies-kenya-lawsuit.

11. For instance, see the "Never-Ending Book Quiz," by Goodreads, available at https:// www.goodreads.com/trivia.

12. Some of the names have been changed in this section due to the school owners' request for anonymity. .

13. James Tooley and David Longfield, *Education, War, and Peace: The Surprising Success of Private Education in War-Torn Countries* (London: IEA, 2017).

14. This section has been adapted with some alterations from James Tooley and David Longfield, "Affordability of Private Schools: Exploration of a Conundrum and Towards a Definition of 'Low-cost,'" *Oxford Review of Education* 42, no. 4 (July 2016): 444–59.

15. Day Ashley et al., *The Role and Impact of Private Schools in Developing Countries*.

16. Day Ashley et al., *The Role and Impact of Private Schools in Developing Countries*, 29.

17. Day Ashley et al., "The Role and Impact of Private Schools in Developing Countries," 28.

18. Joanna Härmä, "Can Choice Promote Education for All? Evidence from Growth in Private Primary Schooling in India," *Compare: A Journal of Comparative and International Education* 39, no. 2 (March 2009): 151–165.

19. Asayo Ohba, "Do Low-Cost Private School Leavers in the Informal Settlement Have a Good Chance of Admission to a Government Secondary School? A Study from Kibera in Kenya," *Compare: A Journal of Comparative and International Education* 43, no. 6 (Published online November 2012): 763–82.

20. Härmä, "Can Choice Promote Education for All?," 163; Prachi Srivastava, "The Shadow Institutional Framework: Towards a New Institutional Understanding of an

Emerging Private School Sector in India," *Research Papers in Education* 23, no. 4 (October 2008): 454.

21. Srivastava, "The Shadow Institutional Framework," 454.

22. Jandhyala B. G. Tilak, *Determinants of Household Expenditure on Education in Rural India* (New Delhi, India: National Council for Applied Economic Research, 2002), 38.

23. These refer to US$1.25 or US$2 per person per day, at purchasing power parity (PPP), using 2005 data. The World Bank set a global poverty line of US$1.25 PPP per day in 2005 as the extreme poverty line typical of the world's poorest countries. The US$2 per day poverty line (in 2005 dollars at PPP) is the median poverty line for all developing countries.

24. Ten percent is inspired by discussion in Keith Lewin's 2007 paper, "The Limits to Growth of Non-Government Private Schooling in Sub-Saharan Africa."

25. We will not go into the full details of these calculations here. Interested readers can refer to previous papers: James Tooley, *School Choice in Lagos State* (Lagos: DFID, 2013); James Tooley, "Challenging Educational Injustices: 'Grassroots' Privatisation in South Asia and Sub-Saharan Africa," *Oxford Review of Education* 39, no. 4 (July 2013); Tooley and Longfield, *Education, War, and Peace.*

Chapter 2: Quality and Value for Money

1. Shreya Roy Chowdhury, "Private Schools Are Not Adding Value: Study," *Times of India*, February 27, 2015, https://timesofindia.indiatimes.com/home/education/news/Private-schools-are-not-adding-value-Study/articleshow/46392725.cms.

2. Lant Pritchett, *The Rebirth of Education: Schooling Ain't Learning* (Washington, DC: Center for Global Development, 2013).

3. For a critique, see Tooley and Longfield, *The Role and Impact of Low-Cost Private Schools.*

4. Day Ashley et al., *The Role and Impact of Private Schools in Developing Countries*, 15.

5. Karthik Muralidharan and Venkatesh Sundararaman, "The Aggregate Effect of School Choice: Evidence from a Two-Stage Experiment in India," *Quarterly Journal of Economics* 130, no. 3 (February 2015): 1013. This section adapts and extends material found in James Tooley, "Extending Access to Low-Cost Private Schools Through Vouchers: An Alternative Interpretation of a Two-Stage 'School Choice' Experiment in India," *Oxford Review of Education* 42, no. 5 (August 2016): 579–93.

6. See, for example, Rajeev Mantri and Harsh Gupta, "Azim Premji, Please Listen to Steve Jobs and Bill Gates: Not about Technology, but about Your Educational Philanthropy," *Mint*, January 6, 2014, http://www.livemint.com/Opinion/301G41LuZJGgs8qLE3clxN/Azim-Premji-please-listen-to-Steve-Jobs-and-Bill-Gates.html.

7. The study was conducted before the bifurcation of this state, which now consists of two states—Telangana, and the other which kept the erstwhile name.

8. D. D. Karopady, "Does School Choice Help Rural Children from Disadvantaged Sections? Evidence from Longitudinal Research in Andhra Pradesh," *Economic and Political Weekly* 49, no. 51 (December 2014): 51.

9. Shreya Roy Chowdhury, "Private Schools Are Not Adding Value," *Times of India*, February 27, 2015.

10. Parth Shah, "Private Schools Are Not Adding Value: You Be the Judge," Spontaneous Order, February 27, 2015, https://web.archive.org/web/20150228184815/http://spontaneous-order.in/private-schools-are-not-adding-value-you-be-the-judge/.

11. Muralidharan and Sundararaman, "The Aggregate Effect of School Choice," 1039, 1027. Children in private schools were predicted to score 0.65 standard deviations higher than those in public schools.

12. Muralidharan and Sundararaman, "The Aggregate Effect of School Choice," 1012.

13. Muralidharan and Sundararaman, "The Aggregate Effect of School Choice," 1012.

14. Muralidharan and Sundararaman, "The Aggregate Effect of School Choice," 1012.

15. Karthik Muralidharan, personal communication.

16. Karopady, "Does School Choice Help Rural Children?," 49.

17. Karopady, "Does School Choice Help Rural Children?," 52; emphasis added.

18. James Tooley, Pauline Dixon, and S. V. Gomathi, "Private Schools and the Millennium Development Goal of Universal Primary Education: A Census and Comparative Survey in Hyderabad, India," *Oxford Review of Education* 33, no. 5 (October 2007): 539–60.

19. Muralidharan and Sundararaman, "The Aggregate Effect of School Choice," 1028.

20. See, for example, Geeta Kingdon, "The Quality and Efficiency of Private and Public Education: A Case Study in Urban India," *Oxford Bulletin of Economics and Statistics* 58, no. 1 (February 1996): 57–82; Sajitha Bashir, "The Cost Effectiveness of Public and Private Schools: Knowledge Gaps, New Research Methodologies and an Application in India," in *Marketizing Education and Health in Developing Countries: Miracle or Mirage?*, ed. Christopher Colclough (Oxford: Clarendon Press, 1997), 124–64; Pauline Dixon, "The Regulation of Private Schools for Low-Income Families in Andhra Pradesh, India: An Austrian Economic Approach" (PhD diss., Newcastle University, Australia, 2003).

21. See, for example, Assessment of Performance Unit (APU), *Mathematical Development: A Review of Monitoring in Mathematics, 1978–1982*, Parts I and II (Slough, UK: NFER, 1988).

22. Karopady, "Does School Choice Help Rural Children?," 49.

23. Karthik Muralidharan, personal communication.

24. For recondite econometric reasons (see Muralidharan and Sundararaman, "The Aggregate Effect of School Choice," 1047–55), these findings may not be as statistically robust as the earlier findings outlined. However, they are all we can use from this study, so we can at least point to their suggestive implications.

25. The mean impact across all subjects is 0.53 percent, statistically significant. Muralidharan and Sundararaman, "The Aggregate Effect of School Choice," 1051.

26. Muralidharan and Sundararaman, "The Aggregate Effect of School Choice," 1052. The mean impact is only slightly lower, 0.50 percent, significant at the 10 percent level.

27. Angus Deaton and Nancy Cartwright, "Understanding and Misunderstanding Randomized Control Trials," National Bureau of Economic Research (NBER) Working Paper No. 22595, issued in September 2016, revised in October 2017, http://www.nber.org/papers/w22595.

28. Tahir Andrabi et al., *Pakistan: Learning and Educational Achievements in Punjab Schools (LEAPS): Insights to Inform the Education Policy Debate* (Cambridge, MA: Harvard Kennedy School, Evidence for Policy Design, 2007), 9.

29. Andrabi et al., *Pakistan: Learning and Educational Achievements*, 6.

30. Andrabi et al., *Pakistan: Learning and Educational Achievements*, 11.

31. Andrabi et al., *Pakistan: Learning and Educational Achievements*, 40.

32. Andrabi et al., *Pakistan: Learning and Educational Achievements*, 40.

33. Andrabi et al., *Pakistan: Learning and Educational Achievements*, 41.

34. Andrabi et al., *Pakistan: Learning and Educational Achievements*, 12.

35. See James Tooley and David Longfield, *Private Primary Education in Western Area, Sierra Leone* (Newcastle, UK: E. G. West Centre and People's Educational Association, 2014).

Chapter 3: Equity and Choice

1. Shahzada Zulfiqar, "Balochistan's Boko Haram," *Newsline*, June 25, 2014, http://www.newslinemagazine.com/2014/06/balochistans-boko-haram/.

2. Tahir Andrabi, Jishnu Das, and Asim Ijaz Khwaja, "A Dime a Day: The Possibilities and Limits of Private Schooling in Pakistan," *Comparative Education Review* 52, no. 3 (August 2008): 329–55.

3. Zulfiqar, "Balochistan's Boko Haram."

4. "Boko Haram Seized 300 Children in 2nd 2014 School Attack: Locals, HRW," *Vanguard*, March 30, 2016, https://www.vanguardngr.com/2016/03/boko-haram-seized-300-children-2nd-2014-school-attack-locals-hrw/.

5. Colin Freeman, "Why Nigeria Is the World's Most Dangerous Place to Be ... a Geography Teacher," *Daily Telegraph*, April 11, 2016, https://www.telegraph.co.uk/news/2016/04/11/why-nigeria-is-the-worlds-most-dangerous-place-to-be-a-geography/.

6. Africa Check, "Education for the Girl Child in Northern Nigeria," 2017, https://africacheck.org/wp-content/uploads/2017/03/July-info-graphic.pdf.

7. Segun Adebowale, "60% of Out of School Children in Nigeria Are Girls—UNICEF," Eagle Online, October 20, 2015, https://theeagleonline.com.ng/60-of-out-of-school-children-in-nigeria-are-girls-unicef/.

8. Flexible Learning Strategies, "Sokoto Has Highest Out-of-School Children in Nigeria—UNICEF," January 21, 2016, http://www.flexlearnstrategies.net/sokoto-has-highest-out-of-school-children-in-nigeria-unicef.

9. Prachi Srivastava, "Low-Fee Private Schools and Poor Children: What Do We Really Know?," *Guardian*, August 12, 2015, https://www.theguardian.com/global-development-professionals-network/2015/aug/12/low-fee-private-schools-poverty-development-economist.

10. Day Ashley et al., *The Role and Impact of Private Schools in Developing Countries*, 24. This section draws on my response to this report. See Tooley and Longfield, *The Role and Impact of Low-Cost Private Schools in Developing Countries*.

11. Kari A. Hartwig, "Using a Social Justice Framework to Assess Educational Quality in Tanzanian Schools," *International Journal of Educational Development* 33, no. 5 (September 2013): 494; emphasis added.

12. Day Ashley et al., *The Role and Impact of Private Schools in Developing Countries*, 24.

13. Day Ashley et al., *The Role and Impact of Private Schools in Developing Countries*, 24.

14. Sarmistha Pal, "Public Infrastructure, Location of Private Schools and Primary School Attainment in an Emerging Economy," *Economics of Education Review* 29, no. 5 (October 2010): 790; emphasis added.

15. Monazza Aslam, "The Relative Effectiveness of Government and Private Schools in Pakistan: Are Girls Worse Off?," *Education Economics* 17, no. 3 (August 2009): 333.

16. Sarmistha Pal and Geeta Kingdon, *Can Private School Growth Foster Universal Literacy? Panel Evidence from Indian Districts* (Bonn: Institute for the Study of Labor, 2010): 14.

17. Andrabi, Das, and Khwaja, "A Dime a Day," 341–42.

18. See Joanna Härmä, "Low Cost Private Schooling in India: Is It Pro Poor and Equitable?," *International Journal of Educational Development* 31, no. 4 (May 2011): 350–56.

19. J. Härmä, "Access or Quality? Why Do Families Living in Slums Choose Low-Cost Private Schools in Lagos, Nigeria?," *Oxford Review of Education* 39, no. 4 (2013): 557; emphasis added.

20. Tooley and Longfield, *The Role and Impact of Low-Cost Private Schools in Developing Countries*, 32.

21. J. Härmä, "Low Cost Private Schooling in India: Is It Pro Poor and Equitable?," *International Journal of Educational Development* 31, no. 4 (2011): 353.

22. Härmä, "Low Cost Private Schooling in India," 353; emphasis in the original.

23. See James Tooley, "Challenging Educational Injustices: 'Grassroots' Privatisation in South Asia and Sub-Saharan Africa," *Oxford Review of Education*, special issue on "Privatisation of Education and Social Justice," ed. Geoffrey Walford, 2013; David Longfield and James Tooley, "School Choice and Parental Preferences in a Poor Area of Monrovia," *International Journal of Educational Development* 53 (March 2017): 117–27.

24. Härmä, *School Choice for the Poor?*, 14.

25. Härmä, *School Choice for the Poor?*, 14.

26. Härmä, *School Choice for the Poor?*, 14.

27. Härmä, *School Choice for the Poor?*, 15.

28. Benjamin Zeitlyn and Joanna Härmä, *The Limits of Marketisation of Primary Education in India*," *CREATE India Policy Brief* 2 (January 2011): 3.

29. J. Härmä, "Can Choice Promote Education for All? Evidence from Growth in Private Primary Schooling in India," *Compare: A Journal of Comparative and International Education* 39, no. 2 (2009): 163; emphases added.

30. Härmä, "Can Choice Promote Education for All?," 163.

31. Amartya Sen, *The Idea of Justice* (London: Allen Lane, 2009), 5–6.

32. Sen, *The Idea of Justice*, 20.

33. Sen, *The Idea of Justice*, 16.

34. See James Tooley, *School Choice in Lagos State* (Lagos: DFID, 2013), for more discussion.

35. Day Ashley et al., *The Role and Impact of Private Schools in Developing Countries*, 30.

36. Day Ashley et al., *The Role and Impact of Private Schools in Developing Countries*, 31.

37. Day Ashley et al., *The Role and Impact of Private Schools in Developing Countries*, 31.

38. Day Ashley et al., *The Role and Impact of Private Schools in Developing Countries*, 34.

Chapter 4: Sustainability and the Rise of Educational Entrepreneurs

1. I wrote up my first inquiries about the profitability of the schools in James Tooley, "Could For-Profit Private Education Benefit the Poor? Some *a Priori* Considerations Arising from Case Study Research in India," *Journal of Education Policy* 22, no. 3 (May 2007): 341–42; there's more in James Tooley, *The Beautiful Tree: A Personal Journey into How the World's Poorest People Are Educating Themselves* (New Delhi, India: Penguin, 2009).

2. This was an edit of the final chapter of *The Beautiful Tree*, which I finished writing in 2006 (although it was not published until 2009).

3. C. K. Prahalad, *The Fortune at the Bottom of the Pyramid: Eradicating Poverty Through Profits* (Upper Saddle River, NJ: Prentice Hall, 2005), 13.

4. James Tooley, "Educating Amaretch: Private Schools for the Poor and the New Frontier for Investors," IFC and the Financial Times First Annual Essay Competition, mimeo (2006); republished in *Economic Affairs* 27, no. 2 (June 2007): 37–43.

5. Tooley, "Educating Amaretch."

6. Tooley, "Educating Amaretch."

7. Tooley, "Educating Amaretch."

8. Prahalad, *The Fortune at the Bottom of the Pyramid*, 37.

9. Tooley, "Educating Amaretch."

10. James Tooley, "Low-Cost Schools in Poor Nations Seek Investors," *Financial Times*, September 17, 2006, https://www.ft.com/content/379b98c4-4670-11db-ac52-0000779e2340.

11. Edwin G. West, *Education and the State: A Study in Political Economy* (Indianapolis, IN: Liberty Fund, 1974), 173.

12. James Tooley, "Lessons from Nigeria's Private School Revolution," Institute of Economic Affairs, October 18, 2018, https://iea.org.uk/lessons-from-nigerias-private-school-revolution/.

13. See John Hattie, *Visible Learning: A Synthesis of Over 800 Meta-Analyses Relating to Achievement* (Abingdon, UK: Routledge, 2009).

14. See, for example, Rebecca Ratcliffe and Afua Hirsch, "UK Urged to Stop Funding 'Ineffective and Unsustainable' Bridge Schools," *Guardian*, August 3, 2017, https://www.theguardian.com/global-development/2017/aug/03/uk-urged-to-stop-funding-ineffective-and-unsustainable-bridge-academies.

15. The income tax withholding system in the UK is called "Pay As You Earn," or PAYE, hence this acronym.

Chapter 5: Education, Corruption, and Domination

1. Transparency International, "Corruption Perception Index 2017," https://www.transparency.org/news/feature/corruption_perceptions_index_2017#table.

2. For example, "Education Corruption: 'Illegal' Appointments Challenged in Sindh High Court," *The Express Tribune*, October 4, 2012, https://tribune.com.pk/story/446620/education-corruption-illegal-appointments-challenged-insindh-high-court; Ibrahim Khatete and Dorcah Asiago, "Effectiveness of the Board of Governors in the Recruitment of Secondary School Teachers in Gucha District," *Journal of Education and Practice* 4, no. 28 (2013): 63–68; "Teachers Allege Rot, Bribery, Extortion at Education," *Swazi Observer*, 2015, accessed November 25, 2015, https://web.archive.org/web/20150914135253/http://www.observer.org.sz/news/75374-teachers-allege-rot-bribery-extortion-at-education.html.

3. See, for example, Natalie Pearl, "Leh Di Pipul Dem Tok [Let the People Talk]," *Peace Review* 15, no. 3 (September 2003): 309–16.

4. Truth and Reconciliation Commission, *Final Report of the Truth and Reconciliation Commission of Sierra Leone* (Freetown, Sierra Leone: 2004), 16; emphasis added.

5. Inter-Agency Network for Education in Emergencies (INEE), *Minimum Standards for Education: Preparedness, Response, Recovery* (New York: INEE, 2010), 32.

6. INEE, *Minimum Standards for Education*, 33.

7. Daron Acemoglu and James A. Robinson, *Why Nations Fail: The Origins of Power, Prosperity, and Poverty* (London: Profile Books, 2013), 111. See also James Tooley and David Longfield, *Education, War, and Peace: The Surprising Success of Private Education in War-Torn Countries* (London: IEA, 2017).

8. United Nations Educational, Scientific and Cultural Organization (UNESCO), *EFA Global Monitoring Report—The Hidden Crisis: Armed Conflict and Education* (Paris: UNESCO, 2011), 16.

9. UNESCO, *EFA Global Monitoring Report*, 160.

10. UNESCO, *EFA Global Monitoring Report*, 16.

11. UNESCO, *EFA Global Monitoring Report*, 160.

12. UNESCO, *EFA Global Monitoring Report*, 17.

13. UNESCO, *EFA Global Monitoring Report*, 160.

14. Marc Sommers, *Islands of Education: Schooling, Civil War, and the Southern Sudanese (1983–2004)* (Paris: International Institute for Educational Planning, UNESCO, 2005), 36, 96.

15. Sommers, *Islands of Education*, 245, 246.

16. Organisation for Economic Co-operation and Development (OECD), *Service Delivery in Fragile Situations: Key Concepts, Findings, and Lessons* (Paris: OECD, 2008), 9.

17. Alex Traub, "India's Dangerous New Curriculum," *New York Review of Books*, December 6, 2018, https://www.nybooks.com/articles/2018/12/06/indias-dangerous-new-curriculum/.

18. Traub, "India's Dangerous New Curriculum."

19. Traub, "India's Dangerous New Curriculum."

20. Gujarat State Board of School Textbooks, *History, Standard 12*, 1st ed. (Gandhinagar, India: H. N. Chavda, 2017); emphasis added.

21. Traub, "India's Dangerous New Curriculum."

22. James Boyd Stanfield, "Private Schools for the Poor and the Right to Education: A Study in Political Economy" (PhD diss., University of Newcastle upon Tyne, 2014), accessed November 24, 2018, https://ethos.bl.uk/OrderDetails.do?did=2&uin=uk.bl.ethos.658367.

23. UNESCO, *World Education Report 2000: The Right to Education* (Paris: UNESCO, 2000), 93; emphasis added.

24. Stanfield, "Private Schools for the Poor and the Right to Education," 123–24.

25. Stanfield, "Private Schools for the Poor and the Right to Education," 113.

26. Stanfield, "Private Schools for the Poor and the Right to Education," 113.

27. UNESCO, *World Education Report 2000*, 99.

28. UNESCO, *World Education Report 2000*, 105.

Chapter 6: Great Expectations

1. Abhijit V. Banerjee and Esther Duflo, *Poor Economics: A Radical Rethinking of the Way to Fight Global Poverty* (New York: PublicAffairs, 2011), 83. This section is adapted from parts of James Tooley, "Big Questions and *Poor Economics*: Banerjee and Duflo on Schooling in Developing Countries," *Econ Journal Watch* 9, no. 3 (September 2012): 170–85. Since I wrote this, Banerjee and Duflo went on to win the 2019 Sveriges Riksbank Prize in Economic Sciences in Memory of Alfred Nobel (commonly known as the Nobel Prize for Economics).

2. Banerjee and Duflo, *Poor Economics*, 84.

3. Banerjee and Duflo, *Poor Economics*, 84.

4. Banerjee and Duflo, *Poor Economics*, 86.

5. Banerjee and Duflo, *Poor Economics*, 86; emphasis in original.

6. Banerjee and Duflo, *Poor Economics*, 87.

7. Banerjee and Duflo, *Poor Economics*, 89; emphasis added.

8. Banerjee and Duflo, *Poor Economics*, 89–90.

9. Banerjee and Duflo, *Poor Economics*, 94.

10. I've done that in James Tooley, *From Village School to Global Chain: Changing the World through Education* (London: Profile Books, 2012).

11. Caplan, *The Case against Education*, 1–2; emphasis in original.

12. Caplan, *The Case against Education*, 2.

13. Caplan, *The Case against Education*, 192.

14. Caplan, *The Case against Education*, 3; emphasis in original.

15. Caplan, *The Case against Education*, 18.

16. Caplan, *The Case against Education*, 39.

17. Caplan, *The Case against Education*, 39.

18. Caplan, *The Case against Education*, 40; emphasis in original.

19. Caplan, *The Case against Education*, 49.

20. Caplan, *The Case against Education*, 50.

21. Caplan, *The Case against Education*, 51, 59.

22. See Walter Mischel, *The Marshmallow Test: Understanding Self-Control and How to Master It* (London: Penguin Random House, 2014).

23. Caplan, *The Case against Education*, 64.

24. Caplan, *The Case against Education*, 5; emphasis in original.

25. Caplan, *The Case against Education*, 6.

26. Caplan, *The Case against Education*, 198; emphasis in original.

27. Caplan, *The Case against Education*, 103–4.

28. Ronald Dore, *The Diploma Disease: Education, Qualification, and Development* (London: George Allen and Unwin, 1976), 23.

29. Dore, *The Diploma Disease*, 24.

30. Wikipedia, s.v. "Chartered Institute of Library and Information Professionals," last modified November 9, 2020, https://en.wikipedia.org/wiki/Chartered_Institute_of_Library _and Information Professionals.

31. Dore, *The Diploma Disease*, 24.

32. Dore, *The Diploma Disease*, 26; emphasis in original.

33. Caplan, *The Case against Education*, 4–5; emphasis in original.

34. Dore, *The Diploma Disease*, 74.

35. At one point, it appears that Caplan is disagreeing with this and the analysis below. He asks, "Is Credentialism a Creature of the State?" (pp. 85ff), which appears to be the same question we are addressing, and his conclusion is negative. However, in this section, he is exploring the question: When the state is *an employer*, is it better or worse than private employers in using credentials? But that is not the question we are addressing here.

36. Caplan, *The Case against Education*, 6; emphasis in original.

37. Caplan, *The Case against Education*, 6; emphasis in original.

38. Caplan, *The Case against Education*, 213; emphasis in original.

39. Caplan, *The Case against Education*, 213.

40. Caplan, *The Case against Education*. 213.

41. Caplan, *The Case against Education*, 214.

42. Caplan, *The Case against Education*, 204.

43. Caplan, *The Case against Education*, 205–6.

44. Caplan, *The Case against Education*, 206.

45. Caplan, *The Case against Education*, 289.

46. Caplan, *The Case against Education*, 200.

47. Caplan, *The Case against Education*, 206.

48. Caplan, *The Case against Education*, 280.

49. Caplan, *The Case against Education*, 200; emphasis in original.

50. Caplan, *The Case against Education*, 265.

Chapter 7: The Unbearable Burden of Learning

1. See James Tooley, *Imprisoned in India: Corruption and Extortion in the World's Largest Democracy* (London: Biteback Publishing, 2016).

2. Matthew Arnold, *Culture and Anarchy* (Oxford: Oxford University Press, 2009).

3. Rabindranath Tagore, "The Parrot's Training," in *Rabindranath Tagore: Pioneer in Education*, ed. V. Bhatia (New Delhi, India: Sahitya Chayan, 1994).

4. Ken Robinson and Lou Aronica, *Creative Schools* (London: Penguin Random House, 2015), x.

5. Carmine Gallo, *Talk Like TED: The 9 Public Speaking Secrets of the World's Top Minds* (New York: St. Martin's Press, 2014).

6. Ken Robinson, *Changing Education Paradigms* (animation), Cognitive and RSA, 2010, accessed November 24, 2018, https://www.wearecognitive.com/rsa-work/changing-education-paradigms.

7. Ken Robinson and Lou Aronica, *The Element: How Finding Your Passion Changes Everything* (London: Penguin Books, 2009).

8. Robinson and Aronica, *Creative Schools*, 75.

9. Robinson and Aronica, *Creative Schools*, 76.

10. Robinson and Aronica, *The Element*.

11. Robinson, *Changing Education Paradigms*.

12. Robinson and Aronica, *Creative Schools*, xi.

13. Robinson and Aronica, *Creative Schools*, xi.

14. Robinson and Aronica, *Creative Schools*, xvii, xx.

15. Robinson and Aronica, *Creative Schools*, 251.

16. Robinson and Aronica, *Creative Schools*, xx.

17. Robinson and Aronica, *Creative Schools*, 116.

18. See Michelle Manno, "Idaho Embracing 'Flipped' Classrooms with Khan Academy," Teach.com, March 11, 2013, https://teach.com/blog/idaho-embracing-flipped-classrooms-with-khan-academy/; Adam Cotterell, "48 Idaho Schools 'Flip the Classroom' and Pilot Khan Academy Online Learning," NPR, September 3, 2013, http://boisestatepublicradio.org/post/48-idaho-schools-flip-classroom-and-pilot-khan-academy-online-learning#stream/0.

19. See Tooley, *From Village School to Global Chain*.

20. Sir Ken Robinson, "How to Escape Education's Death Valley," TED Talks Education, 2013, 14:02; emphasis added, https://www.ted.com/talks/ken_robinson_how_to_escape_education_s_death_valley/transcript?language=en.

21. Ken Robinson, *Changing Education Paradigms*.

22. Robinson and Aronica, *Creative Schools*, ix.

23. Robinson and Aronica, *Creative Schools*, xiv; emphasis added.

24. Robinson and Aronica, *Creative Schools*, 71.

25. Robinson and Aronica, *Creative Schools*, 226.

26. Robinson and Aronica, *Creative Schools*, 246.

27. Robinson and Aronica, *Creative Schools*, 247.

28. Robinson and Aronica, *Creative Schools*, 248.

29. Robinson and Aronica, *Creative Schools*, 249.

30. Robinson and Aronica, *Creative Schools*, xiii.

31. Robinson and Aronica, *Creative Schools*, 132.

32. For example, Michael Naish, "Education and Essential Contestability Revisited," *Journal of Philosophy of Education* 18, no. 2 (December 1984): 141–53; Christopher Winch, "Quality and Education," *Journal of the Philosophy of Education* 30, no. 1 (June 1996): 25–26.

33. Margaret Thatcher, *The Downing Street Years* (London: HarperCollins Publishers, 1993), 593.

34. Terry Moe and John Chubb, *Politics, Markets, and America's Schools* (San Francisco: John Wiley & Sons, 2009), 42–43.

35. Richard Aldrich, "Educational Legislation of the 1980s in England: An Historical Analysis," *History of Education* 21, no. 1 (1992): 57–69.

36. Moe and Chubb, *Politics, Markets, and America's Schools*, 31.

37. Moe and Chubb, *Politics, Markets, and America's Schools*, 31.

38. Moe and Chubb, *Politics, Markets, and America's Schools*, 34; emphasis added

39. Moe and Chubb, *Politics, Markets, and America's Schools*, 34; emphasis added.

40. Moe and Chubb, *Politics, Markets, and America's Schools*, 34–35.

41. Robinson, "How to Escape Education's Death Valley," 8:30.

42. Robinson, "How to Escape Education's Death Valley," 6:20.

43. Robinson and Aronica, *Creative Schools*, xvii.

44. Robinson and Aronica, *Creative Schools*, 65; also see 222–25.

45. Robinson and Aronica, *Creative Schools*, 255.

46. Sadly, Sir Ken Robinson passed away as the manuscript was heading to press. I was very fond of Sir Ken and hope that the playfulness in my approach to him is taken in the spirit in which it was intended.

Chapter 8: Five Problems in Search of a Solution

1. Salman Khan, *The One World Schoolhouse: Education Reimagined* (London: Hodder & Stoughton, 2012), 57.

2. Caplan, *The Case against Education*, 135; emphasis in original.

3. Caplan, *The Case against Education*, 135.

4. "About Us," Trinity College London, http://www.trinitycollege.com/site/?id=6.

5. For their US website, see Associated Board of the Royal Schools of Music (ABRSM), https://us.abrsm.org/en/home#.

6. "Information and Regulations," ABRSM, https://gb.abrsm.org/en/our-exams/information-and-regulations/.

7. The World Martial Arts Center explains the significance of the belt colors on their website, see http://www.wmacenter.com/page/purpose-of-the-belts.

8. Abhijit V. Banerjee and Esther Duflo, *Poor Economics: A Radical Rethinking of the Way to Fight Global Poverty* (New York: Public Affairs, 2011), 95, 96–97.

9. All India Council for Technical Education (AICTE), *Norms and Standards*, New Delhi, All India Council for Technical Education, Section 10(n), 1999.

10. "Theory of Knowledge," International Baccalaureate (IB), accessed October 3, 2019, https://www.ibo.org /programmes/diploma-programme/curriculum/theory-of-knowledge/; and "Creativity, Activity, Service," https://ibo.org /programmes/diploma-programme/curriculum/creativity-activity-and-service/.

11. Department of Education and Science and the Welsh Office, *National Curriculum: Task Group on Assessment and Testing*, December 24, 1987, http://www.educationengland .org.uk/documents/pdfs/1988-TGAT-report.pdf.

Chapter 9: A Thought Experiment in Educational Freedom

1. *The Encyclopaedia of Political Science*, s.v. "Withering Away of the State," ed. George Thomas Kurian (Washington, DC: CQ Press, 2011), http://sk.sagepub.com/cqpress/the -encyclopedia-of-political-science.

2. Chris Whittle, *Crash Course: Imagining a Better Future for Public Education* (New York: Riverhead Books, 2005), 110.

3. Whittle, *Crash Course*, 111.

4. Whittle, *Crash Course*, 112–13.

5. Online Etymology Dictionary, s.v. "apocalypse," accessed June 2, 2018, https://www .etymonline.com/word/apocalypse.

6. Moira Young, "Why Is Dystopia So Appealing to Young Adults?," *Guardian*, October 23, 2011, https://www.theguardian.com/books/2011/oct/23/dystopian-fiction.

7. R. S. Peters, *Ethics and Education* (London: George Allen & Unwin Ltd., 1966).

8. Lewis Dartnell, *The Knowledge: How to Rebuild Our World from Scratch* (London: Bodley Head, 2014), 1.

9. Dartnell, *The Knowledge*, 2.

10. Dartnell, *The Knowledge*, 5.

11. Dartnell, *The Knowledge*, 3.

12. Dartnell, *The Knowledge*, 3.

13. Dartnell, *The Knowledge*, 4.

14. Dartnell, *The Knowledge*, 7.

15. Dartnell, *The Knowledge*, 17.

16. Dartnell, *The Knowledge*, 17.

17. Arnold, *Culture and Anarchy*. See Anthony O'Hear and Marc Sidwell, *The School of Freedom: A Liberal Education Reader from Plato to the Present Day* (Exeter, UK: Imprint Academic, 2009).

Chapter 10: A New Measure of Education

1. Michael Moore, *Where to Invade Next*, directed by Michael Moore (2015; New York: Dog Eat Dog Films, 2016), http://wheretoinvadenext.com/.

2. Tony Wagner and Ted Dintersmith, *Most Likely to Succeed: Preparing Our Kids for the Innovation Era* (New York: Scribner, 2015), 34, 54, 120.

3. Robinson and Aronica, *Creative Schools*, 61, 60.

4. Robinson and Aronica, *Creative Schools*, 60.

5. Robinson and Aronica, *Creative Schools*, 7.

6. Robinson and Aronica, *Creative Schools*, 9.

7. Hilton, Bade, and Bade, *More Human*, 74.

8. Hilton, Bade, and Bade, *More Human*, 73.

9. Ministry of Education and Culture, *The Results of PISA 2012*, accessed June 2, 2018, http://minedu.fi/en/pisa-2012-en.

10. See James Tooley, "The World Loves Our Grammar Schools—So Why Don't We?," *Spectator*, May 27, 2017, https://www.spectator.co.uk/2017/05/the-world-loves-our-grammar -school-system-so-why-dont-we.

11. Sirkku Kupianinen, Jarkko Hautamäki, and Rommi Karjalainen, *The Finnish Education System and PISA* (Helsinki: Ministry of Education Publications, 2009), 14–15.

12. See, for example, Avinash Agarwal, "Why Ignore PISA, the Olympics of Education?," LinkedIn, August 29, 2016, https://www.linkedin.com/pulse/why-ignore-pisa-olympics-education-avinash-agarwal/; *Western Independent* (blog), "Testing Nations: Olympics and PISA," August 17, 2012, https://westernindependent.blogspot.com/2012 /08/testing-nations-olympics-and-pisa.html; Debra Viadero, "Potential of Global Tests Seen as Unrealized Scholars Urged to Scour TIMSS, PISA for Policy Insights," *Education Week*, November 22, 2006, https://www.edweek.org/ew/articles/2006/11/29 /13international.h26.html.

13. *Western Independent*, "Testing Nations: Olympics and PISA."

14. Lant Pritchett, *The Rebirth of Education: Schooling Ain't Learning* (Washington, DC: Center for Global Development, 2013), 13.

15. Robinson and Aronica, *Creative Schools*, xvi; emphasis in original.

16. Ben Williamson, "PISA for Personality Testing—the OECD and the Psychometric Science of Social-Emotional Skills," *Code Acts in Education*, January 16 2018, https:// codeactsineducation.wordpress.com/2018/01/16/pisa-for-personality-testing/.

17. Wagner and Dintersmith, *Most Likely to Succeed*, 56.

18. Ian Morris, *Why the West Rules—for Now: The Patterns of History, and What They Reveal About the Future* (London: Profile Books, 2010), 147.

19. Conference Board, "Total Economy Database - Key Findings," 2018, accessed November 25, 2018, https://www.conference-board .org/data/economydatabase/.

20. Economist Intelligence Unit (EIU), "The Economist Intelligence Unit's Democracy Index," 2018, https://infographics.cconomist.com/2018/DemocracyIndex/.

21. See John R. Lott Jr., "Juvenile Delinquency and Education: A Comparison of Public and Private Provision," *International Review of Law and Economics* 7, no. 3 (December 1987): 163–75.

22. Numbeo, "Crime Index by Country, 2018," accessed June 3, 2018, https://www .numbeo.com/crime/rankings_by_country.jsp.

23. World Health Organization (WHO), "Global Health Observatory Data," "Suicide Rates per 100,000 Population," "Age Standardized Rates by Country," WHO, 2018, http:// www.who.int/gho/mental_health/suicide_rates/en/.

24. World Bank, "World Development Indicators," 2018, https://datacatalog.worldbank .org/dataset/world-development-indicators.

25. Morris, *Why the West Rules—for Now*, 151.

26. See Tooley, "The World Loves Our Grammar Schools."

Part 3: Off to America

1. As for the question "Why should we want to move away from public education?," there have been many pointers to this argument throughout Parts 1 and 2; further, substantial arguments are given in James Tooley, *E. G. West: Economic Liberalism and the Role of Government in Education* (London: Continuum, 2008); Tooley, *The Beautiful Tree*; James Tooley, *Disestablishing the School* (Aldershot, UK: Avebury Press, 1995).

Chapter 11: Some Problems with American Education

1. Charles Murray, *Real Education: Four Simple Truths for Bringing America's Schools Back to Reality* (New York: Crown Forum, 2008), 11.

2. Murray, *Real Education*, 55.

3. Murray, *Real Education*, 12.

4. Murray, *Real Education*, 11.

5. Tooley, *Disestablishing the School*.

6. Murray, *Real Education*, 12.

7. Murray, *Real Education*, 20.

8. Murray, *Real Education*, 21.

9. Murray, *Real Education*, 21.

10. Murray, *Real Education*, 22; emphasis added.

11. Murray, *Real Education*, 44.

12. Murray, *Real Education*, 39.

13. Murray, *Real Education*, 39.

14. Murray, *Real Education*, 39.

15. This is not quite accurate, although accurate enough for most purposes. Suppose a is the share of the population that knows the answer, b is the share that doesn't know the answer but guesses, and c is the share of the population that omits the answer or checks "Don't know." Then (equation 1) $a + b + c = 1$. Furthermore, suppose S is the share of the population that actually comes up with the correct answer, and N is the number of options on the multiple-choice questions. Also assume that those who don't know and guess are equally likely to guess any of the options. Then (equation 2) $a + b/N = S$. Substituting for b gives (equation 3) $a = (SN - 1 + c)/(N - 1)$. In his calculations, Murray has assumed $c = 0$.

16. Murray, *Real Education*, 42.

17. Murray, *Real Education*, 43.

18. Murray, *Real Education*, 43.

19. Murray, *Real Education*, 43.

20. John Locke, *Some Thoughts Concerning Education* (A. and J. Churchill, 1693), Sections 126 and 129, accessed November 25, 2018, https://books.google.bg/books?id=OCUCA AAAQAAJ&hl=bg&pg=PP7#v=onepage&q&f=false.

21. "Can't Be Asked: Effort, Not Ability, May Explain the Gap Between American and Chinese Pupils," *Economist*, August 17, 2017, https://www.economist.com/news/united -states/21726745-when-greenbacks-are-offer-american-schoolchildren-seem-try-harder- effort-not.

22. Erich Von Däniken, *Chariots of the Gods?* (New York: G. P. Putnam's Sons, 1968).

23. BBC, "Grammar Schools: Who Will Get In?," 2018, https://www.bbc.co.uk/programmes/bob57ynx.

24. Murray, *Real Education*, 36.

25. Murray, *Real Education*, 36.

26. Channel 4, *Indian Summer School*, 2018, https://www.channel4.com/programmes/indian-summer-school.

27. Lant Pritchett, *The Rebirth of Education: Schooling Ain't Learning* (Washington, DC: Center for Global Development, 2013), 29.

28. Pritchett, *The Rebirth of Education*, 83; emphasis added.

29. Murray, *Real Education*, 39.

30. Murray, *Real Education*, 40.

31. Pritchett, *The Rebirth of Education*, 2, quoted.

32. Pritchett, *The Rebirth of Education*, 3, quoted.

33. Pritchett, *The Rebirth of Education*, 3–4.

34. Murray, *Real Education*, 40.

35. Murray, *Real Education*, 40.

36. Murray, *Real Education*, 41; emphasis added.

37. Murray, *Real Education*, 153.

38. Andrew Bell, *Mutual Tuition and Moral Discipline; or, Manual of Instructions for Conducting Schools Through the Agency of the Scholars Themselves* (London: Hatchard and Son, 1823; 7th ed. 1896), 58–59.

39. Murray, *Real Education*, 56; emphasis added.

40. Murray, *Real Education*, 140.

41. Murray, *Real Education*, 141; emphasis added.

42. Murray, *Real Education*, 145.

Chapter 12: The Theory and Practice of School Vouchers

1. This chapter adapts and updates material from James Tooley, "The Role of Government in Education Revisited: The Theory and Practice of Vouchers, with Pointers to Another Solution for American Education," *Social Philosophy and Policy* 31, no. 1 (January 2014): 204–28.

2. Friedman, *Capitalism and Freedom*.

3. Murray, *Real Education*, 152.

4. Pritchett, *The Rebirth of Education*, 189.

5. John A. Allison, *The Financial Crisis and the Free Market Cure* (New York: McGraw-Hill, 2013), 233–34.

6. Allison, *The Financial Crisis*, 247.

7. Allison, *The Financial Crisis*, 234.

8. Allison, *The Financial Crisis*, 234, 247, 235.

9. A. C. F. Beales et al., "Appraisal," in *Education: A Framework for Choice* (London: Institute of Economic Affairs, 1967), xiv, xv; emphasis added.

10. Pritchett, *The Rebirth of Education*, 190.

11. See Tooley, *From Village School to Global Chain*, ch. 4.

12. Milton Friedman, "The Role of Government in Education," in *Liberty and Learning: Milton Friedman's Voucher Idea at Fifty*, ed. Robert Enlow and Lenore Ealy (Washington, DC: Cato Institute, 2006).

13. Mark Blaug, "Economic Aspects of Vouchers for Education," in A. C .F. Beales, Mark Blaug, Sir Douglas Veale, and E. G. West, *Education: A Framework for Choice. Papers on Historical, Economic, and Administrative Aspects of Choice in Education and Its Finance*, 2nd ed., Readings in Political Economy 1 (London: Institute of Economic Affairs, 1970), 26.

14. E. G. West, *Education and the State: A Study in Political Economy* (Indianapolis: Liberty Fund, 1994), 3.

15. E. G. West, "Resource Allocation and Growth in Early Nineteenth-Century British Education," *Economic History Review* 23, no. 1 (April 1970): 68–95.

16. Friedman, *Capitalism and Freedom*, 30.

17. Friedman, *Capitalism and Freedom*, 86.

18. Friedman, *Capitalism and Freedom*, 89.

19. Friedman, *Capitalism and Freedom*, 89.

20. Milton Friedman, "Epilogue: School Choice Turns 50, but the Fun Is Just Beginning," in *Liberty and Learning: Milton Friedman's Voucher Idea at Fifty*, ed. Robert C. Enlow and Lenore T. Ealy (Washington, DC: Cato Institute, 2006), 157.

21. Friedman, *Capitalism and Freedom*, 89; emphasis added.

22. F. A. Hayek, *The Constitution of Liberty* (London: Routledge & Kegan Paul, 1960), 377.

23. Hayek, *The Constitution of Liberty*, 379.

24. Hayek, *The Constitution of Liberty*, 380.

25. Hayek, *The Constitution of Liberty*, 380; emphasis added.

26. Hayek, *The Constitution of Liberty*, 381.

27. Hayek, *The Constitution of Liberty*, 376.

28. Tooley, "The Role of Government in Education Revisited."

29. Tooley, *From Village School to Global Chain*.

30. Friedman Foundation for Educational Choice, *The ABCs of School Choice: The Comprehensive Guide to Every Private School Choice Program in America* (Indianapolis, IN: Friedman Foundation for Educational Choice, 2017), 3.

31. Friedman Foundation for Educational Choice, *The ABCs of School Choice*, 6.

32. Friedman Foundation for Educational Choice, *The ABCs of School Choice*, 37.

33. Friedman Foundation for Educational Choice, *The ABCs of School Choice*, 3.

34. Friedman Foundation for Educational Choice, *The ABCs of School Choice*, 13.

35. Friedman Foundation for Educational Choice, *The ABCs of School Choice*, 15.

36. Michelle Rindels, "Nevada Supreme Court Suspends School Choice Program," *Reno Gazette Journal*, September 29, 2016, https://eu.rgj.com/story/news/education/2016/09/29/school-choice-program-unconstitutional-nevada-supreme-court-says/91278708/.

37. Friedman Foundation for Educational Choice, *The ABCs of School Choice*, 80.

38. Friedman Foundation for Educational Choice, *The ABCs of School Choice*, 124.

39. Milton Friedman, "Prologue: A Personal Retrospective," in *Liberty and Learning: Milton Friedman's Voucher Idea at Fifty*, ed. Robert C. Enlow and Lenore T. Ealy (Washington, DC: Cato Institute, 2006), ix.

40. Friedman, "Prologue," ix.

41. Friedman, "Prologue," ix.

42. Friedman, "Prologue," x.

43. Friedman, "Epilogue," 156.

44. Friedman, "Epilogue," 157.

45. Tooley, *E. G. West*, 225; emphasis in original.

46. Tooley, *E. G. West*, 225.

47. Tooley, *E. G. West*, 225.

48. Tooley, *E. G. West*, 225–26.

49. See chapter 4 of this book.

50. Arthur Seldon, *The Riddle of the Voucher: An Inquiry Into the Obstacles of Introducing Choice and Competition in State Schools* (London: Institute of Economic Affairs, 1986), 13, 14, 36.

51. Seldon, *The Riddle of the Voucher*, 15.

52. Seldon, *The Riddle of the Voucher*, 40.

53. Seldon, *The Riddle of the Voucher*, 39.

54. Seldon, *The Riddle of the Voucher*, 38.

55. John Merrifield, "Choice as an Education Reform Catalyst: Lessons from Chile, Milwaukee, Florida, Cleveland, Edgewood, New Zealand, and Sweden," in *What America Can Learn from School Choice in Other Countries*," ed. David Salisbury and James Tooley (Washington, DC: Cato Institute, 2005).

56. Peje Emilsson, "The Profit Motive in Swedish Education," in *The Profit Motive in Education*, ed. James Stanfield (London: Institute of Economic Affairs, 2012).

57. Milton Friedman, "Are Externalities Relevant?," in *Nonpublic School Aid: The Law, Economics, and Politics of American Education*," ed. E. G. West (Lexington, MA: Lexington Books, 1976), 92.

58. Friedman, "Are Externalities Relevant?," 92; emphasis added.

59. Milton Friedman and Rose Friedman, *Free to Choose: A Personal Statement* (Harmonsworth, UK: Pelican Books, 1980), 197.

60. Letter from Milton Friedman to E. G. West, n.d., E. G. West Archives, University of Buckingham, UK.

61. Friedman and Friedman, *Free to Choose*, 197.

Chapter 13: Why Milton Friedman Changed His Mind

1. This chapter includes material from James Tooley, *E. G. West: Economic Liberalism and the Role of Government in Education* (London: Bloomsbury, 2014).

2. George Macaulay Trevelyan, *British History in the Nineteenth Century (1782–1901)* (New York and London: Longmans, Green, 1922), 354.

3. Education Commission, *Report of the Commissioners Appointed to Inquire into the State of Popular Education in England,* Vol. 1 (London: George E. Eyre and William Spottiswoode for Her Majesty's Stationery Office, 1861), 79.

4. It seems to be the same issue (noted in the introduction) of how "public" school is used in England today.

5. Education Commission, *Report of the Commissioners,* 16.

6. Education Commission, *Report of the Commissioners,* 33.

7. Education Commission, *Report of the Commissioners,* 84.

8. Education Commission, *Report of the Commissioners,* 84.

9. Education Commission, *Report of the Commissioners,* 85, 86.

10. Education Commission, *Report of the Commissioners,* 293.

11. Poor Law Commission, *The Report of the Poor Law Commissioners* (1941), cited in E. G. West, *Education and the State* (Indianapolis, IN: Liberty Fund, 1994), 161.

12. Statistical Society of London, *Report on the State of Education in the Borough of Kingston upon Hull, Journal of the Statistical Society of London* (July 1841), cited in E. G. West, *Education and the State* (Indianapolis, IN: Liberty Fund, 1994), 162–63.

13. West, *Education and the State,* 164.

14. James Mill, *Edinburgh Review* (October 1813), cited in West, *Education and the State,* 170.

15. *Report from the Select Committee of the House of Commons Appointed to Inquire Into the Education of the Lower Orders in the Metropolis: With the Minutes of Evidence Taken Before the Committee … to which are Subjoined an Addenda and a Digested Index* (1816), cited in West, *Education and the State,* 171.

16. West, *Education and the State,* 171.

17. West, *Education and the State,* 172.

18. Henry Brougham, House of Lords (May 12, 1835), cited in West, *Education and the State,* 172.

19. Brougham, cited in West, *Education and the State,* 173.

20. West, *Education and the State,* 181.

21. See Education Bill, First Reading, H. C. February 17, 1870, Hansard, vol. 99, in West, *Education and the State,* 607–8.

22. T. Wemyss Reid, *Life of the Rt. Hon. W. E. Forster* (New York: Augustus M. Kelly, 1888, 1970), 479, 506.

23. Education Commission, *Report of the Commissioners,* 86.

24. See Tooley, *The Beautiful Tree.*

25. Education Commission, *Report of the Commissioners,* 94.

26. Tooley, *The Beautiful Tree.*

27. Education Commission, *Report of the Commissioners,* 91–92; emphasis added.

28. Prior to decimalization of the British currency in 1970, £1 comprised 20 shillings (s.), each of which comprised 12 pence (d.). So 2s. 6d. is 18 pence. In 1858, 18 pence would have been worth about US$0.87.

29. Education Commission, *Report of the Commissioners,* 92.

30. Education Commission, *Report of the Commissioners,* 92.

31. Education Commission, *Report of the Commissioners*, 92, 94, 96; emphasis added.

32. Education Commission, *Report of the Commissioners*, 90–91; caps in the original.

33. Education Commission, *Report of the Commissioners*, 95, 96.

34. Education Commission, *Report of the Commissioners*, 101.

35. Education Commission, *Report of the Commissioners*, 103.

36. Education Commission, *Report of the Commissioners*, 103.

37. Education Commission, *Report of the Commissioners*, 108.

38. Education Commission, *Report of the Commissioners*, 119.

39. Education Commission, *Report of the Commissioners*, 120.

40. Education Commission, *Report of the Commissioners*, 135.

41. Education Commission, *Report of the Commissioners*, 134.

42. Education Commission, *Report of the Commissioners*, 142.

43. Education Commission, *Report of the Commissioners*, 144.

44. Education Commission, *Report of the Commissioners*, 151.

45. Education Commission, *Report of the Commissioners*, 177.

46. Education Commission, *Report of the Commissioners*, 33.

47. Education Commission, *Report of the Commissioners*, 33.

48. Education Commission, *Report of the Commissioners*, 34.

49. Education Commission, *Report of the Commissioners*, 34; emphasis added.

50. Education Commission, *Report of the Commissioners*, 34.

51. Education Commission, *Report of the Commissioners*, 35; emphasis added.

52. Education Commission, *Report of the Commissioners*, 176.

53. Education Commission, *Report of the Commissioners*, 176.

54. See Tooley, *E. G. West.*

55. Education Commission, *Report of the Commissioners*, 67.

56. Education Commission, *Report of the Commissioners*, 76.

57. Education Commission, *Report of the Commissioners*, 87.

58. Education Commission, *Report of the Commissioners*, 69.

59. Education Commission, *Report of the Commissioners*, 75.

60. West, *Education and the State*, 84; emphasis added..

61. George Randall, *History of the Common School System of the State of New York* (New York: Ivison, Blakemen, Taylor & Co., 1871), cited in West, *Education and the State*, 298; emphasis in West.

62. Randall, cited in West, *Education and the State*, 298.

63. West, *Education and the State*, 299.

64. Randall, cited in West, *Education and the State*, 301.

65. West, *Education and the State*, 302.

66. *Annual Report of the New York Superintendent for Common Schools*, 1836, cited in West, *Education and the State*, 204.

67. Friedman and Friedman, *Free to Choose*, 196; emphasis added.

68. Friedman and Friedman, *Free to Choose*, 196–97; emphasis added.

69. Friedman and Friedman, *Free to Choose*, 197.

70. Friedman and Friedman, *Free to Choose*, 197.

Chapter 14: Two Types of School Choice

1. Education Commission, *Report of the Commissioners*, 73; emphasis added, 74, 300.

2. Wagner and Dintersmith, *Most Likely to Succeed*, 246.

3. Tooley, *From Village School to Global Chain*.

4. Nora Kern and Wentana Gebru, *Waiting Lists to Attend Charter Schools Top 1 Million Names*, National Alliance for Public Charter Schools, May 2014, accessed June 17, 2018, http://www.publiccharters.org/sites/default/files/migrated/wp-content/uploads/2014/05/NAPCS-2014-Wait-List-Report.pdf.

5. For New South Wales, Australia, see Edwin. G. West, "The Benthamites as Educational Engineers: The Reputation and the Record, *History of Political Economy* 24, no. 3 (Fall 1992): 595–621.

6. Center Bureau, "What Are the Poverty Thresholds Today?," Center for Poverty & Inequality Research, University of California, Davis, last updated September 13, 2017, https://poverty.ucdavis.edu/faq/what-are-poverty-thresholds-today.

7. Private School Review, "Average Private School Tuition Cost," accessed on March 20, 2020, https://www.privateschoolreview.com/tuition-stats/private-school-cost-by-state.

8. Jennifer Medina and Robert Gebeloff, "New York Charter Schools Lag in Enrolling Hispanics," *New York Times*, June 14, 2010, https://www.nytimes.com/2010/06/15/education/15charters.html.

9. Ben Chu, "The Charts That Show How Private School Fees Have Exploded Over the Past 25 Years," *Independent*, May 10, 2016, http://www.independent.co.uk/news/uk/home-news/the-charts-that-shows-how-private-school-fees-have-exploded-a7023056.html.

10. Centre for Economics and Business Research, *Asda Income Tracker, Report: February 2017*, (London: Centre for Economics and Business Research, ltd., 2017).

11. Murray, *Real Education*, 65.

12. Murray, *Real Education*, 151.

Chapter 15: Education as Spontaneous Order

1. Adam Smith, *An Inquiry into the Nature and Causes of the Wealth of Nations*, 2 vols. (London: W. Strahan and T. Cadell, 1776), B. I., Ch. 2, paragraph I.2.2.

2. David Boaz, *The Libertarian Mind: A Manifesto for Freedom* (New York: Simon & Schuster, 2015), 55.

3. Boaz, *The Libertarian Mind*, 55, 56.

4. Eustace Davie, *Unchain the Child: Abolish Compulsory Schooling Laws* (Johannesburg, South Africa: Free Market Foundation, 2005).

5. See A. S. Neill, *Summerhill: A Radical Approach to Child-Rearing* (London: Pelican Books, 1985); Richard Bailey, *A. S. Neill* (London: Bloomsbury, 2013).

6. Sugata Mitra, "The Future of Schooling: Children and Learning at the Edge of Chaos," *Prospects* 44 no.4 (December 2014): 550.

7. Mitra, "The Future of Schooling," 556; emphasis added.

8. Mitra, "The Future of Schooling," 549.

9. Mitra, "The Future of Schooling," 549–50.

10. Mitra, "The Future of Schooling," 550.

11. Mitra, "The Future of Schooling," 550.

12. Sugata Mitra, James Tooley, Parimala Inamdar, and Pauline Dixon, "Improving English Pronunciation: An Automated Instructional Approach," *Information Technologies and International Development* 1, no. 1 (Fall 2003): 75–84.

13. Mitra, "The Future of Schooling," 552; emphasis added.

14. Mitra, "The Future of Schooling," 552.

15. Mitra, "The Future of Schooling," 552.

16. Mitra, "The Future of Schooling," 552; emphasis added.

17. Mitra, "The Future of Schooling," 553; emphasis added.

18. Mitra, "The Future of Schooling," 553.

19. Mitra, "The Future of Schooling," 556.

20. Mitra, "The Future of Schooling," 555.

21. Mitra, "The Future of Schooling," 557.

22. Mitra, "The Future of Schooling," 557.

23. Mitra, "The Future of Schooling," 557; emphasis added.

24. Mitra, "The Future of Schooling," 557.

25. Tooley, *From Village School to Global Chain*, 43.

26. Mitra, "The Future of Schooling," 557.

27. Mitra, "The Future of Schooling," 557; emphasis in original.

28. Mitra, "The Future of Schooling," 2.

29. See William Poundstone, *Head in the Cloud: Why Knowing Things Still Matters When Facts Are So Easy to Look Up* (New York: Little, Brown, 2016).

30. Mitra, "The Future of Schooling," 557.

31. Terry Leahy, *Management in Ten Words: Practical Advice from the Man Who Created One of the World's Largest Retailers* (London: Random House Business Books, 2013), 155.

32. Samuel Smiles, quoted in Leahy, *Management in Ten Words*, 156.

33. Mitra, "The Future of Schooling," 549.

34. Mitra, "The Future of Schooling," 558.

35. Anthony Seldon and Oladimejji Abidoye, *The Fourth Education Revolution: Will Artificial Intelligence Liberate or Infantilize Humanity?* (Buckingham, UK: University of Buckingham Press, 2018), 175.

36. Seldon and Abidoye, *The Fourth Education Revolution*, 206.

37. Seldon and Abidoye, *The Fourth Education Revolution*, 205.

38. Seldon and Abidoye, *The Fourth Education Revolution*, 174.

39. See Anthony O'Hear and Marc Sidwell, *The School of Freedom: A Liberal Education Reader from Plato to the Present Day* (Exeter, UK: Imprint Academic, 2009).

40. John Stuart Mill, *On Liberty* (London: J. M. Dent & Sons, 1972), 190.

Selected Bibliography

Acemoglu, Daron, and James A. Robinson. *Why Nations Fail: The Origins of Power, Prosperity, and Poverty*. London: Profile Books, 2013.

Adebowale, Segun. "60% of Out of School Children in Nigeria Are Girls—UNICEF," Eagle Online. October 20, 2015. https://theeagleonline.com.ng /60-of-out-of-school-children-in-nigeria-are-girls-unicef/.

Africa Check. "Education for the Girl Child in Northern Nigeria." 2017. https:// africacheck.org/wp-content/uploads/2017/03/July-info-graphic.pdf.

Agarwal, Avinash. "Why Ignore PISA, the Olympics of Education?" LinkedIn. August 29, 2016. https://www.linkedin.com/pulse/why-ignore-pisa -olympics-education-avinash-agarwal/.

Akaguri, Luke. "Fee-Free Public or Low-Fee Private Basic Education in Rural Ghana: How Does the Cost Influence the Choice of the Poor?" *Compare: A Journal of Comparative and International Education* 44, no. 2 (May 2013): 140–161. DOI: 10.1080/03057925.2013.796816.

Aldrich, Richard. "Educational Legislation of the 1980s in England: An Historical Analysis." *History of Education* 21, no. 1 (1992): 57–69.

Alger, Vicki E. *Failure: The Federal Misedukation of America's Children*. Oakland, CA: Independent Institute, 2016.

Allison, John A. *The Financial Crisis and the Free Market Cure*. New York: McGraw-Hill, 2013.

Andrabi, Tahir, Jishnu Das, and Asim Ijaz Khwaja. "A Dime a Day: The Possibilities and Limits of Private Schooling in Pakistan." *Comparative Education Review* 52, no. 3 (August 2008): 329–55.

Andrabi, Tahir, Jishnu Das, Asim Ijaz Khwaja, Tara Vishwanath, Tristan Zajonc, and the LEAPS Team. *Pakistan: Learning and Educational Achievements in Punjab Schools (LEAPS): Insights to Inform the Education Policy Debate*, Executive Summary. Cambridge, MA: Harvard Kennedy School, Evidence for Policy Design, February 20, 2007.

Arnold, Matthew. *Culture and Anarchy.* Oxford: Oxford University Press, 2009. First published 1869 by Smith, Elder & Co. (London).

ASER India. *Annual Status of Education Report (Rural) 2012.* New Delhi, India: ASER Centre, 2013.

Aslam, Monazza. "The Relative Effectiveness of Government and Private Schools in Pakistan: Are Girls Worse Off?" *Education Economics* 17, no. 3 (August 2009): 329–54.

Assessment of Performance Unit (APU). *Mathematical Development: A Review of Monitoring in Mathematics, 1978–1982.* Parts 1 and 2. Slough, UK: NFER, 1988.

Banerjee, Abhijit V., and Esther Duflo. *Poor Economics: A Radical Rethinking of the Way to Fight Global Poverty.* New York: PublicAffairs, 2011.

Bashir, Sajitha. "The Cost Effectiveness of Public and Private Schools: Knowledge Gaps, New Research Methodologies and an Application in India." In *Marketizing Education and Health in Developing Countries: Miracle or Mirage?*, edited by Christopher Colclough, 124–64. Oxford: Clarendon Press, 1997.

Beales, A. C. F., Mark Blaug, Sir Douglas Veale, and E. G. West. "Appraisal." In *Education: A Framework for Choice: Papers on Historical, Economic, and Administrative Aspects of Choice in Education and Its Finance.* 2nd ed. London: Institute of Economic Affairs, 1970.

Bell, Andrew. *Mutual Tuition and Moral Discipline; or, Manual of Instructions for Conducting Schools Through the Agency of the Scholars Themselves.* 7th ed. London: Hatchard and Son, 1896.

Bhatia, V. "The Parrot's Training." In *Rabindranath Tagore: Pioneer in Education.* New Delhi, India: Sahitya Chayan, 1994.

Blaug, Mark. "Economic Aspects of Vouchers for Education." In *Education: A Framework for Choice. Papers on Historical, Economic, and Administrative Aspects of Choice in Education and Its Finance*, edited by A. C. F. Beales, Mark Blaug, Sir Douglas Veale, and E. G. West. 2nd ed. London: Institute of Economic Affairs, 1970.

Boaz, David. *The Libertarian Mind: Manifesto for Freedom, Revised and Updated Edition of Libertarianism: A Primer.* New York: Simon & Schuster, 2015.

British Broadcasting Corporation (BBC). "Grammar Schools: Who Will Get In?" 2018. https://www.bbc.co.uk/programmes/b0b57ynx.

———. "Malala Yousafzai: 'Education for Every Child.'" July 12, 2013. https://www.bbc.com/news/av/world-asia-23274568/malala-yousafzai-education-for-every-child.

Caplan, Bryan. *The Case against Education: Why the Education System Is a Waste of Time and Money.* Princeton, NJ: Princeton University Press, 2018.

CapPlus. *Banking on Education, Nairobi.* 2016. http://capplus.org/files/2016/12/Banking-on-Education-in-Nairobi-05.01.pdf.

————. *Banking on Education, Accra*. 2018. http://capplus.org/files/2018/03/Banking -on-Education-in-Accra-2018-03-20.pdf.

————. *Low Fee Private Schools in Low-Income Districts of Kampala, Uganda*. 2017. http://capplus.org/files/2017/04/Kampala-Private-Schools-Market-Study -2017-03-24.pdf.

Center for Poverty Research. "What Are the Poverty Thresholds Today?" University of California, Davis. Last updated September 13, 2017. https://poverty.ucdavis.edu /faq/what-are-poverty-thresholds-today.

Centre for Economics and Business Research. *Asda Income Tracker, Report: February 2017*. London: Centre for Economics and Business Research, ltd., 2017.

Channel 4. "Indian Summer School." 2018. https://www.channel4.com/programmes /indian-summer-school.

Chowdhury, Shreya Roy. "Private Schools Are Not Adding Value: Study." *Times of India*. February 27, 2015.

Cobbett, William. *Advice to Young Men*. London: n.p., 1829.

Conference Board. "Total Economy Database - Key Findings." 2018. https://www .conference-board.org/data/economydatabase/#GDP_perHourWorked.

————. "Total Economy Database - Key Findings." 2018. Accessed November 25, 2018. https://www.conference-board.org/data/economydatabase/.

Cotterell, Adam. "48 Idaho Schools 'Flip the Classroom' and Pilot Khan Academy On-line Learning." NPR, September 3, 2013. http://boisestatepublicradio.org/post/48 -idaho-schools-flip-classroom-and-pilot-khan-academy-online-learning#stream/0.

Dartnell, Lewis. *The Knowledge: How to Rebuild Our World from Scratch*. London: Bodley Head, 2014.

Davie, Eustace. *Unchain the Child: Abolish Compulsory Schooling Laws*. Johannesburg, South Africa: Free Market Foundation, 2005.

Day Ashley, Laura, Claire Mcloughlin, Monazza Aslam, Jakob Engel, Joseph Wales, Shenila Rawal, Richard Batley, Geeta Kingdon, Susan Nicolai, Pauline Rose. *The Role and Impact of Private Schools in Developing Countries: A Rigorous Review of the Evidence*. Final report. *Education Rigorous Literature Review*. London: Department for International Development, 2014.

Deaton, Angus, and Nancy Cartwright. "Understanding and Misunderstanding Randomized Controlled Trials." National Bureau of Economic Research (NBER) Working Paper No. 22595. Issued in September 2016, revised in October 2017. http:// www.nber.org/papers/w22595.

Department of Education and Science and the Welsh Office. *National Curriculum: Task Group on Assessment and Testing*. 1987. Accessed November 24, 2018. http://www .educationengland.org.uk/documents/pdfs/1988-TGAT-report.pdf.

Desai, Sonalde, Amaresh Dubey, Reeve Vanneman, and Rukmini Banerji. *Private Schooling in India: A New Educational Landscape.* College Park: University of Maryland, 2008.

Dixon, Pauline. "The Regulation of Private Schools for Low-Income Families in Andhra Pradesh, India: An Austrian Economic Approach." PhD diss., Newcastle University, Australia, 2003.

————. *International Aid and Private Schools for the Poor: Smiles, Miracles, and Markets.* Cheltenham, UK: Edward Elgar, 2013.

Dore, Ronald. *The Diploma Disease: Education, Qualification, and Development.* London: George Allen and Unwin, 1976.

Economist. "Can't Be Asked—Effort, Not Ability, May Explain the Gap Between American and Chinese Pupils: When Greenbacks Are on Offer, American Schoolchildren Seem to Try Harder." *The Economist.* August 17, 2017. https://www.economist.com /news/united-states/21726745-when-greenbacks-are-offer-american-schoolchildren -seem-try-harder-effort-not.

————. "A Report Card for Liberia's Charter Schools." *The Economist.* September 7, 2017. https://www.economist.com/middle-east-and-africa/2017/09/07/a-report-card-for -liberias-charter-schools.

Economist Intelligence Unit (EIU). "The Economist Intelligence Unit's Democracy Index." *The Economist.* 2018. https://infographics.economist.com/2018 /DemocracyIndex/.

Education Commission. *Report of the Commissioners Appointed to Inquire into the State of Popular Education in England.* Vol. 1. London: George E. Eyre and William Spottiswoode for Her Majesty's Stationery Office ("The Newcastle Commission"), 1861.

Emilsson, Peje. "The Profit Motive in Swedish Education." In *The Profit Motive in Education: Continuing the Revolution,* edited by James Stanfield. London: Institute of Economic Affairs, 2012.

Enlow, Robert C., and Lenore T. Ealy, eds. *Liberty and Learning: Milton Friedman's Voucher Idea at Fifty.* Washington, DC: Cato Institute, 2006.

Flexible Learning Strategies. "Sokoto Has Highest Out-of-School Children in Nigeria—UNICEF." January 21, 2016. http://www.flexlearnstrategies.net/sokoto -has-highest-out-of-school-children-in-nigeria-unicef.

Foko, Borel, Beifith Kouak Tiyab, and Guillaume Husson. *Household Education Spending: An Analytical and Comparative Perspective for 15 African Countries.* Dakar, Senegal: UNESCO-BREDA, 2012.

Free to Choose. "Victoria's Chance." YouTube. January 12, 2011. https://www.youtube .com/watch ?v=5Hewo7jZQ_4.

Freeman, Colin. "Why Nigeria Is the World's Most Dangerous Place to Be ... a Geography Teacher." *Daily Telegraph.* April 11, 2016.

French, Robert, and Geeta Kingdon. *The Relative Effectiveness of Private and Government Schools in Rural India: Evidence from ASER Data*. London: Institute of Education, 2010.

Friedman Foundation for Educational Choice. *The ABCs of School Choice: The Comprehensive Guide to Every Private School Choice Program in America—2013 Edition*. Indianapolis, IN: Friedman Foundation for Educational Choice, 2013.

————. *The ABCs of School Choice: The Comprehensive Guide to Every Private School Choice Program in America—2017 Edition*. Indianapolis, IN: Friedman Foundation for Educational Choice, 2017.

Friedman, Milton. "Are Externalities Relevant?" In *Nonpublic School Aid: The Law, Economics, and Politics of American Education*, edited by E. G. West. Lexington, MA: Lexington Books, D. C. Heath and Company, 1976.

————. *Capitalism and Freedom*. Chicago: University of Chicago Press, 1962.

————. "Epilogue: School Choice Turns 50, but the Fun Is Just Beginning." In *Liberty and Learning: Milton Friedman's Voucher Idea at Fifty*, edited by Robert C. Enlow and Lenore T. Ealy. Washington, DC: Cato Institute, 2006.

————. "Prologue: A Personal Retrospective." In *Liberty and Learning: Milton Friedman's Voucher Idea at Fifty*, edited by Robert C. Enlow and Lenore T. Ealy. Washington, DC: Cato Institute, 2006.

————. "The Role of Government in Education." In *Economics and the Public Interest*, edited by Robert A. Solo. New Brunswick, NJ: Rutgers University Press, 1955.

Friedman, Milton, and Rose Friedman. *Free to Choose: A Personal Statement*. Harmonsworth, UK: Pelican Books, 1980.

Gallo, Carmine. *Talk Like TED: The 9 Public Speaking Secrets of the World's Top Minds*. New York: St. Martin's Press, 2014.

Gates Foundation. "Bill & Melinda Gates Foundation Request for Proposals: Self-Help Group (SHG) Portfolio Evaluation." April 13, 2018. https://www.gatesfoundation.org/~/media/GFO/How-We-Work/RFP/SHG-Portfolio-Evaluation--RFP--online-version.docx?la=en.

Goyal, Sangeeta, and Priyanka Pandey. *How Do Government and Private Schools Differ? Findings from Two Large Indian States*. Washington, DC: World Bank, 2009.

Gujarat State Board of School Textbooks. *History, Standard 12*. 1st ed. Gandhinagar, India: H. N. Chavda, 2017.

Härmä, Joanna. "Access or Quality? Why Do Families Living in Slums Choose Low-Cost Private Schools in Lagos, Nigeria?" *Oxford Review of Education* 39, no. 4 (August 2013): 548–66.

————. "Can Choice Promote Education for All? Evidence from Growth in Private Primary Schooling in India." *Compare: A Journal of Comparative and International Education* 39, no. 2 (March 2009): 151–65.

_____. "Low Cost Private Schooling in India: Is It Pro Poor and Equitable?" *International Journal of Educational Development* 31, no. 4 (May 2011): 350–56.

_____. *School Choice for the Poor? The Limits of Marketisation of Primary Education in Rural India.* CREATE Pathways to Access, Research Monograph No. 23. Brighton, UK: University of Sussex, Centre for International Education, 2010.

Härmä, Joanna, and Folasade Adefisayo. "Scaling Up: Challenges Facing Low-Fee Private Schools in the Slums of Lagos, Nigeria." In *Low-Fee Private Schooling: Aggravating Equity or Mitigating Disadvantage?*, edited by P. Srivastava. Oxford: Symposium Books, 2013.

Hartwig, Kari A. "Using a Social Justice Framework to Assess Educational Quality in Tanzanian Schools." *International Journal of Educational Development* 33, no. 5 (September 2013): 487–96.

Hattie, John. *Visible Learning: A Synthesis of Over 800 Meta-Analyses Relating to Achievement,* Abingdon, UK: Routledge, 2009.

Hayek, Friedrich A. *The Constitution of Liberty.* London: Routledge & Kegan Paul, 1960.

_____. *Law, Legislation, and Liberty.* 3 vols. London: Routledge & Kegan Paul, 1982.

Herrnstein, Richard J., and Charles Murray. *The Bell Curve: Intelligence and Class Structure in American Life.* New York: Free Press, 1994.

Hilton, Steve, Scott Bade, and Jason Bade. *More Human.* 2nd ed. London: W. H. Allen; New York: PublicAffairs, 2016.

Inter-Agency Network for Education in Emergencies (INEE). *Minimum Standards for Education: Preparedness, Response, Recovery.* New York: INEE, 2010. Accessed June 20, 2020. http://toolkit.ineesite.org/toolkit/INEEcms/uploads/1012/INEE_GuideBook_EN_2012%20LoRes.pdf.

International Monetary Fund (IMF). *World Economic Outlook Database.* 2012. Accessed May 13, 2013. http://www.imf.org/external/pubs/ft/weo/2012/02/weodata/index.aspx.

_____. *World Economic Outlook Database.* 2014. Accessed October 16, 2014. http://www.imf.org/external/pubs/ft/weo/2014/02/weodata/weorept.aspx?sy=2005&ey=2015&scsm=1&ssd=1&sort=country&ds=.&br=1&c=724%2C652%2C534%2C668&s=PCPI%2CPCPIPCH%2CPCPIE%2CPCPIEPCH&grp=0&a=&pr.x=59&pr.y=8.

Karopady, D. D. "Does School Choice Help Rural Children from Disadvantaged Sections? Evidence from Longitudinal Research in Andhra Pradesh." *Economic and Political Weekly* 49, no. 51 (December 20, 2014): 46–52.

Kern, Nora, and Wentana Gebru. *Waiting Lists to Attend Charter Schools Top 1 Million Names.* National Alliance for Public Charter Schools. May 2014. Accessed June 17, 2018. http://www.publiccharters.org/sites/default/files/migrated/wp-content/uploads/2014/05/NAPCS-2014-Wait-List-Report.pdf.

Khan, Salman. *The One World Schoolhouse: Education Reimagined*. London: Hodder & Stoughton, 2012.

Khatete, Ibrahim, and Dorcah Asiago. "Effectiveness of the Board of Governors in the Recruitment of Secondary School Teachers in Gucha District." *Journal of Education and Practice* 4, no. 28 (2013): 63–68.

Kingdon, Geeta. *The Private Schooling Phenomenon in India: A Review*. CSAE Working Paper WPS/2017-04. London: IZA Institute of Labor Economics. February 2017. http://www.csae.ox.ac.uk /materials/papers/csae-wps-2017-04.pdf.

———. "The Quality and Efficiency of Private and Public Education: A Case Study in Urban India." *Oxford Bulletin of Economics and Statistics* 58, no. 1 (February 1996): 57–82.

Kremer, Michael, and Karthik Muralidharan. "Public and Private Schools in Rural India." In *School Choice International: Exploring Public-Private Partnerships*, edited by Paul E. Peterson and Rajashri Chakrabarti. Cambridge, MA: MIT Press, 2008.

Kupianinen, Sirkku, Jarkko Hautamäki, and Tommi Karjalainen. *The Finnish Education System and PISA*. Helsinki, Finland: Ministry of Education Publications, 2009.

Leahy, Terry. *Management in Ten Words: Practical Advice from the Man Who Created One of the World's Largest Retailers*. London: Random House Business Books, 2013.

Lewin, Keith M. *The Limits to Growth of Non-Government Private Schooling in Sub-Saharan Africa*. CREATE *Pathways to Access*, Research Monograph No. 5. Brighton, UK: University of Sussex, Centre for International Education, June 2007.

Liberia Institute of Statistics and Geo-Information Services (LISGIS). *National Population and Housing Census: Final Results*. Monrovia, Liberia: LISGIS, 2008.

Locke, John. *Some Thoughts Concerning Education*. A. and J. Churchill, 1693. Accessed November 25, 2018. https://books.google.bg/books?id=OCUCAAAAQAAJ&hl -bg&pg-PP7#v-onepage&q&f=false.

Longfield, David, and James Tooley. "School Choice and Parental Preferences in a Poor Area of Monrovia," *International Journal of Educational Development* 53 (March 2017): 117–27.

———. *A Survey of Schools in Juba, South Sudan*. Newcastle, UK: E. G. West Centre, 2013. Accessed March 25, 2015. http://egwestcentre.files.wordpress.com/2014/07/00 -report-south-sudan-2013-11-30.pdf.

Lott, John R., Jr. "Juvenile Delinquency and Education: A Comparison of Public and Private Provision." *International Review of Law and Economics* 7, no. 3 (December 1987): 163–75.

Macpherson, Ian, Susan Robertson, and Geoffrey Walford, eds. *Education, Privatization, and Social Justice: Case Studies from Africa, South Asia, and South East Asia*. Oxford: Symposium Books, 2014.

Maitra Pushkar, Sarmistha Pal, and Anurag Sharma. *Reforms, Growth and Persistence of Gender Gap: Recent Evidence from Private School Enrolment in India*. Bonn, Germany: Institute for the Study of Labor, 2011.

Manno, Michelle. "Idaho Embracing 'Flipped' Classrooms with Khan Academy." Teach.com, March 11, 2013. https://teach.com/blog/idaho-embracing-flipped -classrooms-with-khan-academy/.

Mantri, Rajeev, and Harsh Gupta. "Azim Premji, Please Listen to Steve Jobs and Bill Gates: Not about Technology, but about Your Educational Philanthropy." *Mint*, January 6, 2014. http://www.livemint.com/Opinion/301G41LuZJGgs8qLE3clxN/Azim -Premji-please-listen-to-Steve-Jobs-and-Bill-Gates.html.

Math Solutions. "The Challenge of Teaching Math to English Learners," 2019. https:// mathsolutions.com/uncategorized/the-challenges-of-teaching-math-to-english -language-learners/.

Mcloughlin, Claire. *Low-Cost Private Schools: Evidence, Approaches, and Emerging Issues.* EPS-Peaks, 2013.

McVeigh, Karen, and Kate Lyons. "Beyond Justification: Teachers Decry UK Backing for Private Schools in Africa." *Guardian*, May 8, 2017. https://www.theguardian.com /global-development/2017/may/05/beyond-justification-teachers-decry-uk-backing -private-schools-africa-bridge-international-academies-kenya-lawsuit.

Merrifield, John. "Choice as an Education Reform Catalyst: Lessons from Chile, Milwaukee, Florida, Cleveland, Edgewood, New Zealand, and Sweden." In *What America Can Learn from School Choice in Other Countries*, edited by David Salisbury and James Tooley. Washington, DC: Cato Institute, 2005.

––––––. *School Choices: True and False*. Oakland, CA: Independent Institute, 2002.

Mill, John Stuart. *On Liberty*. London: J. M. Dent & Sons, 1972. First published 1859 by J. W. Parker & Son (London).

Ministry of Education and Culture (Finland). "Finland and PISA." 2018. Accessed June 2, 2018. https://minedu.fi/en/pisa-en.

––––––. *The Results of PISA 2012*. 2012. Accessed June 2, 2018. http://minedu.fi/en /pisa-2012-en.

––––––. *The Results of PISA 2015*. 2015. Accessed June 2, 2018. http://minedu.fi/en /pisa-2015-en.

Mischel, Walter. *The Marshmallow Test: Understanding Self-Control and How to Master It*. London: Penguin Random House, 2014.

Mitra, Sugata. "The Future of Schooling: Children and Learning at the Edge of Chaos." *Prospects* 44, no. 4 (December 2014): 547–58.

Mitra, Sugata, James Tooley, Parimala Inamdar, and Pauline Dixon. "Improving English Pronunciation: An Automated Instructional Approach." *Information Technologies and International Development* 1, no. 1 (Fall 2003): 75–84.

Moe, Terry M., and John E. Chubb. *Liberating Learning: Technology, Politics, and the Future of American Education.* San Francisco: John Wiley & Sons, 2009.

Moore, Michael, dir. *Where to Invade Next.* 2015; New York: Dog Eat Dog Films, 2016. DVD. http://wheretoinvadenext.com/.

Morris, Ian. *Why the West Rules—for Now: The Patterns of History, and What They Reveal About the Future.* London: Profile Books, 2010.

Muralidharan, Karthik, and Venkatesh, Sundararaman. "The Aggregate Effect of School Choice: Evidence from a Two-Stage Experiment in India." *Quarterly Journal of Economics* 130, no. 3 (February 2015): 1011–66.

Murray, Charles. *Real Education: Four Simple Truths for Bringing America's Schools Back to Reality.* New York: Crown Forum, 2008.

Naish, Michael. "Education and Essential Contestability Revisited." *Journal of Philosophy of Education* 18, no. 2 (December 1984): 141–53.

Numbeo. "Crime Index by Country, 2018." Accessed June 3, 2018. https://www.numbeo.com/crime/rankings_by_country.jsp.

Oakeshott, Michael. "Education: The Engagement and Its Frustration." In *Michael Oakeshott and Education,* edited by T. Fuller. New Haven, CT: Yale University Press, 1972.

Oakeshott, Michael. *Rationalism in Politics and Other Essays.* London: Methuen, 1962.

OECD. *Service Delivery in Fragile Situations: Key Concepts, Findings, and Lessons.* Paris: Organisation for Economic Co-operation and Development, 2008.

Ohba, Asayo. "Do Low-Cost Private School Leavers in the Informal Settlement Have a Good Chance of Admission to a Government Secondary School? A Study from Kibera in Kenya." *Compare: A Journal of Comparative and International Education* 43, no. 6 (Published online November 2012): 763–82.

O'Hear, Anthony, and Marc Sidwell. *The School of Freedom: A Liberal Education Reader from Plato to the Present Day.* Exeter, UK: Imprint Academic, 2009.

Pal, Sarmistha. "Public Infrastructure, Location of Private Schools and Primary School Attainment in an Emerging Economy." *Economics of Education Review* 29, no. 5 (October 2010): 783–94.

Pal, Sarmistha, and Geeta Kingdon. *Can Private School Growth Foster Universal Literacy? Panel Evidence from Indian Districts.* Bonn, Germany: Institute for the Study of Labor, 2010.

Pearl, Natalie. "Leh Di Pipul Dem Tok [Let the People Talk]." *Peace Review* 15, no. 3 (September 2003): 309–16.

Peters, R. S. *Ethics and Education.* London: George Allen & Unwin, 1966.

———. "Philosophy of Education." In *Educational Theory and Its Foundation Disciplines,* edited by P. H. Hirst. London: Routledge and Kegan Paul, 1983.

Pilling, David. "Liberia Is Outsourcing Education, Can It Work?" *Financial Times,* April 21, 2017. https://www.ft.com/content/291b7fca-2487-11e7-a34a-538b4cb30025.

Poundstone, William. *Head in the Cloud: Why Knowing Things Still Matters When Facts Are So Easy to Look Up*. New York: Little, Brown and Company, 2016.

Prahalad, C. K. *The Fortune at the Bottom of the Pyramid: Eradicating Poverty Through Profits*. Upper Saddle River, NJ: Prentice Hall, 2005.

Pring, Richard. *Closing the Gap: Liberal Education and Vocational Preparation*. London: Hodder & Stoughton, 1995.

_____. *Knowledge and Schooling*. London: Open Books, 1976.

Pritchett, Lant. *The Rebirth of Education: Schooling Ain't Learning*. Washington, DC: Center for Global Development, 2013.

Randall, George. *History of the Common School System of the State of New York*. New York: Ivison, Blakemen, Taylor, 1871.

Ratcliffe, Rebecca, and Afua Hirsh. "U.K. Urged to Stop Funding 'Ineffective and Unsustainable' Bridge Schools." *Guardian*, August 3, 2017. https://www.theguardian .com/global-development/2017/aug/03/uk-urged-to-stop-funding-ineffective-and -unsustainable-bridge-academies.

Reid, T. Wemyss. *Life of the Rt. Hon. W. E. Forster*. New York: Kelley, 1970. First published 1888 by Chapman & Hall (London).

Rindels, Michelle. "Nevada Supreme Court Suspends School Choice Program." *Reno Gazette Journal*, September 29, 2016. https://eu.rgj.com/story/news/education/2016/09/29 /school-choice-program-unconstitutional-nevada-supreme-court-says/91278708/.

Robinson, Ken. *Changing Education Paradigms* (animation). Cognitive and RSA. 2010. Accessed November 24, 2018. https://www.wearecognitive.com/rsa-work /changing-education-paradigms.

Robinson, Ken. "How to Escape Education's Death Valley." TED Talks Education, 2013, 14:02. https://www.ted.com/talks/ken_robinson_how_to_escape_education_s _death_valley/transcript?language=en.

Robinson, Ken, and Lou Aronica. *Creative Schools*. London: Penguin Random House, 2015.

_____. *The Element: How Finding Your Passion Changes Everything*. London: Penguin Books, 2009.

Rolleston, Caine, and Modupe Adefeso-Olateju. "De Facto Privatization of Basic Education in Africa: A Market Response to Government Failure? A Comparative Study of the Cases of Ghana and Nigeria." In *Education, Privatisation and Social Justice: case studies from Africa, South Asia and South East Asia*, edited by Ian Macpherson, Susan Robertson, and Geoffrey Walford, 25–44. Oxford: Symposium Books, 2014.

Seldon, Anthony, and Abidoye Oladimejji. *The Fourth Education Revolution: Will Artificial Intelligence Liberate or Infantilize Humanity?* Buckingham, UK: University of Buckingham Press, 2018.

Seldon, Arthur. *The Riddle of the Voucher: An Inquiry into the Obstacles of Introducing Choice and Competition in State Schools.* London: Institute of Economic Affairs, 1986.

Sen, Amartya. *The Idea of Justice.* London and New York: Allen Lane, 2009.

Shah, Bina. "Boko Haram Beyond Nigeria: Girls' Education Under Threat." *Al Jazeera.* June 3, 2014. http://www.aljazeera.com/indepth/opinion/2014/06/boko-haram-nigeria -education-20146363912922864.html.

Shah, Parth. "Private Schools Are Not Adding Value: You Be the Judge." Spontaneous Order. February 27, 2015. https://web.archive.org/web/20150228184815/http:// spontaneousorder.in/private-schools-are-not-adding-value-you-be-the-judge/.

Singh, Renu, and Sudipa Sarkar. *Teaching Quality Counts: How Student Outcomes Relate to Quality of Teaching in Private and Public Schools in India,* Working Paper 91. Oxford: Young Lives, 2012.

Smith, Adam. *An Inquiry into the Nature and Causes of the Wealth of Nations.* 2 vols. London: W. Strahan and T. Cadell, 1776.

_____. *An Inquiry into the Nature and Causes of the Wealth of Nations.* 2 vols. Book IV. Edited by R. H. Campbell, A. S. Skinner, and W. B. Todd. Oxford: Clarendon Press, 1976.

Sommers, Marc. *Islands of Education: Schooling, Civil War, and the Southern Sudanese (1983–2004).* Paris: International Institute for Educational Planning (IIEP), UNESCO, 2005.

Srivastava, Prachi. "Low-Fee Private Schools and Poor Children: What Do We Really Know?" *Guardian,* August 12, 2015. https://www.theguardian.com/global -development-professionals-network/2015/aug/12/low-fee-private-schools-poverty -development-economist.

Srivastava, Prachi. "School Choice in India: Disadvantaged Groups and Low-Fee Private Schools." In *The Globalisation of School Choice?,* edited by Martin Forsey, Scott Davies, and Geoffrey Walford, 185–208. Oxford: Oxford Studies in Comparative Education, 2008.

_____. "The Shadow Institutional Framework: Towards a New Institutional Understanding of an Emerging Private School Sector in India." *Research Papers in Education* 23, no. 4 (October 2008): 451–75.

Srivastava, Prachi, ed. *Low-Fee Private Schooling: Aggravating Equity or Mitigating Disadvantage?* Oxford, UK: Symposium Books, 2013.

Srivastava, Prachi, and Geoffrey Walford, eds. *Private Schooling in Less Economically Developed Countries: Asian and African Perspectives.* Oxford: Symposium Books, 2007.

Stanfield, James Boyd. "Private Schools for the Poor and the Right to Education: A Study in Political Economy." PhD diss., University of Newcastle upon Tyne, 2014. Accessed November 24, 2018. https://ethos.bl.uk/OrderDetails.do?did=2&uin=uk .bl.ethos.658367.

Swazi Observer. "Teachers Allege Rot, Bribery, Extortion at Education." 2015. Accessed November 25, 2015. https://web.archive.org/web/20150914135253/http://www .observer.org.sz/news/75374-teachers-allege-rot-bribery-extortion-at-education.html.

Tagore, Rabindranath. "The Parrot's Training." In *Rabindranath Tagore: Pioneer in Education*, edited by V. Bhatia. New Delhi, India: Sahitya Chayan, 1994.

Thatcher, Margaret. *The Downing Street Years*. London: HarperCollins Publishers, 1993.

The Express Tribune. "Education Corruption: 'Illegal' Appointments Challenged in Sindh High Court." October 4, 2012. https://tribune.com.pk/story/446620 /education-corruption-illegal-appointments-challenged-in-sindh-high-court.

Tilak, Jandhyala B. G. *Determinants of Household Expenditure on Education in Rural India*. New Delhi, India: National Council of Applied Economic Research, 2002.

Tooley, James. *The Beautiful Tree: A Personal Journey into How the World's Poorest People Are Educating Themselves*. Washington, DC: Cato Institute, 2009.

————. "Big Questions and *Poor Economics*: Banerjee and Duflo on Schooling in Developing Countries." *Econ Journal Watch* 9, no. 3 (September 2012): 170–85.

————. "Challenging Educational Injustices: 'Grassroots' Privatisation in South Asia and Sub-Saharan Africa." *Oxford Review of Education* 39, no. 4 (July 2013), special issue on "Privatisation of Education and Social Justice," edited by Geoffrey Walford.

————. "Could For-Profit Private Education Benefit the Poor? Some *a Priori* Considerations Arising from Case Study Research in India." *Journal of Education Policy* 22, no. 3 (May 2007): 321–42.

————. *Disestablishing the School*. Aldershot, UK: Avebury Press, 1995.

————. "Educating Amaretch: Private Schools for the Poor and the New Frontier for Investors." *Economic Affairs* 27, no. 2 (June 2007): 37–43.

————. *E. G. West: Economic Liberalism and the Role of Government in Education*. London: Continuum, 2008.

————. "Extending Access to Low-Cost Private Schools through Vouchers: An Alternative Interpretation of a Two-Stage 'School Choice' Experiment in India." *Oxford Review of Education* 42, no. 5 (August 2016): 579–93. DOI: 10.1080 /03054985.2016.1217689.

————. *From Village School to Global Chain: Changing the World through Education*. London: Profile Books, 2012.

————. *Imprisoned in India: Corruption and Extortion in the World's Largest Democracy*. London: Biteback Publishing, 2016.

————. "Lessons from Nigeria's Private School Revolution." Institute of Economic Affairs. October 18, 2018. https://iea.org.uk/lessons-from-nigerias-private-school-revolution/.

————. "Low-Cost Schools in Poor Nations Seek Investors." *Financial Times*, September 17, 2006. https://www.ft.com/content/379b98c4-4670-11db-ac52-0000779e2340.

————. "Private Education: The Poor's Best Chance?" *UNESCO Courier*, November 2000.

————. "Private Schools for the Poor." *Economic Affairs*, June 2000.

————. *Reclaiming Education*. London: Continuum, 2000.

————. "The Role of Government in Education Revisited: The Theory and Practice of Vouchers, with Pointers to Another Solution for American Education." *Social Philosophy and Policy* 31, no. 1 (January 2014): 204–28.

————. *School Choice in Lagos State*. Lagos: DFID, 2013.

————. "The World Loves Our Grammar Schools—So Why Don't We?" *Spectator*, May 27, 2017. https://www.spectator.co.uk/2017/05/the-world-loves-our-grammar -school-system-so-why-dont-we.

Tooley, James, and Pauline Dixon. "'*De Facto*' Privatisation of Education and the Poor: Implications of a Study from Sub-Saharan Africa and India." *Compare: A Journal of Comparative and International Education* 36, no. 4 (December 2006): 443–62.

Tooley, James, Pauline Dixon, and James Stanfield. "Impact of Free Primary Education in Kenya: A Case Study of Private Schools in Kibera." *Educational Management Administration and Leadership* 36, no. 4 (October 2008): 449–69.

Tooley, James, Pauline Dixon, and S. V. Gomathi. "Private Schools and the Millennium Development Goal of Universal Primary Education: A Census and Comparative Survey in Hyderabad, India." *Oxford Review of Education* 33, no. 5 (October 2007): 539–60.

Tooley, James, and David Longfield. "Affordability of Private Schools: Exploration of a Conundrum and Towards a Definition of 'Low-cost.'" *Oxford Review of Education* 42, no. 4 (July 2016): 444–59.

————. *Education, War, and Peace: The Surprising Success of Private Education in War-Torn Countries*. London: Institute of Economic Affairs, 2017.

————. *Private Education in Low-Income Areas of Monrovia: School and Household Surveys*. Newcastle, UK: E. G. West Centre and Development Initiatives Liberia, 2014.

————. *Private Primary Education in Western Area, Sierra Leone*. Newcastle, UK: E. G. West Centre and People's Educational Association, 2014.

————. *The Role and Impact of Low-Cost Private Schools in Developing Countries: A Response to the DFID-Commissioned 'Rigorous Literature Review.'* London: Pearson, 2015.

————. *The Role and Impact of Private Schools in Developing Countries: A Response to DFID's 'Rigorous Literature Review.'* Newcastle, UK: E. G. West Centre, 2014.

Transparency International. "Corruption Perception Index 2017." 2017. Accessed May 20, 2020. https://www.transparency.org/news/feature/corruption _perceptions_index_2017#table.

Traub, Alex. "India's Dangerous New Curriculum." *New York Review of Books*, December 6, 2018. https://www.nybooks.com/articles/2018/12/06/indias-dangerous-new-curriculum/.

Trevelyan, George Macaulay. *British History in the Nineteenth Century (1782–1901)*. New York: Longmans, Green, 1922.

Truth and Reconciliation Commission. *Final Report of the Truth and Reconciliation Commission of Sierra Leone*. Freetown, Sierra Leone: Truth and Reconciliation Commission, 2004. http://www.sierra-leone.org/Other-Conflict/TRCVolume1.pdf.

United Nations Children's Fund (UNICEF). "At a Glance: Liberia." 2013. Accessed November 18, 2018. http://www.unicef.org/infobycountry/liberia_statistics.html.

United Nations Committee on the Elimination of Discrimination Against Women (CEDAW). *Privatization and Its Impact on the Right to Education of Women and Girls*. Written submission. CEDAW. June 27, 2014.

United Nations Educational, Scientific and Cultural Organization (UNESCO). *Building a Better Future: Education for an Independent South Sudan*. Paris: UNESCO, 2011.

————. *The Dakar Framework for Action: Education for All—Meeting Our Collective Commitments (Including Six Regional Frameworks for Action)*. Adopted by the World Education Forum, Dakar. April 26–28. Paris: UNESCO, 2000.

————. *Education in Situations of Emergency, Crisis, and Reconstruction* (ED-2003/WS/48). Paris: UNESCO Strategy, 2003.

————. *EFA Global Monitoring Report—The Hidden Crisis: Armed Conflict and Education*. Paris: UNESCO, 2011.

————. *Guidebook for Planning Education in Emergencies and Reconstruction*. Paris: International Institute for Educational Planning, 2010.

United Nations Statistics Division. "Millennium Development Goals Indicators." 2014. Accessed October 22, 2014. http://mdgs.un.org/unsd/mdg/Metadata.aspx?IndicatorId=0&SeriesId=580.

Vedder, Richard K. *Can Teachers Own Their Own Schools? New Strategies for Educational Excellence*. Oakland, CA: Independent Institute, 2000.

Viadero, Debra. "Potential of Global Tests Seen as Unrealized Scholars Urged to Scour TIMSS, PISA for Policy Insights." *Education Week*, November 22, 2006. https://www.edweek.org/ew/articles/2006/11/29/13international.h26.html.

Von Däniken, Erich. *Chariots of the Gods?* New York: G. P. Putnam's Sons, 1968.

Wagner, Tony, and Ted Dintersmith. *Most Likely to Succeed: Preparing Our Kids for the Innovation Era*. New York: Scribner, 2015.

Watkins, Kevin. "Private Education and Education for All—or How Not to Construct an Evidence-Based Argument: A Reply to Tooley." *Economic Affairs* 24, no. 4 (December 2004).

Weber, Karl, ed. *Waiting for "Superman": How We Can Save America's Failing Public Schools*. New York: PublicAffairs, 2010.

West, Edwin G. "The Benthamites as Educational Engineers: The Reputation and the Record." *History of Political Economy* 24, no. 3 (Fall 1992): 595–621.

———. *Education and the State: A Study in Political Economy*. 3rd ed. Indianapolis, IN: The Liberty Fund, 1994 (1965).

———. *Non-Public School Aid: The Law, Economics, and Politics of American Education*. Lexington, MA: Lexington Books, 1976.

———. "Resource Allocation and Growth in Early Nineteenth-Century British Education." *Economic History Review* 23, no. 1 (April 1970): 68–95.

Western Independent. "Testing Nations: Olympics and PISA." August 17, 2012. https://westernindependent.blogspot.com/2012/08/testing-nations-olympics-and-pisa.html.

Whittle, Chris. *Crash Course: Imagining a Better Future for Public Education*. New York: Riverhead Books, 2005.

Wikipedia. S.v. "Chartered Institute of Library and Information Professionals." Last modified November 9, 2020. https:// en.wikipedia.org/wiki/Chartered_Institute _of_Library_and Information Professionals.

———. "List of Countries by GDP (PPP) per Hour Worked." https://en.wikipedia .org/wiki/List_of_countries_by_GDP_(PPP)_per_hour_worked.

Williamson, Ben. "PISA for Personality Testing—The OECD and the Psychometric Science of Social-Emotional Skills." January 16, 2018. https://codeactsineducation .wordpress.com/2018/01/16/pisa-for-personality-testing/.

Winch, Christopher. "Quality and Education." *Journal of the Philosophy of Education* 30, no. 1 (June 1996), Special Issue: 25–26.

World Bank. "PPP Conversion Factor, Private Consumption (LCU per International $)." 2014. Accessed October 10, 2014. http://data.worldbank.org/indicator/PA.NUS .PRVT.PP.

———. "2005 International Comparison Program, Tables of Final Results." Washington, DC. 2008. Accessed May 13, 2013. http://siteresources.worldbank.org/ICPINT /Resources/icp-finaltables.pdf.

———. "World Development Indicators." 2018. https://datacatalog.worldbank.org /dataset/world-development-indicators.

World Health Organization (WHO). "Global Health Observatory Data," "Suicide Rates per 100,000 Population," "Age-Standardized Rates by Country." WHO. 2018. http:// www.who.int/gho/mental_health/suicide_rates/en/.

XE. "Current and Historic Rate Tables.v" 2013. Accessed May 15, 2013. http://www .xe.com/currencytables/.

Young, Moira. "Why Is Dystopia Reading So Appealing to Young Adults?" *Guardian*. October 23, 2011. https://www.theguardian.com/books/2011/oct/23/dystopian-fiction.

Yousafzai, Malala, with Christina Lamb. *I Am Malala: The Girl Who Stood Up for Education and Was Shot by the Taliban*. London: Weidenfeld & Nicolson, 2013.

Zeitlyn, Benjamin, and Joanna Härmä. *The Limits of Marketisation of Primary Education in India. CREATE India Policy Brief* 2 (January 2011).

Zulfiqar, Shahzada. "Balochistan's Boko Haram." *Newsline*. June 25, 2014. http://www.newslinemagazine.com/2014/06/balochistans-boko-haram/.

Index

About the Author

JAMES TOOLEY IS Vice Chancellor (President) of the University of Buckingham in England, where he also serves as Professor of Educational Entrepreneurship and Policy, and is a Senior Fellow at the Independent Institute. He was formerly Director of the E. G. West Centre and Professor of Education Policy at Newcastle University upon Tyre, and temporarily Global Head of Low Cost Schools for GEMS Education.

Tooley's best-selling book *The Beautiful Tree: A Personal Journey into How the World's Poorest Are Educating Themselves* received the Sir Antony Fisher International Memorial Award. It builds on his groundbreaking research on private education for the poor in India, China, and Africa, for which Tooley was awarded the Gold Prize in the first International Finance Corporation/ *Financial Times* Private Sector Development Competition. He has co-founded chains of low-cost private schools in India, Ghana, Nigeria, Honduras, and England. He is also patron of the Association of Formidable Educational Development and chief mentor of the National Independent Schools Alliance, (large federations of low-cost private schools in Nigeria and India respectively).

His work has been featured in the American PBS documentary *Meet the New Heroes*, profiled alongside the work of Nobel laureate Muhammad Yunus and Grameen Bank. It has also been featured in a documentary for BBC World and on BBC *Newsnight*. *Philanthropy Magazine* has described him as "a 21st-century Indiana Jones" traveling to "the remotest regions on Earth researching something that many regard as mythical: private, parent-funded schools serving the Third World poor."

Tooley is a contributor to numerous scholarly volumes, and his articles have been published in such journals as the *Journal of School Choice, Educational Management, Journal of Comparative Education Research, School Effectiveness and School Improvement, Educational Management, Journal of Education Policy, International Review of Education, International Journal of Educational Development, Economic Affairs, Education Next, Information Technologies and International Development, Journal of Philosophy of Education*, and the *Oxford Review of Education*.

He received his PhD in education from the University of London, and he has previously taught and researched at the Universities of Oxford and Manchester, Simon Fraser University, and University of the Western Cape, South Africa.

Independent Institute Studies in Political Economy

Independent Institute Studies in Political Economy

INDEPENDENT
I N S T I T U T E

100 SWAN WAY, OAKLAND, CA 94621-1428

For further information:

510-632-1366 • orders@independent.org • http://www.independent.org/publications/books/